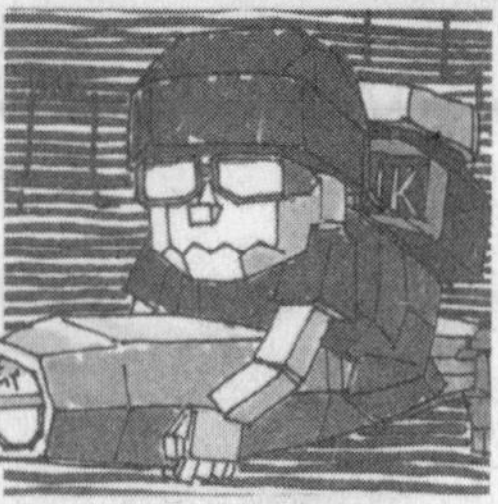

岸本斉史

This volume of Naruto is apparently the first to be created entirely digitally. My guess is that, in the future, manga production will continue to move further and further into this kind of production and away from the more traditional methods.

Both the backgrounds and the characters themselves are created in software as polygons, and once the initial design and programming is done, any imaginable composition is possible. For action sequences, we use motion capture to create and manipulate the coolest poses we can come up with. It's all done on the computer, without using any paper or ink. Our methods will probably continue to change as the technology evolves... but there's one thing that won't ever change: the need to invent good stories!

—*Masashi Kishimoto, 2001*

Author/artist Masashi Kishimoto was born in 1974 in rural Okayama Prefecture, Japan. After spending time in art college, he won the Hop Step Award for new manga artists with his manga **Karakuri** ("Mechanism"). Kishimoto decided to base his next story on traditional Japanese culture. His first version of **Naruto**, drawn in 1997, was a one-shot story about fox spirits; his final version, which debuted in **Weekly Shonen Jump** in 1999, quickly became the most popular ninja manga in Japan.

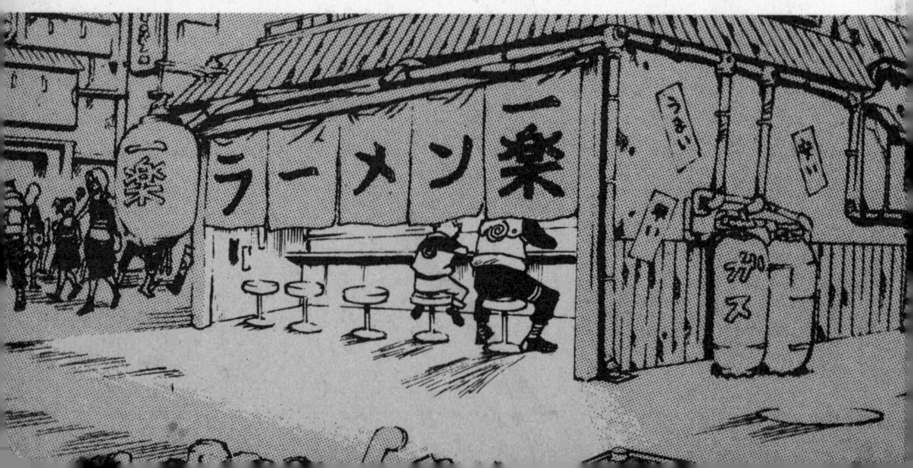
一楽
ラーメン一楽

NARUTO VOL. 7
The SHONEN JUMP Graphic Novel Edition

This graphic novel contains material that was originally published
in English in **SHONEN JUMP** #27-31.

STORY AND ART BY MASASHI KISHIMOTO

English Adaptation/Jo Duffy
Translation/Mari Morimoto
Touch-up Art & Lettering/Heidi Szykowny
Additional Touch-up/Josh Simpson
Design/Sean Lee
Editor/Frances E. Wall

Editor in Chief, Books/Alvin Lu
Editor in Chief, Magazines/Marc Weidenbaum
VP of Publishing Licensing/Rika Inouye
VP of Sales/Gonzalo Ferreyra
Sr. VP of Marketing/Liza Coppola
Publisher/Hyoe Narita

Printed in the U.S.A.

Published by VIZ Media, LLC
P.O. Box 77010
San Francisco, CA 94107

SHONEN JUMP Graphic Novel Edition
10 9 8 7 6
First printing, July 2005
Sixth printing, June 2007

THE WORLD'S
MOST POPULAR MANGA

www.shonenjump.com

SHONEN JUMP GRAPHIC NOVEL

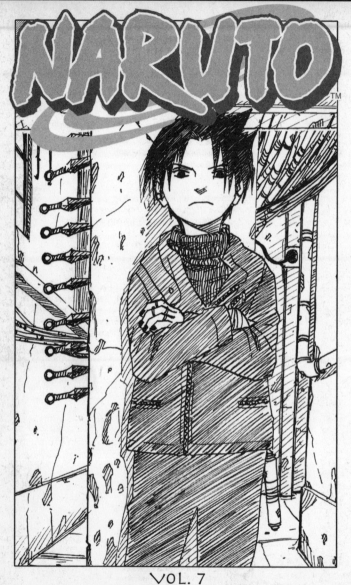

NARUTO

VOL. 7
OROCHIMARU'S CURSE
STORY AND ART BY
MASASHI KISHIMOTO

SAKURA サクラ

Smart and studious, Sakura is the brightest of Naruto's classmates, but she's constantly distracted by her crush on Sasuke. Her goal: to win Sasuke's heart!

NARUTO ナルト

When Naruto was born, a destructive fox spirit was imprisoned inside his body. Spurned by the older villagers, he's grown into an attention-seeking troublemaker. His goal: to become the village's next *Hokage*.

SASUKE サスケ

The top student in Naruto's class, Sasuke comes from the prestigious Uchiha clan. His goal: to get revenge on a mysterious person who wronged him in the past.

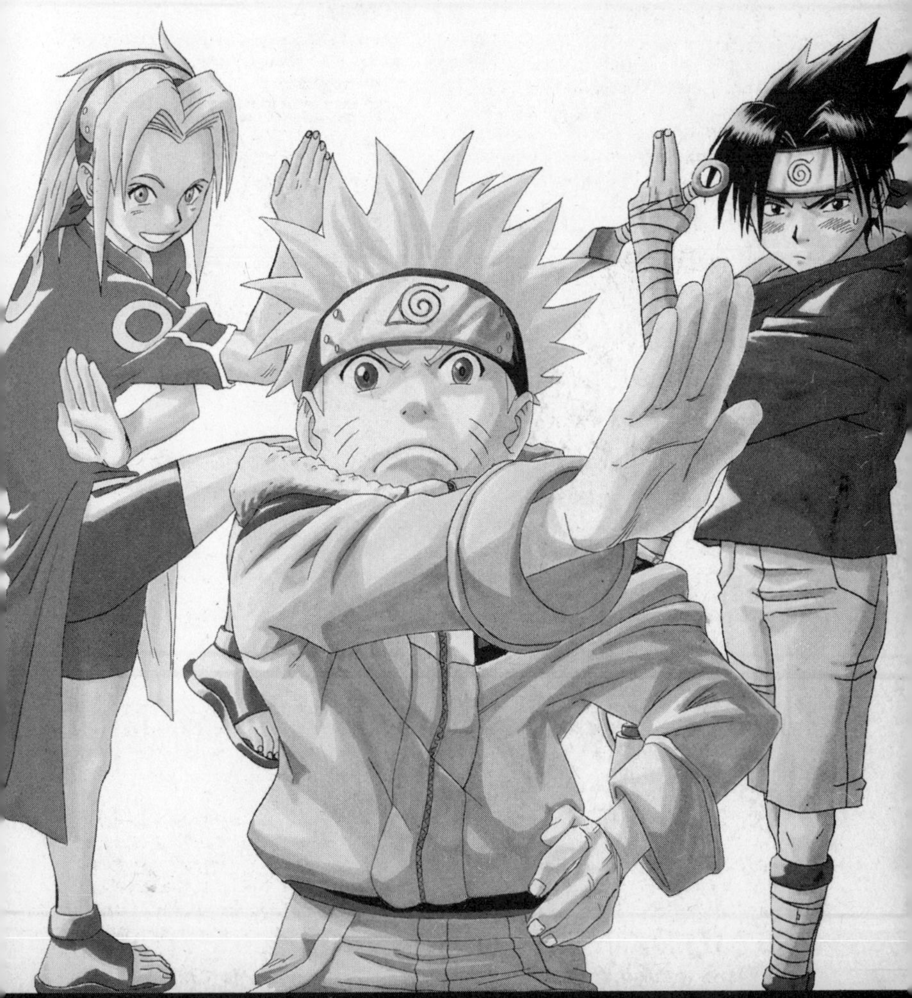

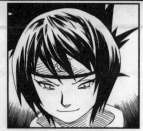

MITARASHI ANKO
みたらしアンコ

The Second Chief Examination Officer, proctor of the test in the Forest of Death! She tried hunting down Orochimaru herself, but since he slipped through her fingers, she has been waiting for the help of the elite Black Ops team she summoned.

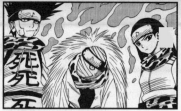

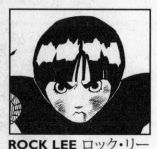

ROCK LEE ロック・リー

Rock Lee is one of the most talented young shinobi around, and he's completely infatuated with Sakura. Separated from his teammates Neji and Tenten in the forest, he tried to act as Sakura's protector but was severely knocked around by the Sound Ninja.

THE SOUND NINJA (OTONIN)音忍

These mysterious ninja are in the forest only to do their master Orochimaru's bidding — to destroy Sasuke!

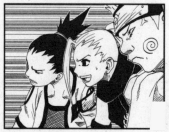

THE ASUMA CELL
Choji チョウジ
Ino いの
Shikamaru シカマル

Choji, Ino and Shikamaru chased after Naruto's team hoping to steal their scroll. Watching from the sidelines as Lee and Sakura fight the Sound Ninja, they've been debating whether to get involved or stay in the shadows…but now Ino is jumping into the fray, coming to her rival Sakura's aid!

THE STORY SO FAR…

Twelve years ago, a destructive nine-tailed fox spirit attacked the ninja village of Konohagakure. The *Hokage*, or village champion, defeated the fox by sealing its soul into the body of a baby boy. Now that boy, Uzumaki Naruto, has grown up to become a ninja-in-training, learning the art of *ninjutsu* with his classmates Sakura and Sasuke.

Naruto, Sasuke and Sakura are deep in the Forest of Death, the site of the second stage of the Chûnin (Journeyman Ninja) Selection Exam…but more urgent concerns have distracted them from collecting the scrolls they need to pass the test. After coming under the attack of the nefarious impostor Orochimaru, Naruto and Sasuke now lie unconscious on the forest floor. Mitarashi Anko, the exam proctor, chases after Orochimaru and learns his intentions: to mold Sasuke into his successor…assuming Sasuke survives the curse that Orochimaru placed on him. Orochimaru's minions, the mysterious Sound Ninja, are also hunting down Sasuke, and they're confused to discover that their leader has already caught his prey. But they're not prepared to back down, so the burden is on Sakura to defend her helpless teammates…

NARUTO

VOL. 7

OROCHIMARU'S CURSE

CONTENTS

Number 55: No Holds Barred!!

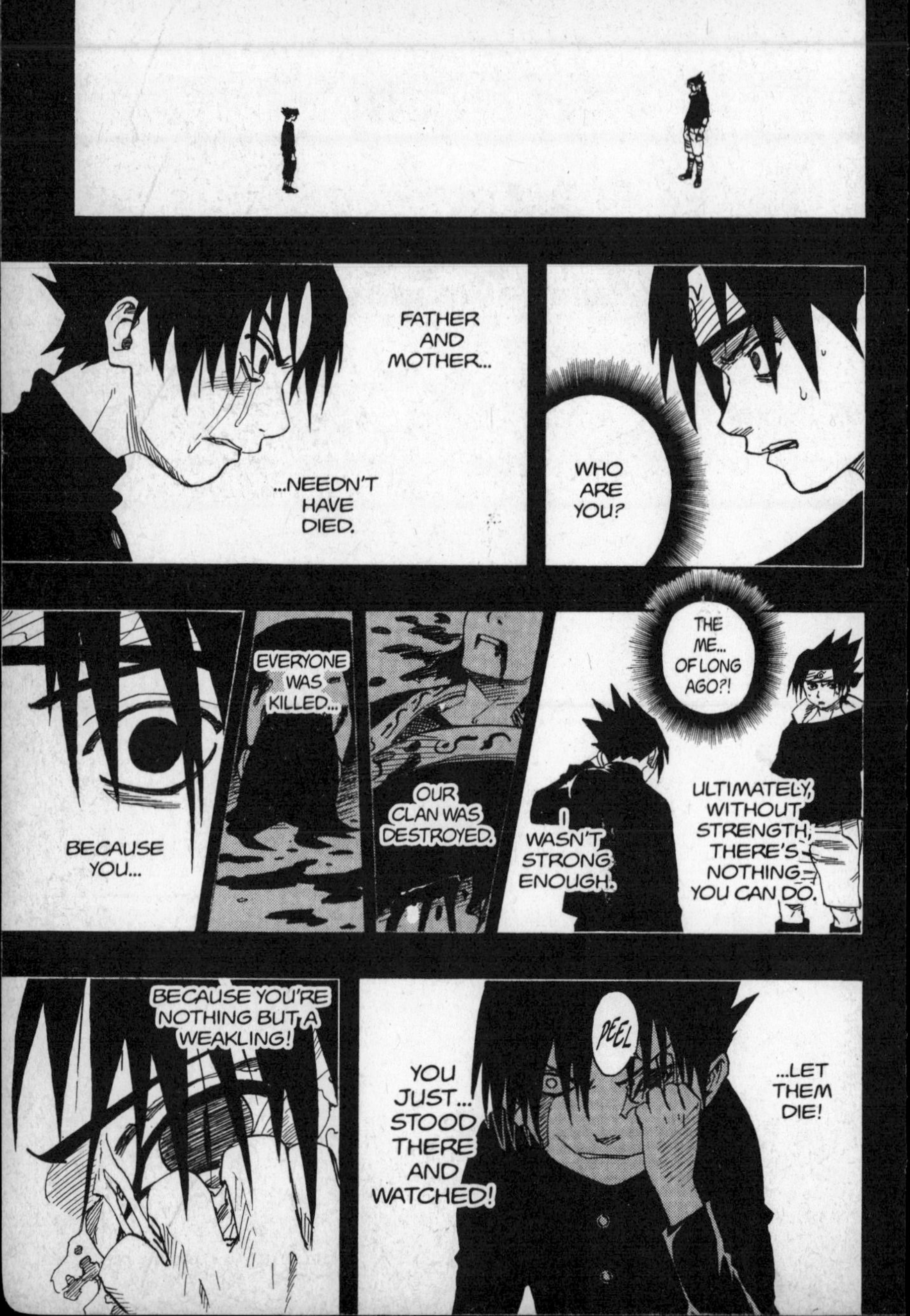
WHO ARE YOU?
FATHER AND MOTHER...
...NEEDN'T HAVE DIED.
THE ME... OF LONG AGO?!
ULTIMATELY, WITHOUT STRENGTH, THERE'S NOTHING YOU CAN DO.
I WASN'T STRONG ENOUGH.
OUR CLAN WAS DESTROYED.
EVERYONE WAS KILLED...
BECAUSE YOU...
PEEL
...LET THEM DIE!
YOU JUST... STOOD THERE AND WATCHED!
BECAUSE YOU'RE NOTHING BUT A WEAKLING!

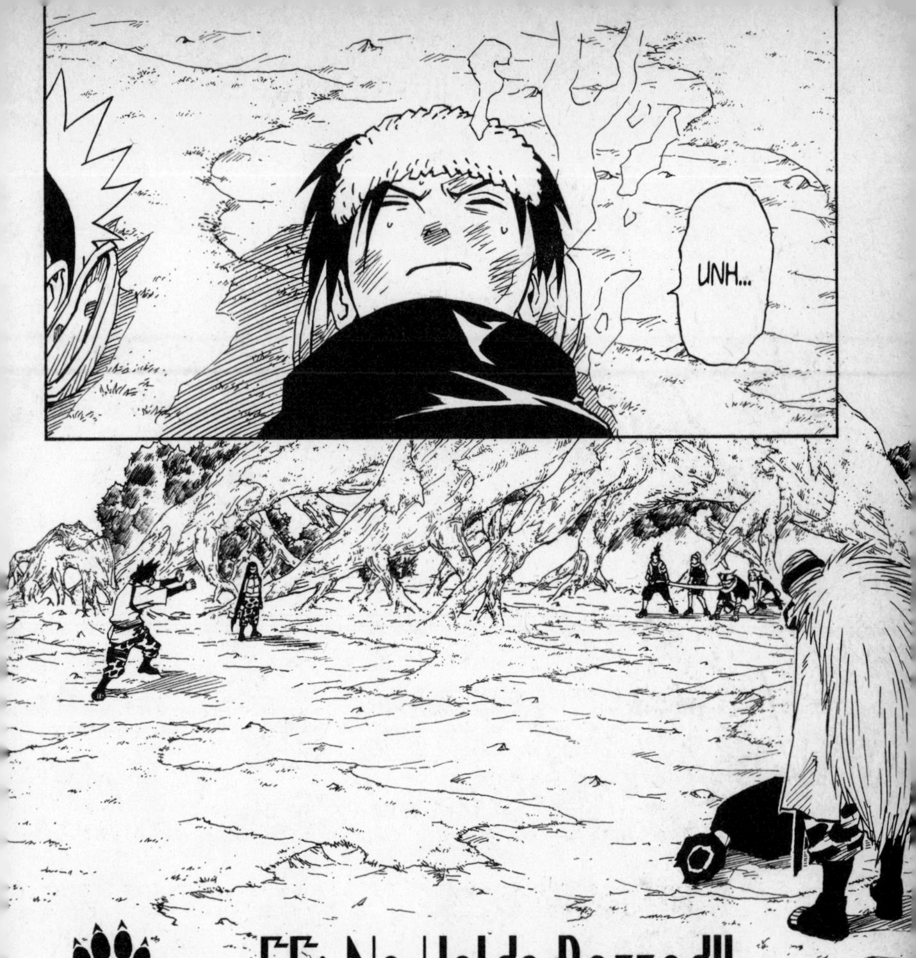
UNH...

Number 55: No Holds Barred!!

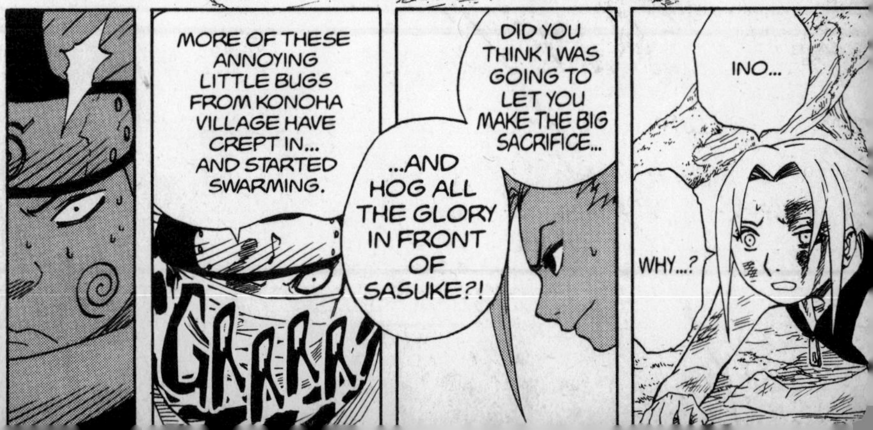
INO...
WHY...?
DID YOU THINK I WAS GOING TO LET YOU MAKE THE BIG SACRIFICE...
...AND HOG ALL THE GLORY IN FRONT OF SASUKE?!
MORE OF THESE ANNOYING LITTLE BUGS FROM KONOHA VILLAGE HAVE CREPT IN... AND STARTED SWARMING.
GRRRR

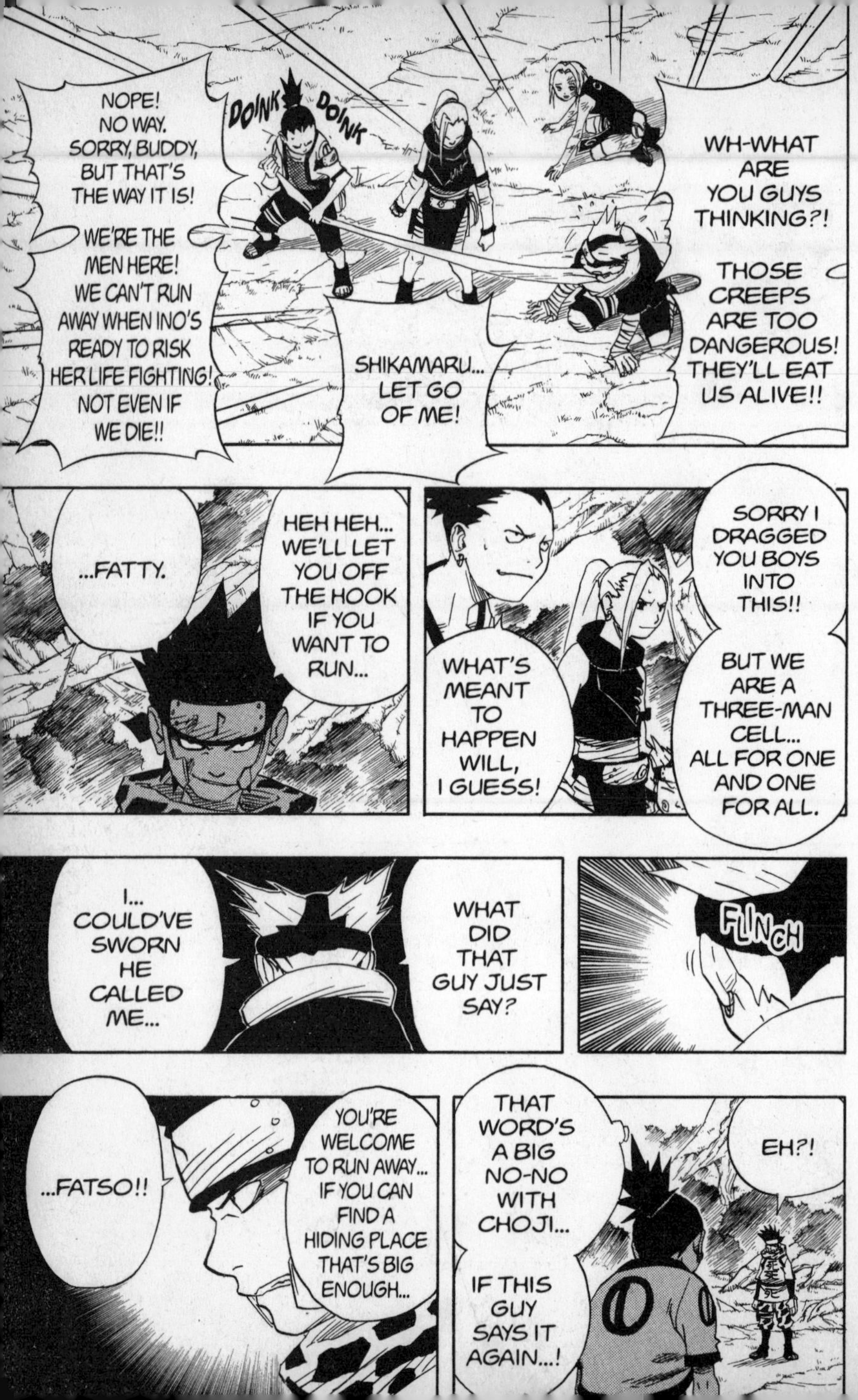
WH-WHAT ARE YOU GUYS THINKING?!
THOSE CREEPS ARE TOO DANGEROUS! THEY'LL EAT US ALIVE!!
SHIKAMARU... LET GO OF ME!
DOINK DOINK
NOPE! NO WAY. SORRY, BUDDY, BUT THAT'S THE WAY IT IS!
WE'RE THE MEN HERE! WE CAN'T RUN AWAY WHEN INO'S READY TO RISK HER LIFE FIGHTING! NOT EVEN IF WE DIE!!
SORRY I DRAGGED YOU BOYS INTO THIS!!
BUT WE ARE A THREE-MAN CELL... ALL FOR ONE AND ONE FOR ALL.
WHAT'S MEANT TO HAPPEN WILL, I GUESS!
HEH HEH... WE'LL LET YOU OFF THE HOOK IF YOU WANT TO RUN...
...FATTY.
FLINCH
WHAT DID THAT GUY JUST SAY?
I... COULD'VE SWORN HE CALLED ME...
EH?!
THAT WORD'S A BIG NO-NO WITH CHOJI...
IF THIS GUY SAYS IT AGAIN...!
YOU'RE WELCOME TO RUN AWAY... IF YOU CAN FIND A HIDING PLACE THAT'S BIG ENOUGH...
...FATSO!!

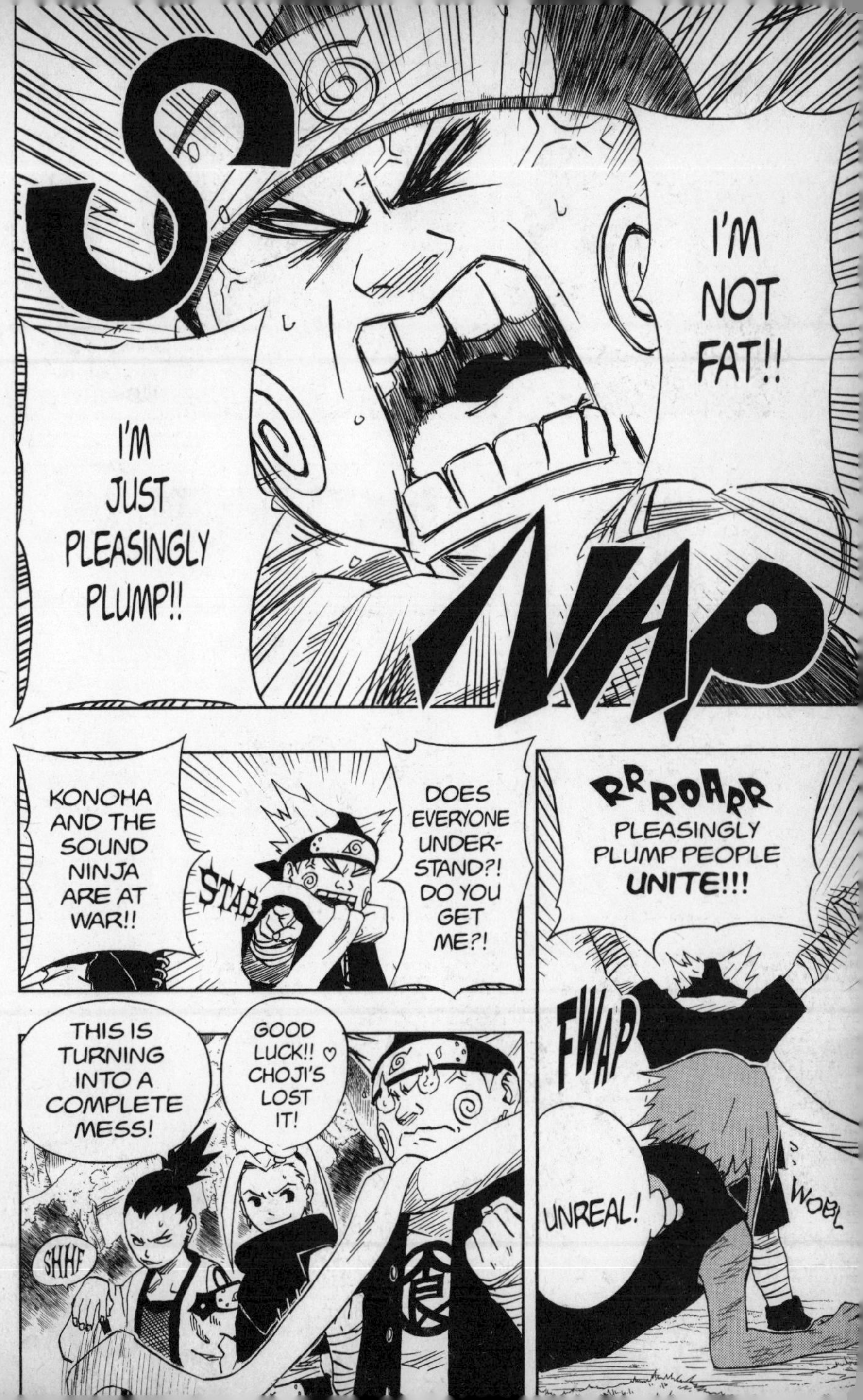
I'M NOT FAT!!
I'M JUST PLEASINGLY PLUMP!!
S
NAP
RRROARR
PLEASINGLY PLUMP PEOPLE UNITE!!!
FWAP
WOBL
UNREAL!
DOES EVERYONE UNDER-STAND?! DO YOU GET ME?!
STAB
KONOHA AND THE SOUND NINJA ARE AT WAR!!
GOOD LUCK!! ♡ CHOJI'S LOST IT!
THIS IS TURNING INTO A COMPLETE MESS!
SHHF

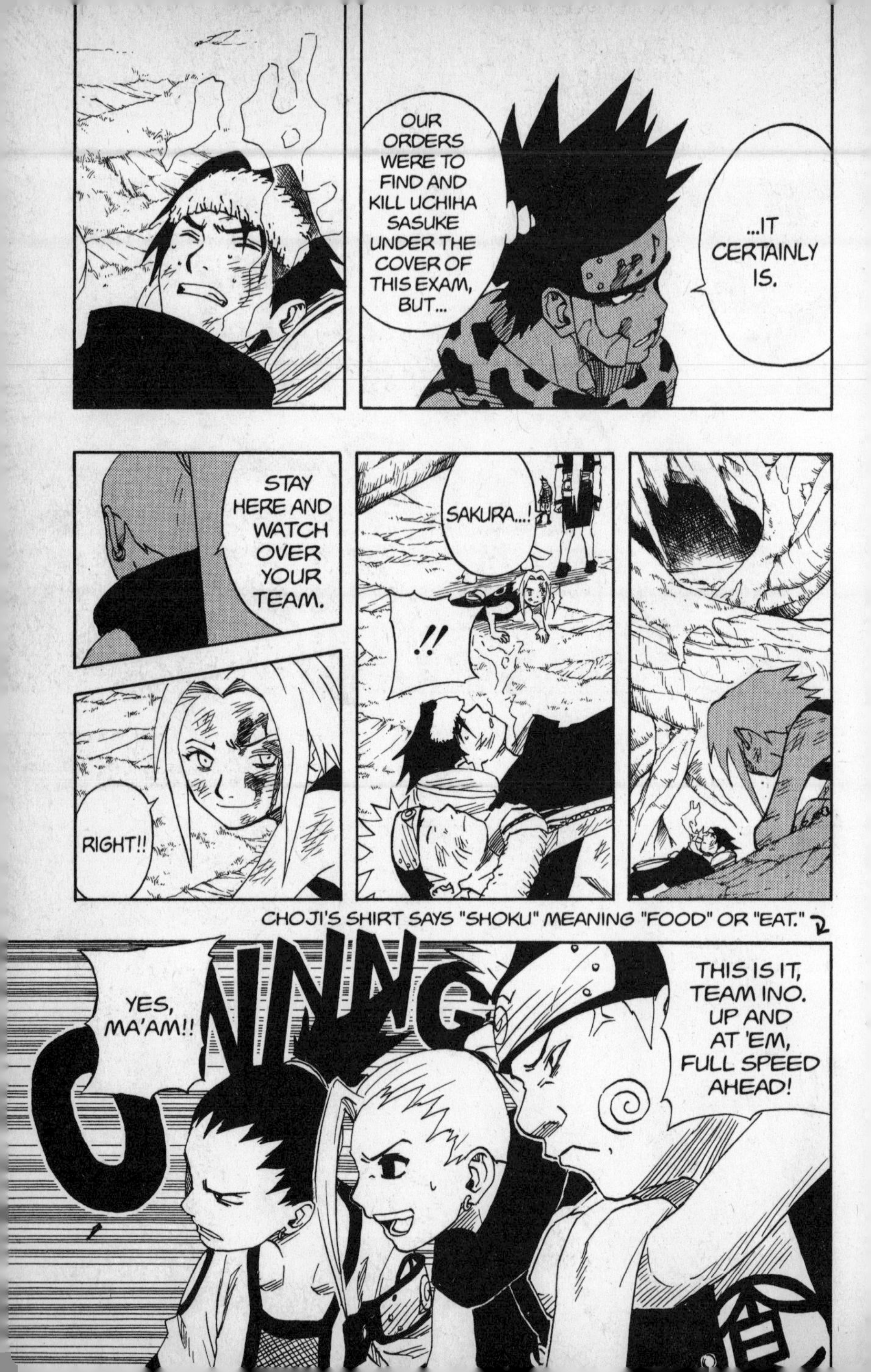

...IT CERTAINLY IS.
OUR ORDERS WERE TO FIND AND KILL UCHIHA SASUKE UNDER THE COVER OF THIS EXAM, BUT...
SAKURA...!
!!
STAY HERE AND WATCH OVER YOUR TEAM.
RIGHT!!
CHOJI'S SHIRT SAYS "SHOKU" MEANING "FOOD" OR "EAT."
THIS IS IT, TEAM INO. UP AND AT 'EM, FULL SPEED AHEAD!
YES, MA'AM!!

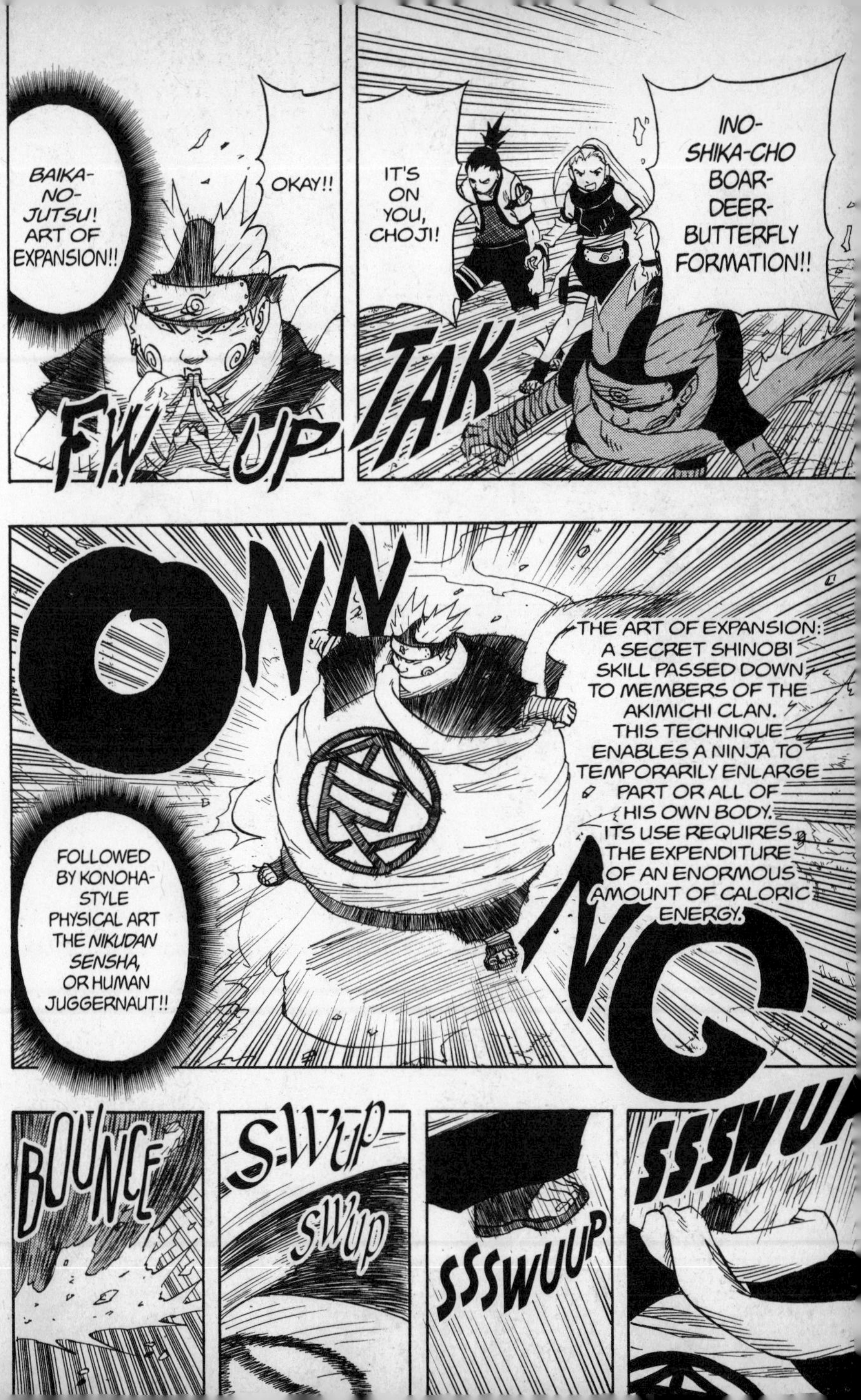
INO-SHIKA-CHO BOAR-DEER-BUTTERFLY FORMATION!!
IT'S ON YOU, CHOJI!
TAK
OKAY!!
BAIKA-NO-JUTSU! ART OF EXPANSION!!
FW UP
THE ART OF EXPANSION: A SECRET SHINOBI SKILL PASSED DOWN TO MEMBERS OF THE AKIMICHI CLAN. THIS TECHNIQUE ENABLES A NINJA TO TEMPORARILY ENLARGE PART OR ALL OF HIS OWN BODY. ITS USE REQUIRES THE EXPENDITURE OF AN ENORMOUS AMOUNT OF CALORIC ENERGY.
ONN NG
FOLLOWED BY KONOHA-STYLE PHYSICAL ART THE *NIKUDAN SENSHA*, OR HUMAN JUGGERNAUT!!
SSSWU
SSSWUUP
S-WUP
SWUP
BOUNCE

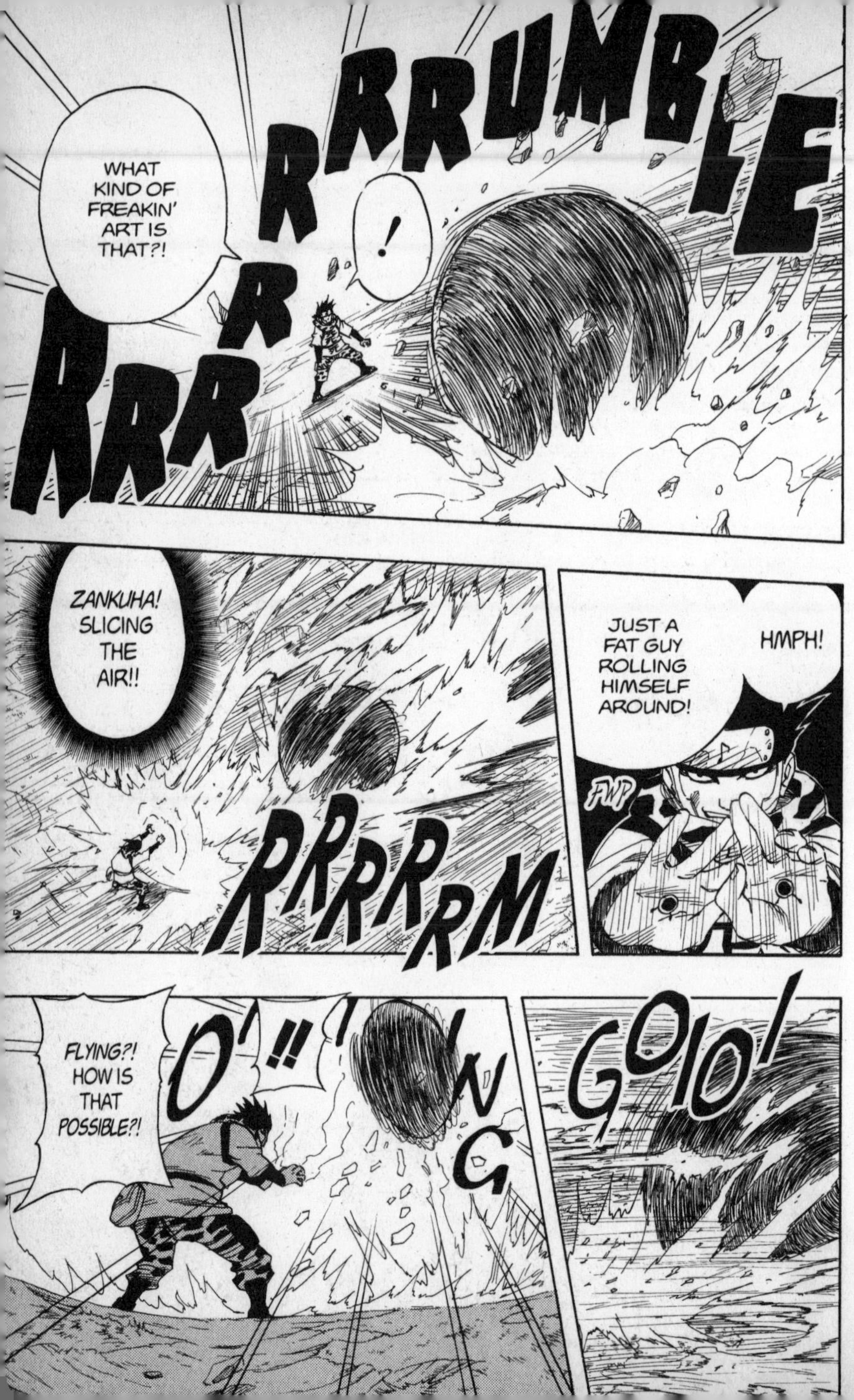
RRRUMBLE
!
WHAT KIND OF FREAKIN' ART IS THAT?!
RRRR
HMPH!
JUST A FAT GUY ROLLING HIMSELF AROUND!
FWP
ZANKUHA! SLICING THE AIR!!
RRRRRM
GOIO!
'NG
O'!!
FLYING?! HOW IS THAT POSSIBLE?!

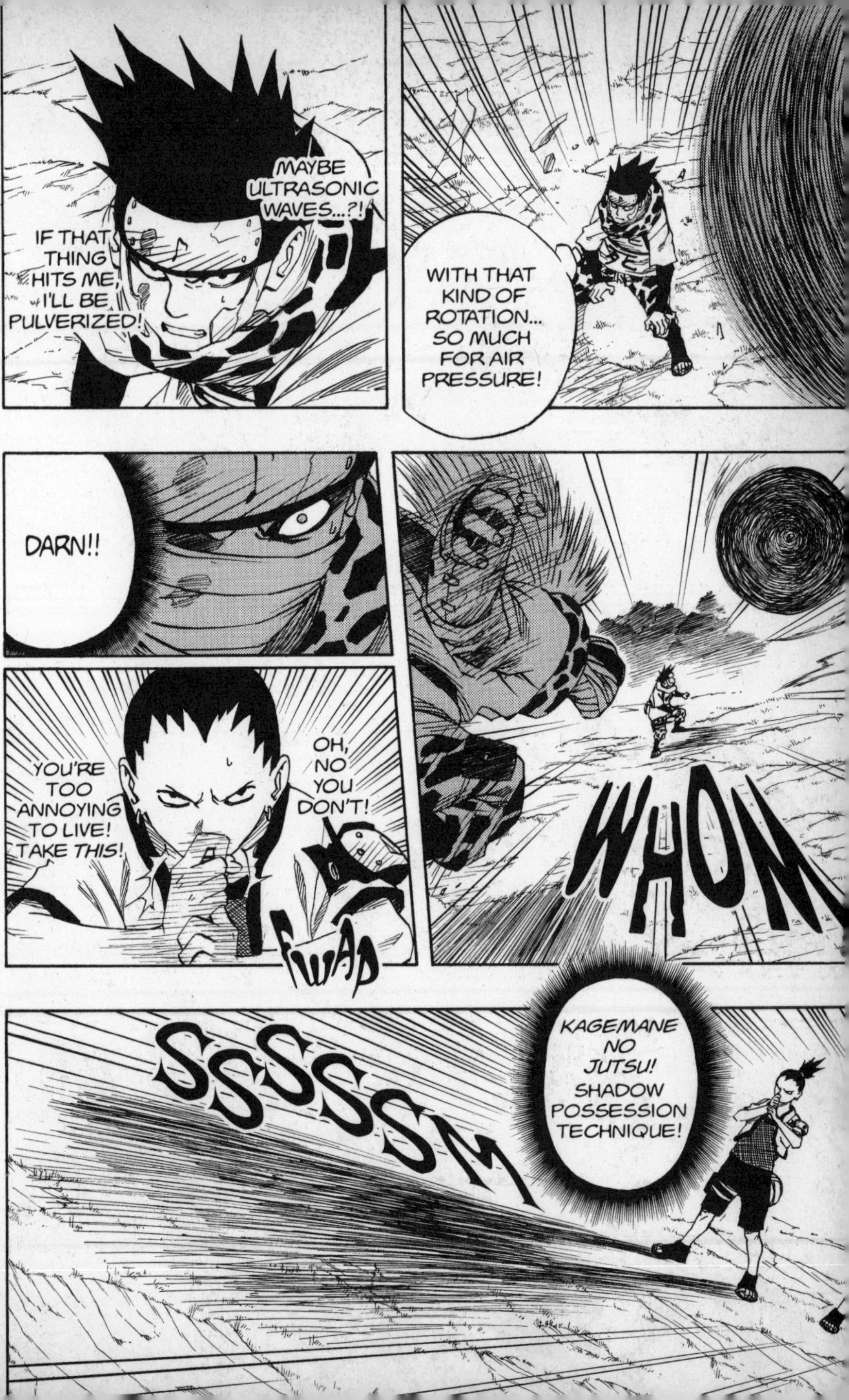
WITH THAT KIND OF ROTATION... SO MUCH FOR AIR PRESSURE!
MAYBE ULTRASONIC WAVES...?!
IF THAT THING HITS ME, I'LL BE PULVERIZED!
WHOM
DARN!!
OH, NO YOU DON'T!
YOU'RE TOO ANNOYING TO LIVE! TAKE THIS!
FWAP
KAGEMANE NO JUTSU! SHADOW POSSESSION TECHNIQUE!
SSSSM

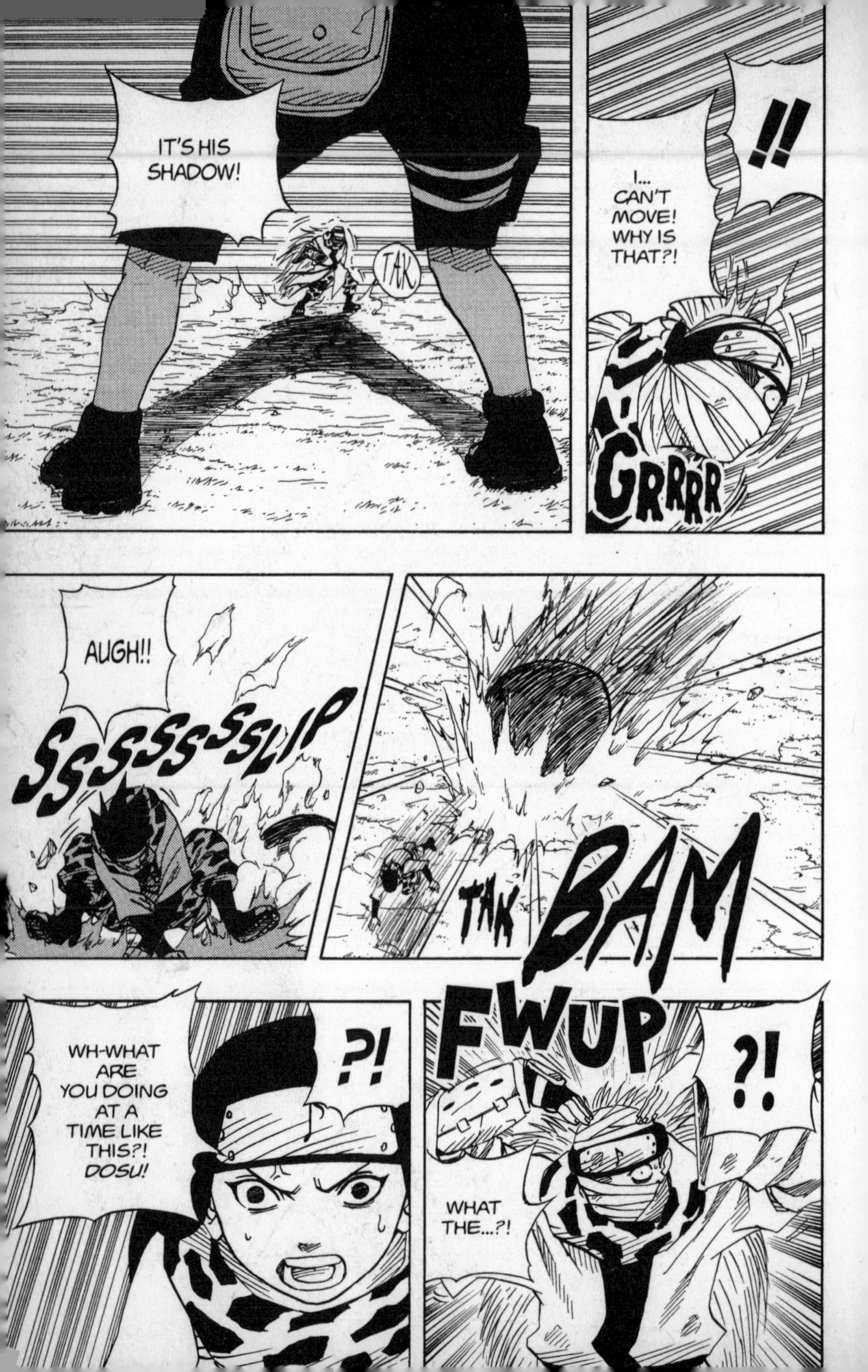
!!
I... CAN'T MOVE! WHY IS THAT?!
GRRRR
IT'S HIS SHADOW!
TAK
TAK
BAM
AUGH!!
SSSSSSSLIP
FWUP
?!
WHAT THE...?!
WH-WHAT ARE YOU DOING AT A TIME LIKE THIS?! DOSU!
?!

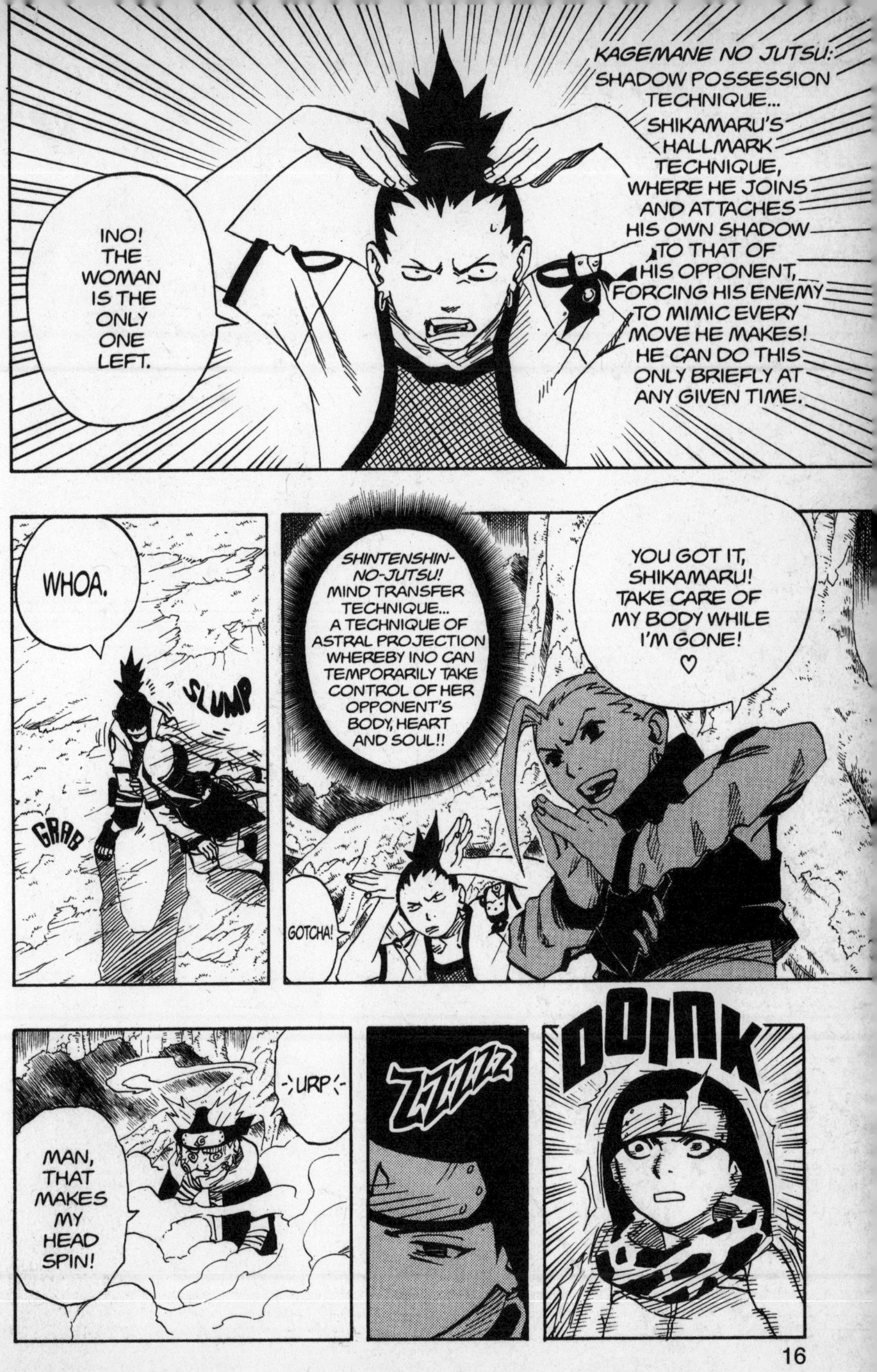
KAGEMANE NO JUTSU: SHADOW POSSESSION TECHNIQUE... SHIKAMARU'S HALLMARK TECHNIQUE, WHERE HE JOINS AND ATTACHES HIS OWN SHADOW TO THAT OF HIS OPPONENT, FORCING HIS ENEMY TO MIMIC EVERY MOVE HE MAKES! HE CAN DO THIS ONLY BRIEFLY AT ANY GIVEN TIME.
INO! THE WOMAN IS THE ONLY ONE LEFT.
YOU GOT IT, SHIKAMARU! TAKE CARE OF MY BODY WHILE I'M GONE! ♡
SHINTENSHIN-NO-JUTSU! MIND TRANSFER TECHNIQUE... A TECHNIQUE OF ASTRAL PROJECTION WHEREBY INO CAN TEMPORARILY TAKE CONTROL OF HER OPPONENT'S BODY, HEART AND SOUL!!
GOTCHA!
WHOA.
SLUMP
GRAB
DOINK
URP
MAN, THAT MAKES MY HEAD SPIN!

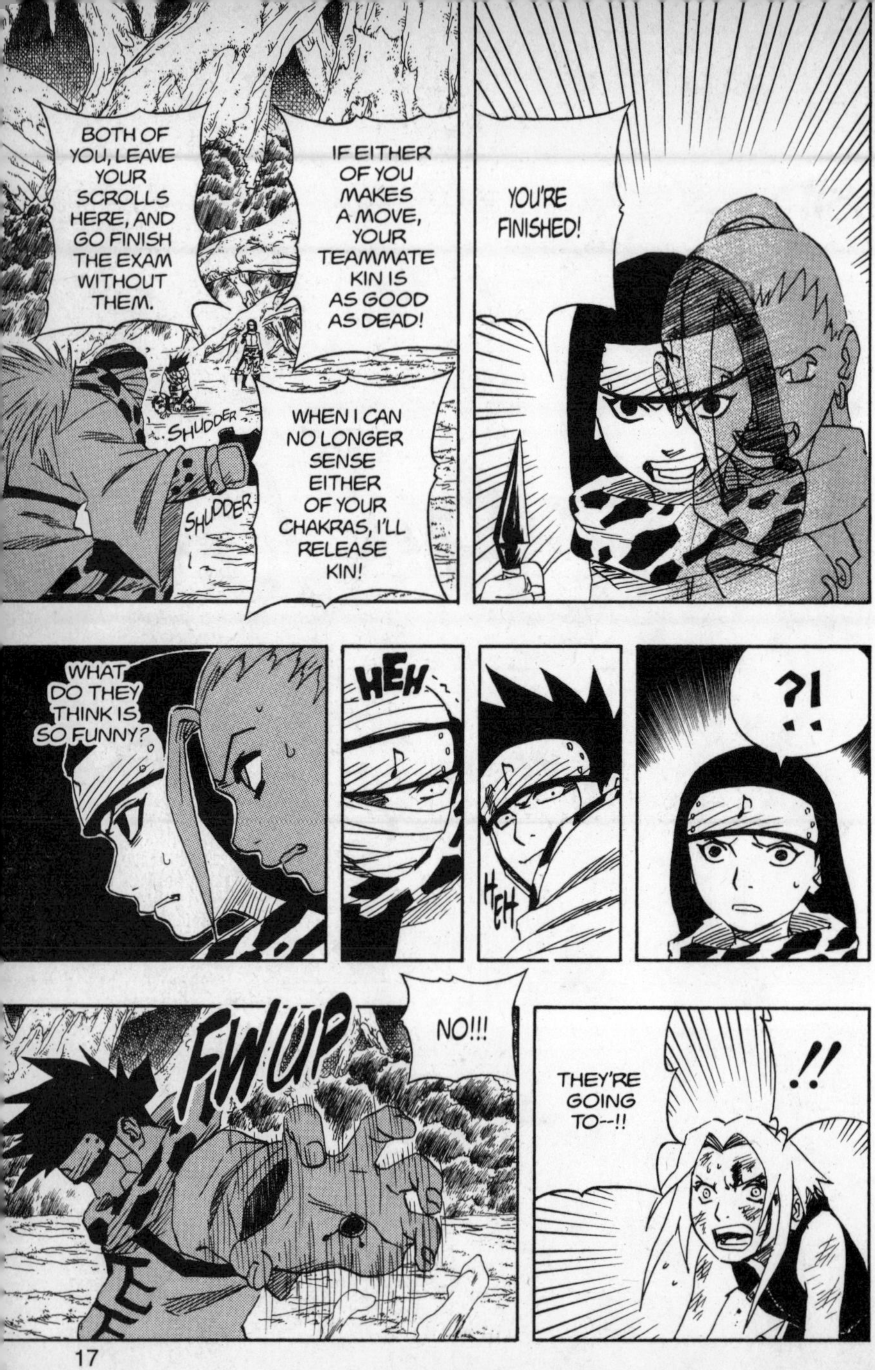
YOU'RE FINISHED!
IF EITHER OF YOU MAKES A MOVE, YOUR TEAMMATE KIN IS AS GOOD AS DEAD!
BOTH OF YOU, LEAVE YOUR SCROLLS HERE, AND GO FINISH THE EXAM WITHOUT THEM.
WHEN I CAN NO LONGER SENSE EITHER OF YOUR CHAKRAS, I'LL RELEASE KIN!
SHUDDER
SHUDDER
?!
HEH
HEH
HEH
WHAT DO THEY THINK IS SO FUNNY?
!!
THEY'RE GOING TO--!!
NO!!!
FWUP

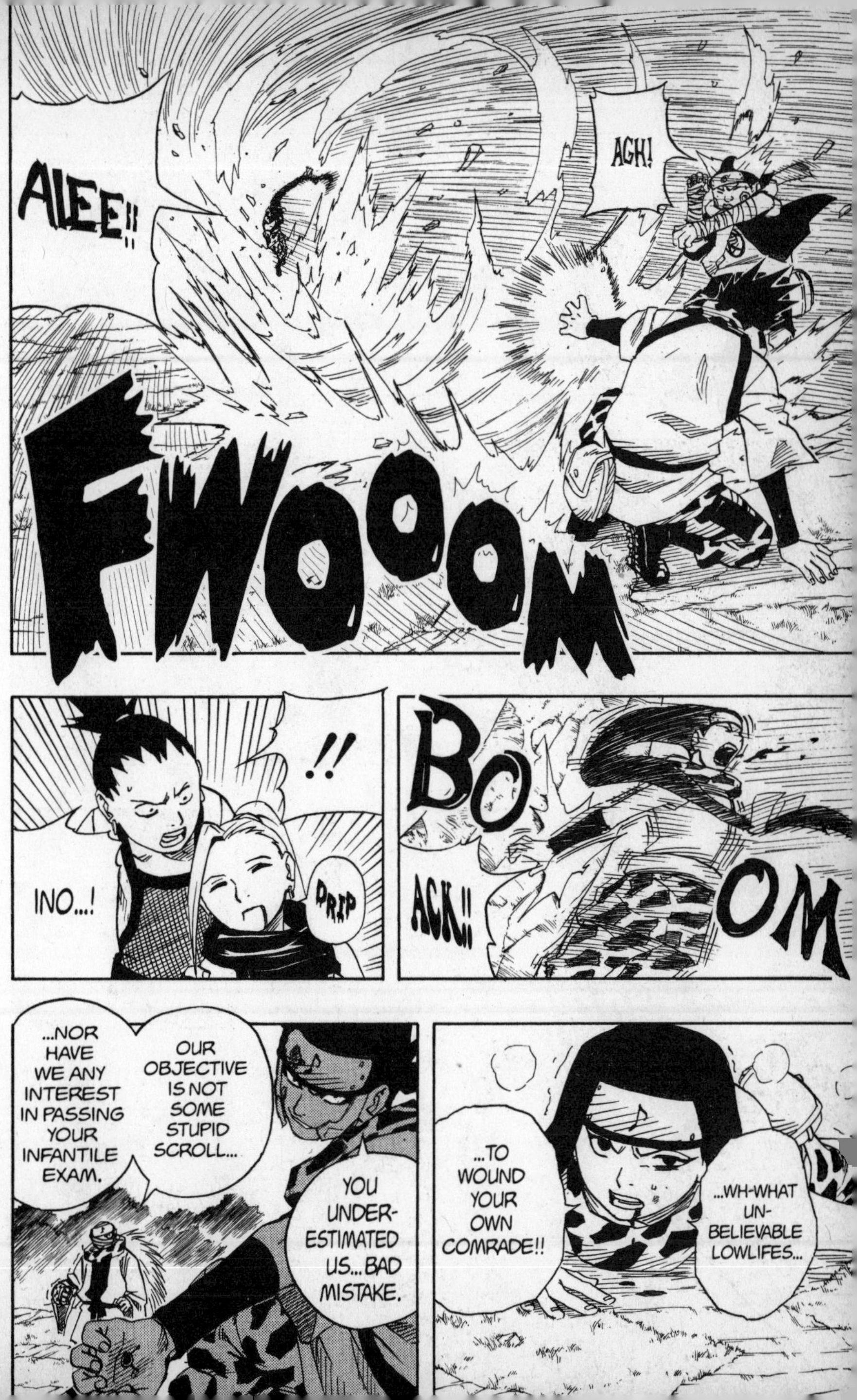
AGH!
AIEE!!
FWOOOM
BOOM
ACK!!
!!
INO...!
DRIP
...WH-WHAT UN-BELIEVABLE LOWLIFES...
...TO WOUND YOUR OWN COMRADE!!
OUR OBJECTIVE IS NOT SOME STUPID SCROLL...
...NOR HAVE WE ANY INTEREST IN PASSING YOUR INFANTILE EXAM.
YOU UNDER-ESTIMATED US... BAD MISTAKE.

READ THIS WAY

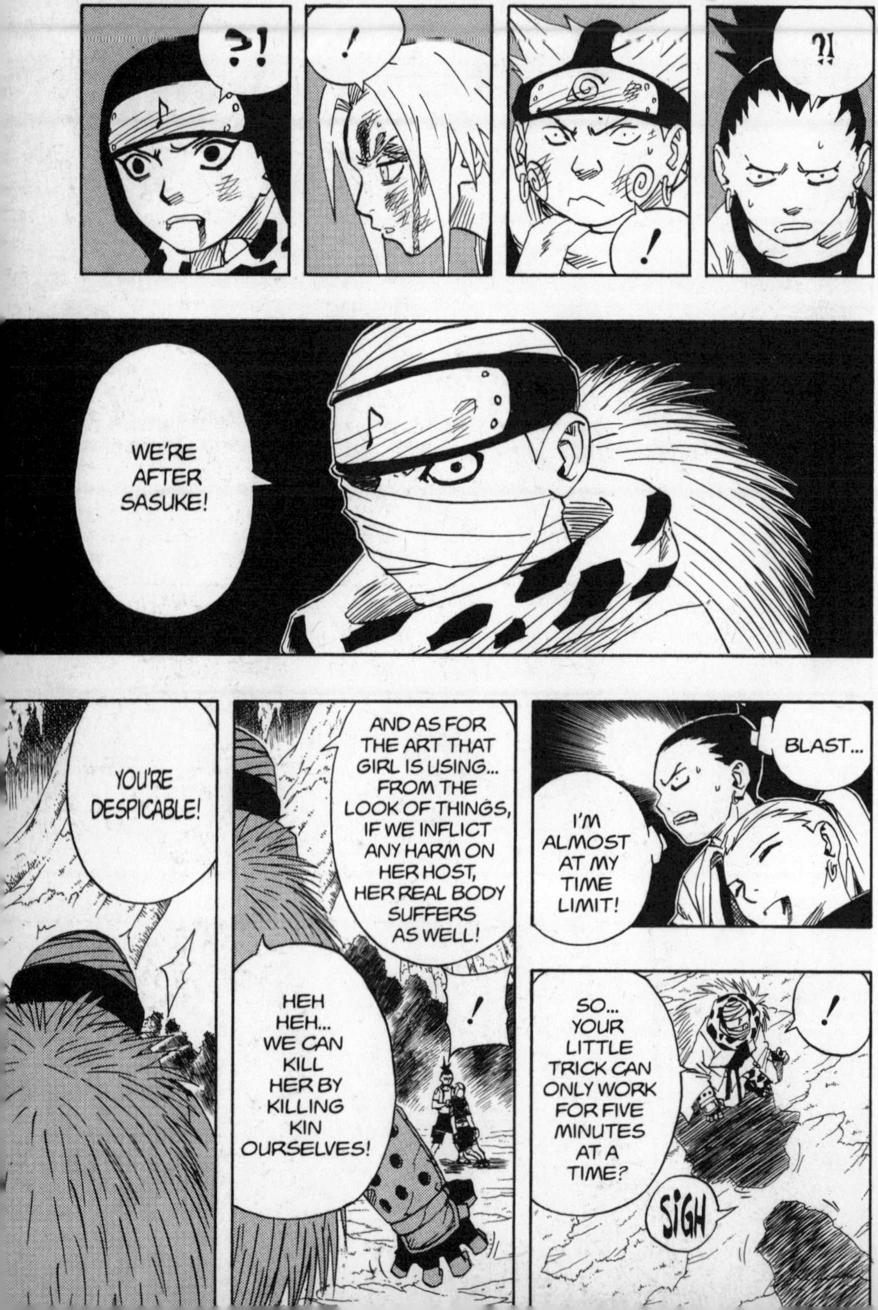
?!
!
!
?!
WE'RE AFTER SASUKE!
BLAST...
I'M ALMOST AT MY TIME LIMIT!
!
SO... YOUR LITTLE TRICK CAN ONLY WORK FOR FIVE MINUTES AT A TIME?
SIGH
AND AS FOR THE ART THAT GIRL IS USING... FROM THE LOOK OF THINGS, IF WE INFLICT ANY HARM ON HER HOST, HER REAL BODY SUFFERS AS WELL!
HEH HEH... WE CAN KILL HER BY KILLING KIN OURSELVES!
!
YOU'RE DESPICABLE!

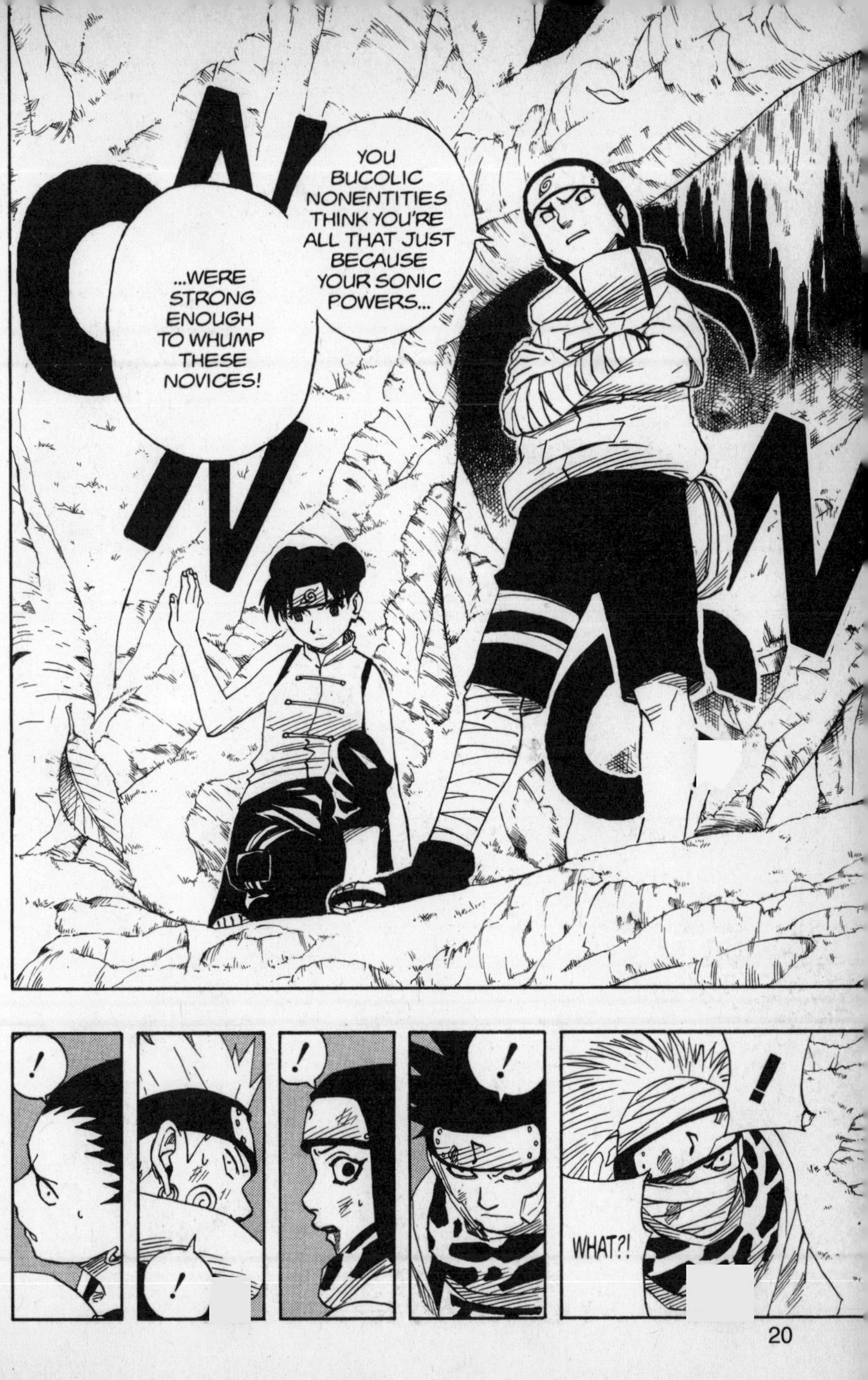
YOU BUCOLIC NONENTITIES THINK YOU'RE ALL THAT JUST BECAUSE YOUR SONIC POWERS...
...WERE STRONG ENOUGH TO WHUMP THESE NOVICES!
!
WHAT?!
!
!
!
!
!

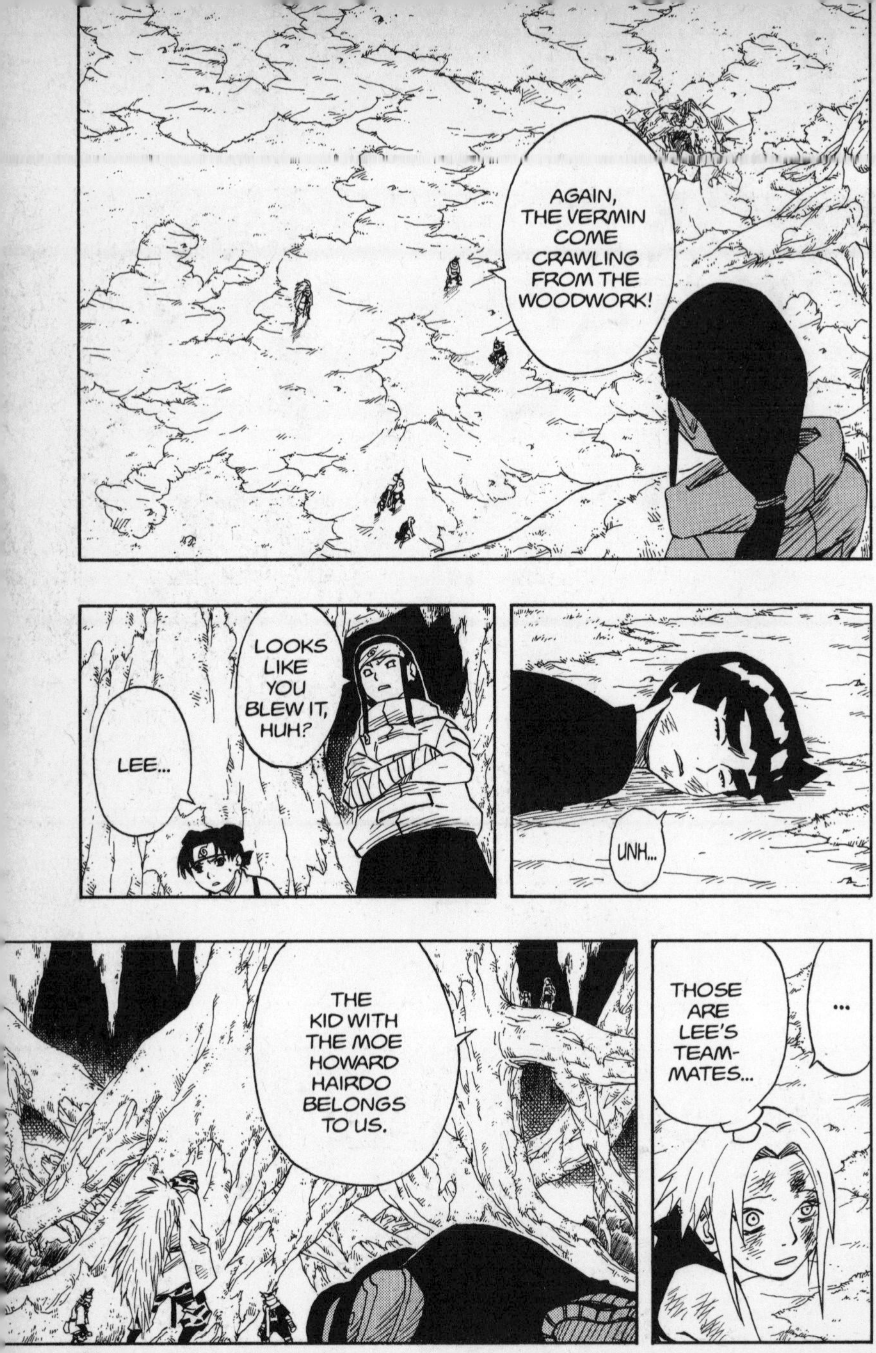
AGAIN, THE VERMIN COME CRAWLING FROM THE WOODWORK!
UNH...
LOOKS LIKE YOU BLEW IT, HUH?
LEE...
...
THOSE ARE LEE'S TEAM-MATES...
THE KID WITH THE MOE HOWARD HAIRDO BELONGS TO US.

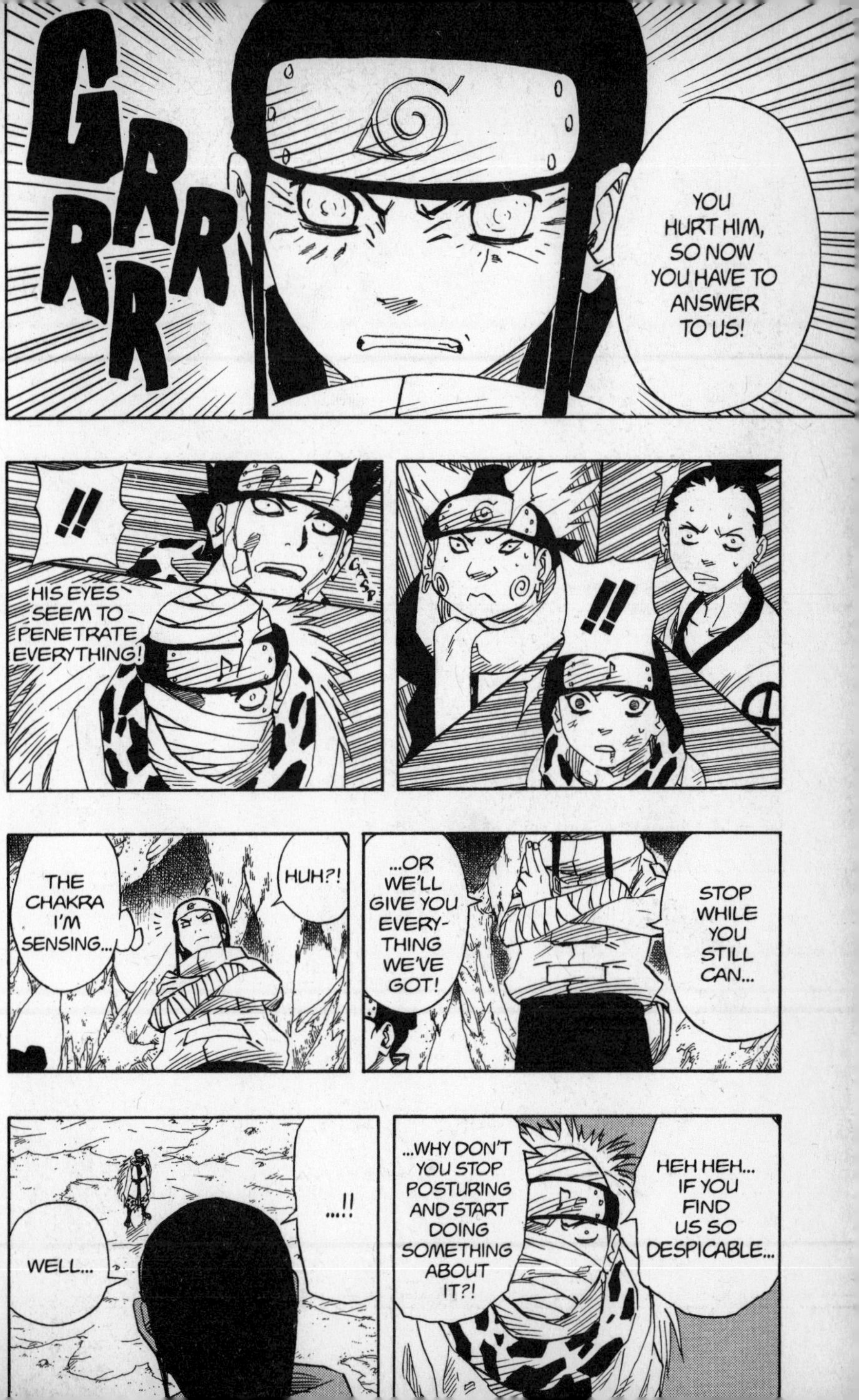
YOU HURT HIM, SO NOW YOU HAVE TO ANSWER TO US!
GRRRR
!!
!!
GASP
HIS EYES SEEM TO PENETRATE EVERYTHING!
STOP WHILE YOU STILL CAN...
...OR WE'LL GIVE YOU EVERY-THING WE'VE GOT!
HUH?!
THE CHAKRA I'M SENSING...
HEH HEH... IF YOU FIND US SO DESPICABLE...
...WHY DON'T YOU STOP POSTURING AND START DOING SOMETHING ABOUT IT?!
...!!
WELL...

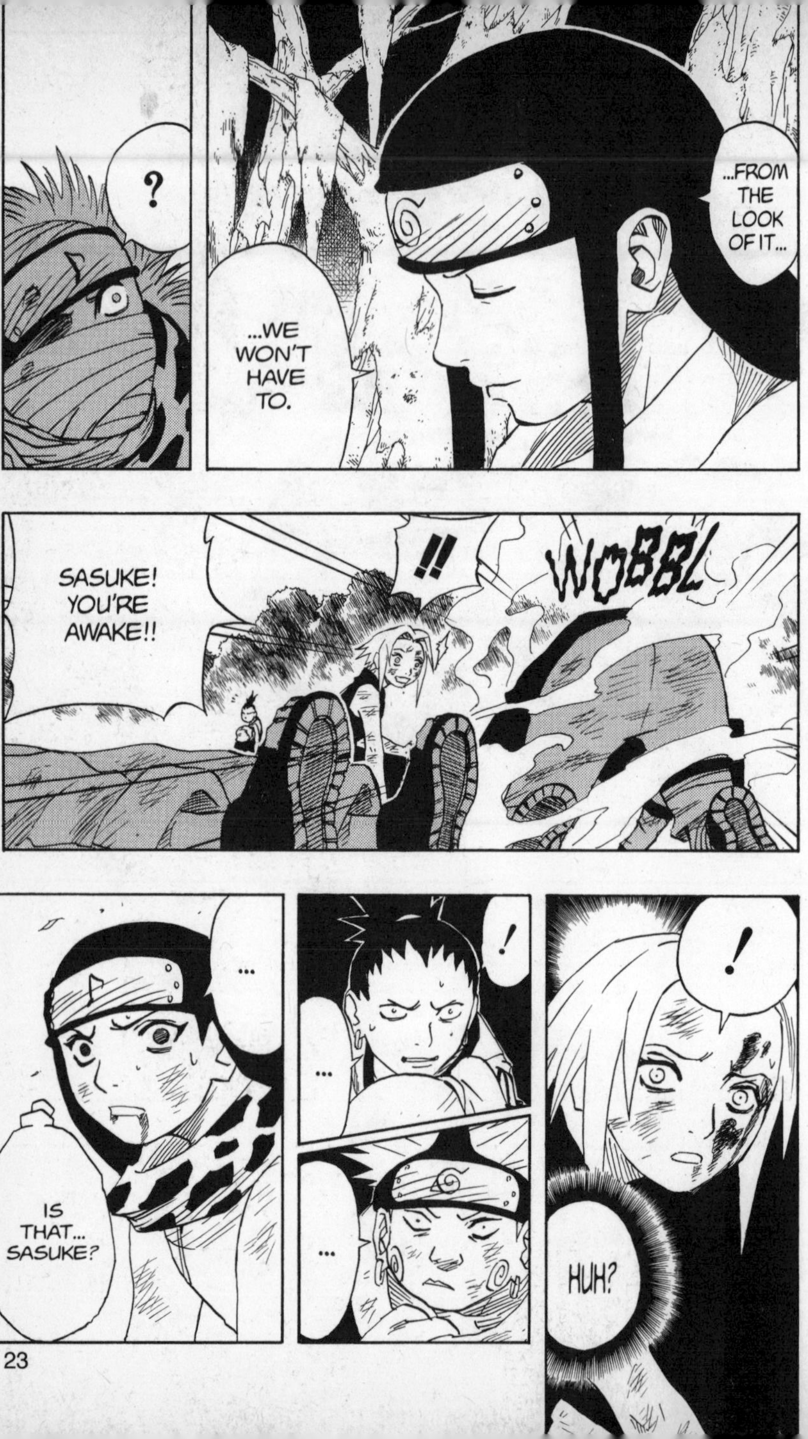
...FROM THE LOOK OF IT...
...WE WON'T HAVE TO.
?
WOBBL
!!
SASUKE! YOU'RE AWAKE!!
!
HUH?
!
...
...
...
IS THAT... SASUKE?

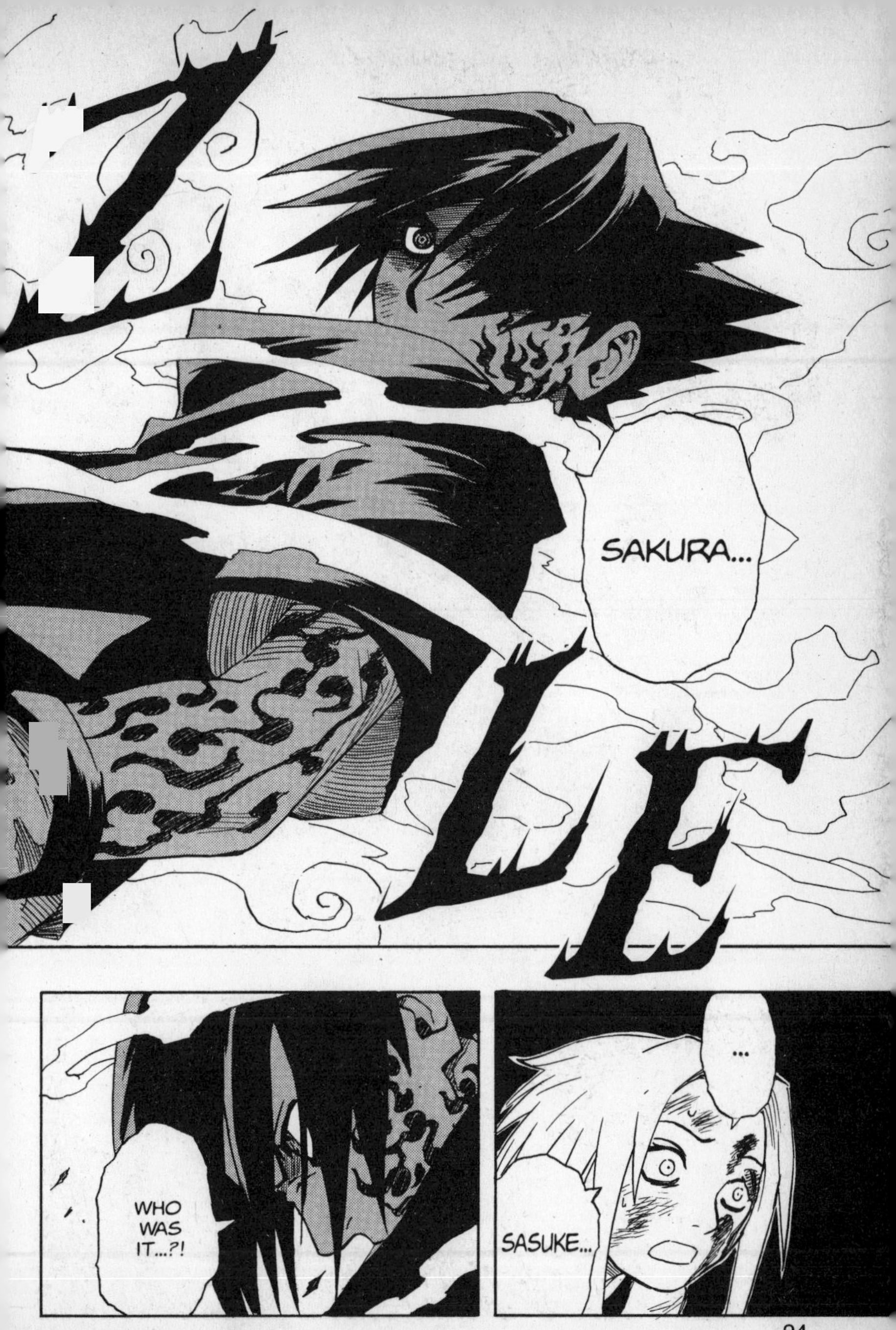
SAKURA...
...
SASUKE...
WHO WAS IT...?!

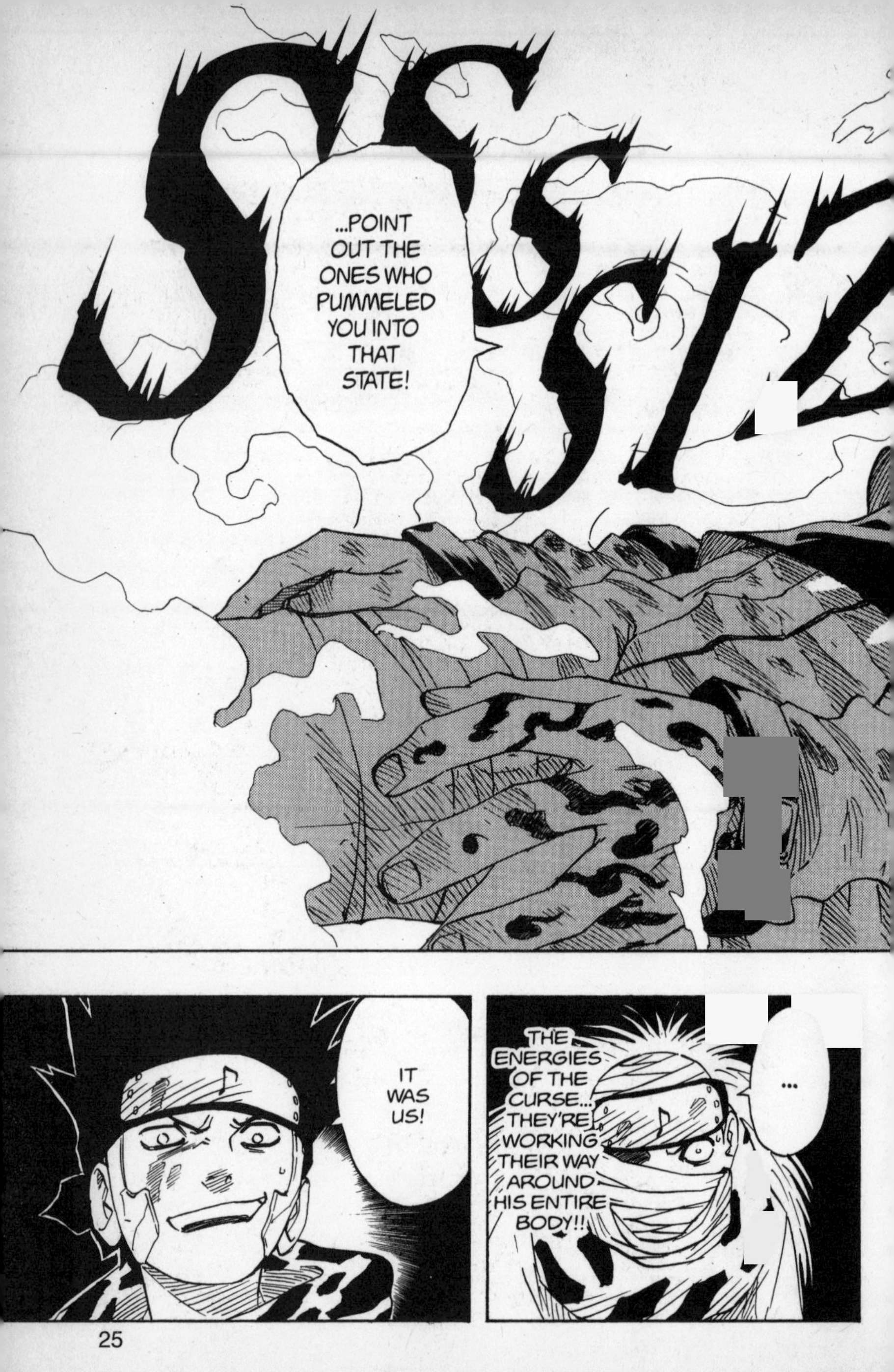
...POINT OUT THE ONES WHO PUMMELED YOU INTO THAT STATE!
...
THE ENERGIES OF THE CURSE... THEY'RE WORKING THEIR WAY AROUND HIS ENTIRE BODY!!
IT WAS US!

THE WORLD OF KISHIMOTO MASASHI
MY PERSONAL HISTORY, PART ONE: GROWING UP

I WAS THE FIRST-BORN OF TWIN BROTHERS IN A TOWN IN OKAYAMA PREFECTURE IN 1974. I WAS EXTREMELY PREMATURE AND HAD TO BE PUT INTO AN INCUBATOR AT ONCE. WITHOUT IT, I WOULD HAVE DIED. MY SURVIVAL WAS A VICTORY FOR SCIENCE. MY HOMETOWN HAS A TRADITION THAT PERSISTS TO THIS DAY WHERE, ON ONE'S FIRST BIRTHDAY, A MOCHI RICE CAKE IS PLACED UPON YOUR BACK AND THREE OBJECTS ARE PLACED BEFORE YOU. DEPENDING ON WHICH OF THOSE THREE A CHILD GRABS FIRST, THAT CHILD'S FUTURE PATH CAN BE DETERMINED. IN FRONT OF MY TWIN AND I, OUR PARENTS PLACED AN ABACUS (TO REPRESENT SCHOLARSHIP), A BRUSH PEN AND MONEY. THE STORY IS THAT AFTER SOME HESITATION, MY YOUNGER BROTHER TOOK HOLD OF THE BRUSH PEN. AND AT THAT SAME MOMENT, I'M TOLD I UNHESITATINGLY WENT FOR THE CASH, LAUGHING ALL THE WAY. WHAT A BRAT! I MAY HAVE BEEN A MERCENARY BABY, BUT AS I GREW OLDER, MY INTERESTS TURNED TOWARD DRAWING... AS DID THOSE OF MY BROTHER. TO THIS DAY, THERE ARE TWO LARGE BROWN STAINS ON THE WALL OF MY PARENTS' HOME. WHEN I ASKED MY MOTHER ABOUT IT, SHE TOLD ME, "WHEN YOU TWO WERE BABIES, YOU USED THE POOP THAT HAD OOZED OUT OF YOUR DIAPERS TO DECORATE THE WALL. WE'VE TRIED TO WASH IT OFF TIME AND TIME AGAIN, BUT THE STAIN REMAINS." THAT'S WHEN I REALIZED I'D WANTED TO BE AN ARTIST MY ENTIRE LIFE.

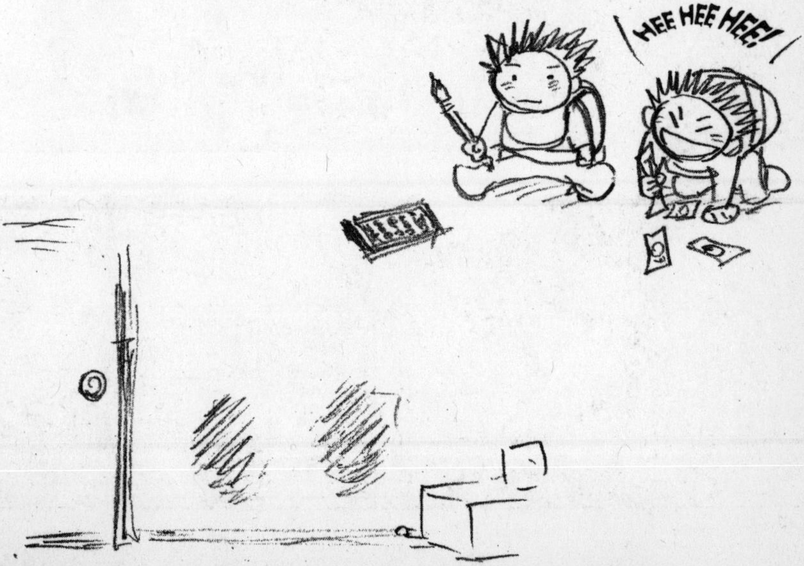
HEE HEE HEE!

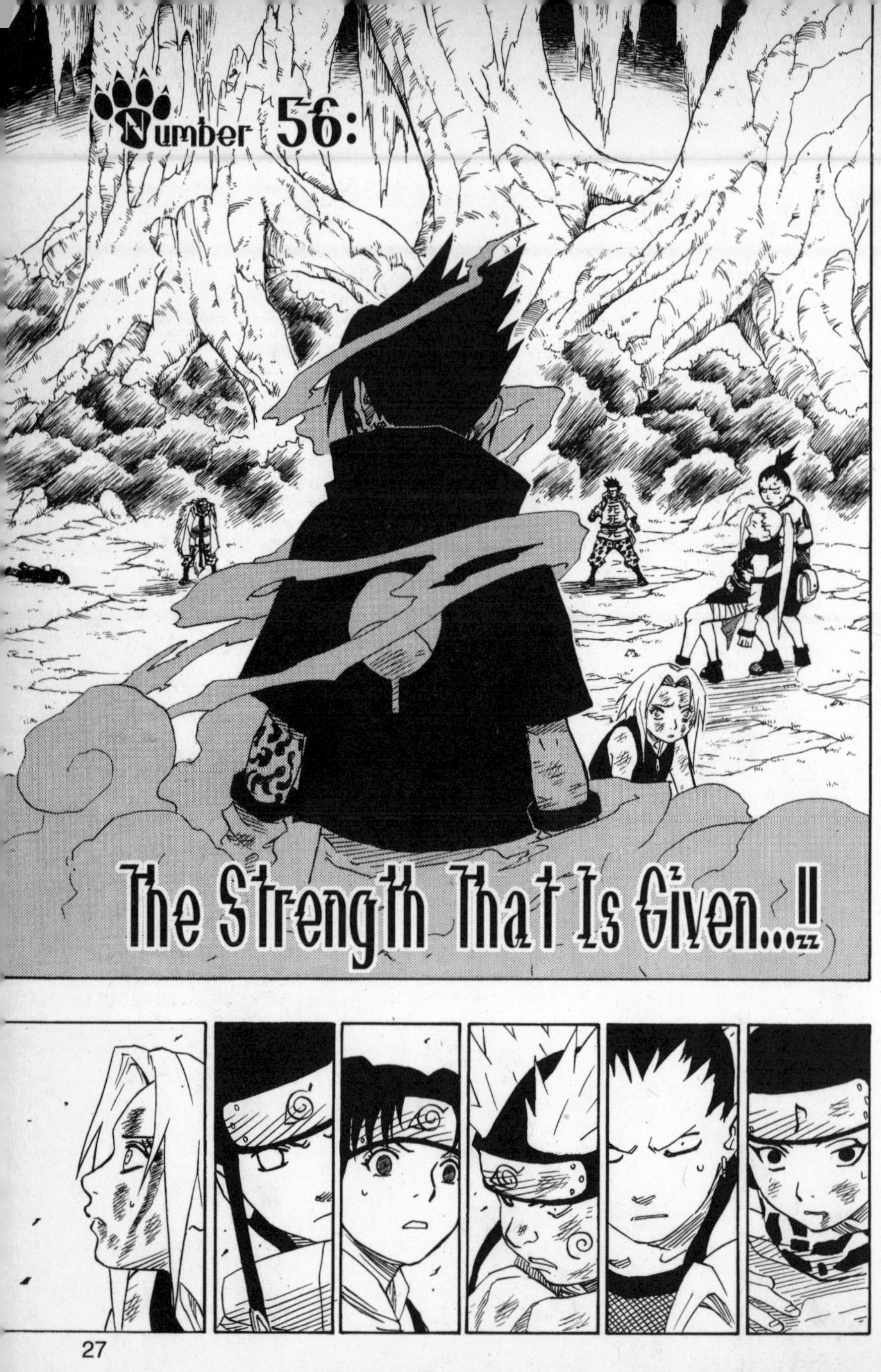
Number 56:
The Strength That Is Given...!!

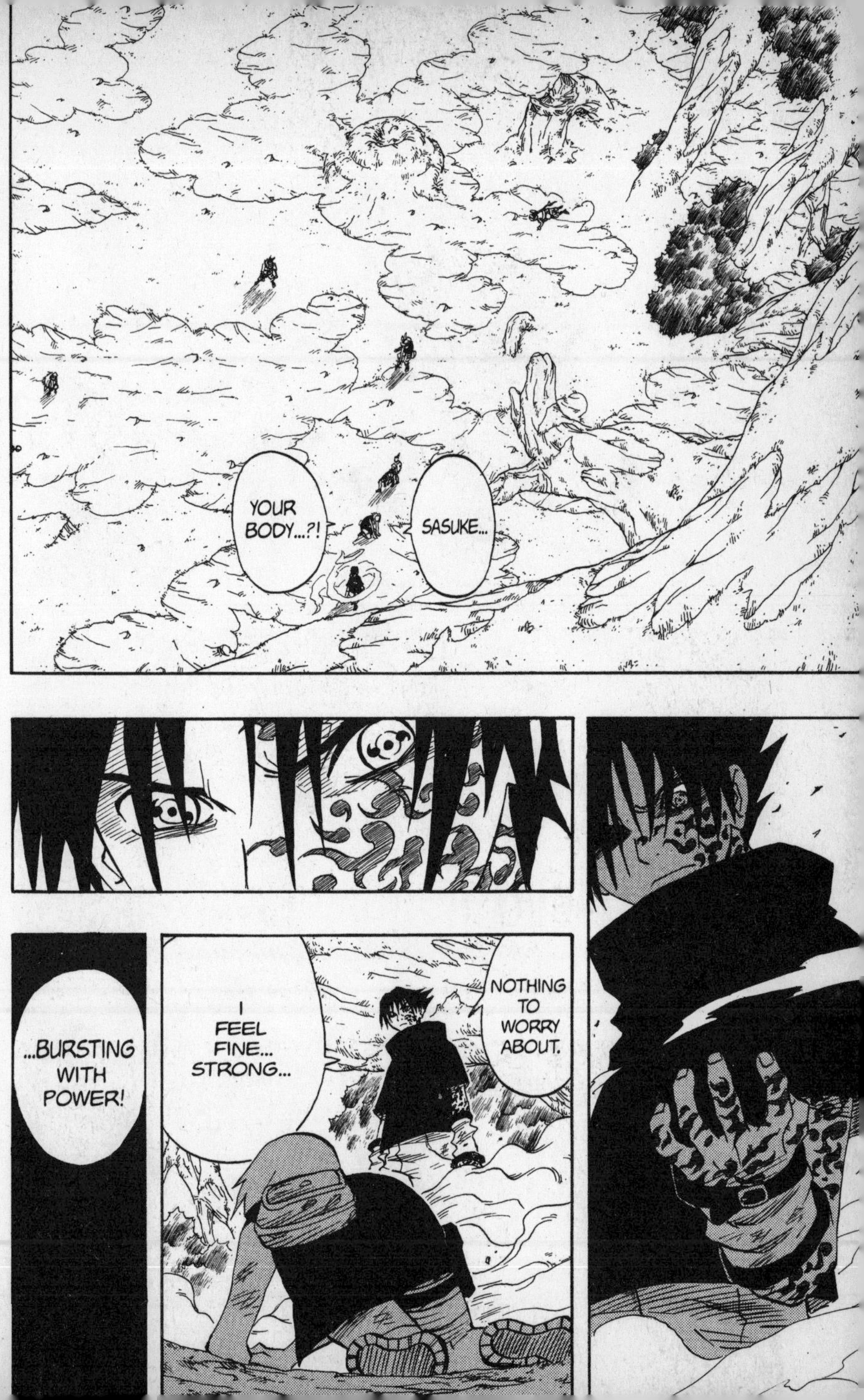
SASUKE...
YOUR BODY...?!
NOTHING TO WORRY ABOUT.
I FEEL FINE... STRONG...
...BURSTING WITH POWER!

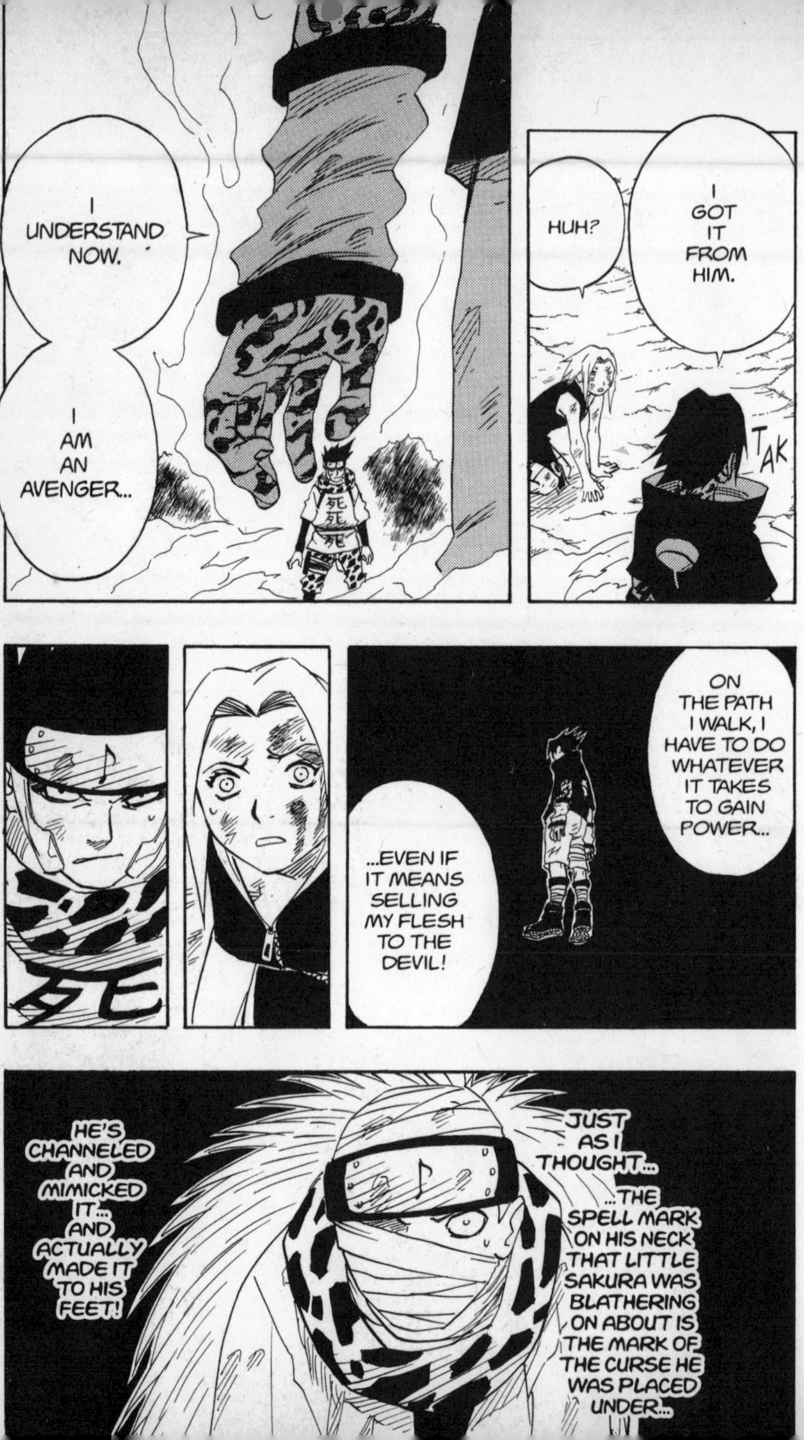
I GOT IT FROM HIM.
HUH?
TAK
I UNDERSTAND NOW.
I AM AN AVENGER...
ON THE PATH I WALK, I HAVE TO DO WHATEVER IT TAKES TO GAIN POWER...
...EVEN IF IT MEANS SELLING MY FLESH TO THE DEVIL!
JUST AS I THOUGHT...
...THE SPELL MARK ON HIS NECK THAT LITTLE SAKURA WAS BLATHERING ON ABOUT IS THE MARK OF THE CURSE HE WAS PLACED UNDER...
HE'S CHANNELED AND MIMICKED IT... AND ACTUALLY MADE IT TO HIS FEET!

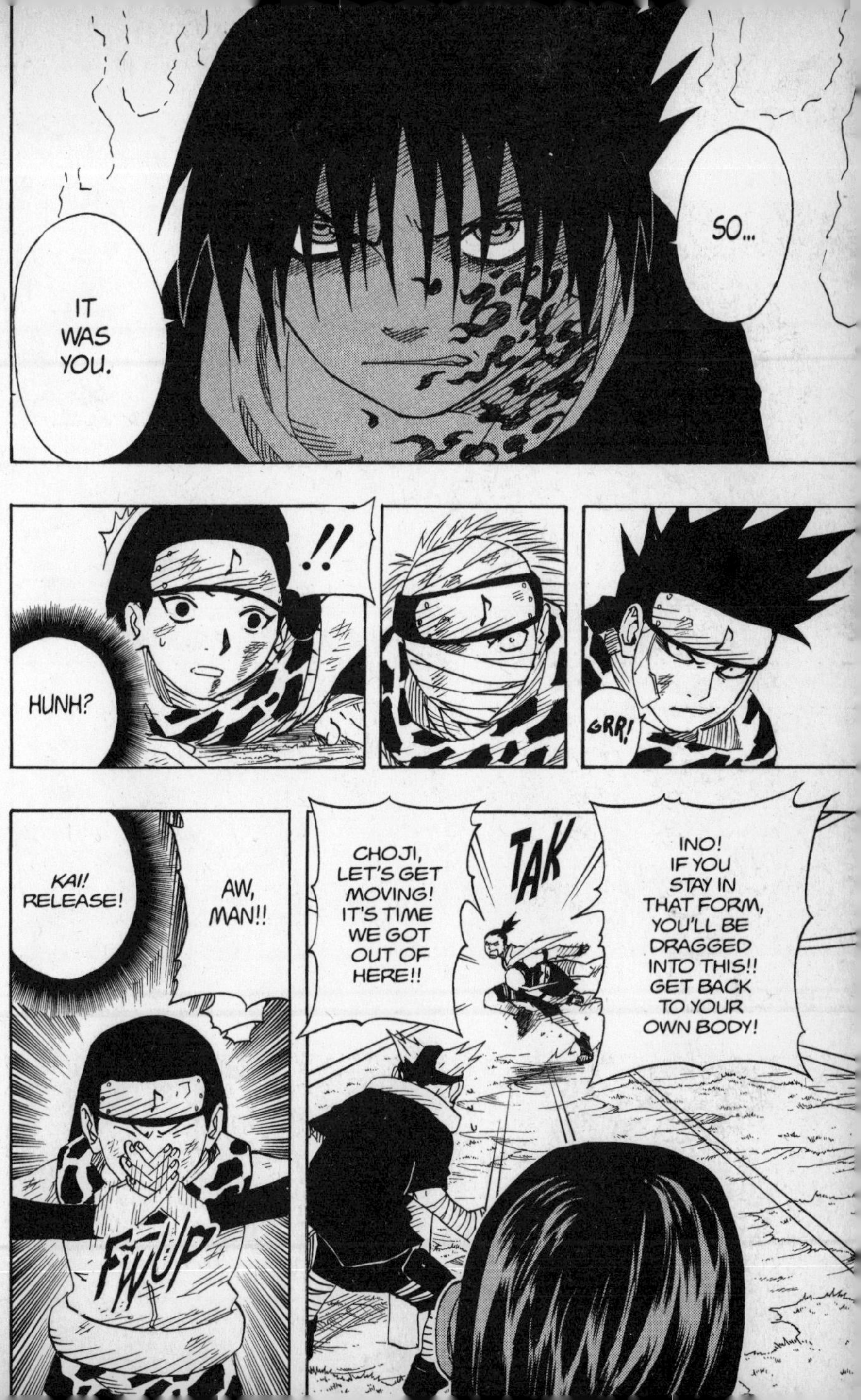
SO...
IT WAS YOU.
GRR!
!!
HUNH?
INO! IF YOU STAY IN THAT FORM, YOU'LL BE DRAGGED INTO THIS!! GET BACK TO YOUR OWN BODY!
TAK
CHOJI, LET'S GET MOVING! IT'S TIME WE GOT OUT OF HERE!!
AW, MAN!!
KAI! RELEASE!
FWUP

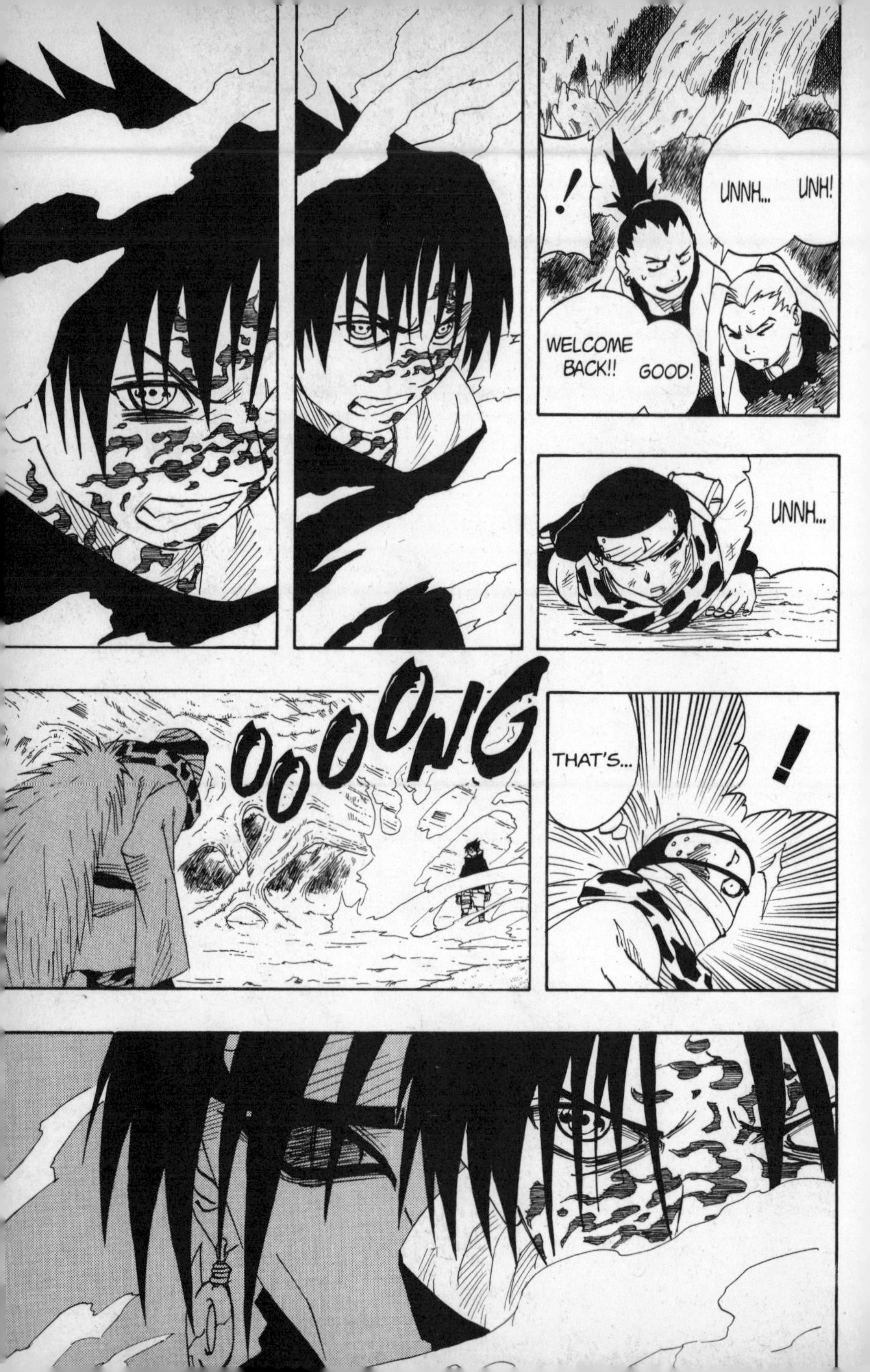
UNNH... UNH!
!
GOOD!
WELCOME BACK!!
UNNH...
!
THAT'S...
OOOONG

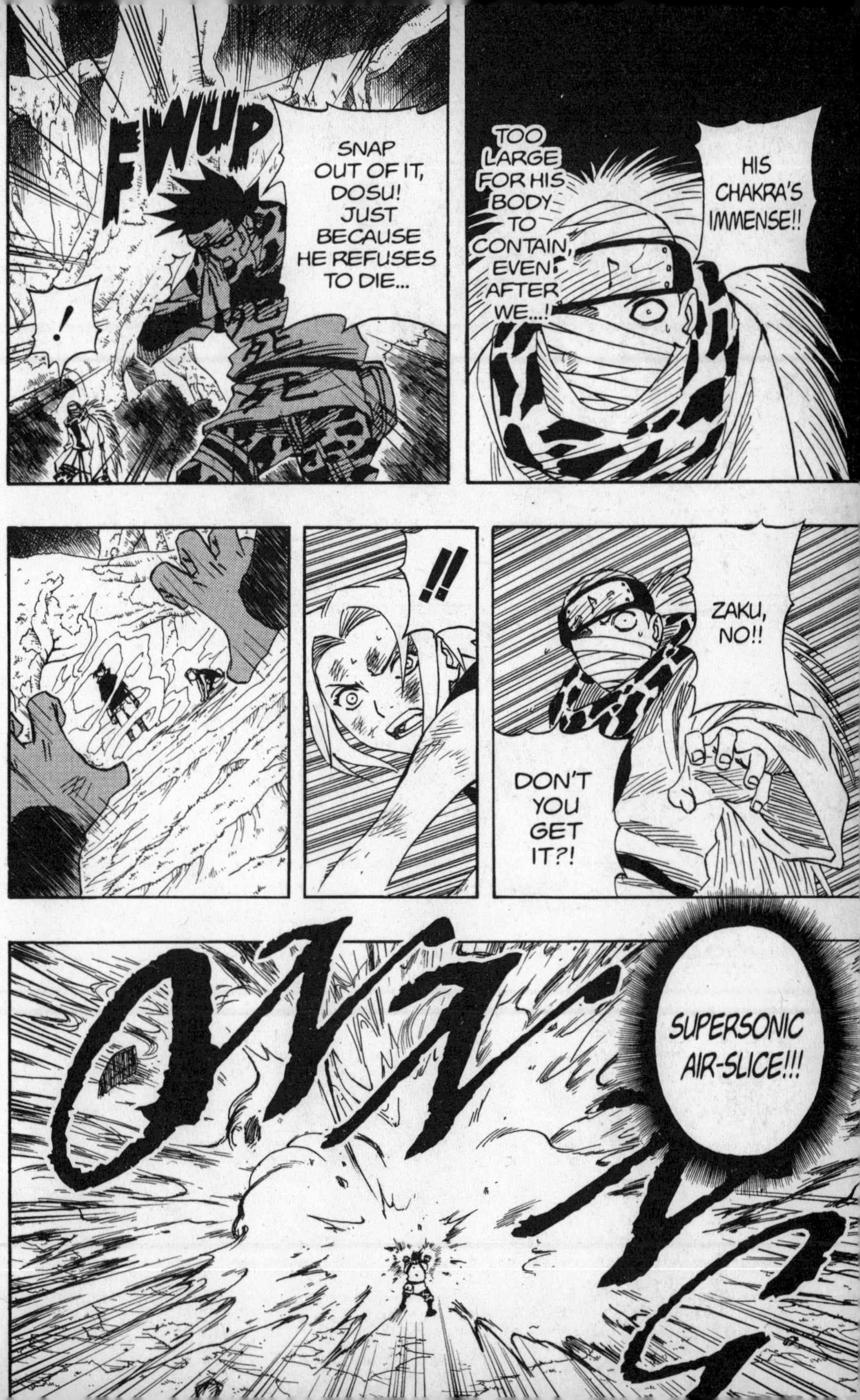
HIS CHAKRA'S IMMENSE!!
TOO LARGE FOR HIS BODY TO CONTAIN, EVEN AFTER WE...!
SNAP OUT OF IT, DOSU! JUST BECAUSE HE REFUSES TO DIE...
FWUP
!
ZAKU, NO!!
DON'T YOU GET IT?!
!!
SUPERSONIC AIR-SLICE!!!

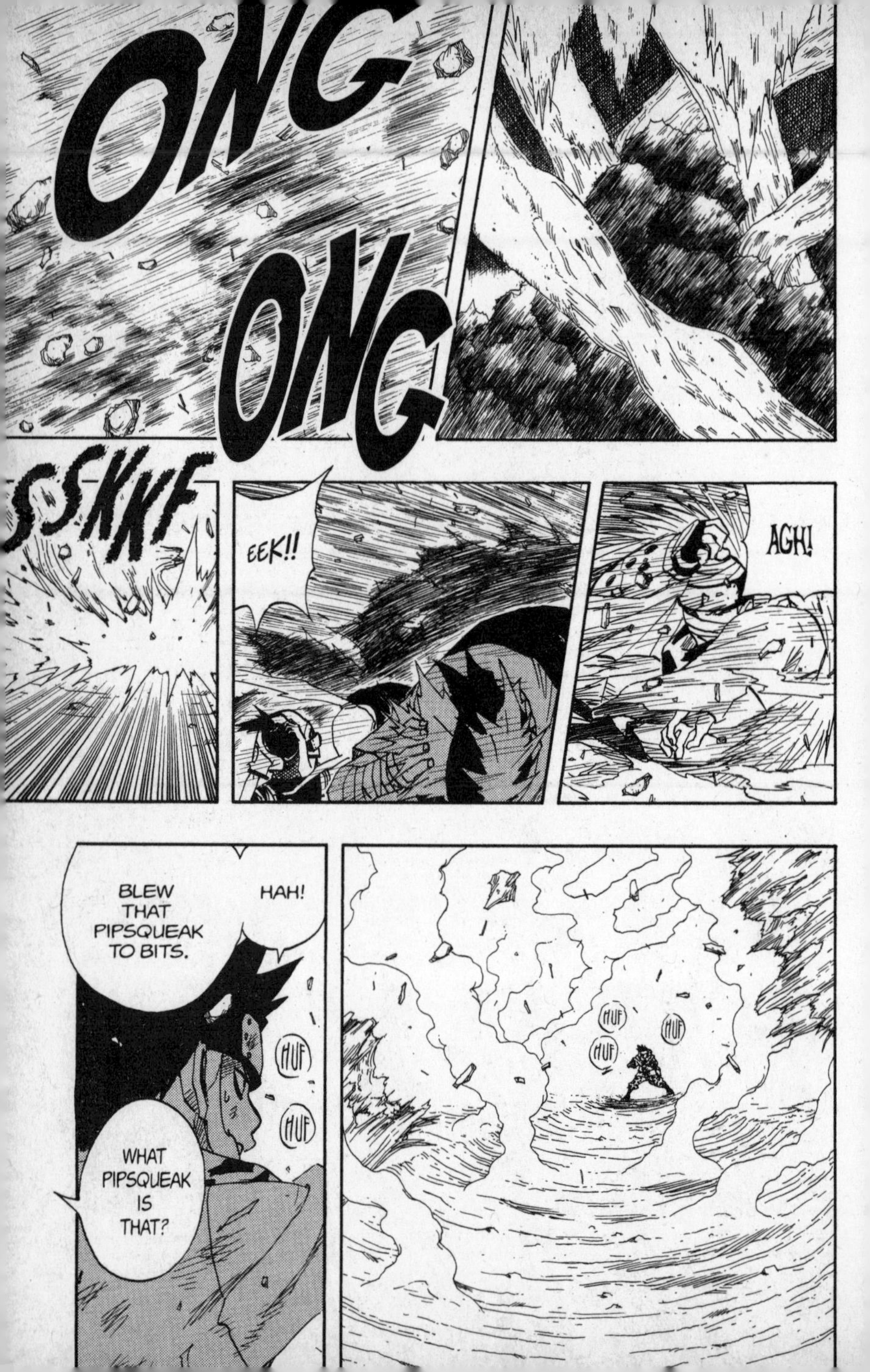
ONG
ONG
AGH!
EEK!!
SSKNF
HUF
HUF
HUF
HAH!
BLEW THAT PIPSQUEAK TO BITS.
HUF
HUF
WHAT PIPSQUEAK IS THAT?

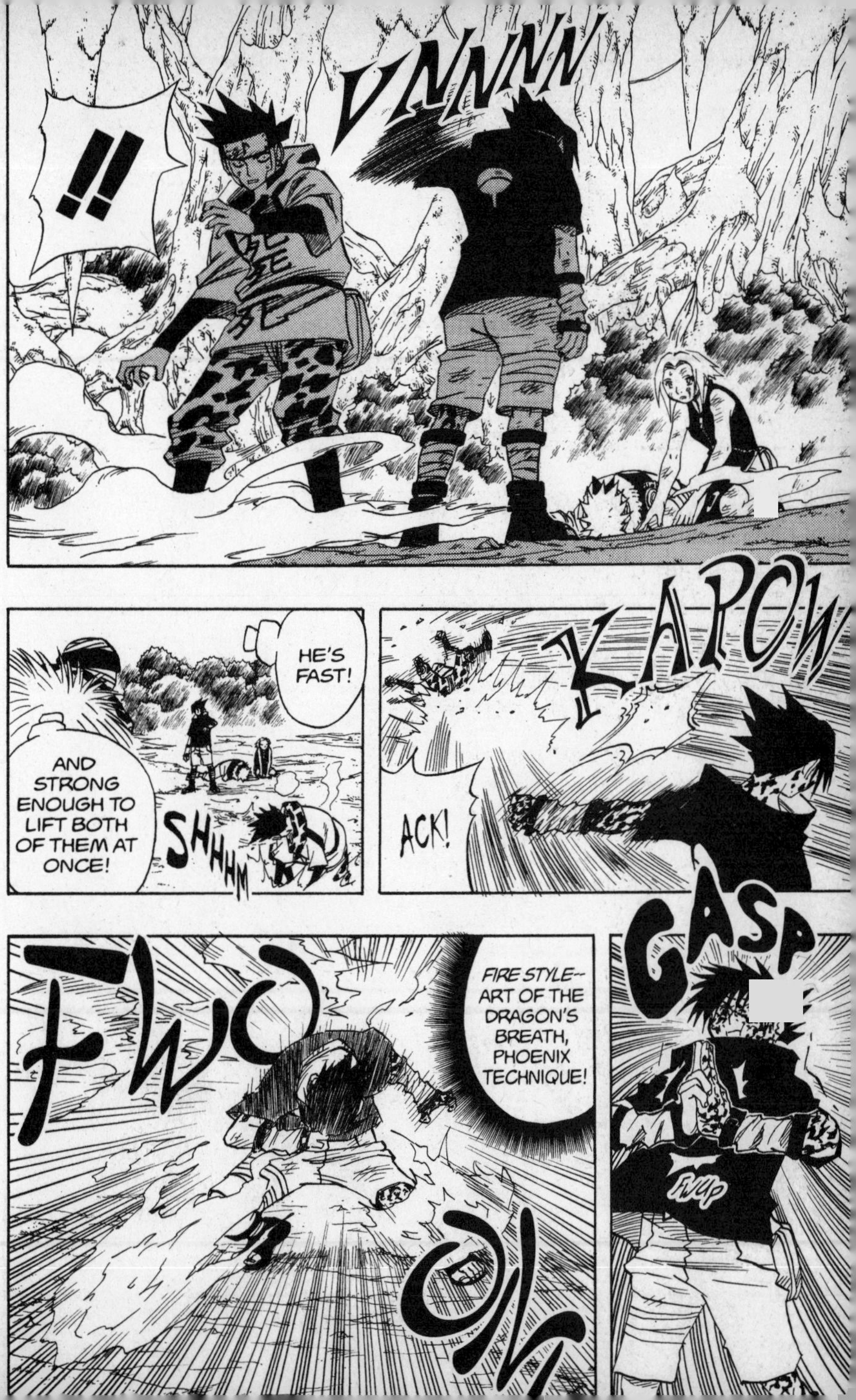
VNNNN
!!
KAROW
ACK!
HE'S FAST!
AND STRONG ENOUGH TO LIFT BOTH OF THEM AT ONCE!
SHHHM
GASP
FWUP
FIRE STYLE-- ART OF THE DRAGON'S BREATH, PHOENIX TECHNIQUE!
FWO

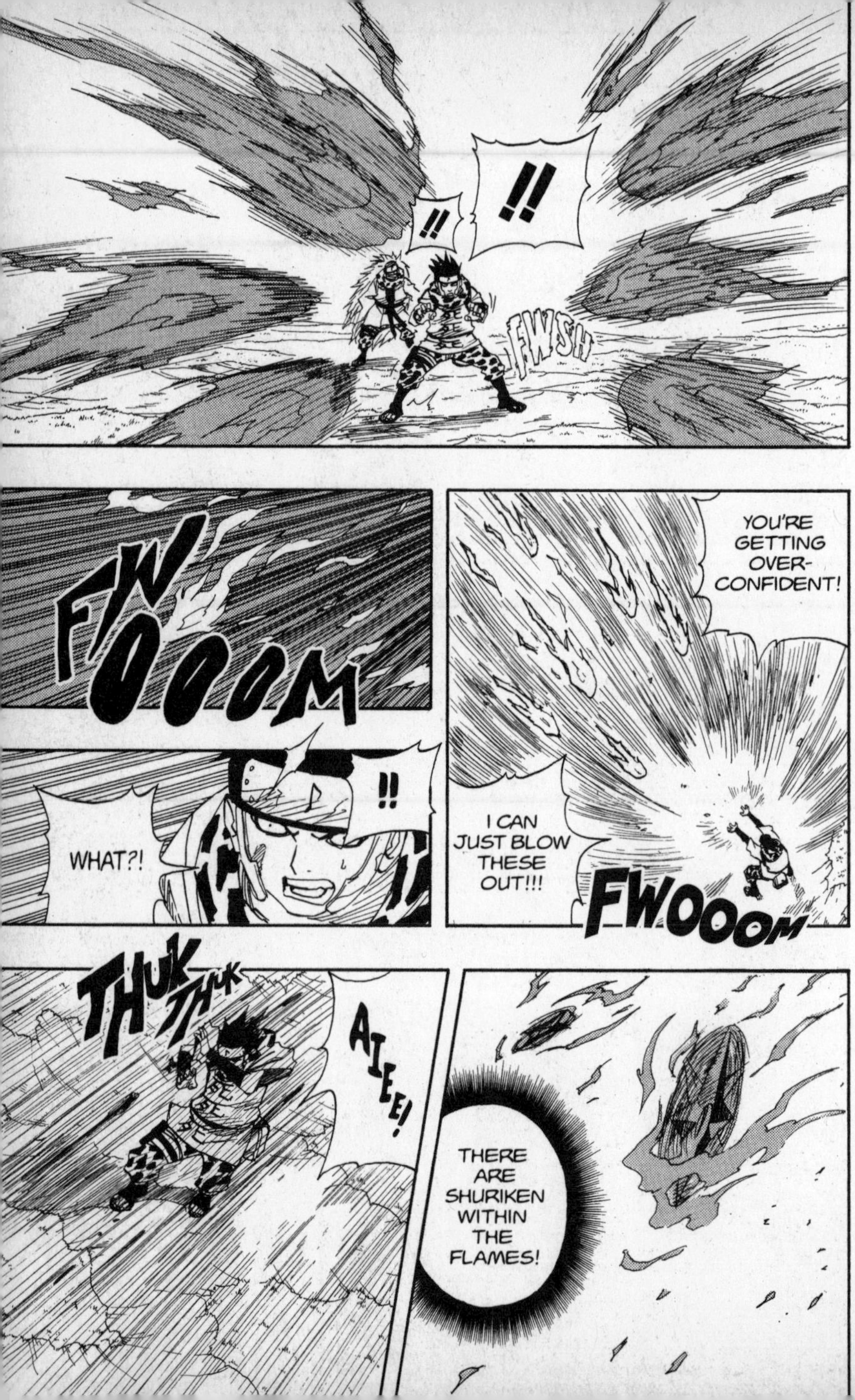
!!
!!
FWSH
YOU'RE GETTING OVER-CONFIDENT!
I CAN JUST BLOW THESE OUT!!!
FWOOOM
FWOOOM
!!
WHAT?!
THERE ARE SHURIKEN WITHIN THE FLAMES!
THUK THUK
AIEEE!

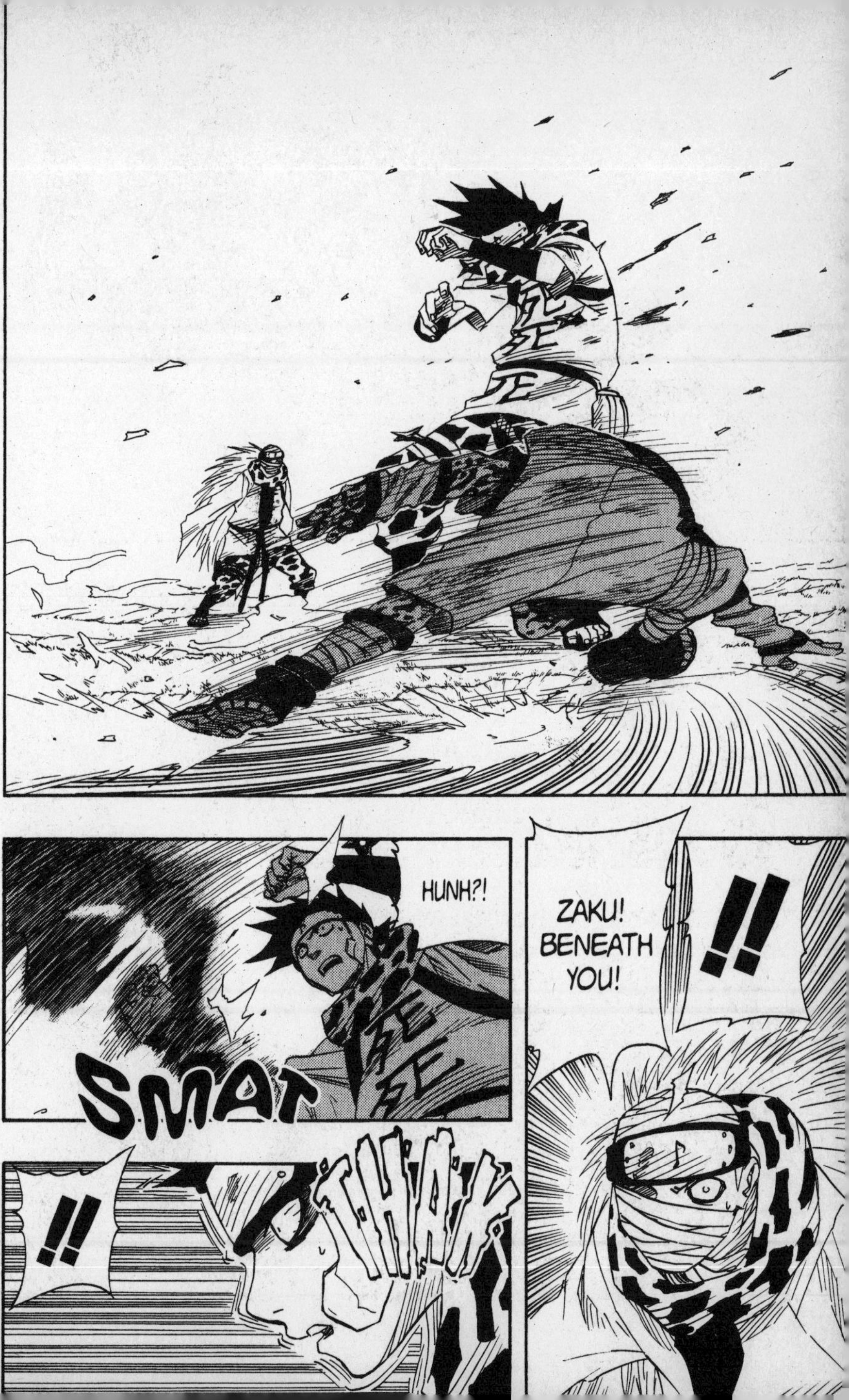
ZAKU! BENEATH YOU!
!!
HUNH?!
SMAT
!!
THAK

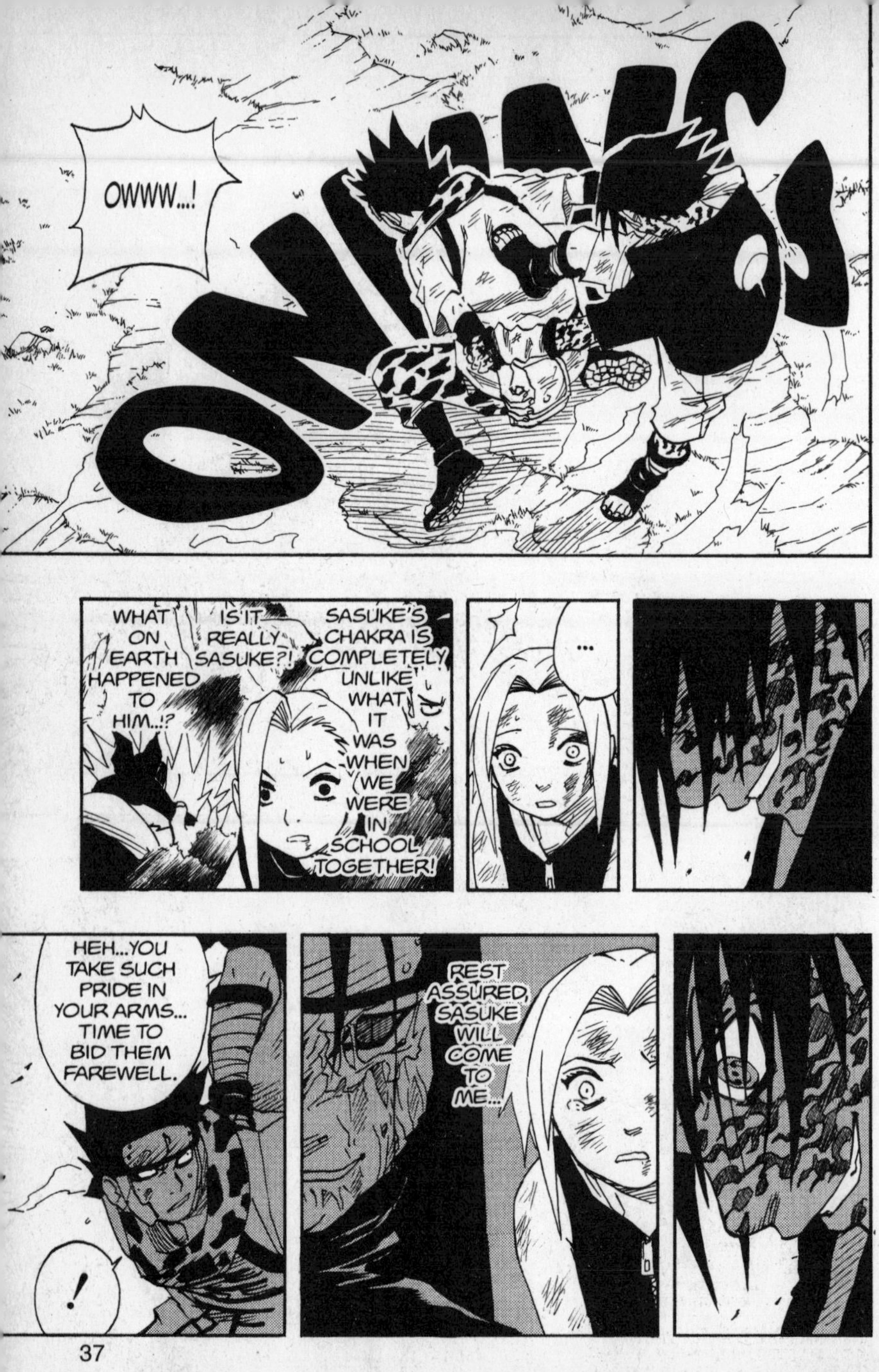
OWWW...!
...
SASUKE'S CHAKRA IS COMPLETELY UNLIKE WHAT IT WAS WHEN WE WERE IN SCHOOL TOGETHER!
IS IT REALLY SASUKE?!
WHAT ON EARTH HAPPENED TO HIM...?
REST ASSURED, SASUKE WILL COME TO ME...
HEH...YOU TAKE SUCH PRIDE IN YOUR ARMS... TIME TO BID THEM FAREWELL.
!

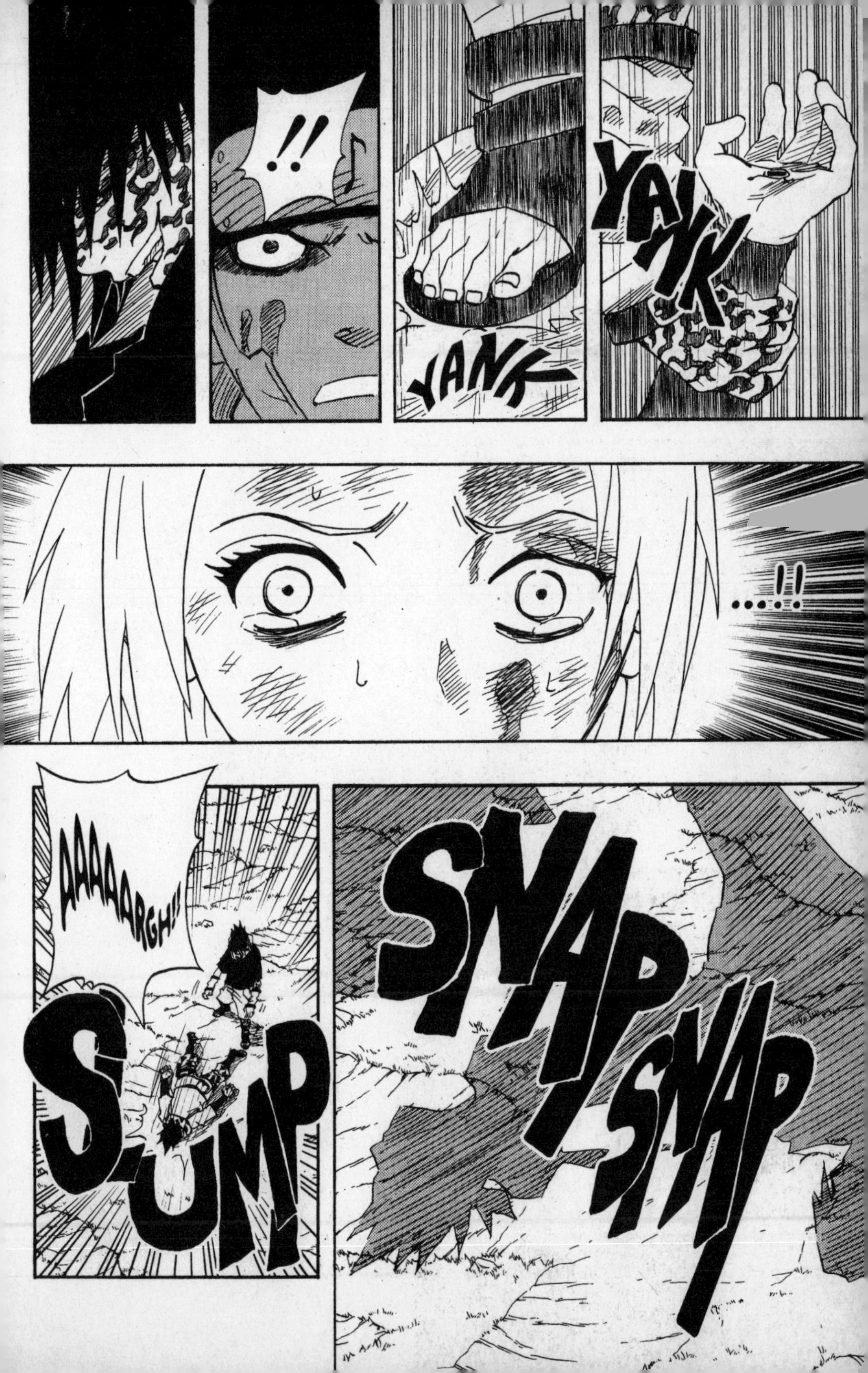
YANK
YANK
!!
...!!
SNAP
SNAP
AAAAARGH!!
SLUMP

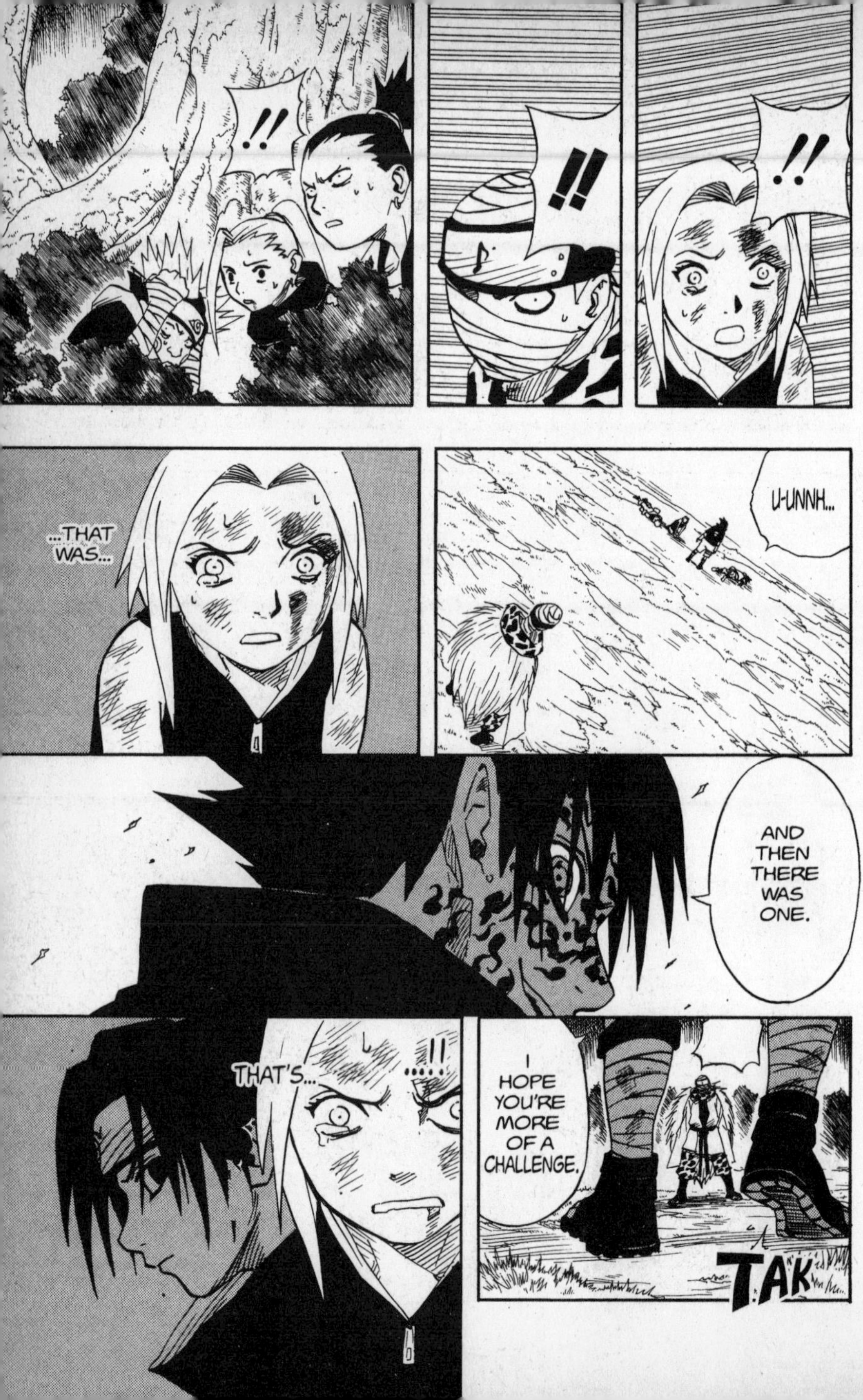

!!
!!
!!
U-UNNH...
...THAT WAS...
AND THEN THERE WAS ONE.
I HOPE YOU'RE MORE OF A CHALLENGE.
TAK
.....!!
THAT'S...

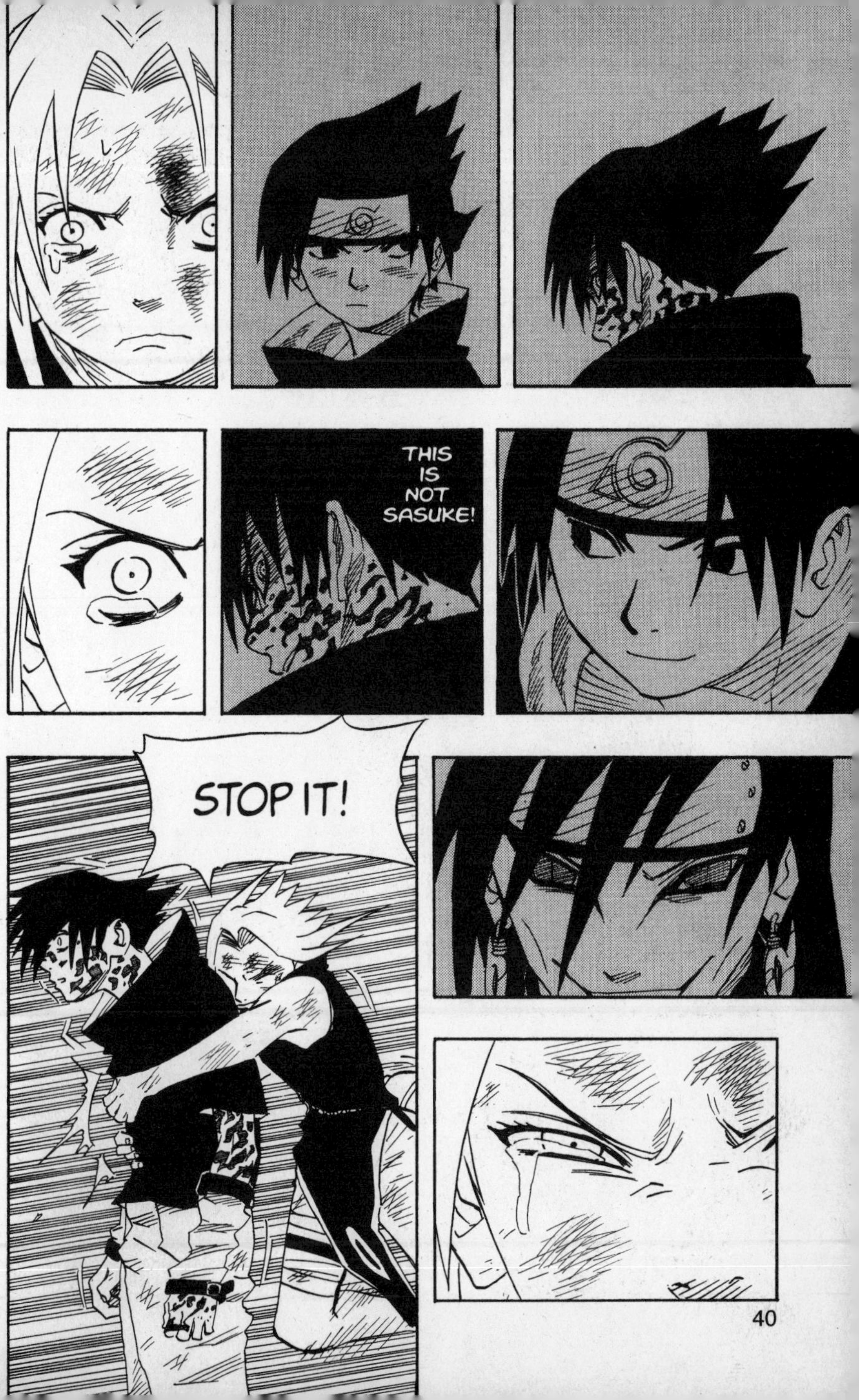
THIS IS NOT SASUKE!
STOP IT!

READ THIS WAY

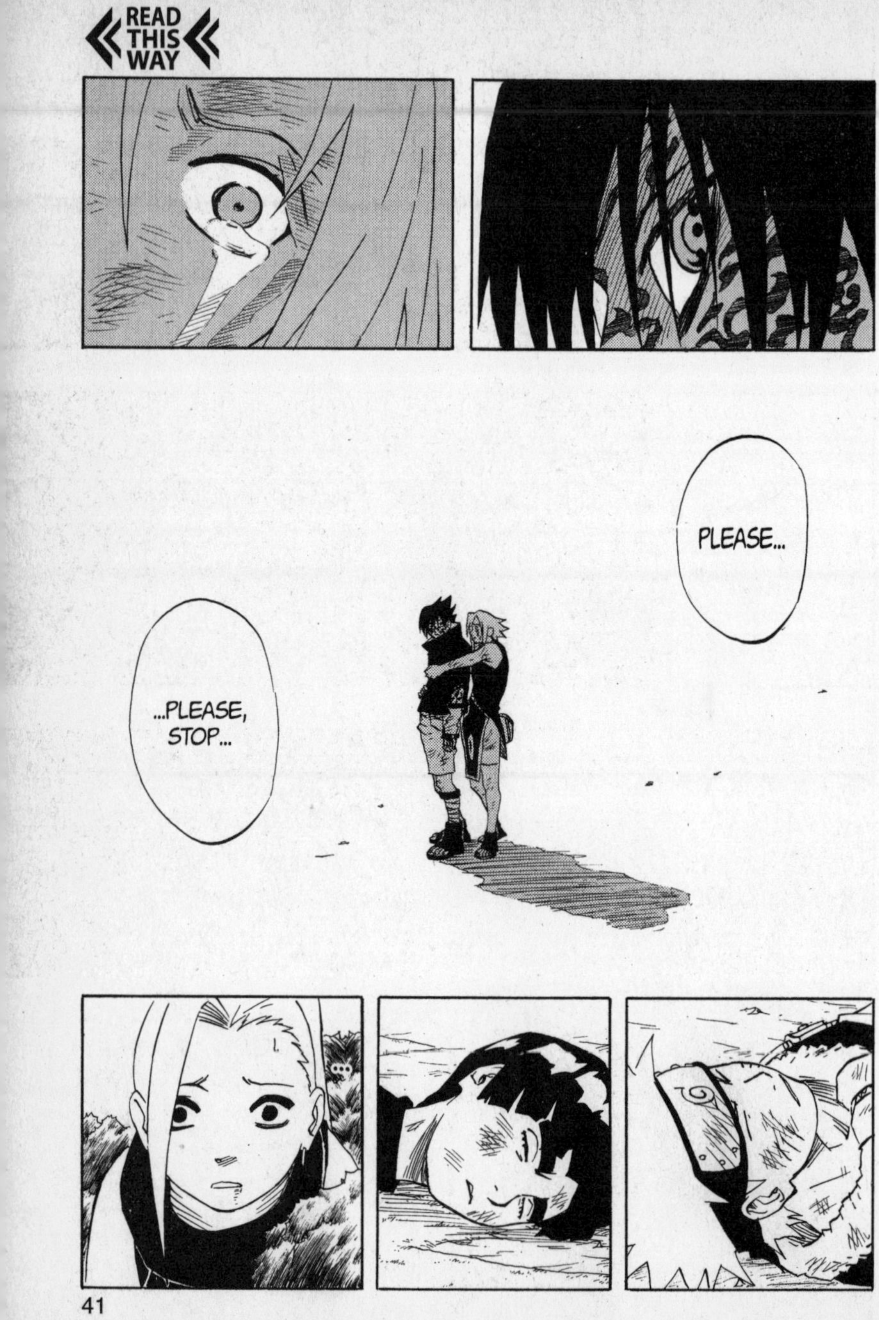
PLEASE...
...PLEASE, STOP...
...

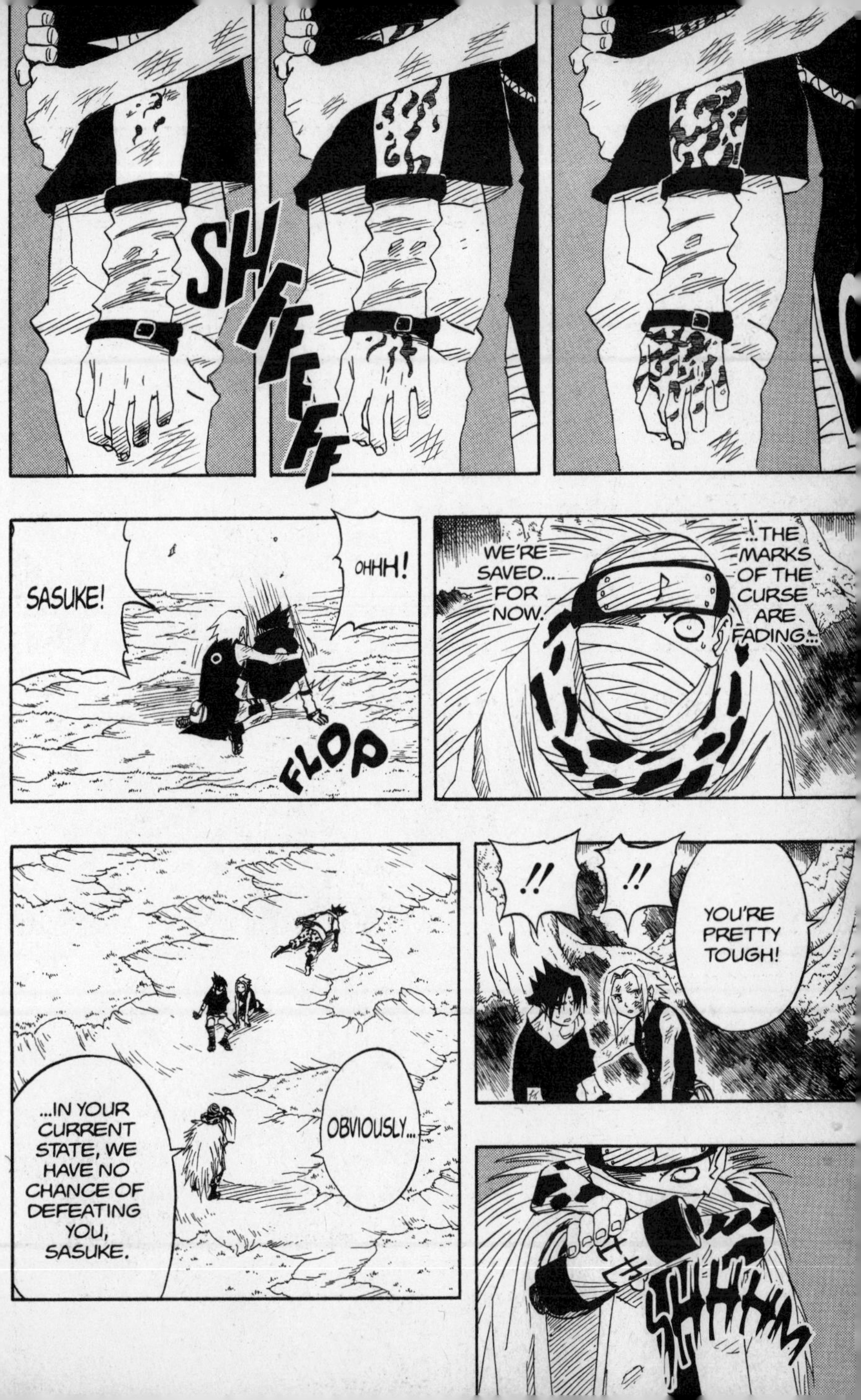
SHFFFFF
...THE MARKS OF THE CURSE ARE FADING...
WE'RE SAVED... FOR NOW.
OHHH!
SASUKE!
FLOP
!!
!!
YOU'RE PRETTY TOUGH!
SHHHM
OBVIOUSLY...
...IN YOUR CURRENT STATE, WE HAVE NO CHANCE OF DEFEATING YOU, SASUKE.

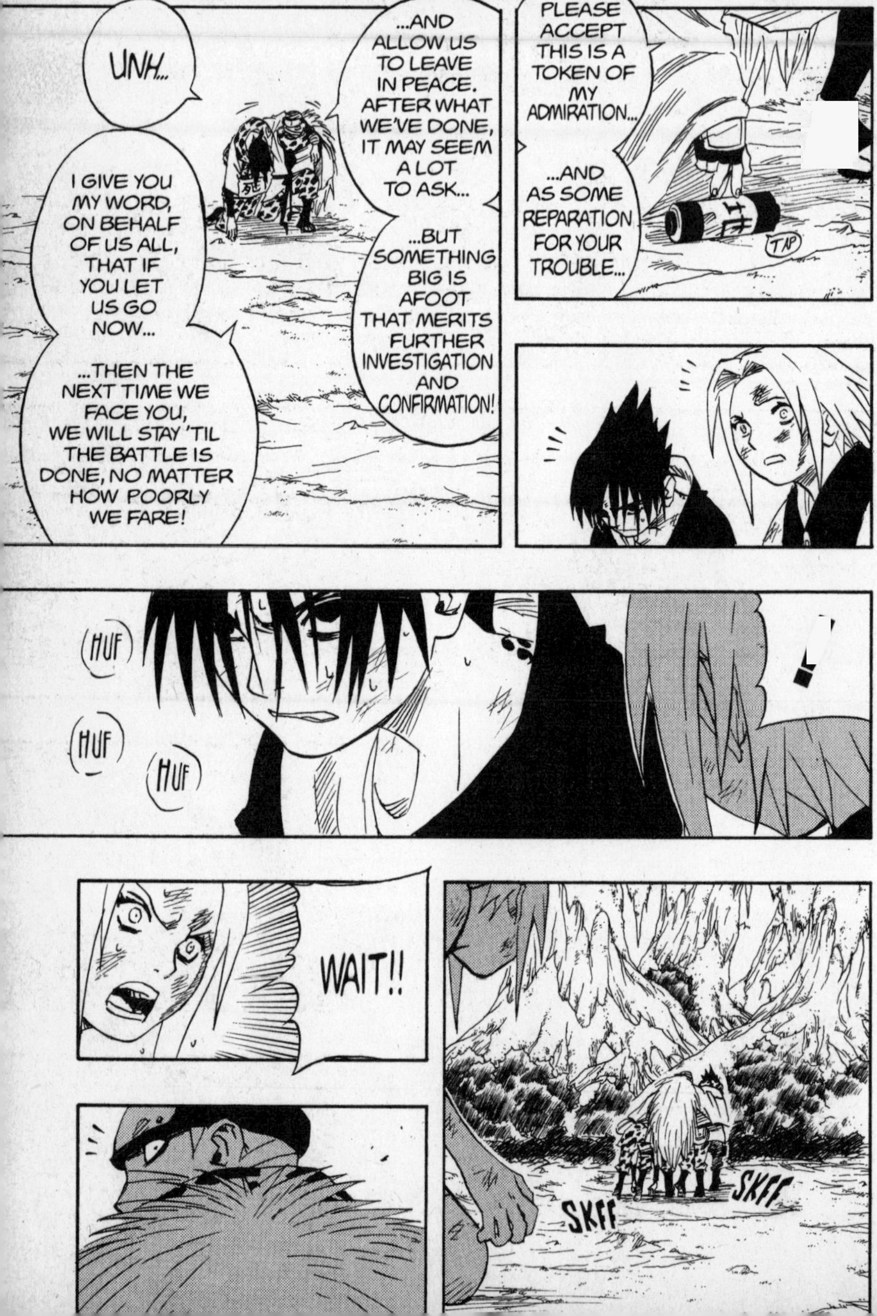
PLEASE ACCEPT THIS IS A TOKEN OF MY ADMIRATION...
...AND AS SOME REPARATION FOR YOUR TROUBLE...
TAP
...AND ALLOW US TO LEAVE IN PEACE. AFTER WHAT WE'VE DONE, IT MAY SEEM A LOT TO ASK...
...BUT SOMETHING BIG IS AFOOT THAT MERITS FURTHER INVESTIGATION AND CONFIRMATION!
UNH...
I GIVE YOU MY WORD, ON BEHALF OF US ALL, THAT IF YOU LET US GO NOW...
...THEN THE NEXT TIME WE FACE YOU, WE WILL STAY 'TIL THE BATTLE IS DONE, NO MATTER HOW POORLY WE FARE!
HUF
HUF
HUF
SKFF
SKFF
WAIT!!

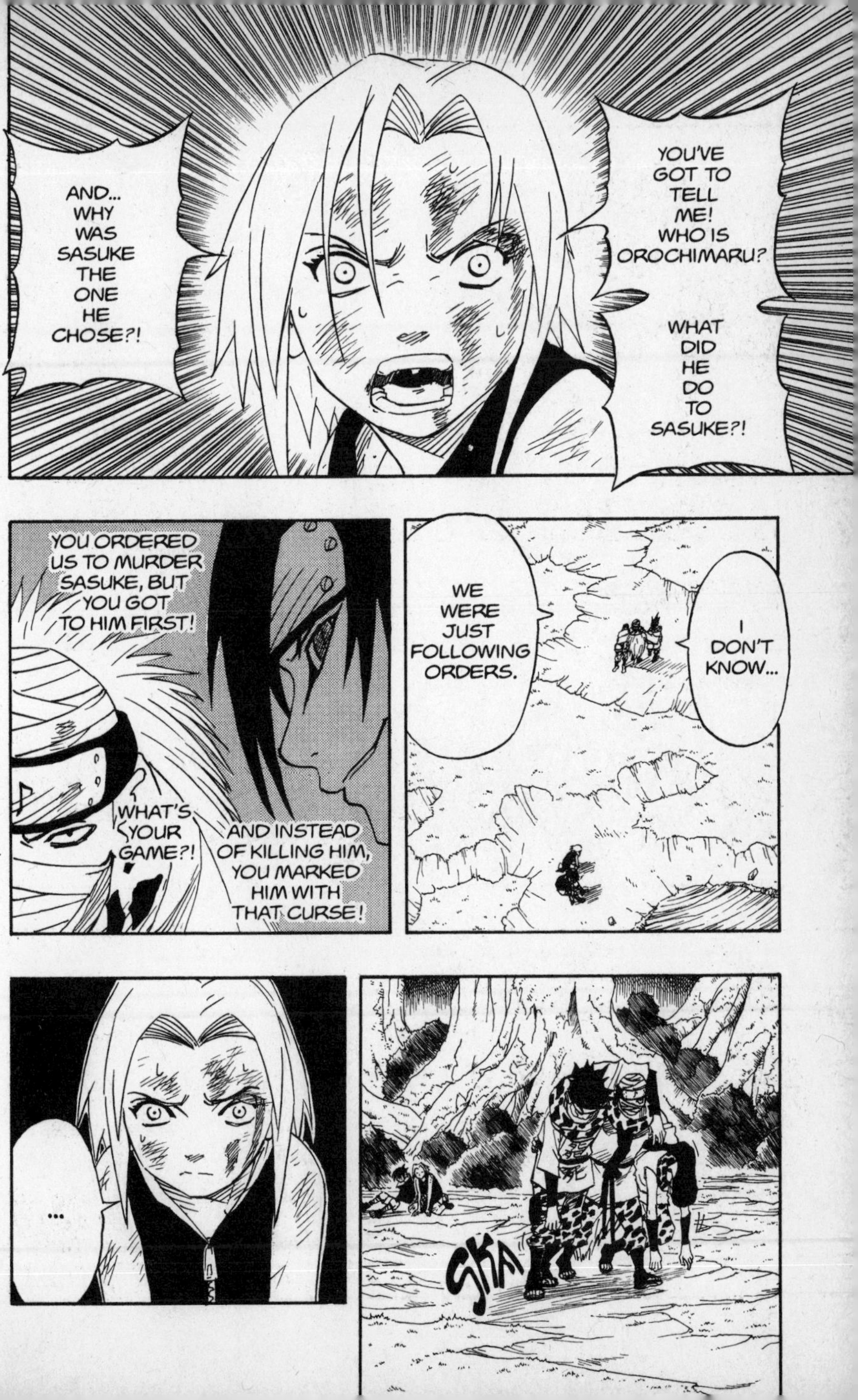
YOU'VE GOT TO TELL ME! WHO IS OROCHIMARU?
WHAT DID HE DO TO SASUKE?!
AND... WHY WAS SASUKE THE ONE HE CHOSE?!
I DON'T KNOW...
WE WERE JUST FOLLOWING ORDERS.
YOU ORDERED US TO MURDER SASUKE, BUT YOU GOT TO HIM FIRST!
AND INSTEAD OF KILLING HIM, YOU MARKED HIM WITH THAT CURSE!
WHAT'S YOUR GAME?!
SKA
...

READ THIS WAY

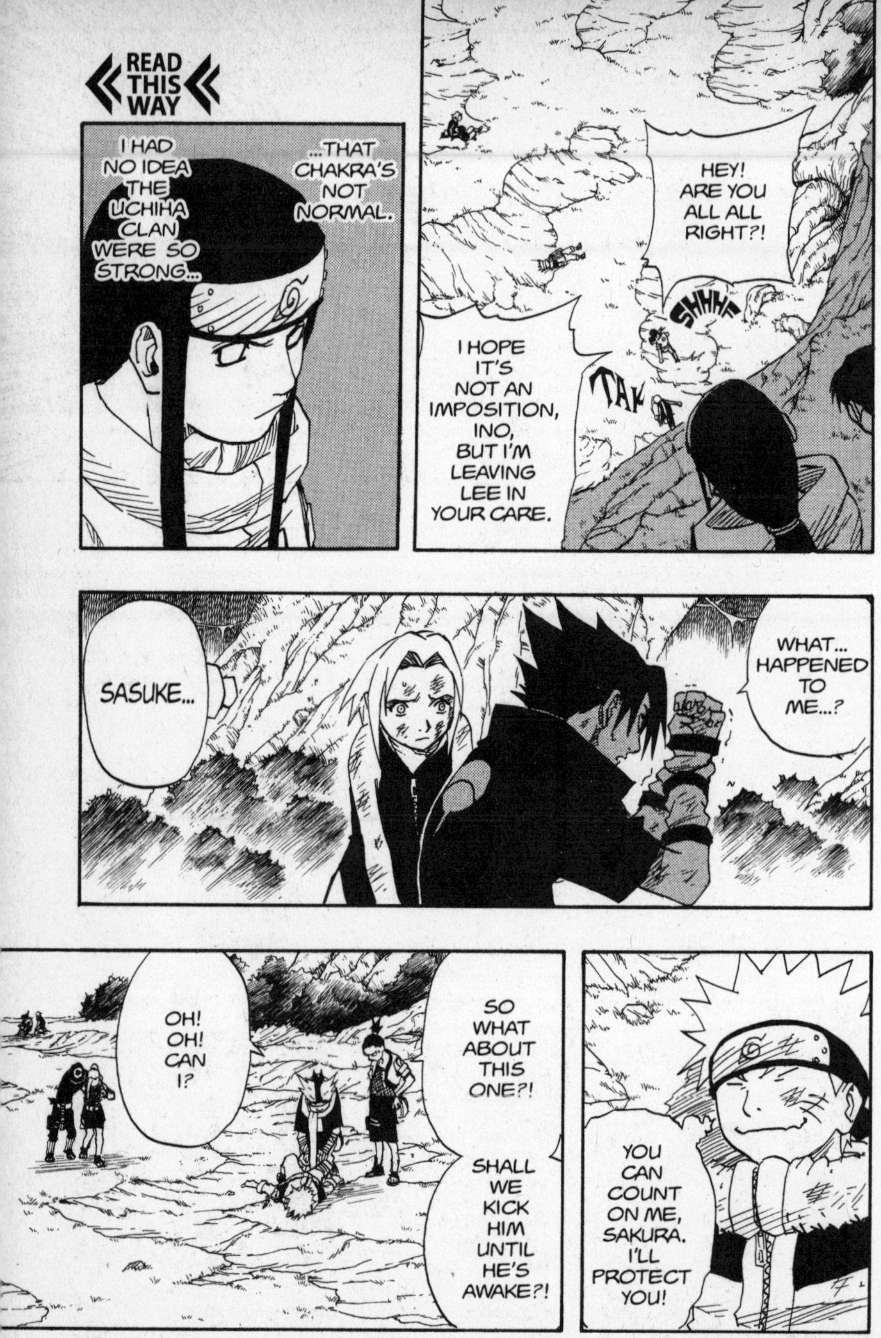

HEY! ARE YOU ALL ALL RIGHT?!
SHHHF
TAK
I HOPE IT'S NOT AN IMPOSITION, INO, BUT I'M LEAVING LEE IN YOUR CARE.
I HAD NO IDEA THE UCHIHA CLAN WERE SO STRONG...
...THAT CHAKRA'S NOT NORMAL.
WHAT... HAPPENED TO ME...?
SASUKE...
YOU CAN COUNT ON ME, SAKURA. I'LL PROTECT YOU!
SO WHAT ABOUT THIS ONE?!
SHALL WE KICK HIM UNTIL HE'S AWAKE?!
OH! OH! CAN I?

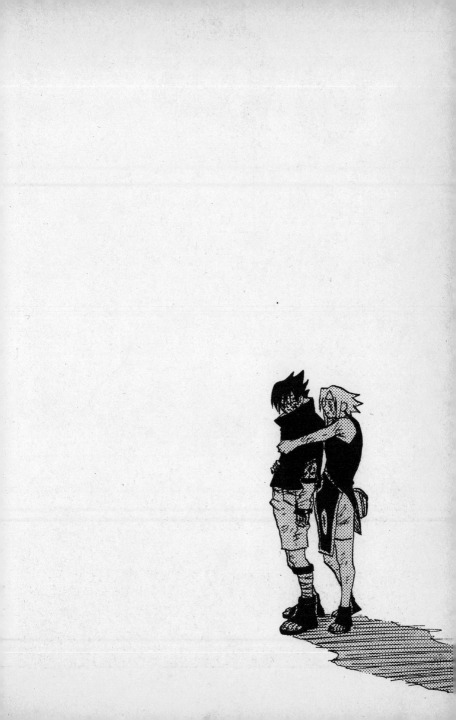

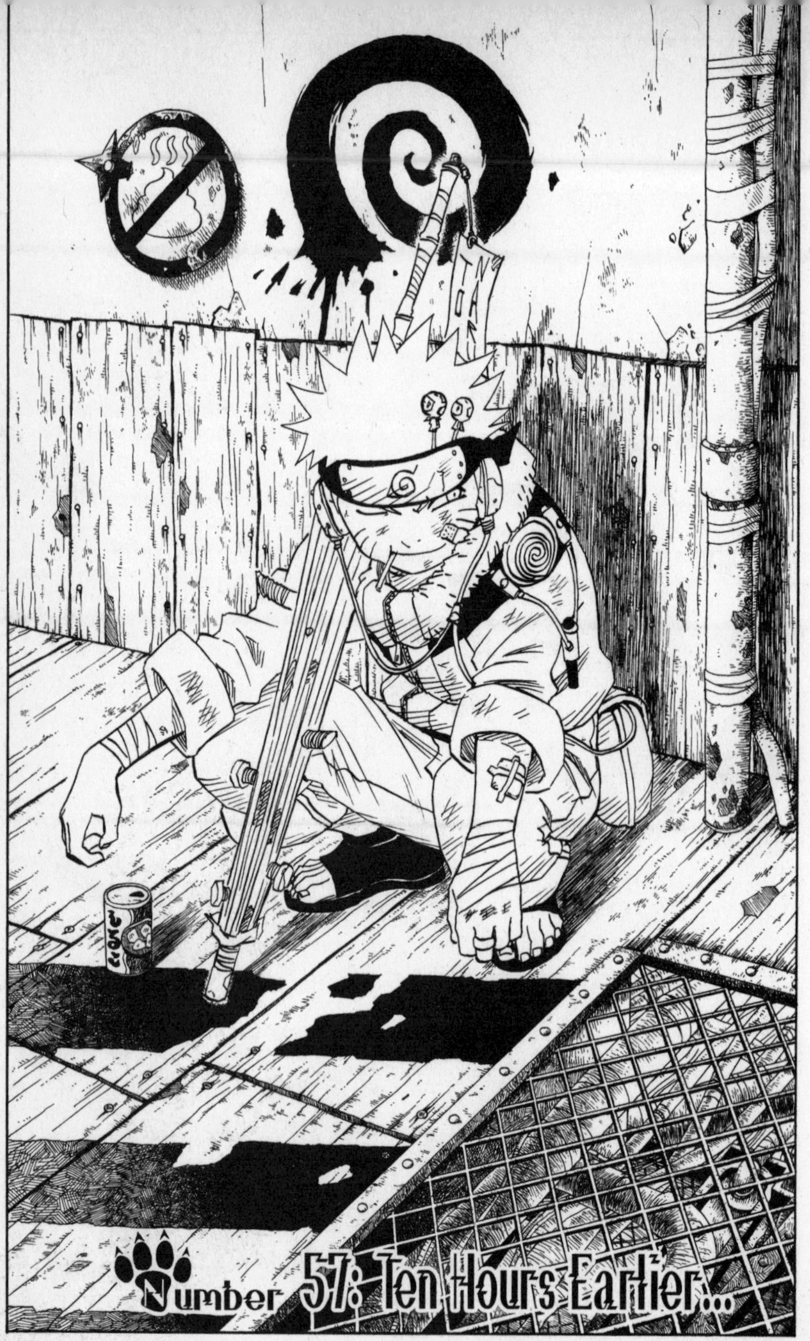
Number 57: Ten Hours Earlier...

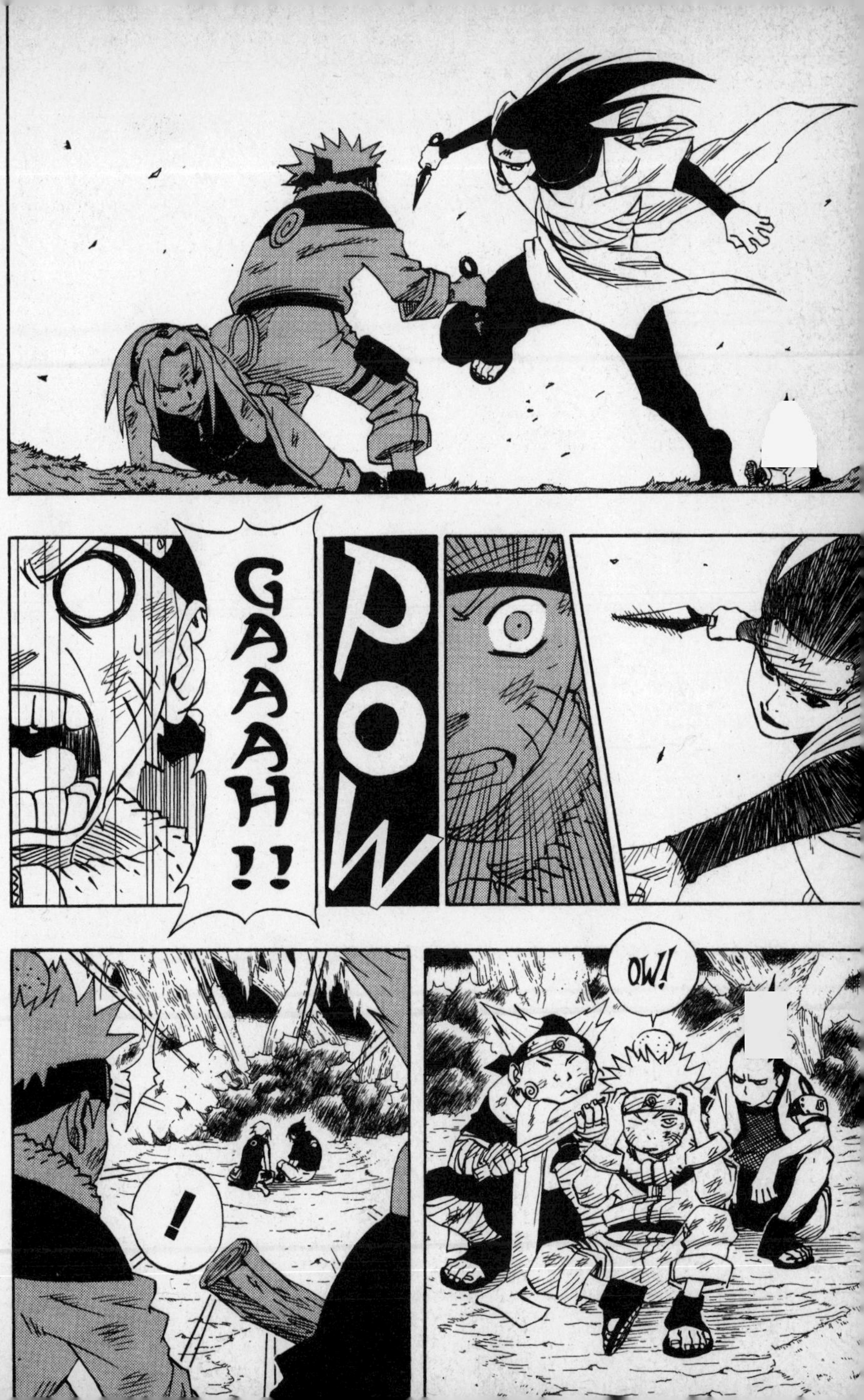
POW
GAAAH!!
OW!
!

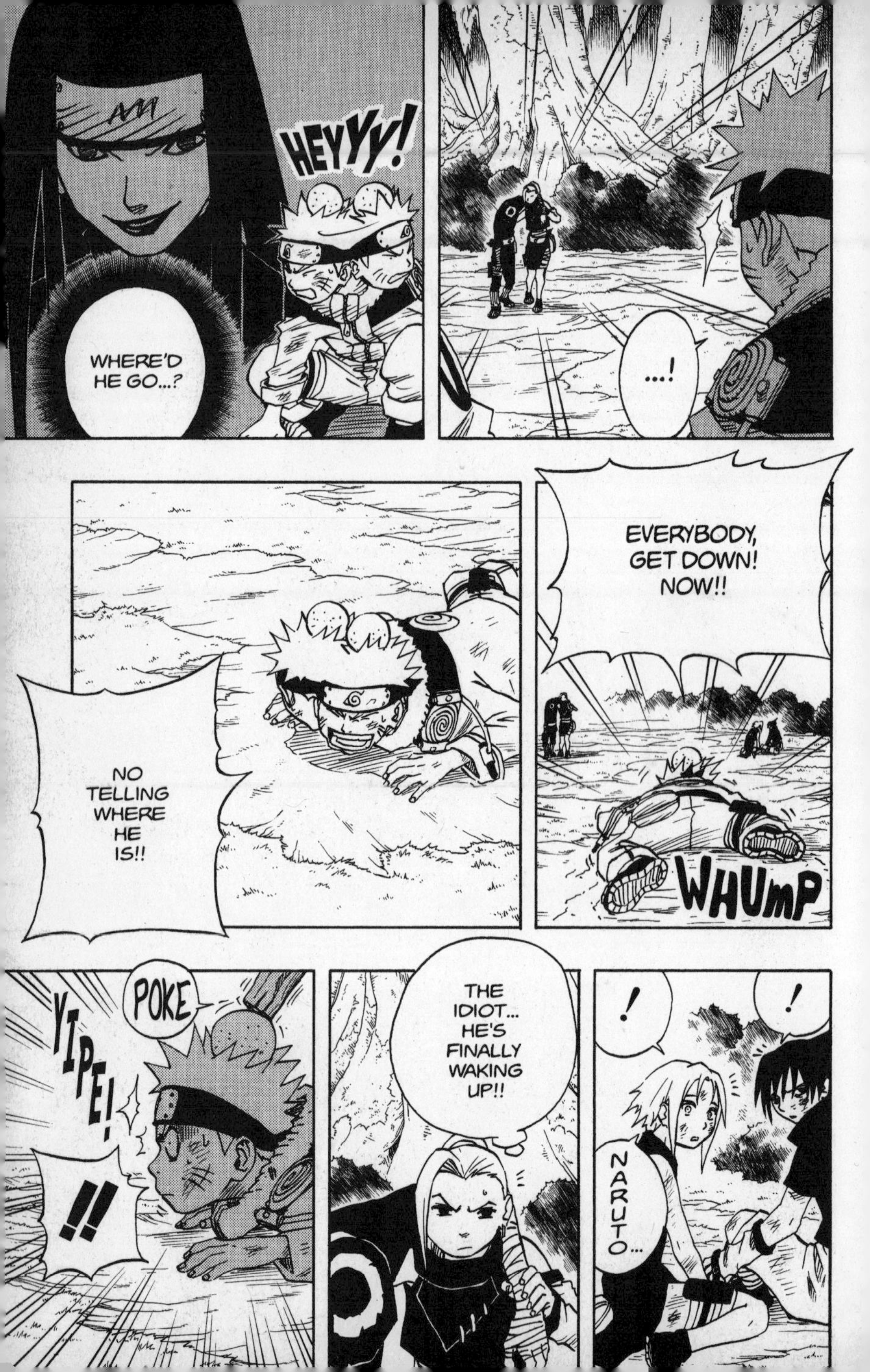
...!
HEYYY!
WHERE'D HE GO...?
EVERYBODY, GET DOWN! NOW!!
WHUMP
NO TELLING WHERE HE IS!!
!
!
NARUTO...
THE IDIOT... HE'S FINALLY WAKING UP!!
POKE
YIPE!
!!

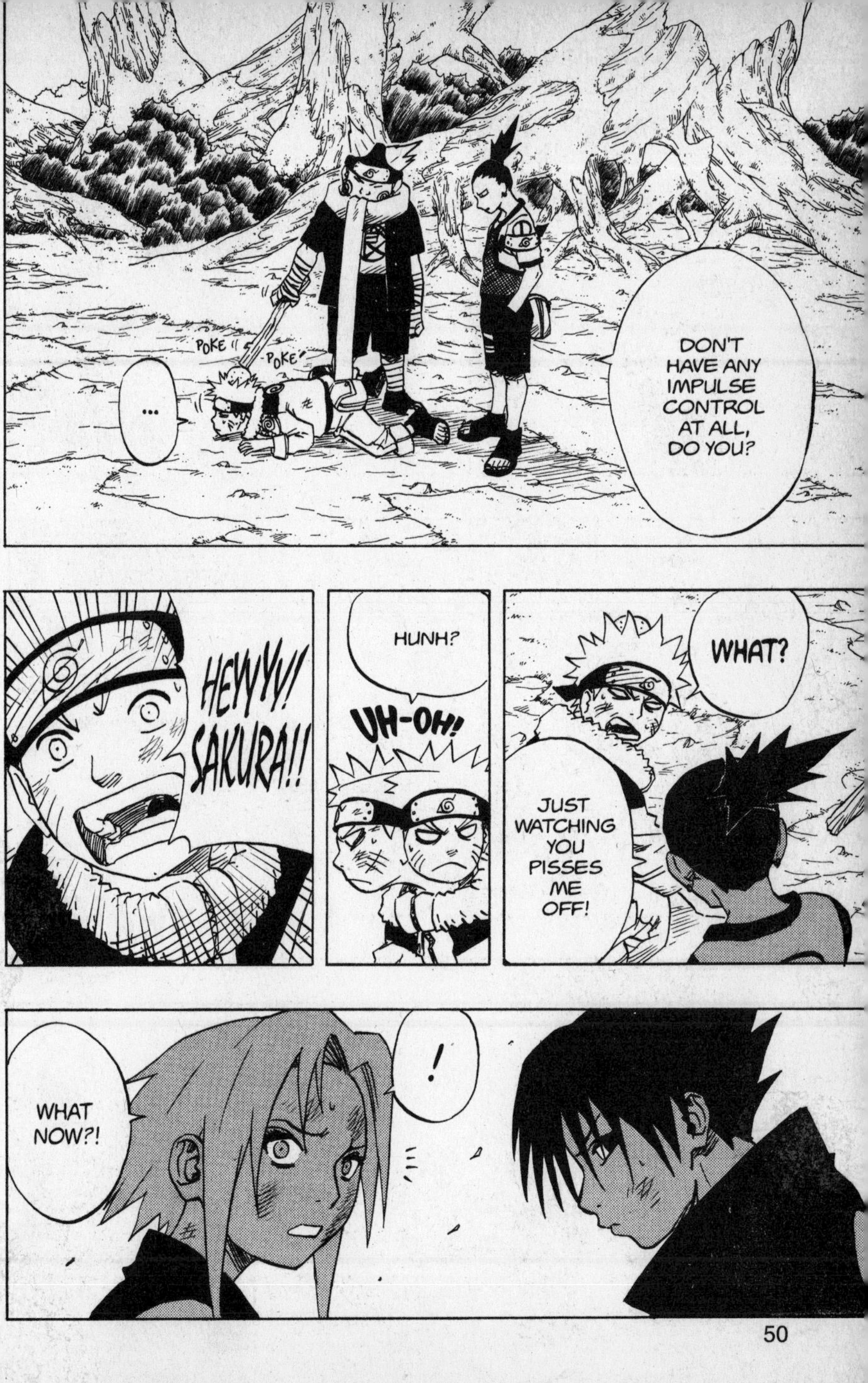
DON'T HAVE ANY IMPULSE CONTROL AT ALL, DO YOU?
POKE
POKE
...
WHAT?
JUST WATCHING YOU PISSES ME OFF!
HUNH?
UH-OH!
HEYYYY! SAKURA!!
!
WHAT NOW?!

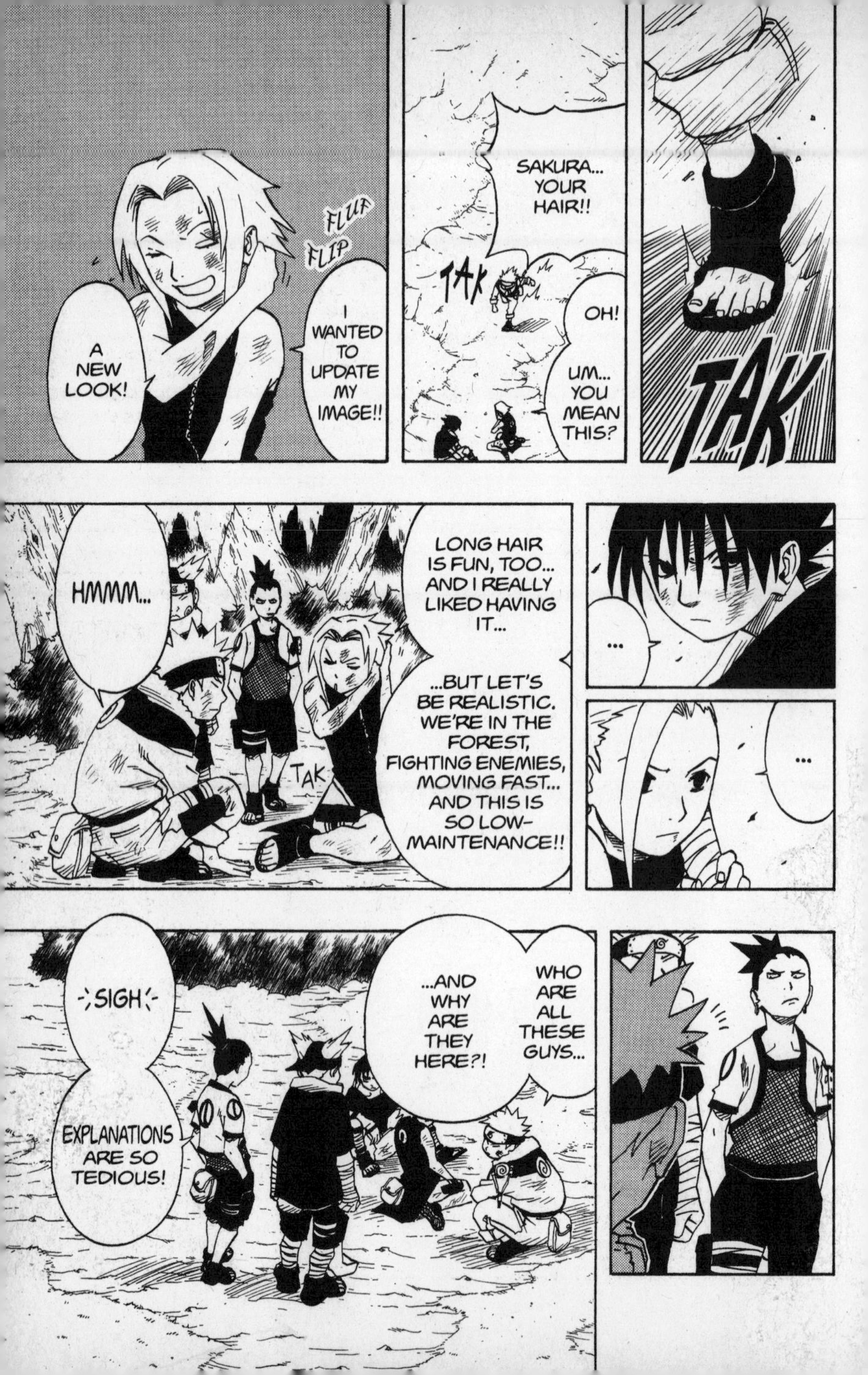
TAK
SAKURA... YOUR HAIR!!
OH!
UM... YOU MEAN THIS?
TAK
FLUP
FLIP
I WANTED TO UPDATE MY IMAGE!!
A NEW LOOK!
...
...
LONG HAIR IS FUN, TOO... AND I REALLY LIKED HAVING IT...
...BUT LET'S BE REALISTIC. WE'RE IN THE FOREST, FIGHTING ENEMIES, MOVING FAST... AND THIS IS SO LOW-MAINTENANCE!!
TAK
HMMM...
WHO ARE ALL THESE GUYS...
...AND WHY ARE THEY HERE?!
SIGH
EXPLANATIONS ARE SO TEDIOUS!

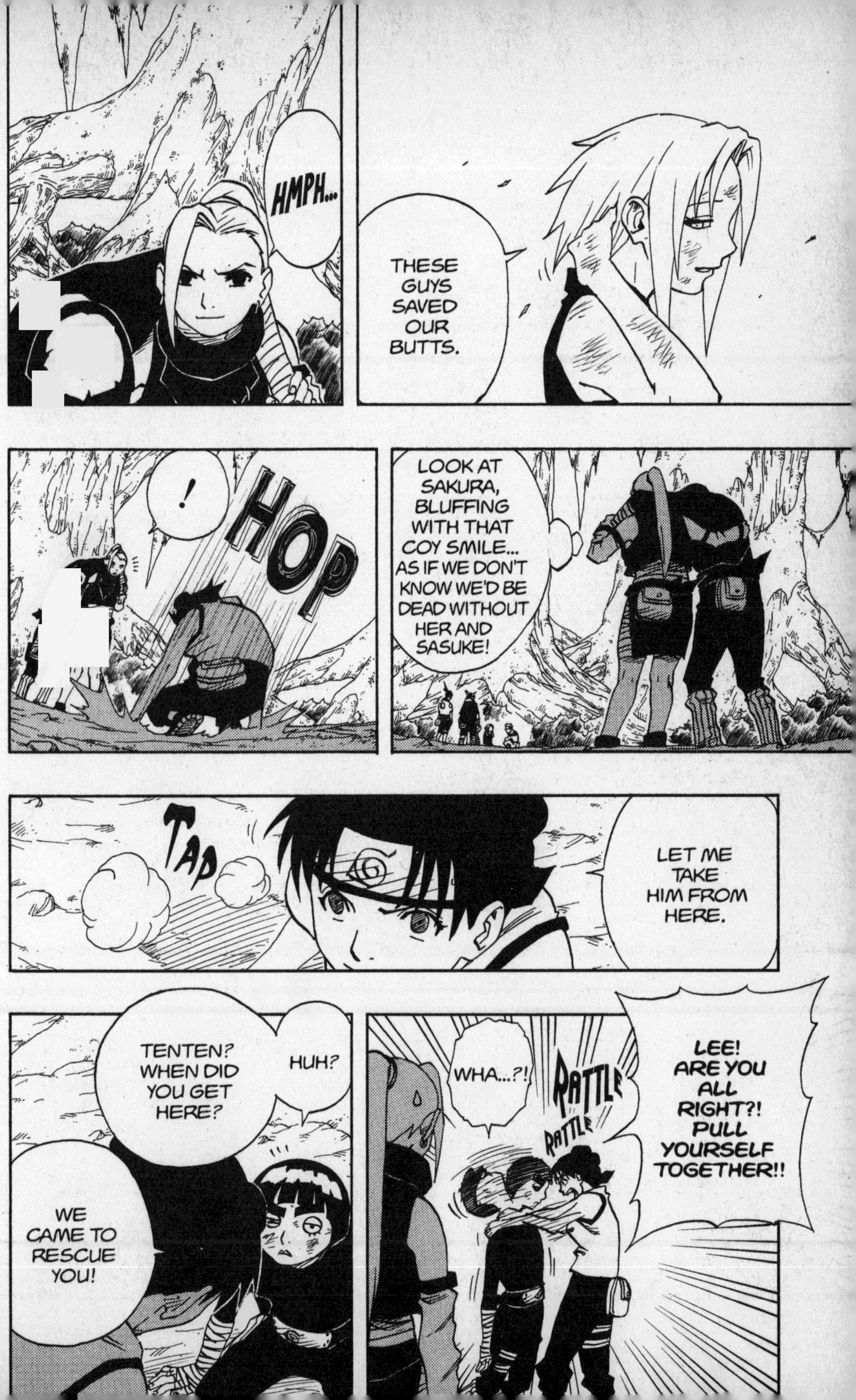
THESE GUYS SAVED OUR BUTTS.
HMPH...
LOOK AT SAKURA, BLUFFING WITH THAT COY SMILE... AS IF WE DON'T KNOW WE'D BE DEAD WITHOUT HER AND SASUKE!
!
HOP
LET ME TAKE HIM FROM HERE.
TAP
LEE! ARE YOU ALL RIGHT?! PULL YOURSELF TOGETHER!!
WHA...?!
RATTLE
RATTLE
HUH?
TENTEN? WHEN DID YOU GET HERE?
WE CAME TO RESCUE YOU!

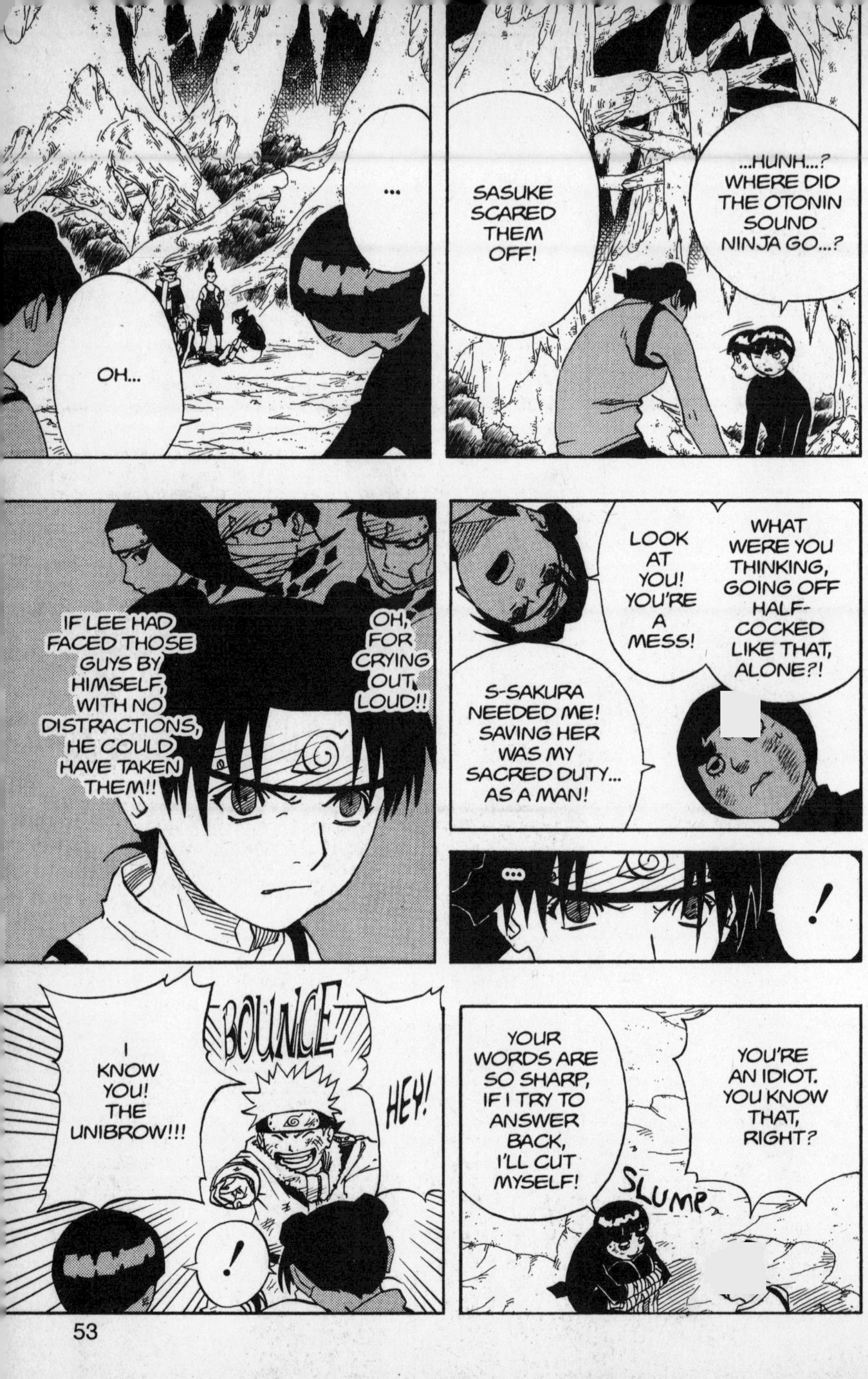

...HUNH...? WHERE DID THE OTONIN SOUND NINJA GO...?
SASUKE SCARED THEM OFF!
...
OH...
WHAT WERE YOU THINKING, GOING OFF HALF-COCKED LIKE THAT, ALONE?!
LOOK AT YOU! YOU'RE A MESS!
S-SAKURA NEEDED ME! SAVING HER WAS MY SACRED DUTY... AS A MAN!
!
...
OH, FOR CRYING OUT LOUD!!
IF LEE HAD FACED THOSE GUYS BY HIMSELF, WITH NO DISTRACTIONS, HE COULD HAVE TAKEN THEM!!
YOU'RE AN IDIOT. YOU KNOW THAT, RIGHT?
YOUR WORDS ARE SO SHARP, IF I TRY TO ANSWER BACK, I'LL CUT MYSELF!
SLUMP
HEY!
BOUNCE
I KNOW YOU! THE UNIBROW!!!
!

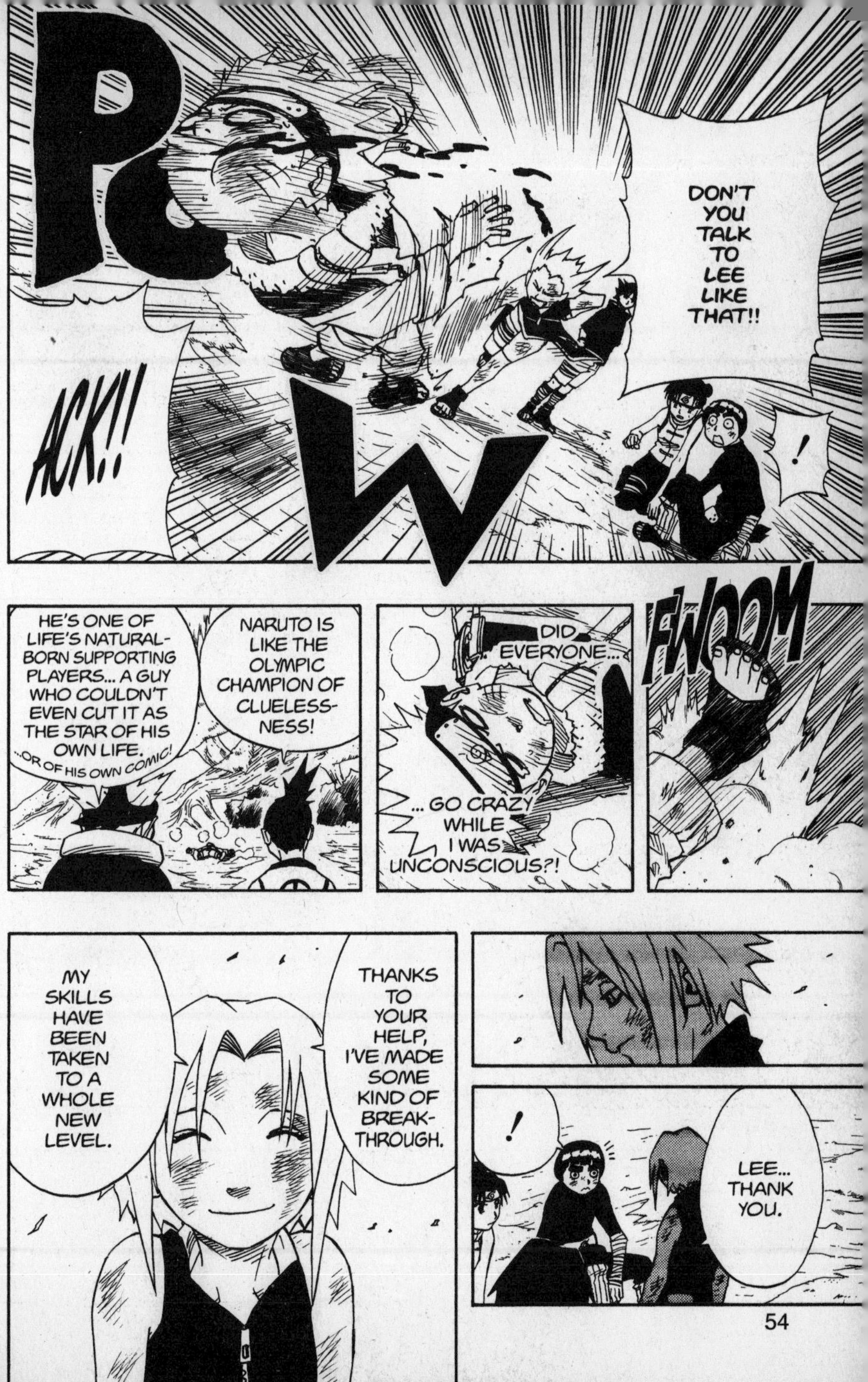
DON'T YOU TALK TO LEE LIKE THAT!!
!
POW
ACK!!
FWOOM
DID EVERYONE...
... GO CRAZY WHILE I WAS UNCONSCIOUS?!
NARUTO IS LIKE THE OLYMPIC CHAMPION OF CLUELESS-NESS!
HE'S ONE OF LIFE'S NATURAL-BORN SUPPORTING PLAYERS... A GUY WHO COULDN'T EVEN CUT IT AS THE STAR OF HIS OWN LIFE.
...OR OF HIS OWN COMIC!
!
LEE... THANK YOU.
THANKS TO YOUR HELP, I'VE MADE SOME KIND OF BREAK-THROUGH.
MY SKILLS HAVE BEEN TAKEN TO A WHOLE NEW LEVEL.

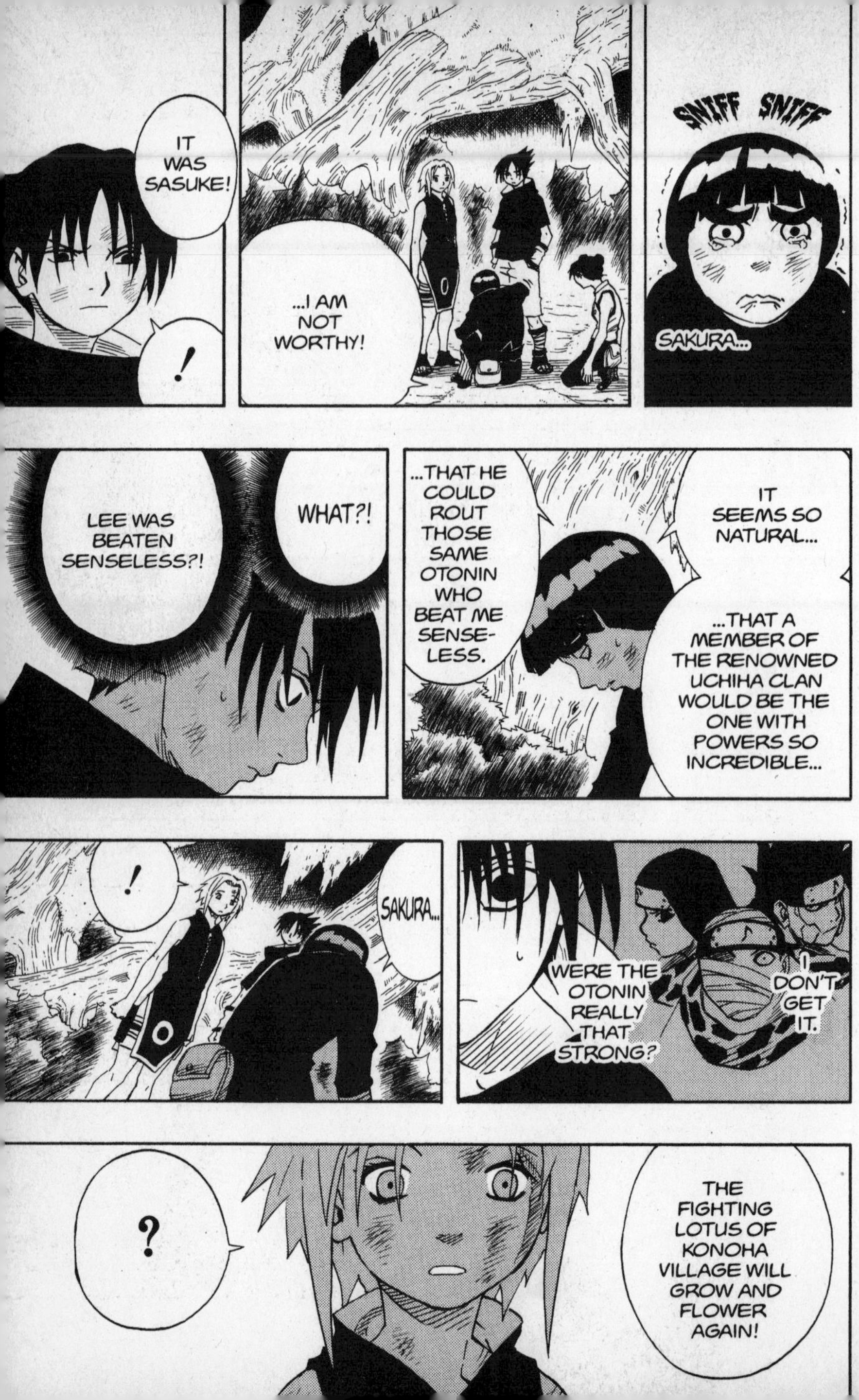
SNIFF SNIFF
SAKURA...
...I AM NOT WORTHY!
IT WAS SASUKE!
!
IT SEEMS SO NATURAL...
...THAT A MEMBER OF THE RENOWNED UCHIHA CLAN WOULD BE THE ONE WITH POWERS SO INCREDIBLE...
...THAT HE COULD ROUT THOSE SAME OTONIN WHO BEAT ME SENSELESS.
WHAT?!
LEE WAS BEATEN SENSELESS?!
I DON'T GET IT.
WERE THE OTONIN REALLY THAT STRONG?
SAKURA...
!
THE FIGHTING LOTUS OF KONOHA VILLAGE WILL GROW AND FLOWER AGAIN!
?

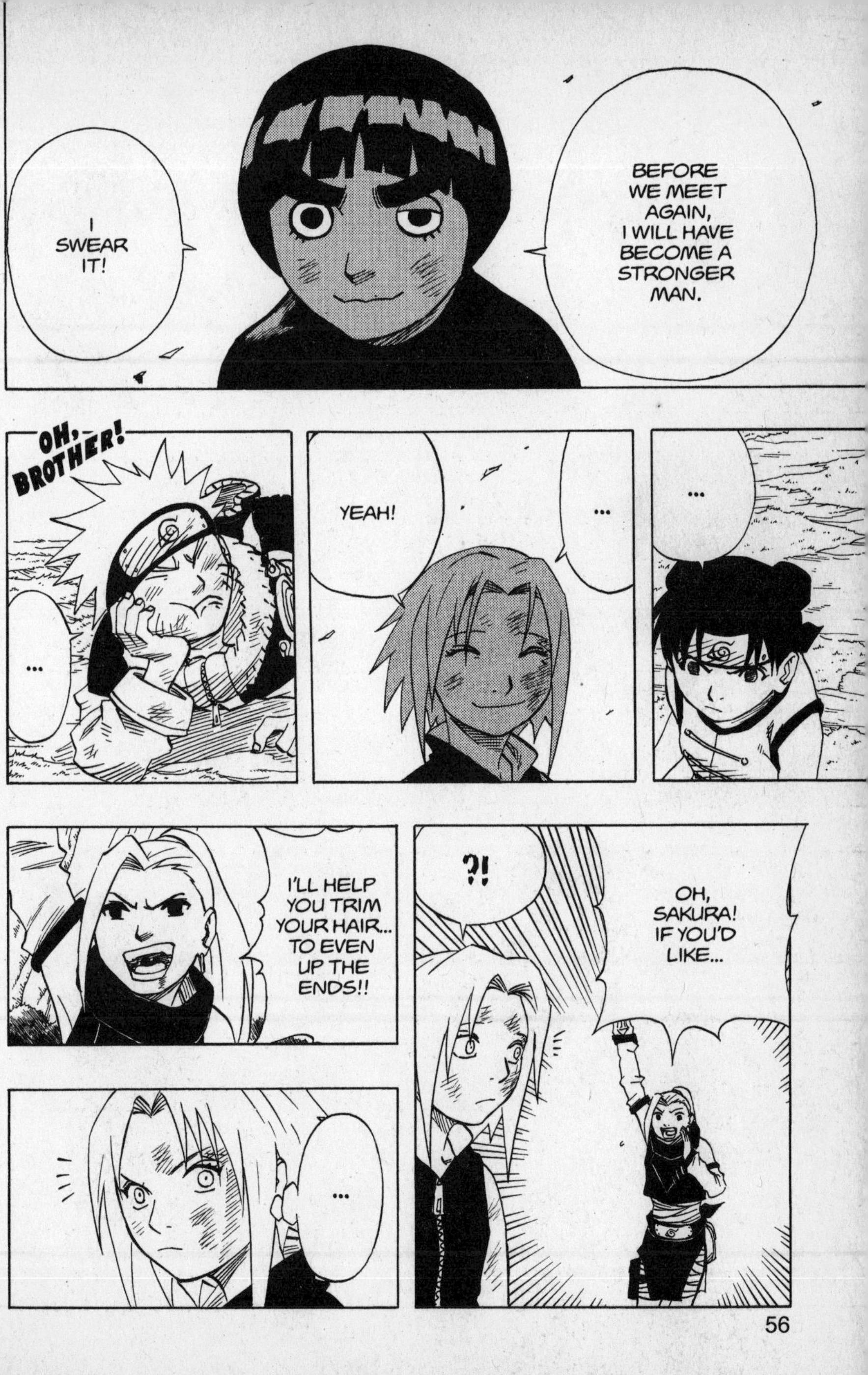
BEFORE WE MEET AGAIN, I WILL HAVE BECOME A STRONGER MAN.
I SWEAR IT!
...
...
YEAH!
OH, BROTHER!
...
OH, SAKURA! IF YOU'D LIKE...
?!
I'LL HELP YOU TRIM YOUR HAIR... TO EVEN UP THE ENDS!!
...

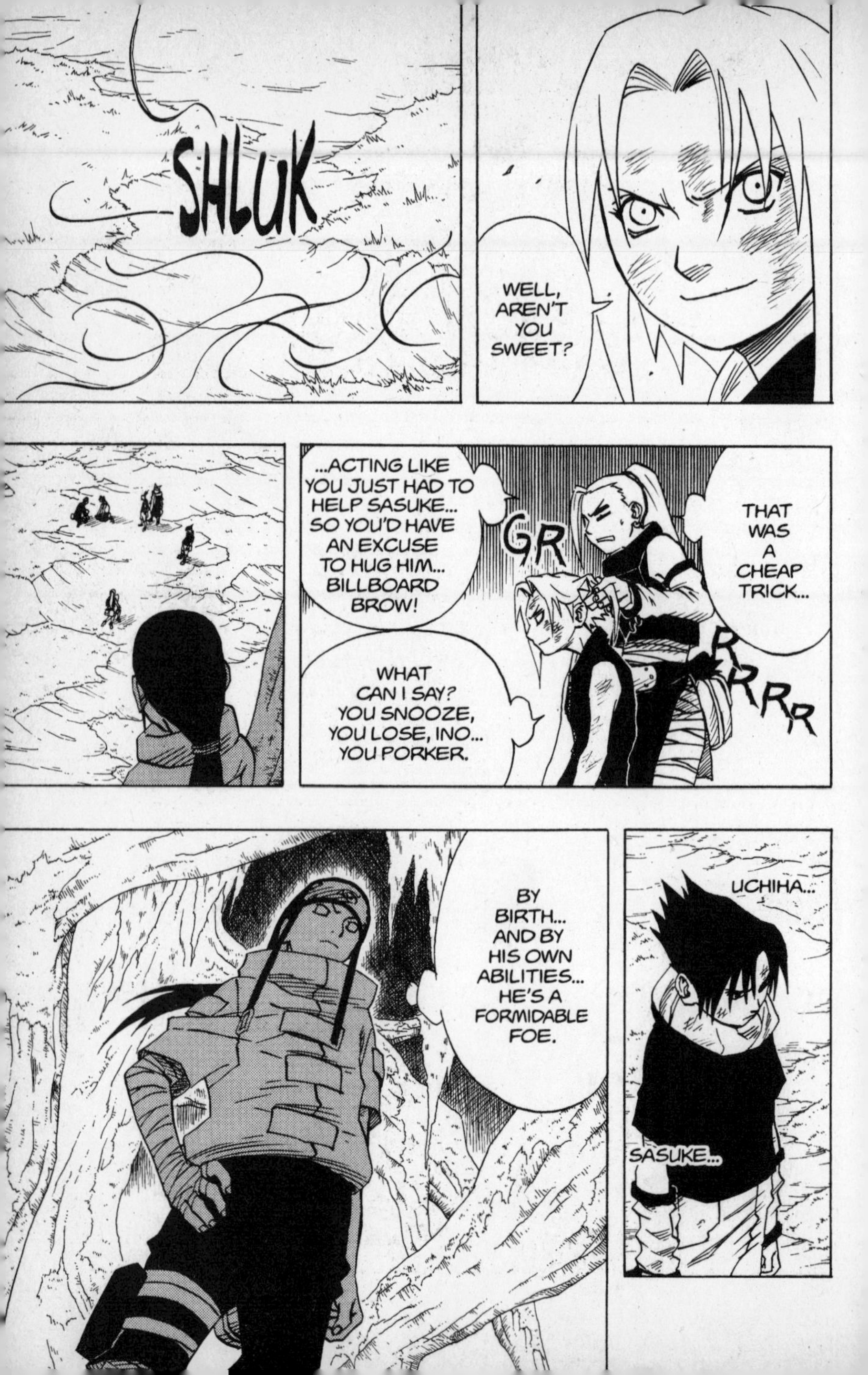
WELL, AREN'T YOU SWEET?
SHLUK
THAT WAS A CHEAP TRICK...
...ACTING LIKE YOU JUST HAD TO HELP SASUKE... SO YOU'D HAVE AN EXCUSE TO HUG HIM... BILLBOARD BROW!
GR
RRRRR
WHAT CAN I SAY? YOU SNOOZE, YOU LOSE, INO... YOU PORKER.
UCHIHA...
SASUKE...
BY BIRTH... AND BY HIS OWN ABILITIES... HE'S A FORMIDABLE FOE.

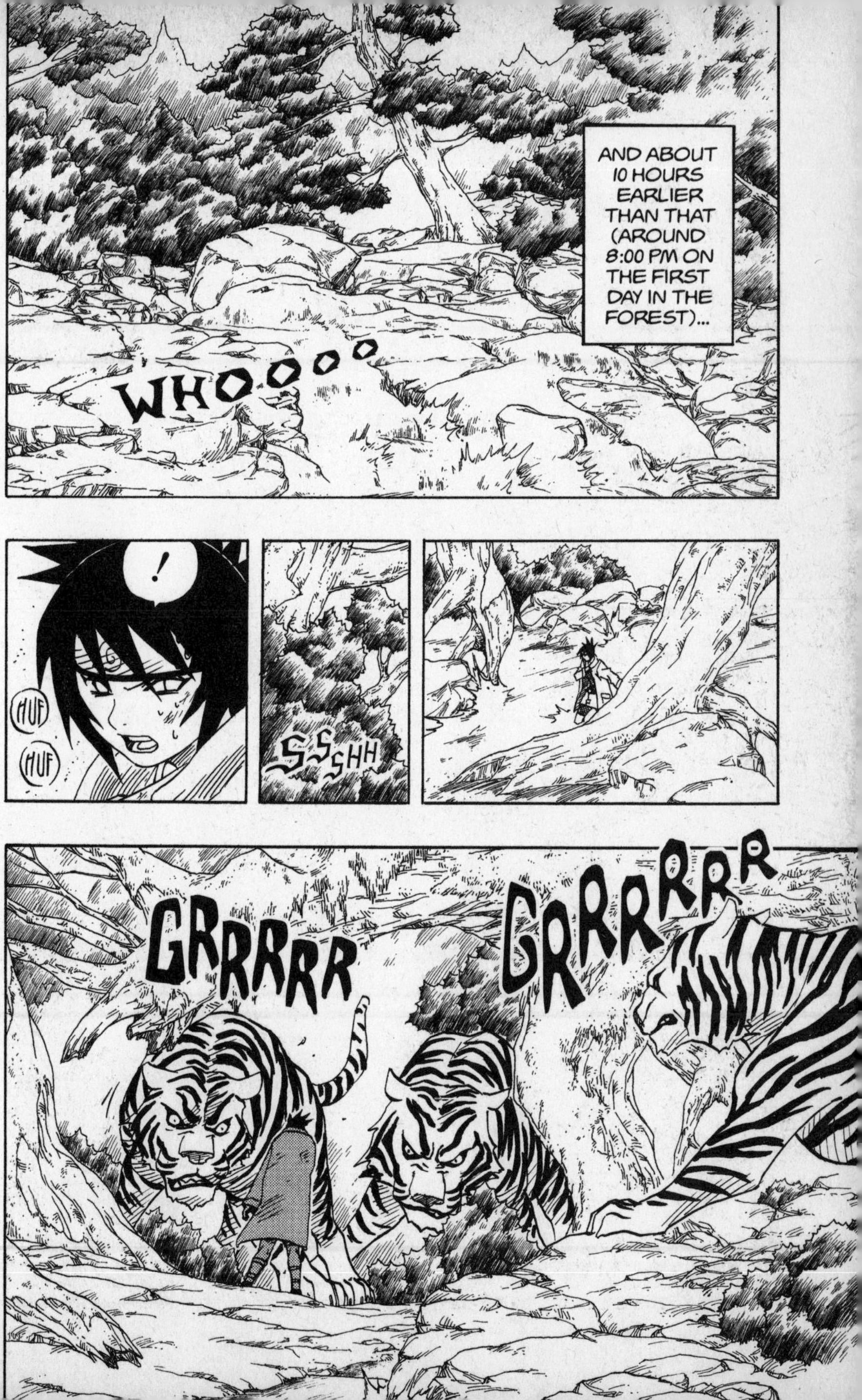
AND ABOUT 10 HOURS EARLIER THAN THAT (AROUND 8:00 PM ON THE FIRST DAY IN THE FOREST)...
WHOOOOO
SSSHH
!
HUF
HUF
GRRRRRRR
GRRRRRR

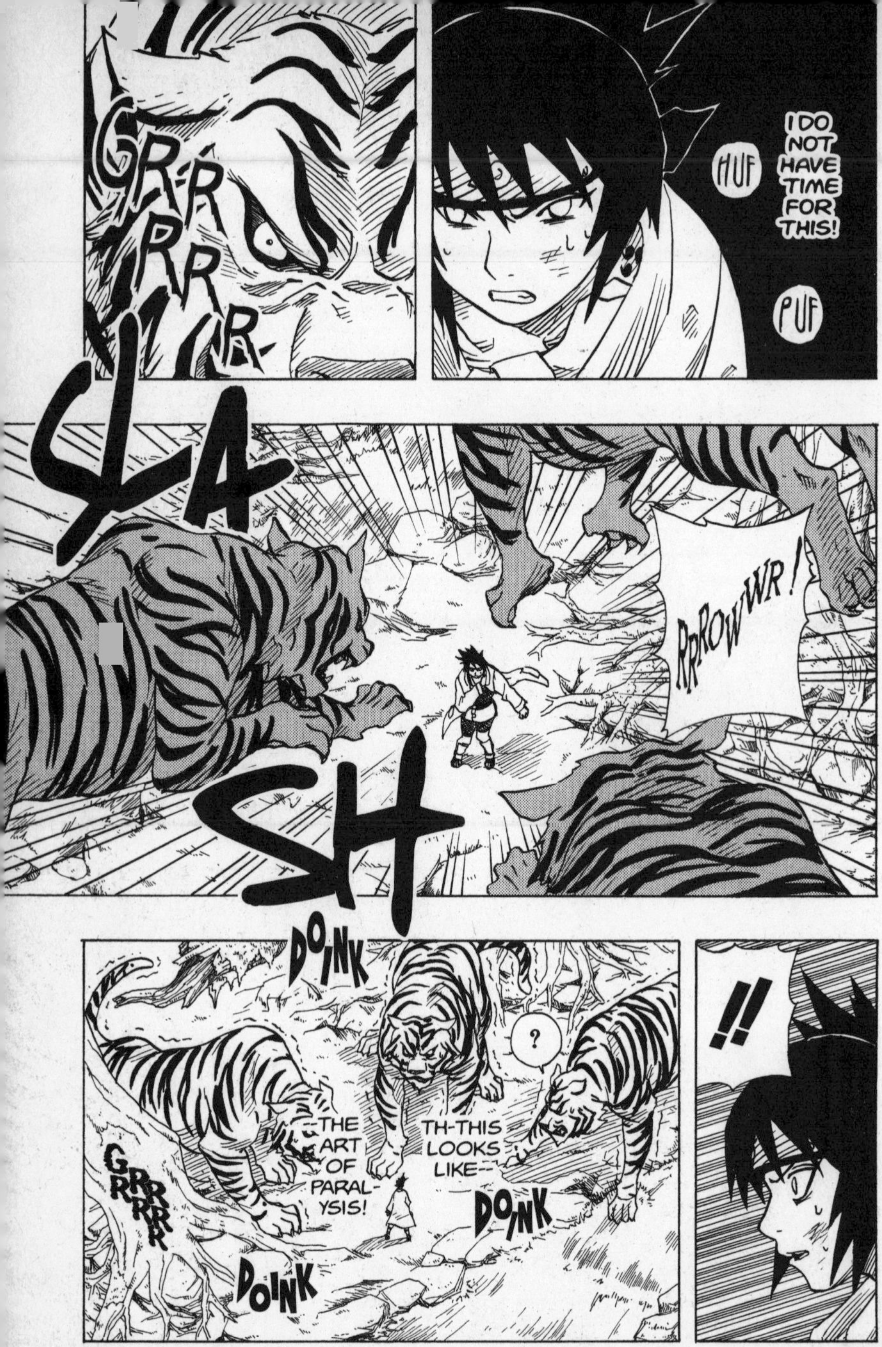
HUF
I DO NOT HAVE TIME FOR THIS!
PUF
GR-R-R-R-R-R
SHASH
RRROWWR!
!!
?
TH-THIS LOOKS LIKE--
THE ART OF PARALYSIS!
DOINK
DOINK
DOINK
GRRRRR

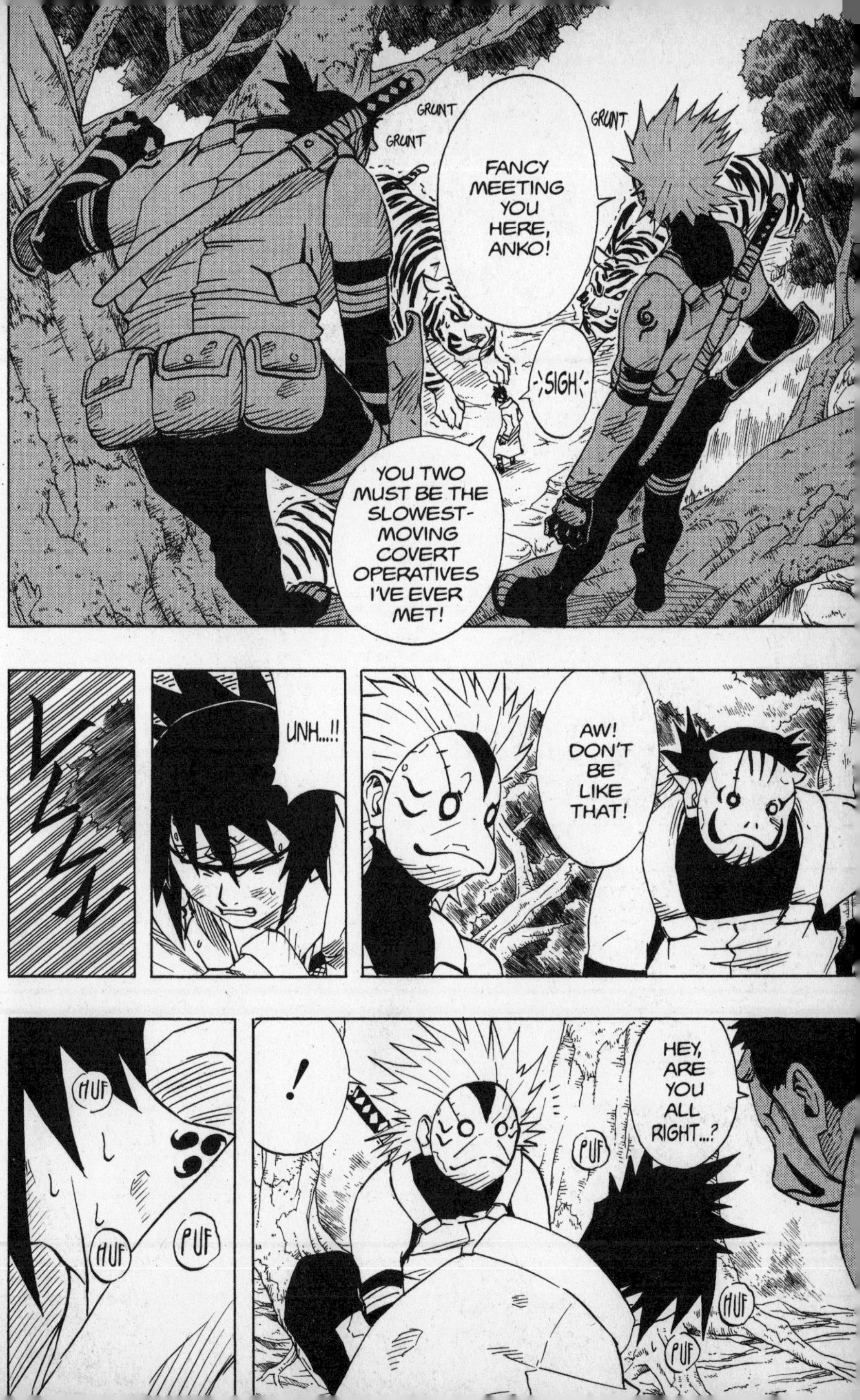
GRUNT
FANCY MEETING YOU HERE, ANKO!
GRUNT
GRUNT
SIGH
YOU TWO MUST BE THE SLOWEST-MOVING COVERT OPERATIVES I'VE EVER MET!
AW! DON'T BE LIKE THAT!
UNH...!!
HEY, ARE YOU ALL RIGHT...?
!
PUF
HUF
PUF
HUF
HUF
PUF

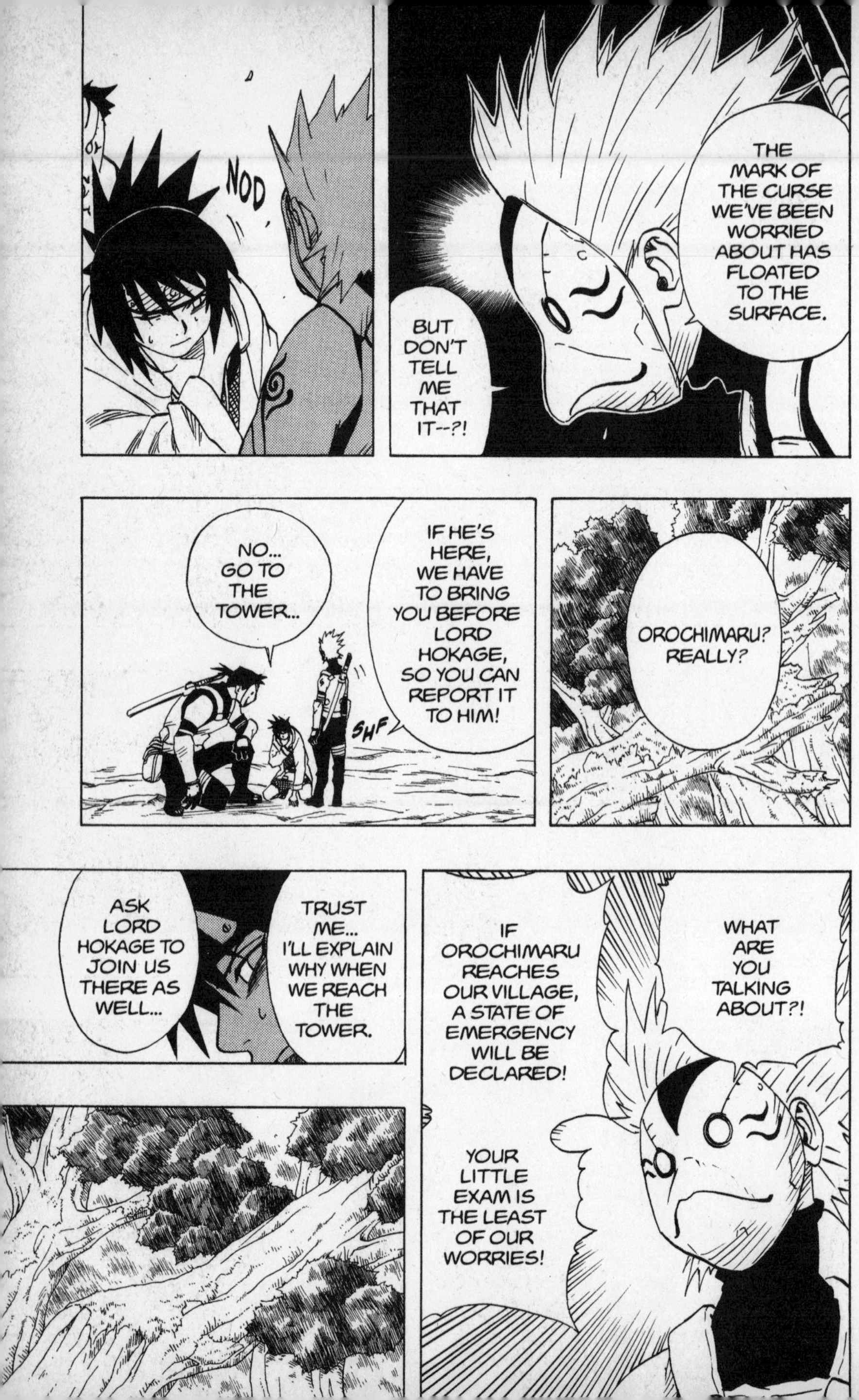
THE MARK OF THE CURSE WE'VE BEEN WORRIED ABOUT HAS FLOATED TO THE SURFACE.
BUT DON'T TELL ME THAT IT--?!
NOD
OROCHIMARU? REALLY?
IF HE'S HERE, WE HAVE TO BRING YOU BEFORE LORD HOKAGE, SO YOU CAN REPORT IT TO HIM!
SHF
NO... GO TO THE TOWER...
WHAT ARE YOU TALKING ABOUT?!
IF OROCHIMARU REACHES OUR VILLAGE, A STATE OF EMERGENCY WILL BE DECLARED!
YOUR LITTLE EXAM IS THE LEAST OF OUR WORRIES!
TRUST ME... I'LL EXPLAIN WHY WHEN WE REACH THE TOWER.
ASK LORD HOKAGE TO JOIN US THERE AS WELL...

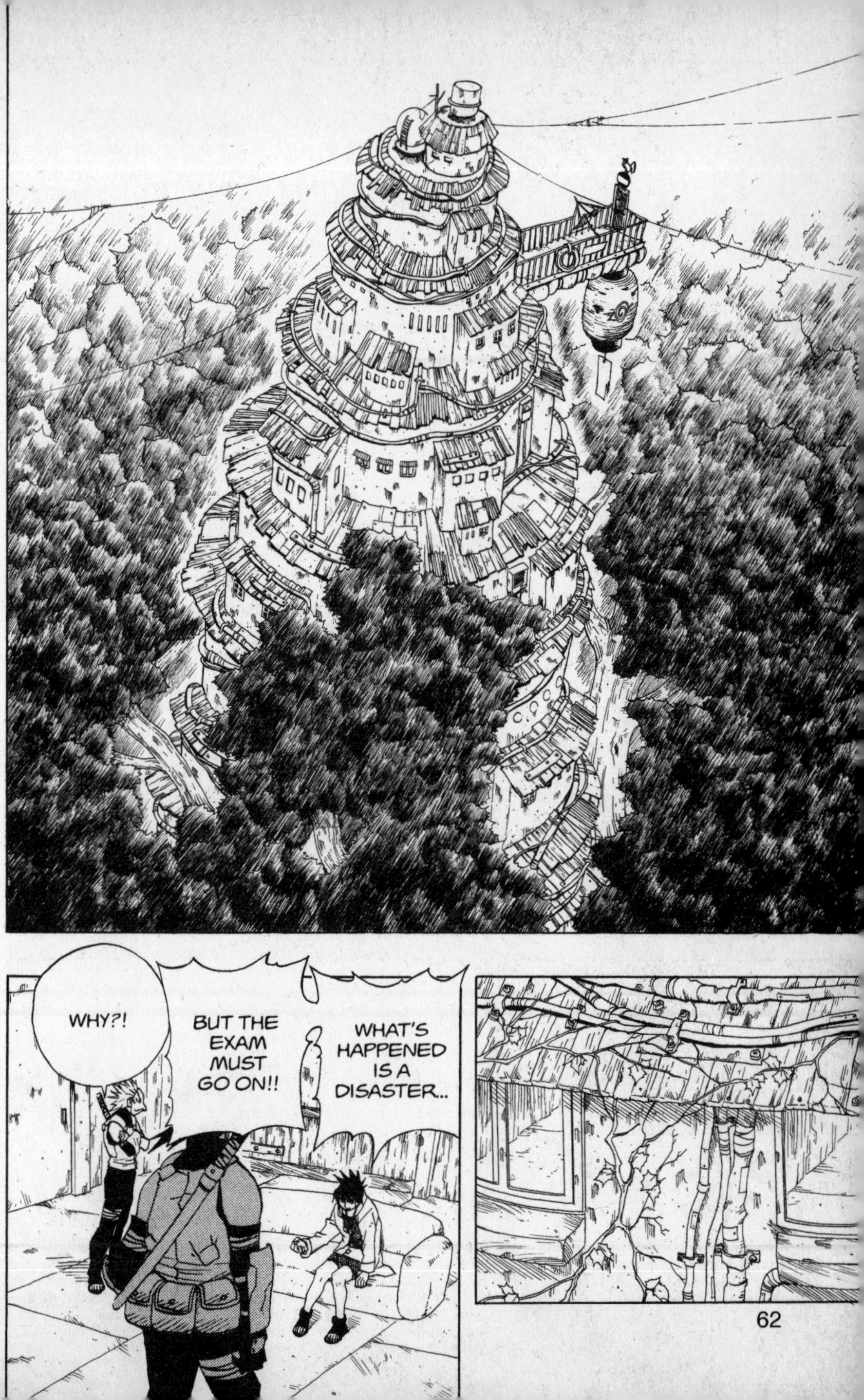
WHAT'S HAPPENED IS A DISASTER...
BUT THE EXAM MUST GO ON!!
WHY?!

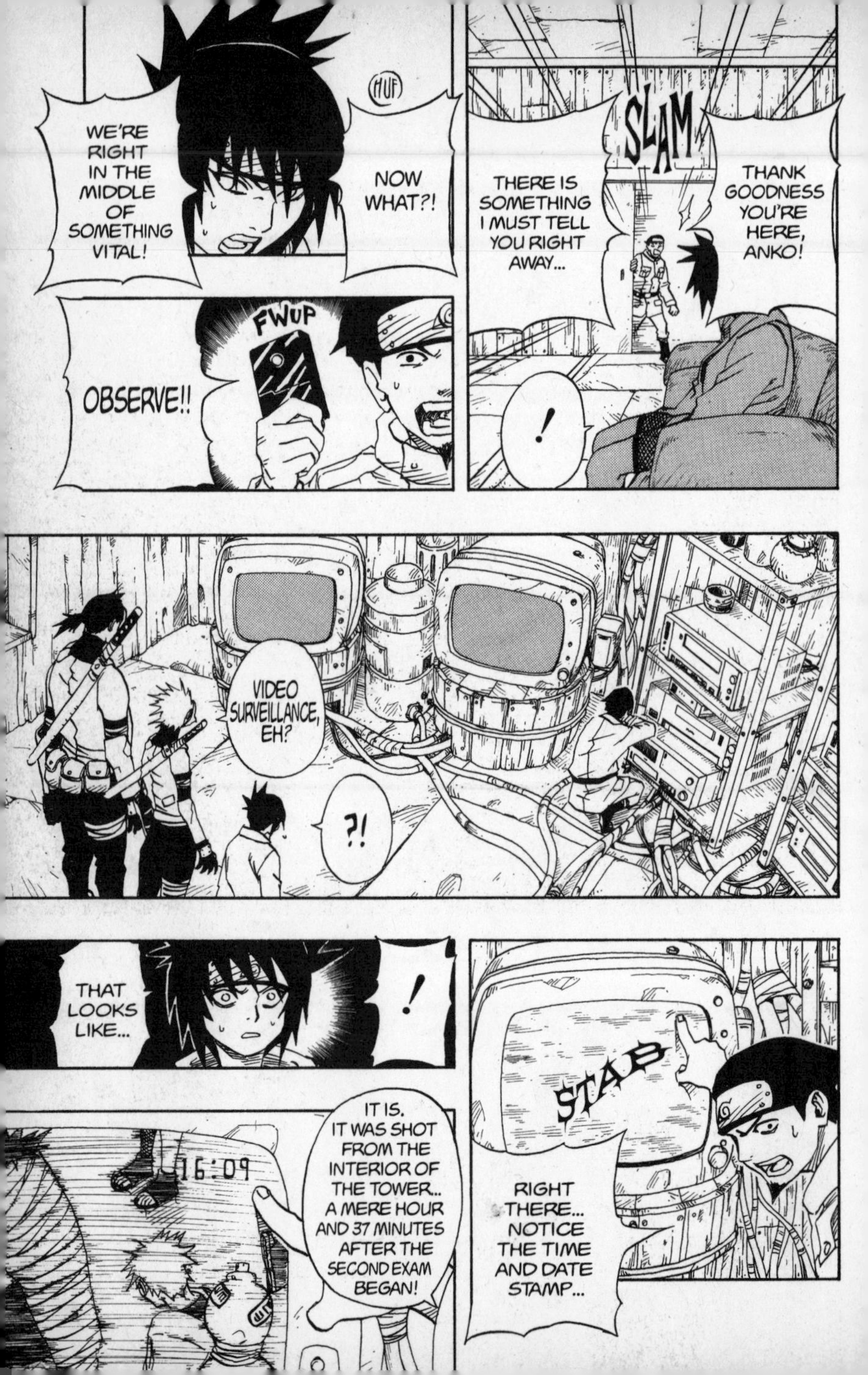
SLAM
THANK GOODNESS YOU'RE HERE, ANKO!
THERE IS SOMETHING I MUST TELL YOU RIGHT AWAY...
HUF
NOW WHAT?!
WE'RE RIGHT IN THE MIDDLE OF SOMETHING VITAL!
!
FWUP
OBSERVE!!
VIDEO SURVEILLANCE, EH?
?!
STAB
RIGHT THERE... NOTICE THE TIME AND DATE STAMP...
!
THAT LOOKS LIKE...
IT IS. IT WAS SHOT FROM THE INTERIOR OF THE TOWER... A MERE HOUR AND 37 MINUTES AFTER THE SECOND EXAM BEGAN!
16:09

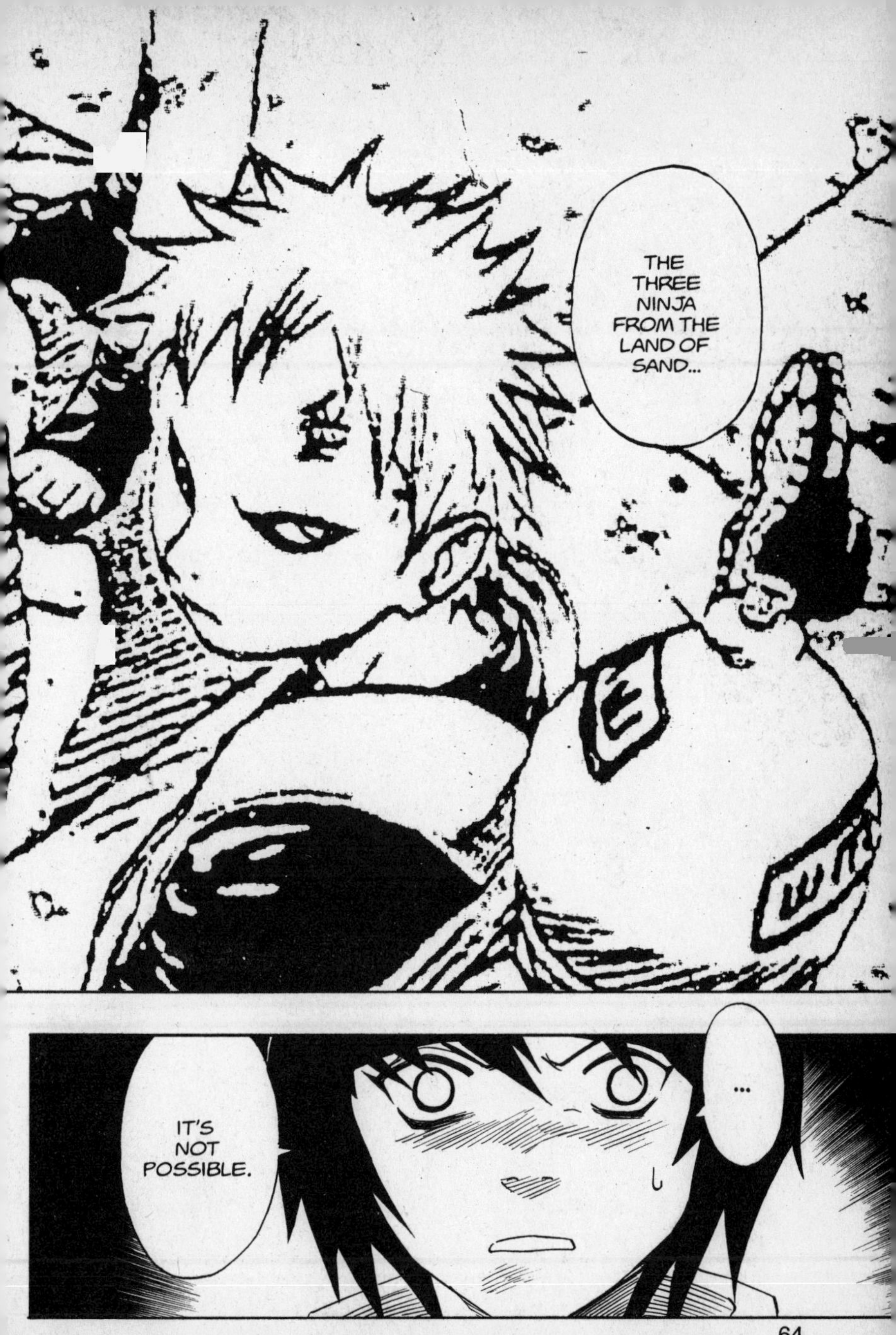
THE THREE NINJA FROM THE LAND OF SAND...
...
IT'S NOT POSSIBLE.

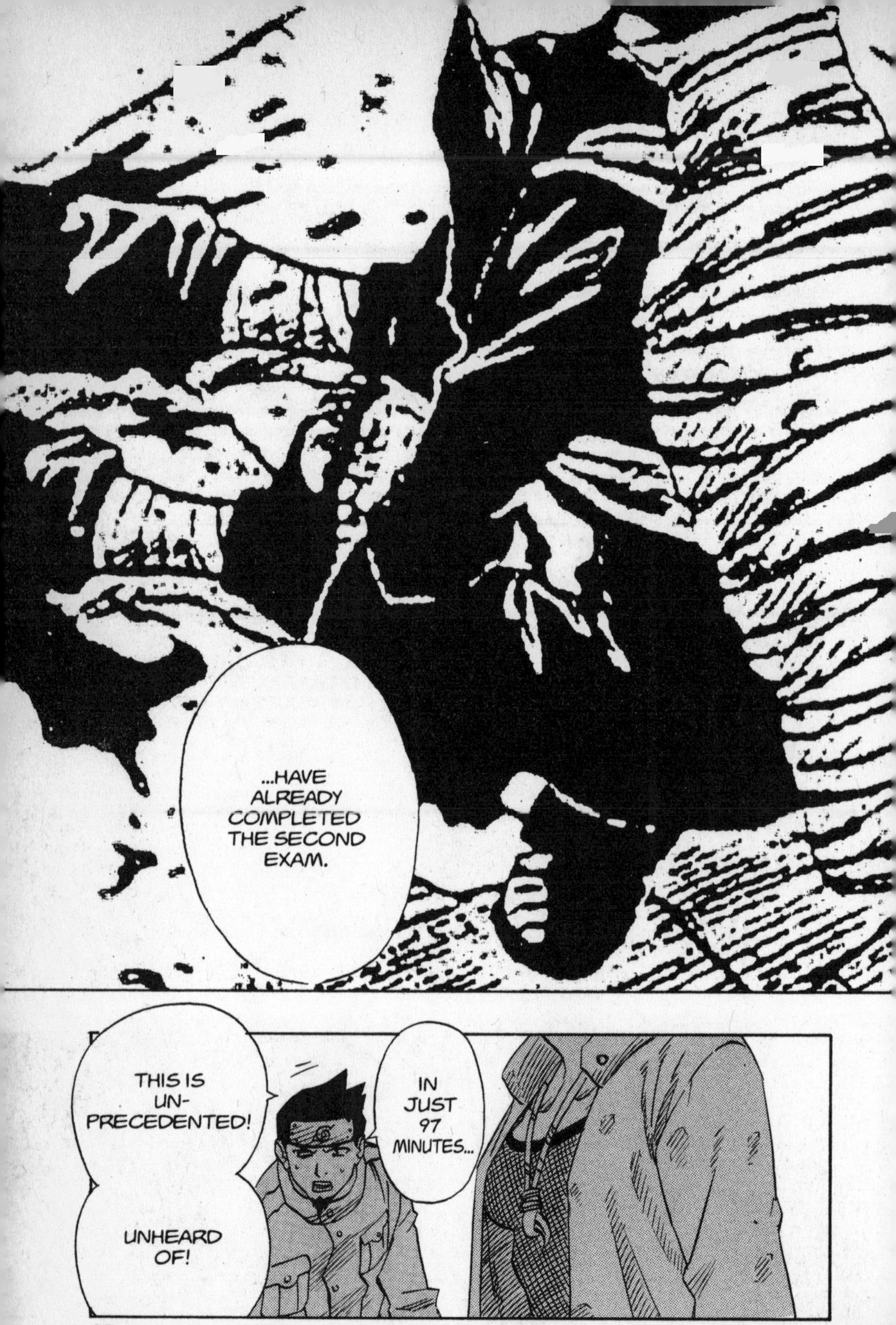
...HAVE ALREADY COMPLETED THE SECOND EXAM.
IN JUST 97 MINUTES...
THIS IS UN-PRECEDENTED!
UNHEARD OF!

THE WORLD OF KISHIMOTO MASASHI
MY PERSONAL HISTORY, PART TWO: STARTING SCHOOL

WHEN I WAS OLD ENOUGH TO GO TO KINDERGARTEN, I BECAME INTERESTED IN A WHOLE VARIETY OF NEW THINGS. BUGS, THE FLOW OF A RIVER... IF SOMETHING CAUGHT MY ATTENTION, IT WOULD HOLD MY FOCUS UNTIL SOMEONE INTERRUPTED ME. I'M TOLD MY MOTHER AND MY TEACHERS HAD TO COME LOOKING FOR ME ALL THE TIME. AT HOME, I DID THE SAME THING. WHEN I WAS WATCHING TV, I'D TUNE OUT THE REST OF THE WORLD. EVEN IF MY FATHER CALLED ME BY MY PET NICKNAME, MABO, AND PHYSICALLY TURNED MY FACE SO HE COULD SEE ME--UNDERSTANDABLY WANTING HIS CHILD TO PAY A LITTLE ATTENTION TO HIM--I STILL CONCENTRATED ON THE SCREEN. HE SAYS THAT MY FOCUS REMAINED SO COMPLETELY ON THE TV AND MY FACE GOT SO INTENSE THAT IT WAS A LITTLE SCARY. AND IT MADE HIM ENVY THE TELEVISION. BACK THEN, TV WAS THE MOST INCREDIBLY THRILLING, STIMULATING THING I COULD IMAGINE. ONE OF MY FAVORITES WAS "DORAEMON." I WOULD DRAW THAT CHARACTER'S FACE OVER AND OVER AGAIN, NO MATTER WHERE I WAS. ACTUALLY, ALL MY KINDERGARTEN CLASSMATES LOVED DORAEMON, TOO, AND ALSO USED TO TRY AND DRAW HIM WITH ME. BUT I WAS A TOTAL STICKLER ABOUT IT, ESPECIALLY ABOUT THE WAY THE CHARACTER'S EYES HAD TO BE DRAWN. THE DIAGRAMS BELOW SHOW WHAT I MEAN. EVERYONE KEPT DRAWING THE CHARACTER THE WAY HE LOOKS IN FIGURE 2...BUT FIGURE 1 IS THE VERSION THAT'S CORRECT! I ALWAYS POINTED THAT OUT TO THEM AND LECTURED THEM ABOUT THE RIGHT WAY TO DO IT. IN RETROSPECT, I'D HAVE TO SAY I WAS AN OBNOXIOUS LITTLE PERFECTIONIST. BACK THEN, I EVEN CONDEMNED ANYONE WHO USED THE "DORAEMON DRAWING SONG"* TO DRAW DORAEMON AS A HERETIC!

*EDITOR'S NOTE: "THE DORAEMON DRAWING SONG" (OR "DORAEMON NO O-EKAKI UTA") GIVES STEP-BY-STEP INSTRUCTIONS FOR HOW TO DRAW DORAEMON; PRESUMABLY, USING THE SONG SEEMED LIKE A COP-OUT TO THE KINDERGARTEN-AGED KISHIMOTO.

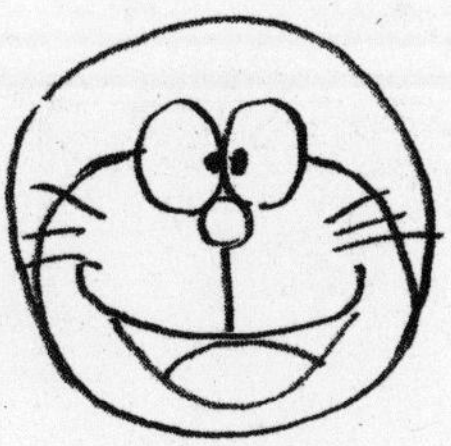

FIG. 1

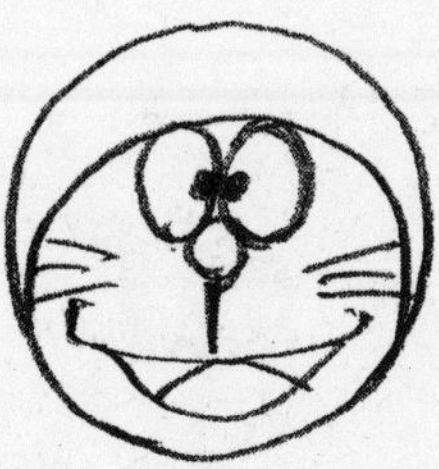

FIG. 2

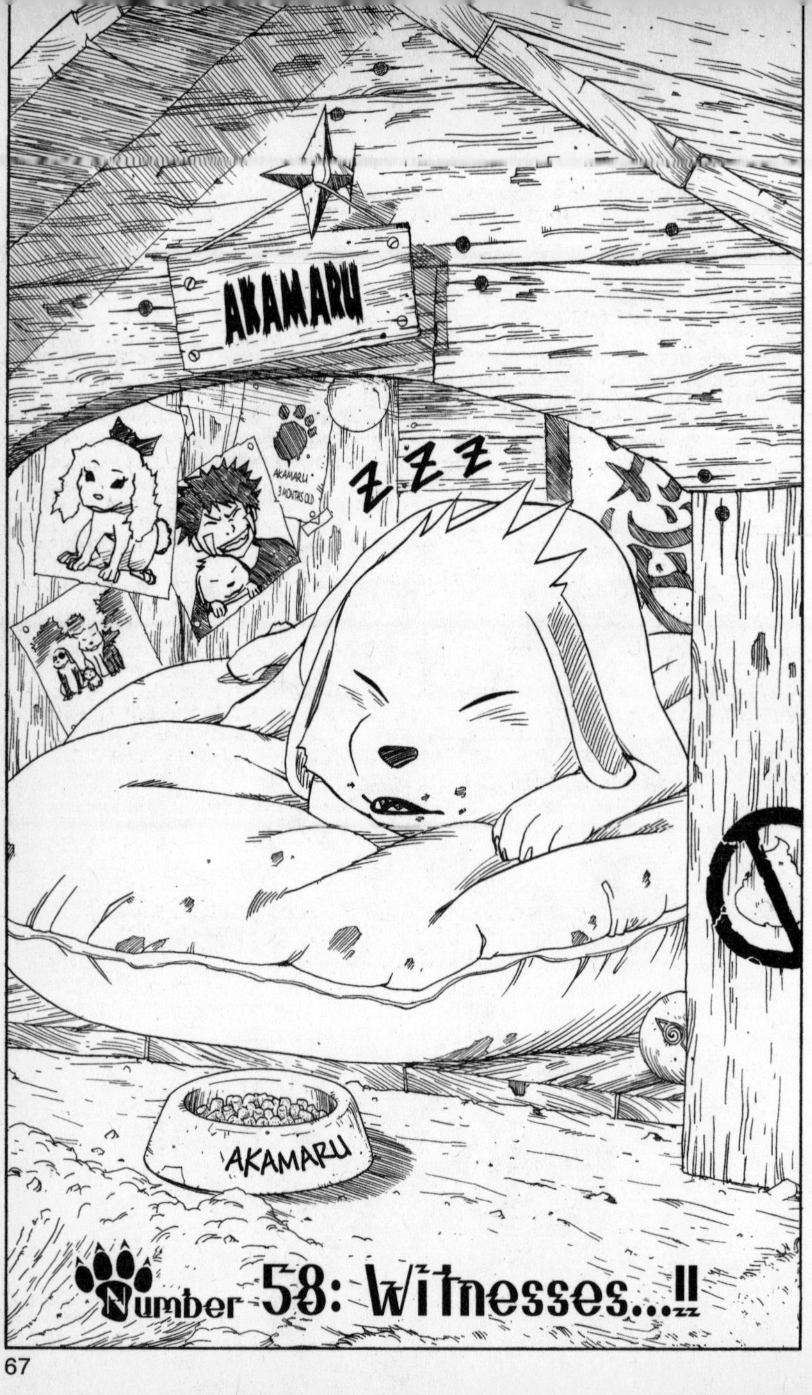
AKAMARU
AKAMARU 3 MONTHS OLD
ZZZ
AKAMARU
Number 58: Witnesses...!!

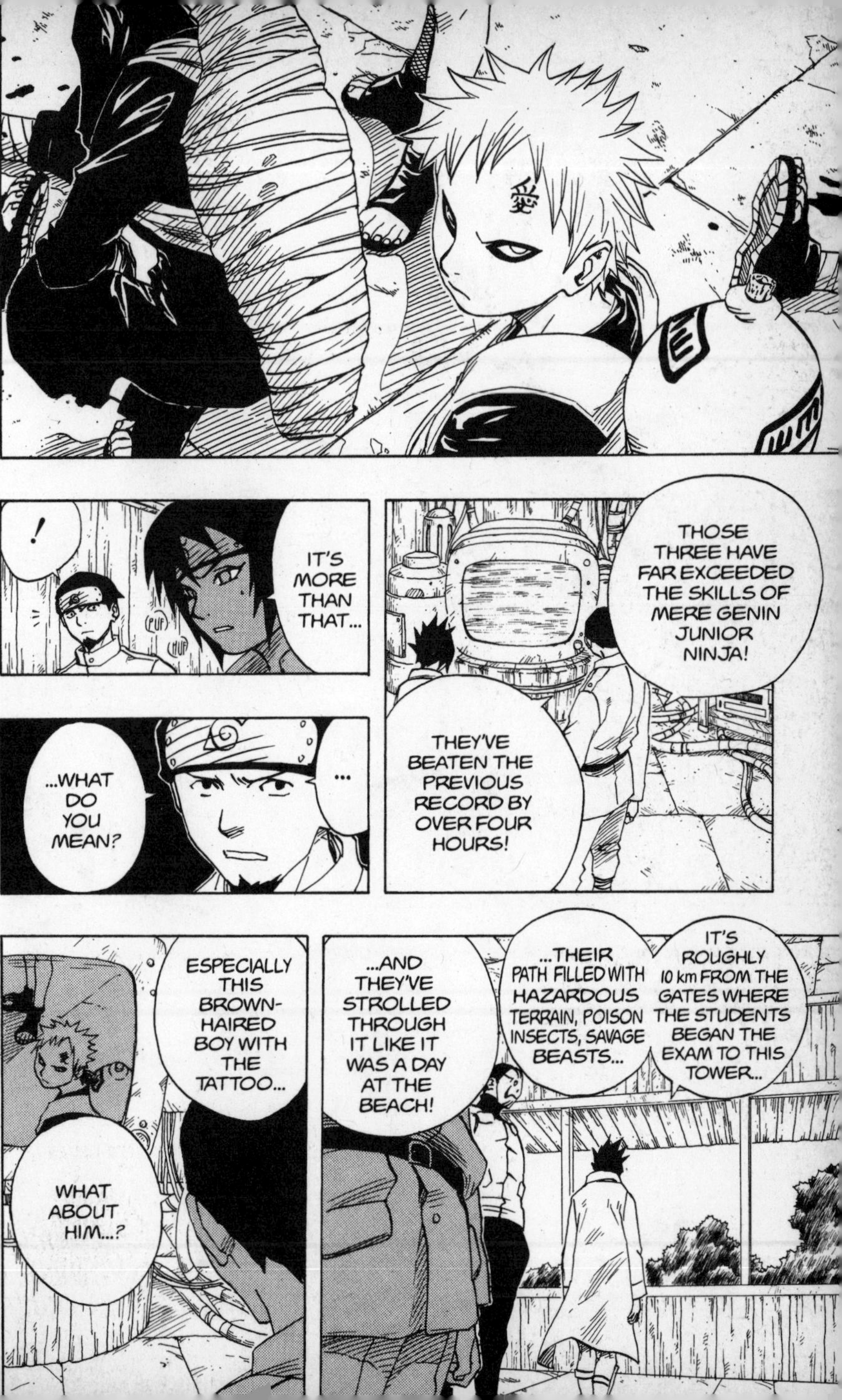
THOSE THREE HAVE FAR EXCEEDED THE SKILLS OF MERE GENIN JUNIOR NINJA!
THEY'VE BEATEN THE PREVIOUS RECORD BY OVER FOUR HOURS!
IT'S MORE THAN THAT...
!
(PUF)
(HUF)
...
...WHAT DO YOU MEAN?
IT'S ROUGHLY 10 km FROM THE GATES WHERE THE STUDENTS BEGAN THE EXAM TO THIS TOWER...
...THEIR PATH FILLED WITH HAZARDOUS TERRAIN, POISON INSECTS, SAVAGE BEASTS...
...AND THEY'VE STROLLED THROUGH IT LIKE IT WAS A DAY AT THE BEACH!
ESPECIALLY THIS BROWN-HAIRED BOY WITH THE TATTOO...
WHAT ABOUT HIM...?

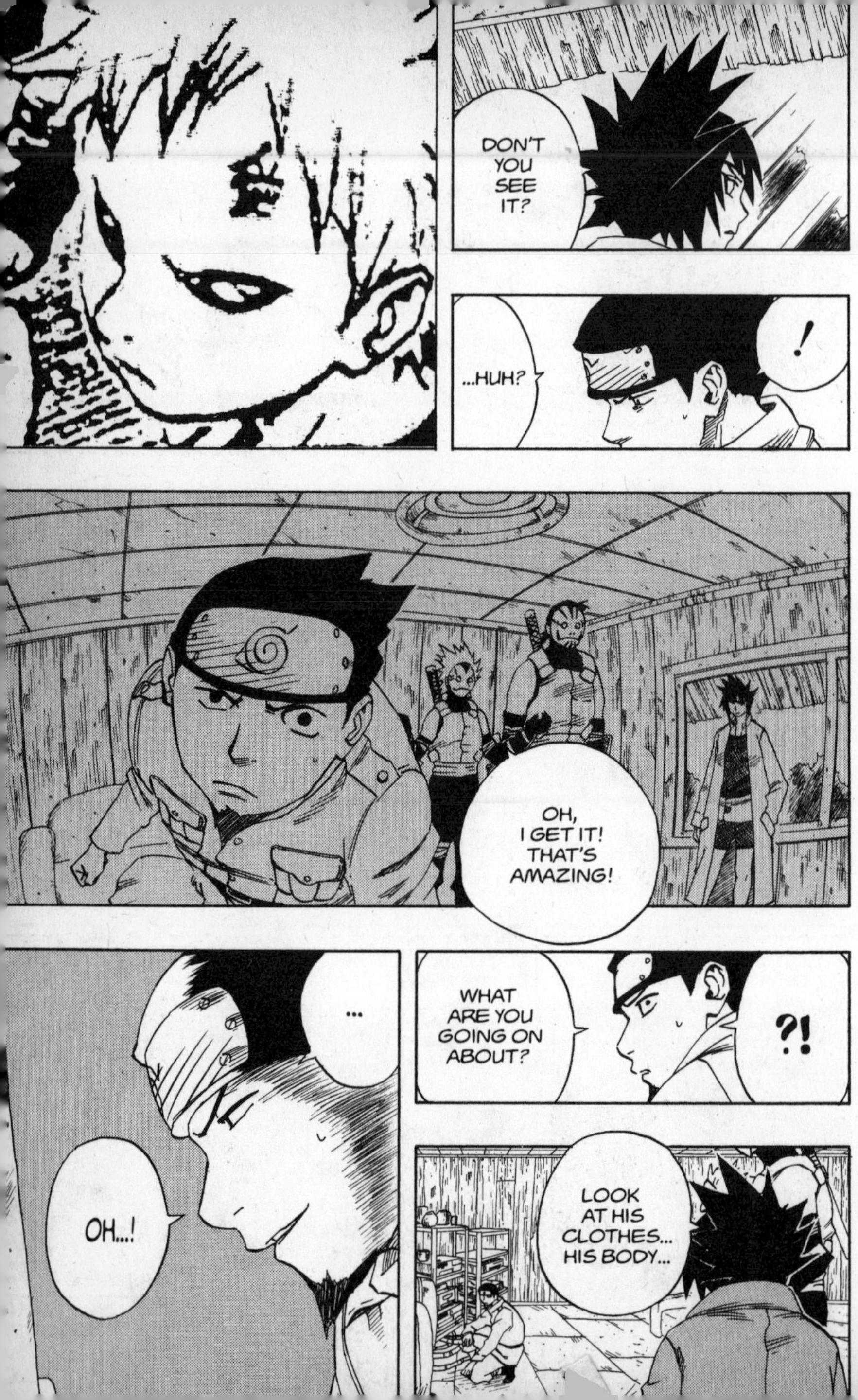
DON'T YOU SEE IT?
!
...HUH?
OH, I GET IT! THAT'S AMAZING!
?!
WHAT ARE YOU GOING ON ABOUT?
LOOK AT HIS CLOTHES... HIS BODY...
...
OH...!

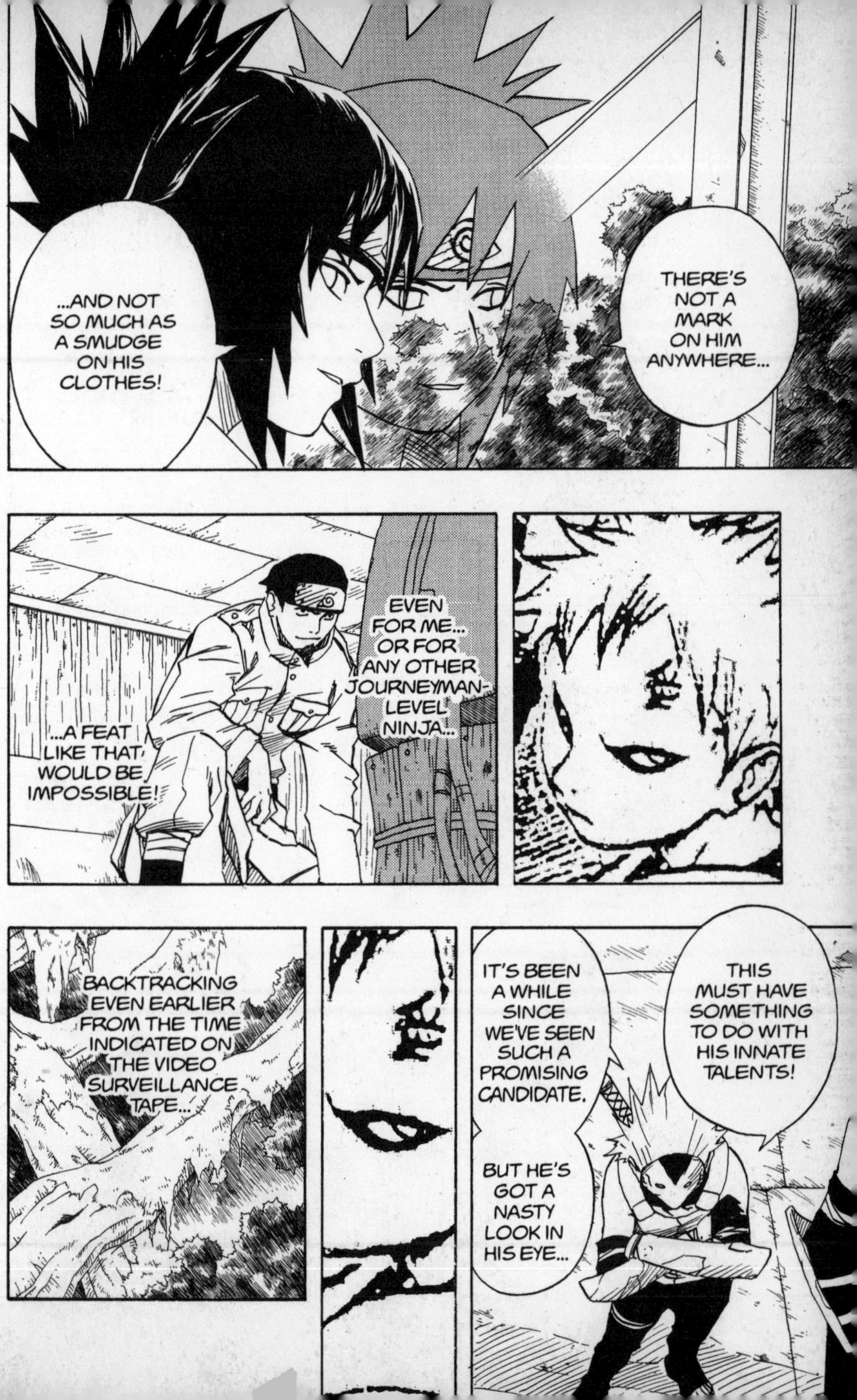
THERE'S NOT A MARK ON HIM ANYWHERE...
...AND NOT SO MUCH AS A SMUDGE ON HIS CLOTHES!
EVEN FOR ME... OR FOR ANY OTHER JOURNEYMAN-LEVEL NINJA...
...A FEAT LIKE THAT WOULD BE IMPOSSIBLE!
THIS MUST HAVE SOMETHING TO DO WITH HIS INNATE TALENTS!
IT'S BEEN A WHILE SINCE WE'VE SEEN SUCH A PROMISING CANDIDATE.
BUT HE'S GOT A NASTY LOOK IN HIS EYE...
BACKTRACKING EVEN EARLIER FROM THE TIME INDICATED ON THE VIDEO SURVEILLANCE TAPE...

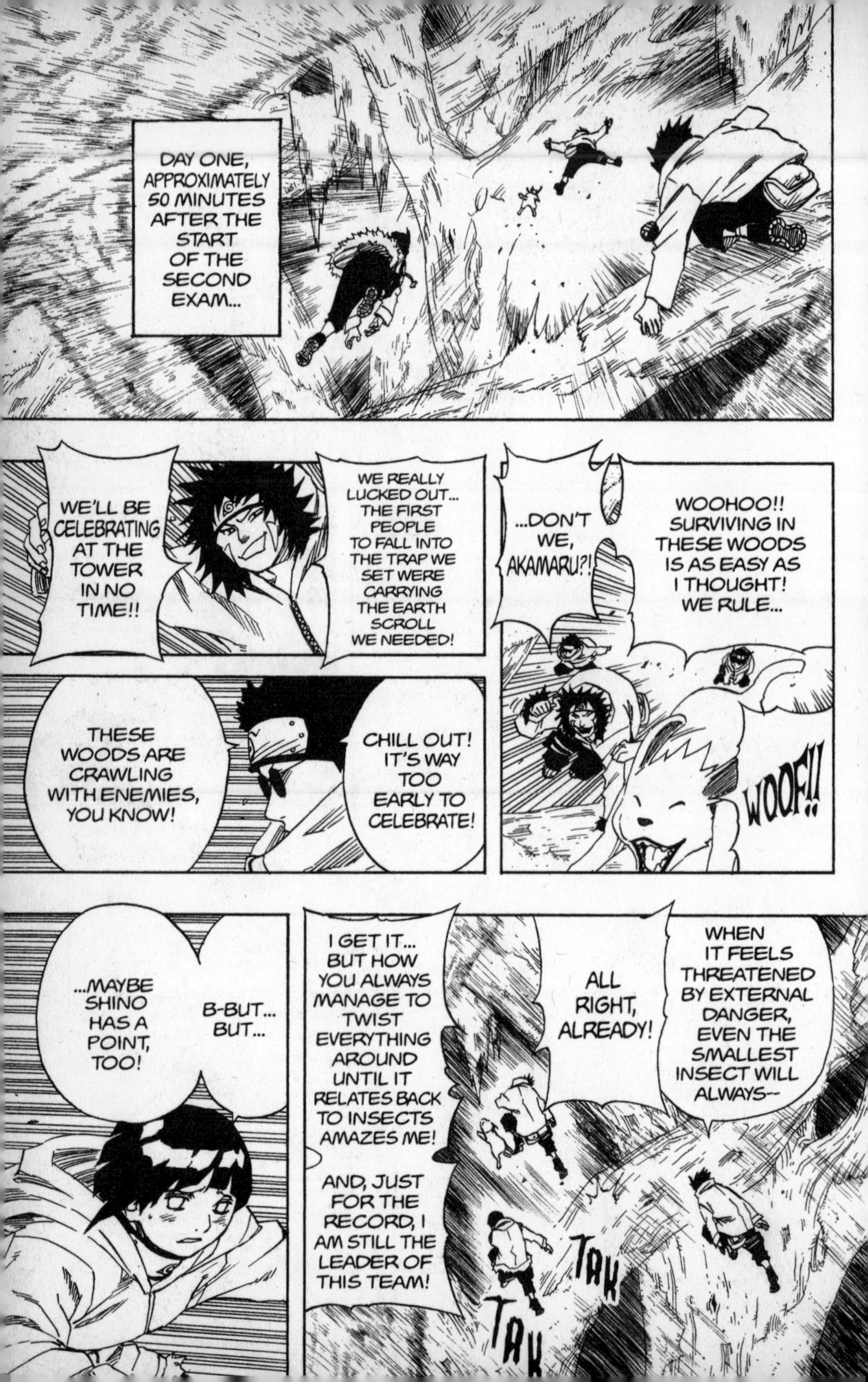
DAY ONE, APPROXIMATELY 50 MINUTES AFTER THE START OF THE SECOND EXAM...
WOOHOO!! SURVIVING IN THESE WOODS IS AS EASY AS I THOUGHT! WE RULE...
...DON'T WE, AKAMARU?!
WOOF!!
WE REALLY LUCKED OUT... THE FIRST PEOPLE TO FALL INTO THE TRAP WE SET WERE CARRYING THE EARTH SCROLL WE NEEDED!
WE'LL BE CELEBRATING AT THE TOWER IN NO TIME!!
CHILL OUT! IT'S WAY TOO EARLY TO CELEBRATE!
THESE WOODS ARE CRAWLING WITH ENEMIES, YOU KNOW!
WHEN IT FEELS THREATENED BY EXTERNAL DANGER, EVEN THE SMALLEST INSECT WILL ALWAYS--
ALL RIGHT, ALREADY!
I GET IT... BUT HOW YOU ALWAYS MANAGE TO TWIST EVERYTHING AROUND UNTIL IT RELATES BACK TO INSECTS AMAZES ME!
AND, JUST FOR THE RECORD, I AM STILL THE LEADER OF THIS TEAM!
TAK
TAK
B-BUT... BUT...
...MAYBE SHINO HAS A POINT, TOO!

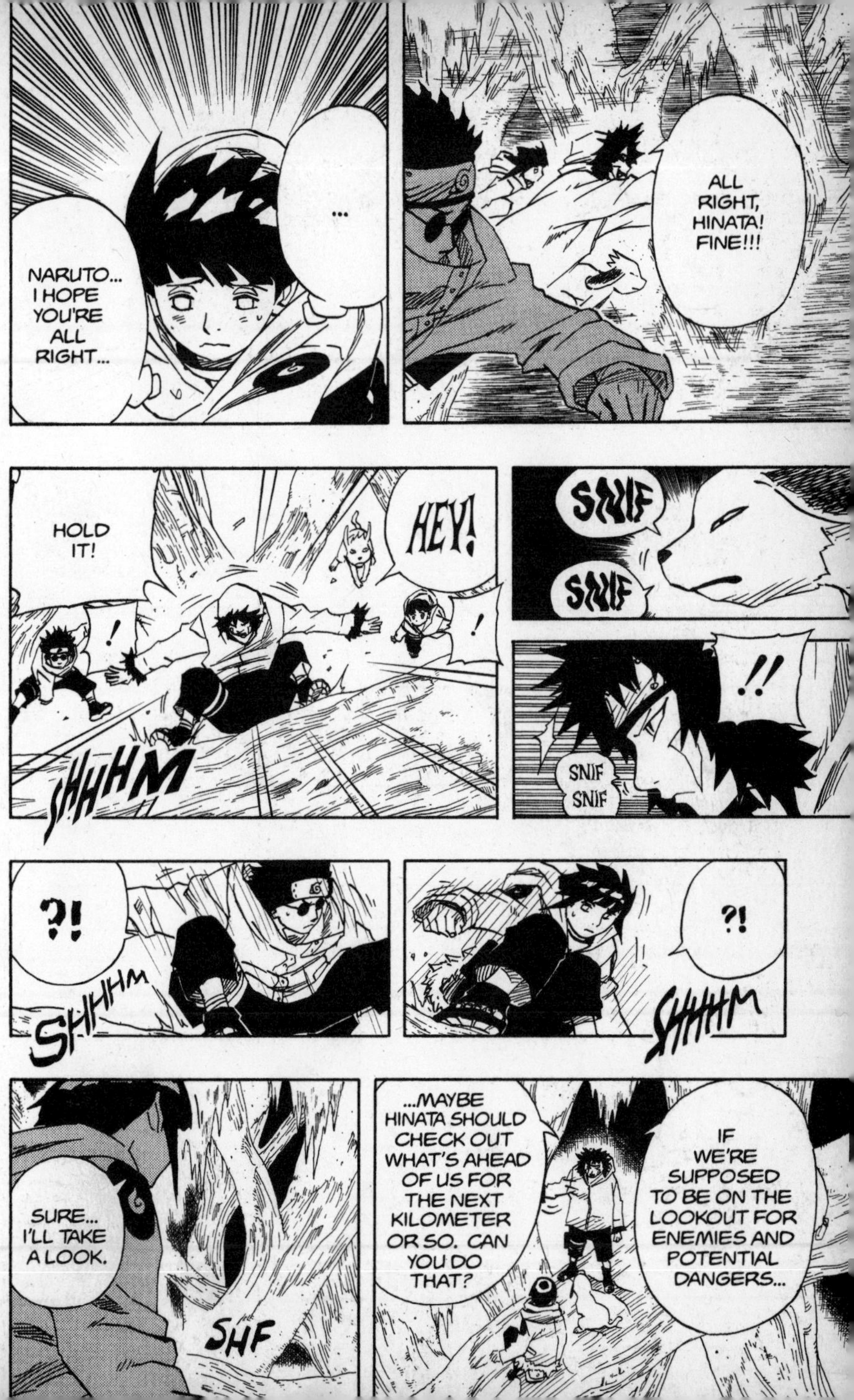
ALL RIGHT, HINATA! FINE!!!
...
NARUTO... I HOPE YOU'RE ALL RIGHT...
SNIF
SNIF
!!
SNIF SNIF
HEY!
HOLD IT!
!
!
SHHHM
?!
SHHHM
?!
SHHHM
IF WE'RE SUPPOSED TO BE ON THE LOOKOUT FOR ENEMIES AND POTENTIAL DANGERS...
...MAYBE HINATA SHOULD CHECK OUT WHAT'S AHEAD OF US FOR THE NEXT KILOMETER OR SO. CAN YOU DO THAT?
SURE... I'LL TAKE A LOOK.
SHF

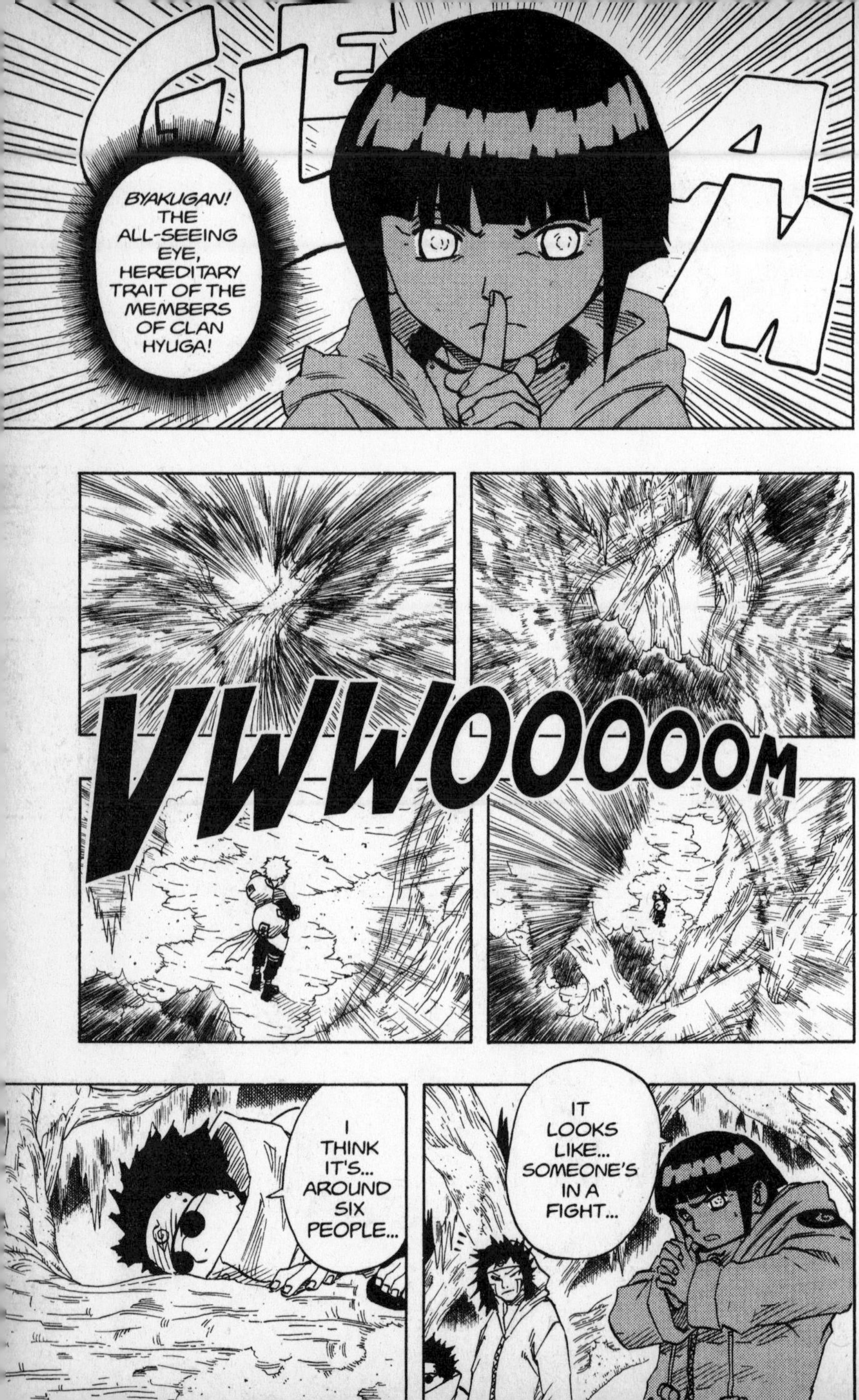
BYAKUGAN! THE ALL-SEEING EYE, HEREDITARY TRAIT OF THE MEMBERS OF CLAN HYUGA!
VWWOOOOOM
IT LOOKS LIKE... SOMEONE'S IN A FIGHT...
I THINK IT'S... AROUND SIX PEOPLE...

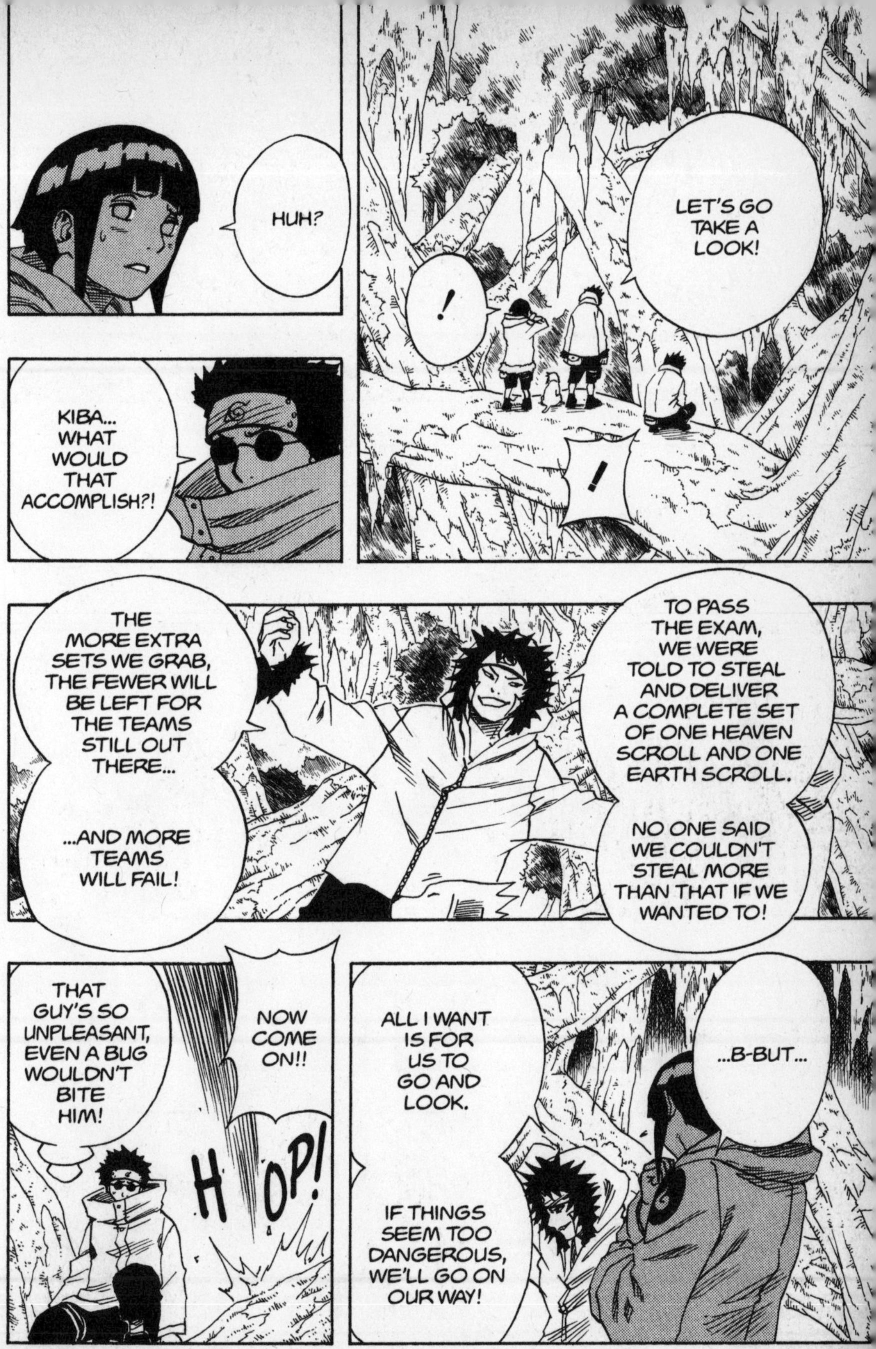
LET'S GO TAKE A LOOK!
!
!
HUH?
KIBA... WHAT WOULD THAT ACCOMPLISH?!
TO PASS THE EXAM, WE WERE TOLD TO STEAL AND DELIVER A COMPLETE SET OF ONE HEAVEN SCROLL AND ONE EARTH SCROLL.
NO ONE SAID WE COULDN'T STEAL MORE THAN THAT IF WE WANTED TO!
THE MORE EXTRA SETS WE GRAB, THE FEWER WILL BE LEFT FOR THE TEAMS STILL OUT THERE...
...AND MORE TEAMS WILL FAIL!
...B-BUT...
ALL I WANT IS FOR US TO GO AND LOOK.
IF THINGS SEEM TOO DANGEROUS, WE'LL GO ON OUR WAY!
NOW COME ON!!
HOP!
THAT GUY'S SO UNPLEASANT, EVEN A BUG WOULDN'T BITE HIM!

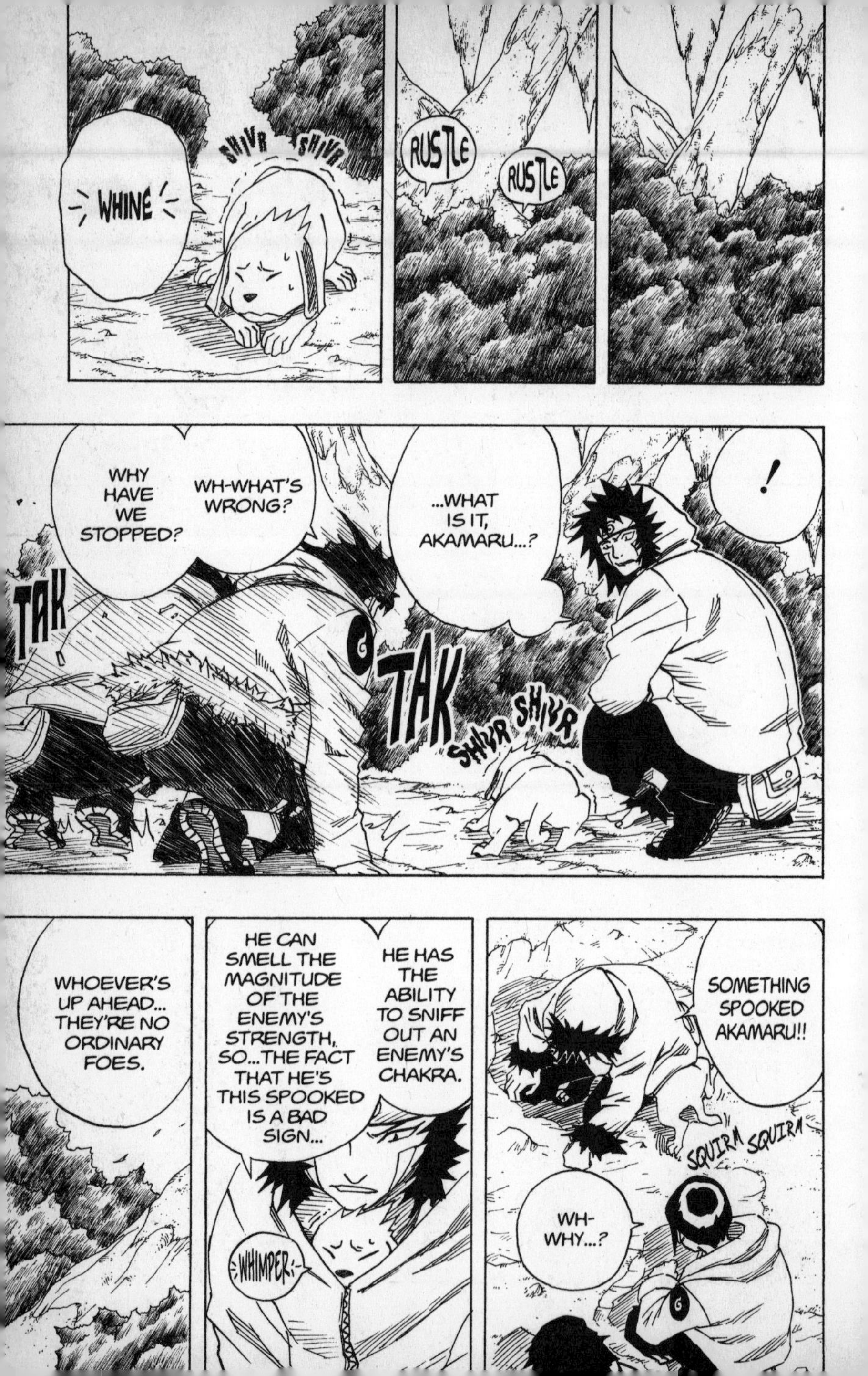
RUSTLE
RUSTLE
WHINE
SHIVR
SHIVR
!
...WHAT IS IT, AKAMARU...?
TAK
SHIVR
SHIVR
WH-WHAT'S WRONG?
WHY HAVE WE STOPPED?
TAK
SOMETHING SPOOKED AKAMARU!!
SQUIRM
SQUIRM
WH-WHY...?
HE HAS THE ABILITY TO SNIFF OUT AN ENEMY'S CHAKRA.
HE CAN SMELL THE MAGNITUDE OF THE ENEMY'S STRENGTH, SO...THE FACT THAT HE'S THIS SPOOKED IS A BAD SIGN...
WHIMPER
WHOEVER'S UP AHEAD... THEY'RE NO ORDINARY FOES.

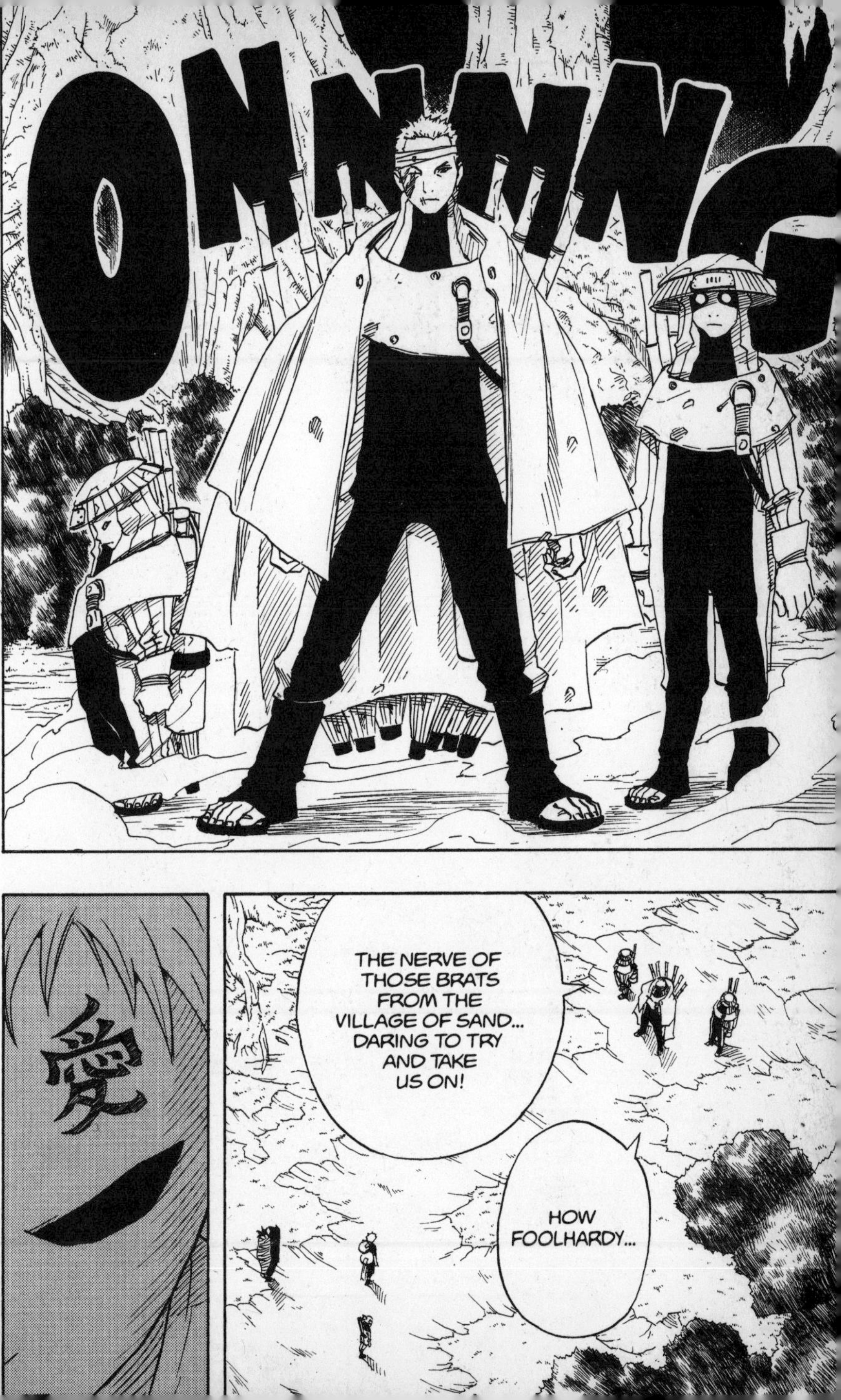
ONNNNG
THE NERVE OF THOSE BRATS FROM THE VILLAGE OF SAND... DARING TO TRY AND TAKE US ON!
HOW FOOLHARDY...
愛

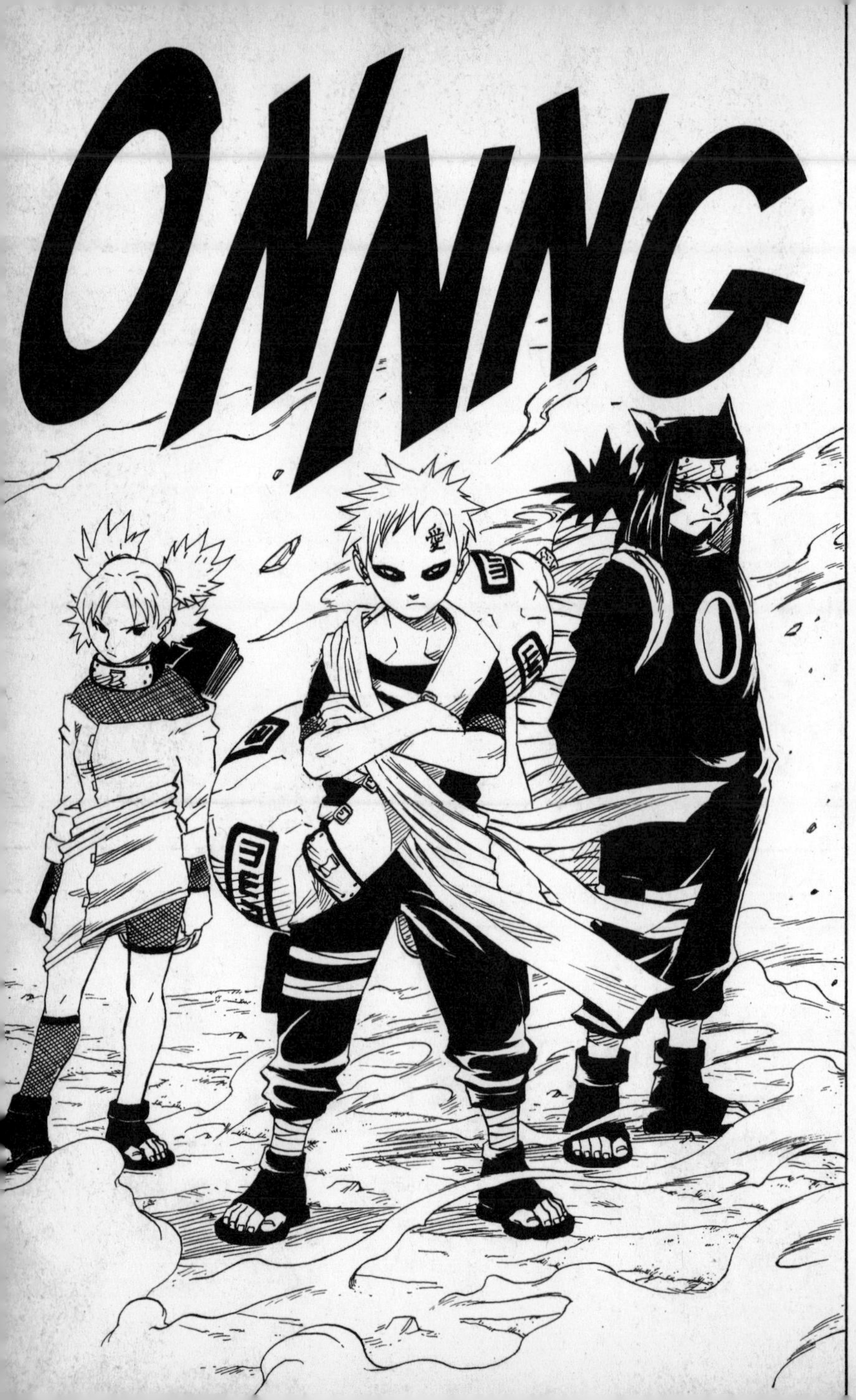
ONNNG

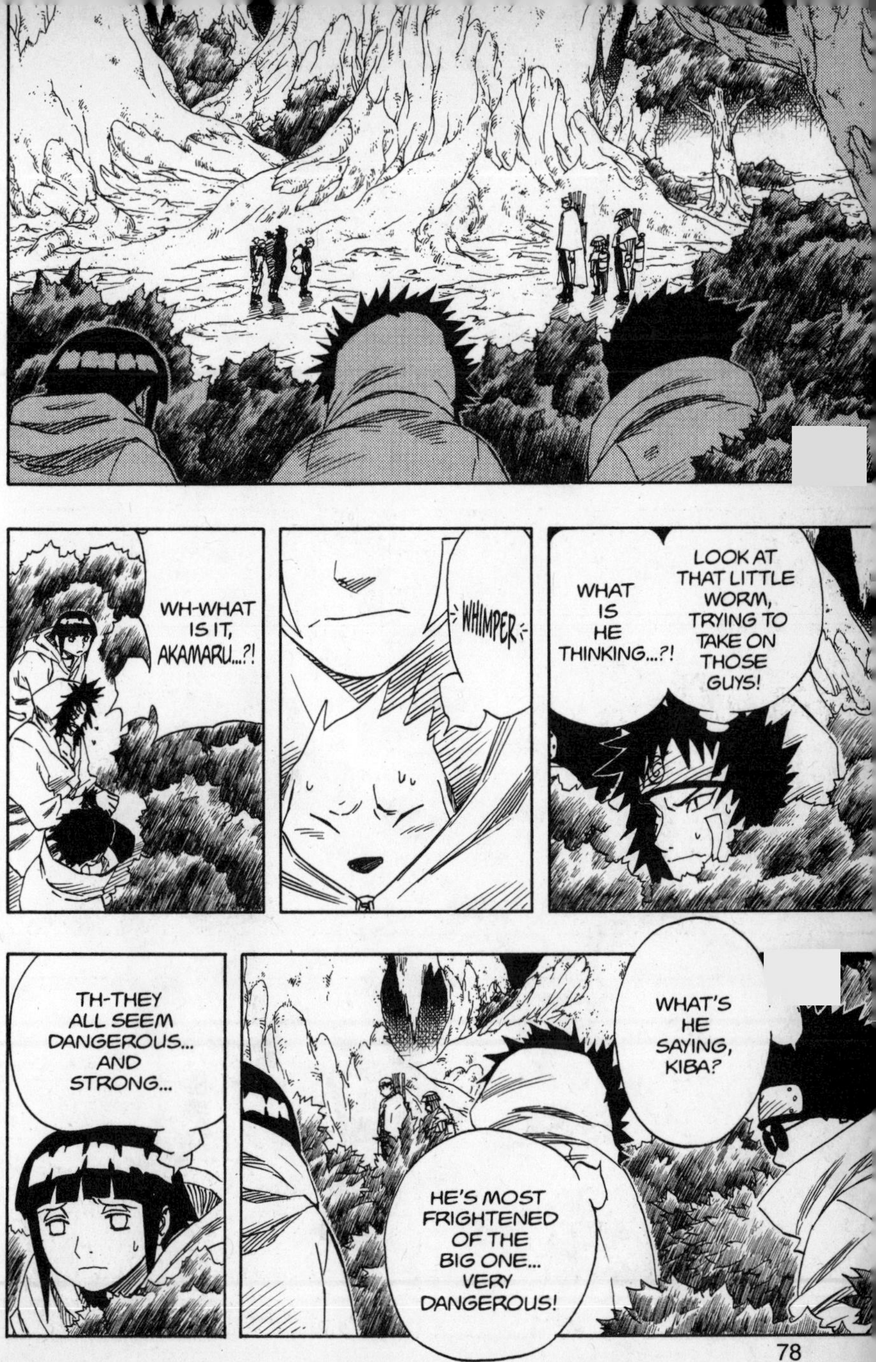
LOOK AT THAT LITTLE WORM, TRYING TO TAKE ON THOSE GUYS!
WHAT IS HE THINKING...?!
WHIMPER
WH-WHAT IS IT, AKAMARU...?!
WHAT'S HE SAYING, KIBA?
HE'S MOST FRIGHTENED OF THE BIG ONE... VERY DANGEROUS!
TH-THEY ALL SEEM DANGEROUS... AND STRONG...

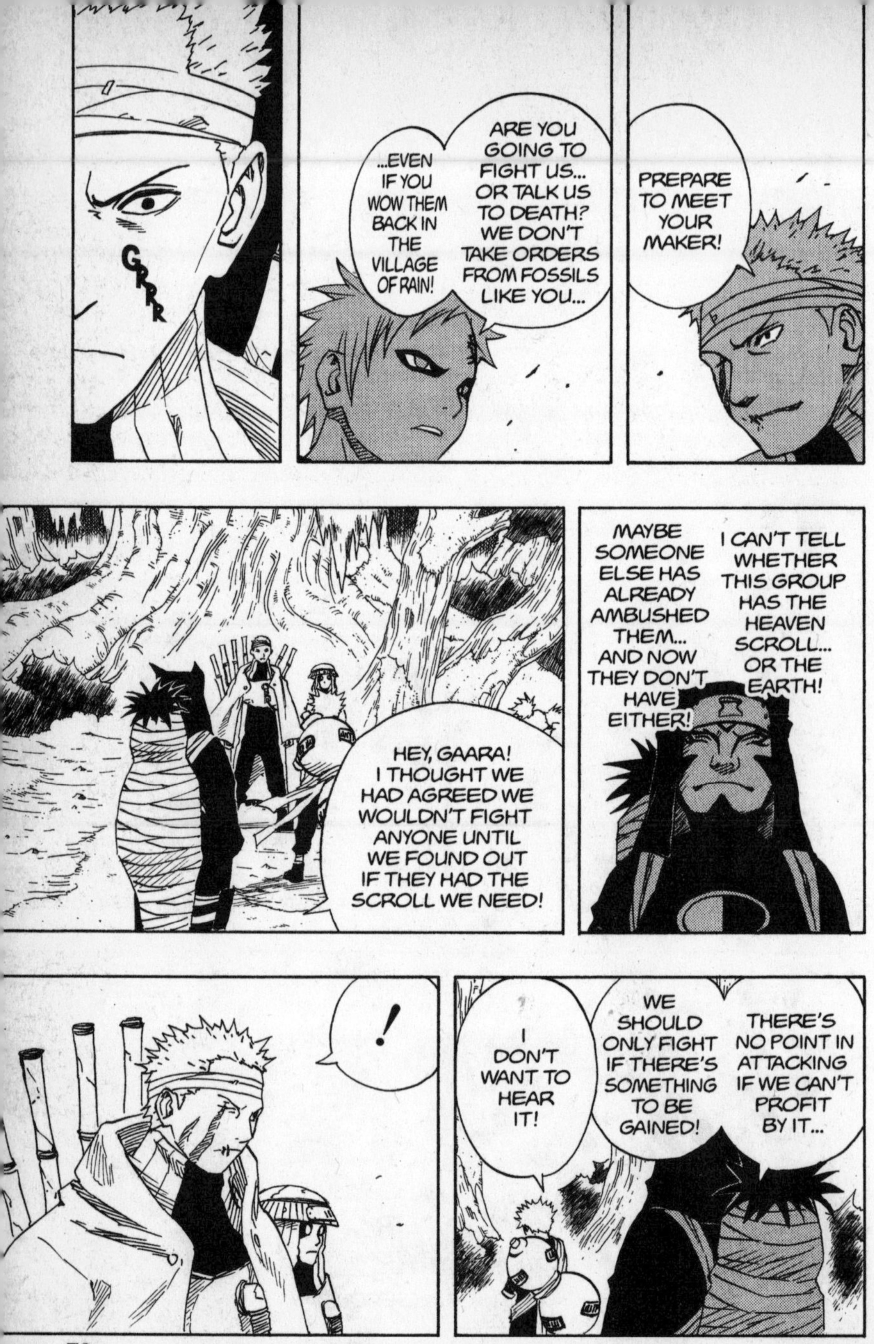
PREPARE TO MEET YOUR MAKER!
ARE YOU GOING TO FIGHT US... OR TALK US TO DEATH? WE DON'T TAKE ORDERS FROM FOSSILS LIKE YOU...
...EVEN IF YOU WOW THEM BACK IN THE VILLAGE OF RAIN!
GRRR
I CAN'T TELL WHETHER THIS GROUP HAS THE HEAVEN SCROLL... OR THE EARTH!
MAYBE SOMEONE ELSE HAS ALREADY AMBUSHED THEM... AND NOW THEY DON'T HAVE EITHER!
HEY, GAARA! I THOUGHT WE HAD AGREED WE WOULDN'T FIGHT ANYONE UNTIL WE FOUND OUT IF THEY HAD THE SCROLL WE NEED!
THERE'S NO POINT IN ATTACKING IF WE CAN'T PROFIT BY IT...
WE SHOULD ONLY FIGHT IF THERE'S SOMETHING TO BE GAINED!
I DON'T WANT TO HEAR IT!
!

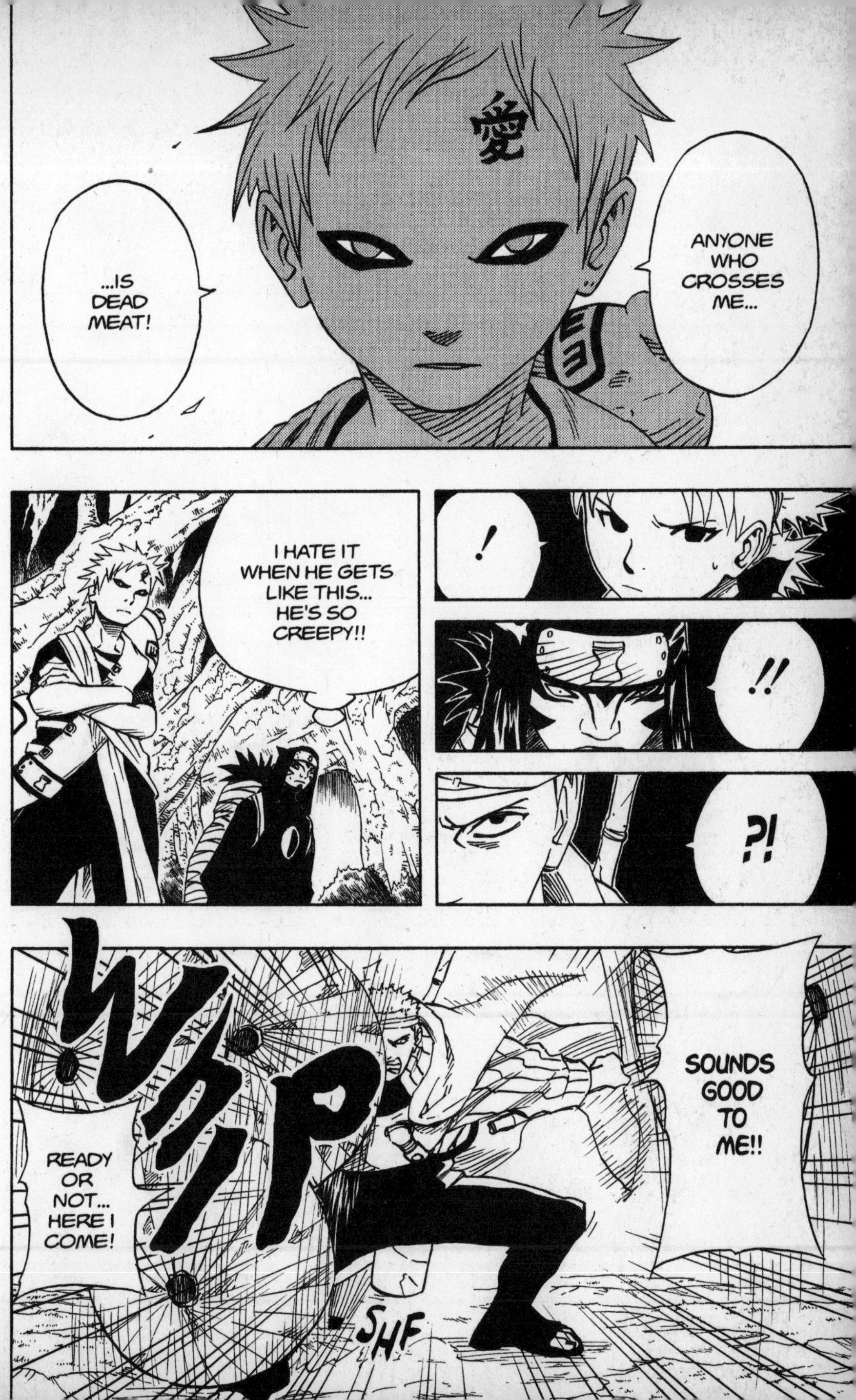
ANYONE WHO CROSSES ME...
...IS DEAD MEAT!
!
!!
?!
I HATE IT WHEN HE GETS LIKE THIS... HE'S SO CREEPY!!
SOUNDS GOOD TO ME!!
WHIP
READY OR NOT... HERE I COME!
SHF

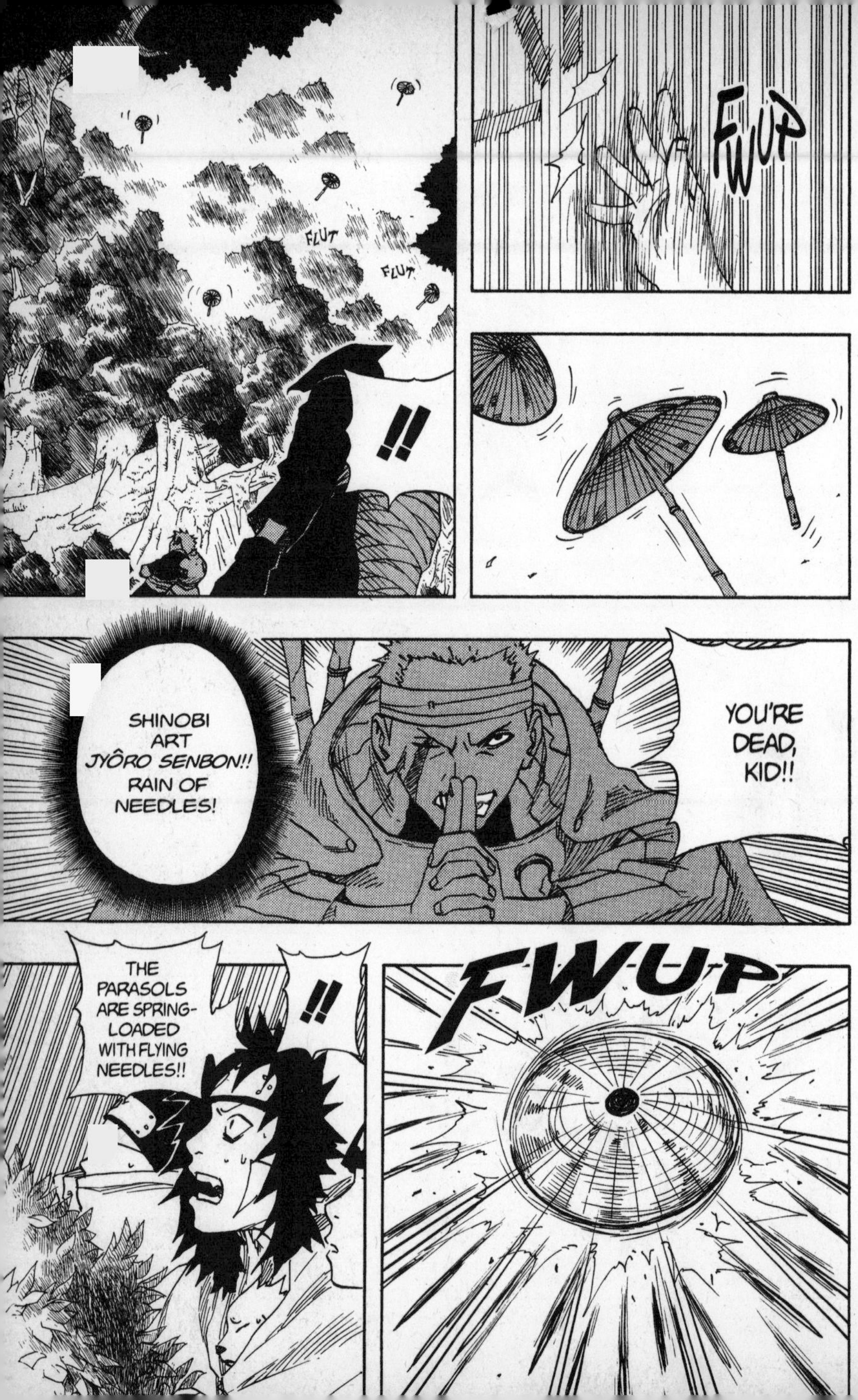
FWUP
FLUT
FLUT
!!
YOU'RE DEAD, KID!!
SHINOBI ART JYÔRO SENBON!! RAIN OF NEEDLES!
FWUP
!!
THE PARASOLS ARE SPRING-LOADED WITH FLYING NEEDLES!!

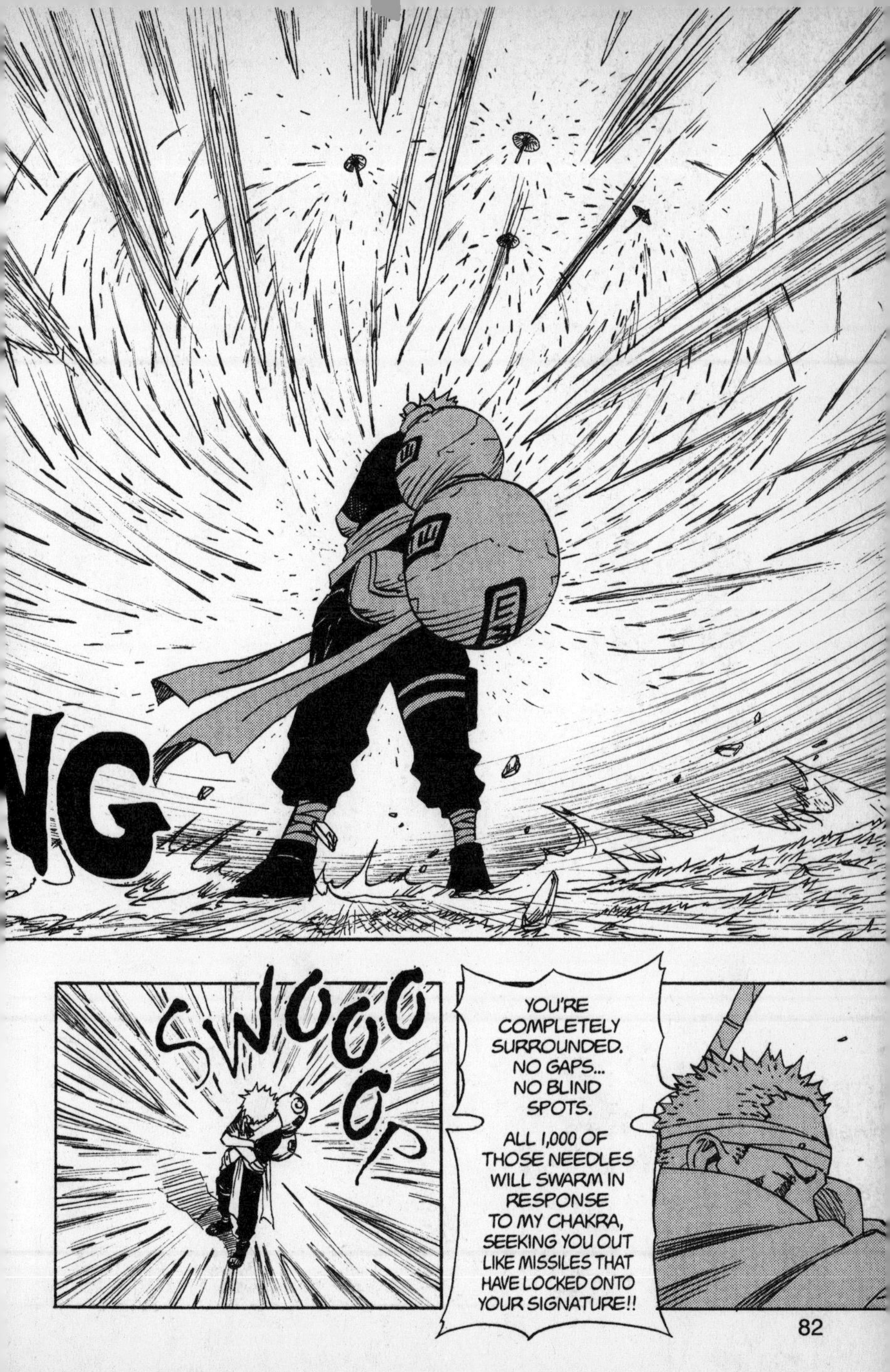
NG
YOU'RE COMPLETELY SURROUNDED. NO GAPS... NO BLIND SPOTS.
ALL 1,000 OF THOSE NEEDLES WILL SWARM IN RESPONSE TO MY CHAKRA, SEEKING YOU OUT LIKE MISSILES THAT HAVE LOCKED ONTO YOUR SIGNATURE!!
SWOOOOP

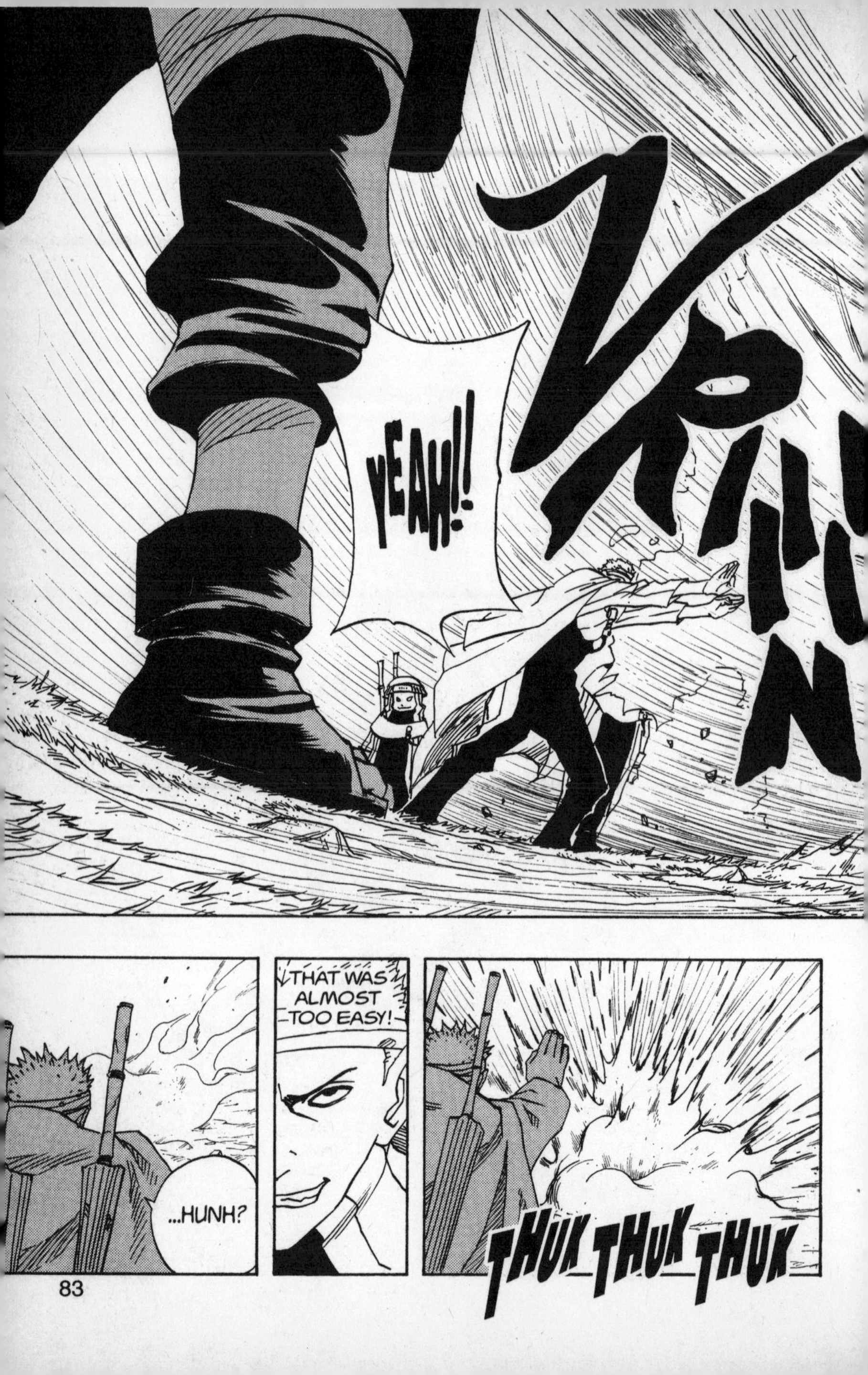
YEAH!!
THUK THUK THUK
THAT WAS ALMOST TOO EASY!
...HUNH?

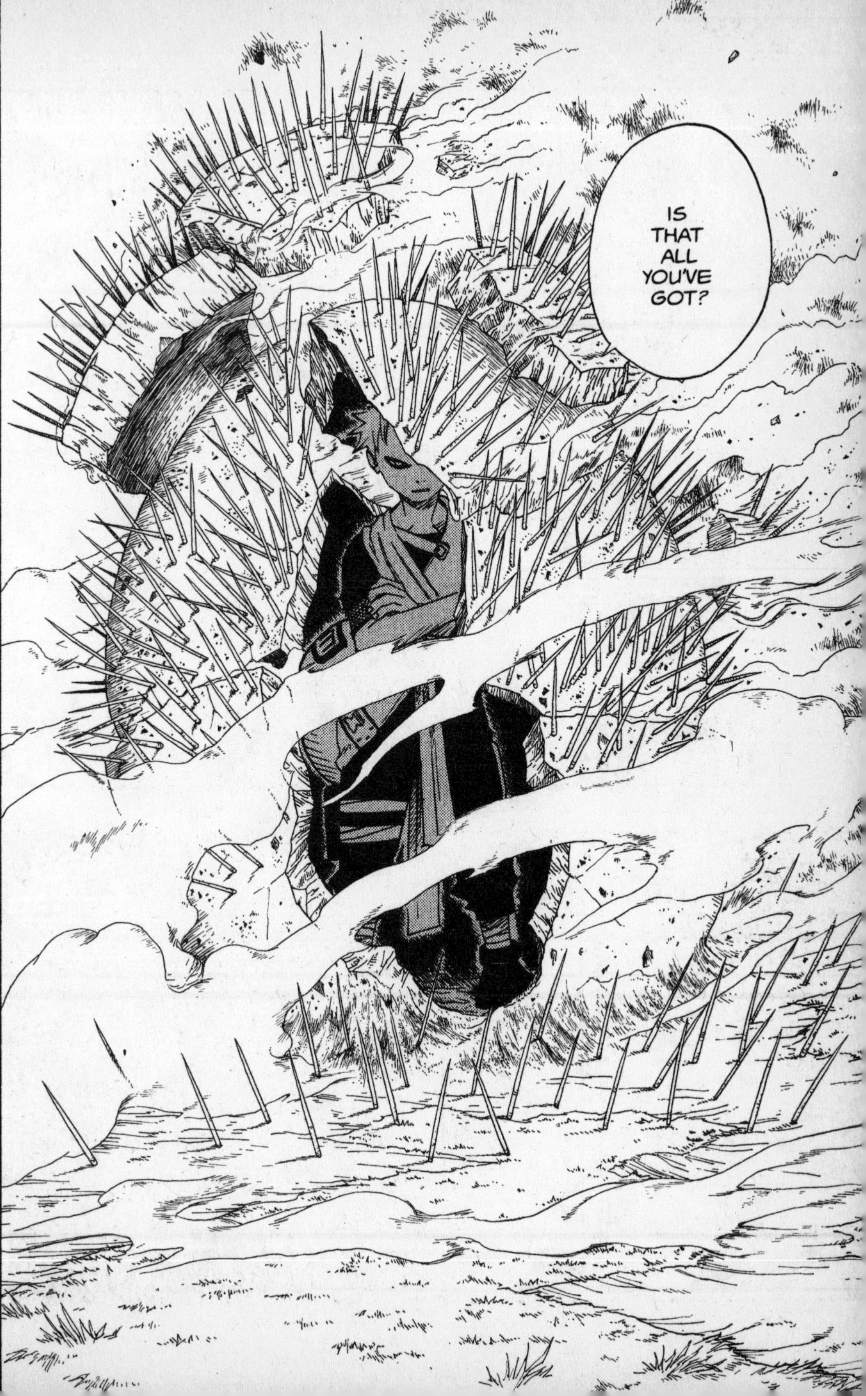
IS THAT ALL YOU'VE GOT?

READ THIS WAY

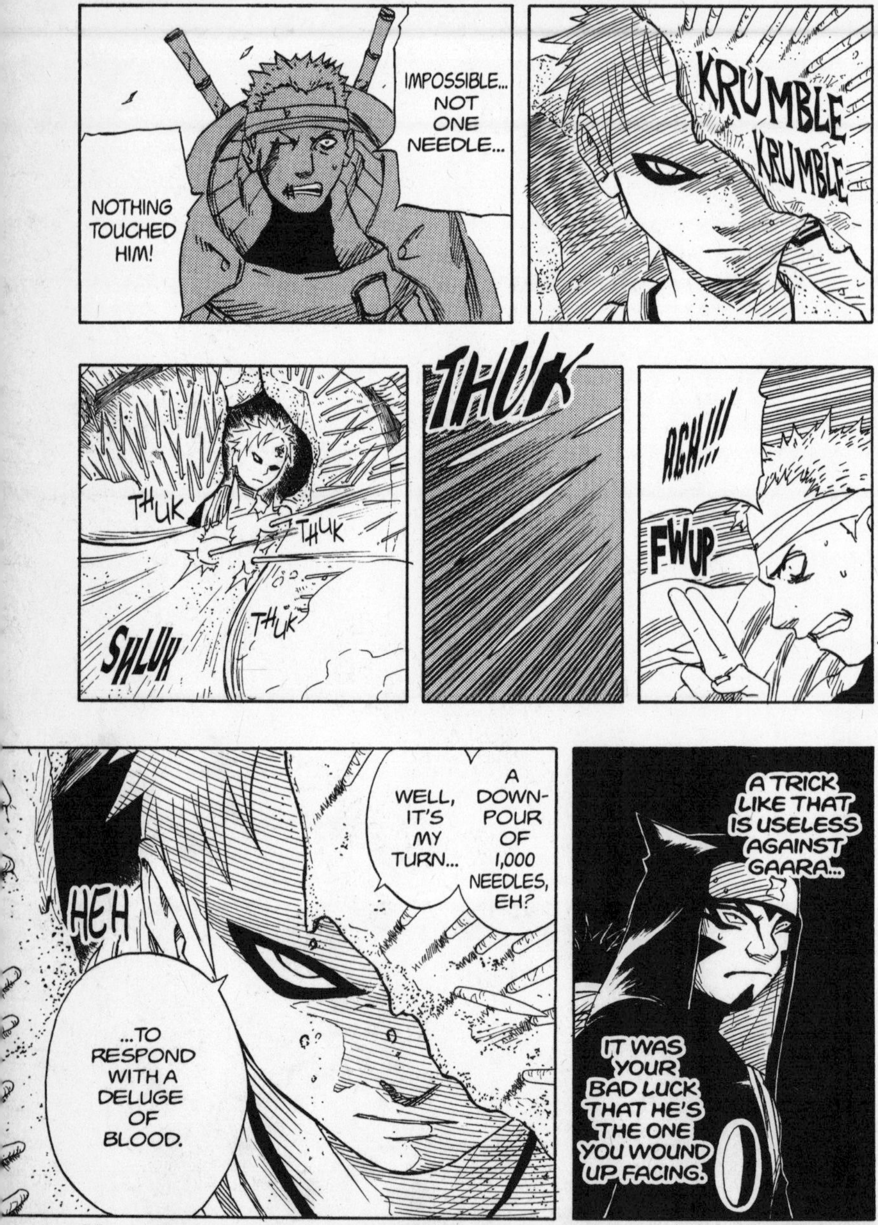
KRUMBLE
KRUMBLE
IMPOSSIBLE... NOT ONE NEEDLE...
NOTHING TOUCHED HIM!
AGH!!!
FWUP
THUK
THUK
THUK
THUK
SHLUK
A TRICK LIKE THAT IS USELESS AGAINST GAARA...
IT WAS YOUR BAD LUCK THAT HE'S THE ONE YOU WOUND UP FACING.
A DOWNPOUR OF 1,000 NEEDLES, EH?
WELL, IT'S MY TURN...
HEH
...TO RESPOND WITH A DELUGE OF BLOOD.

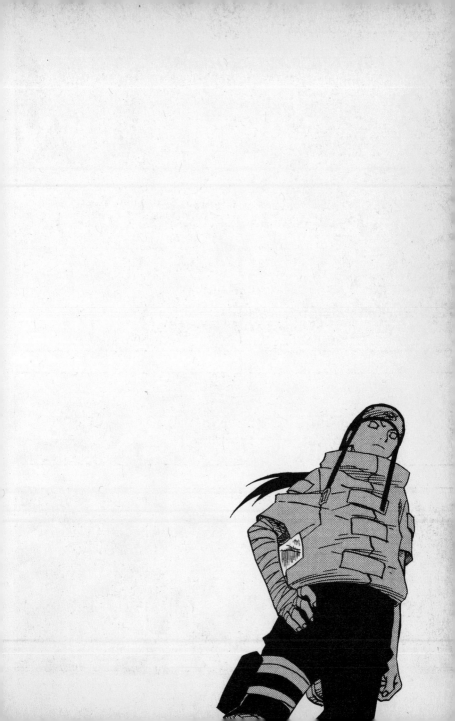

Number 59: The Tragedy of the Sand!!

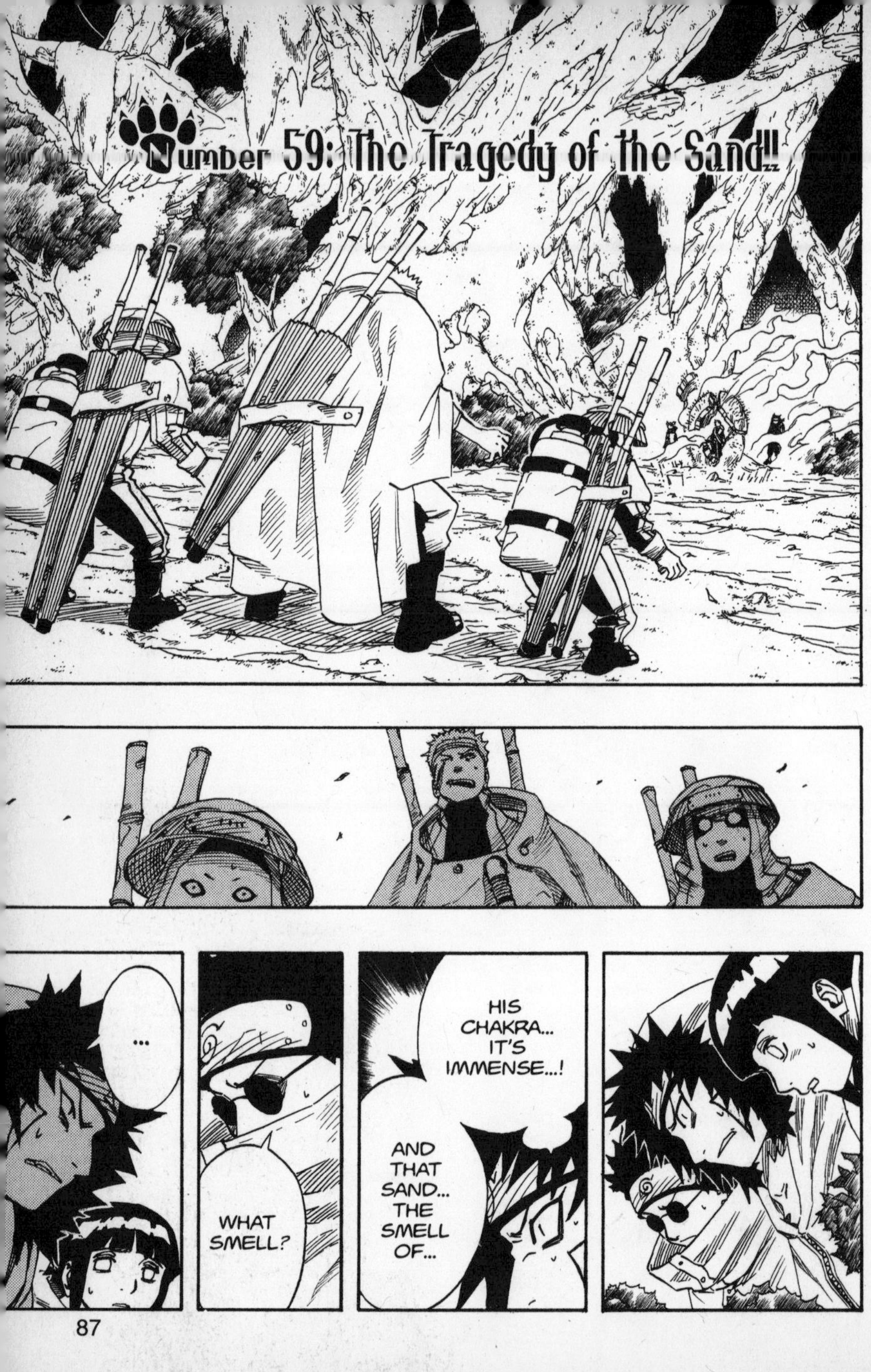
HIS CHAKRA... IT'S IMMENSE...!
AND THAT SAND... THE SMELL OF...
WHAT SMELL?
...

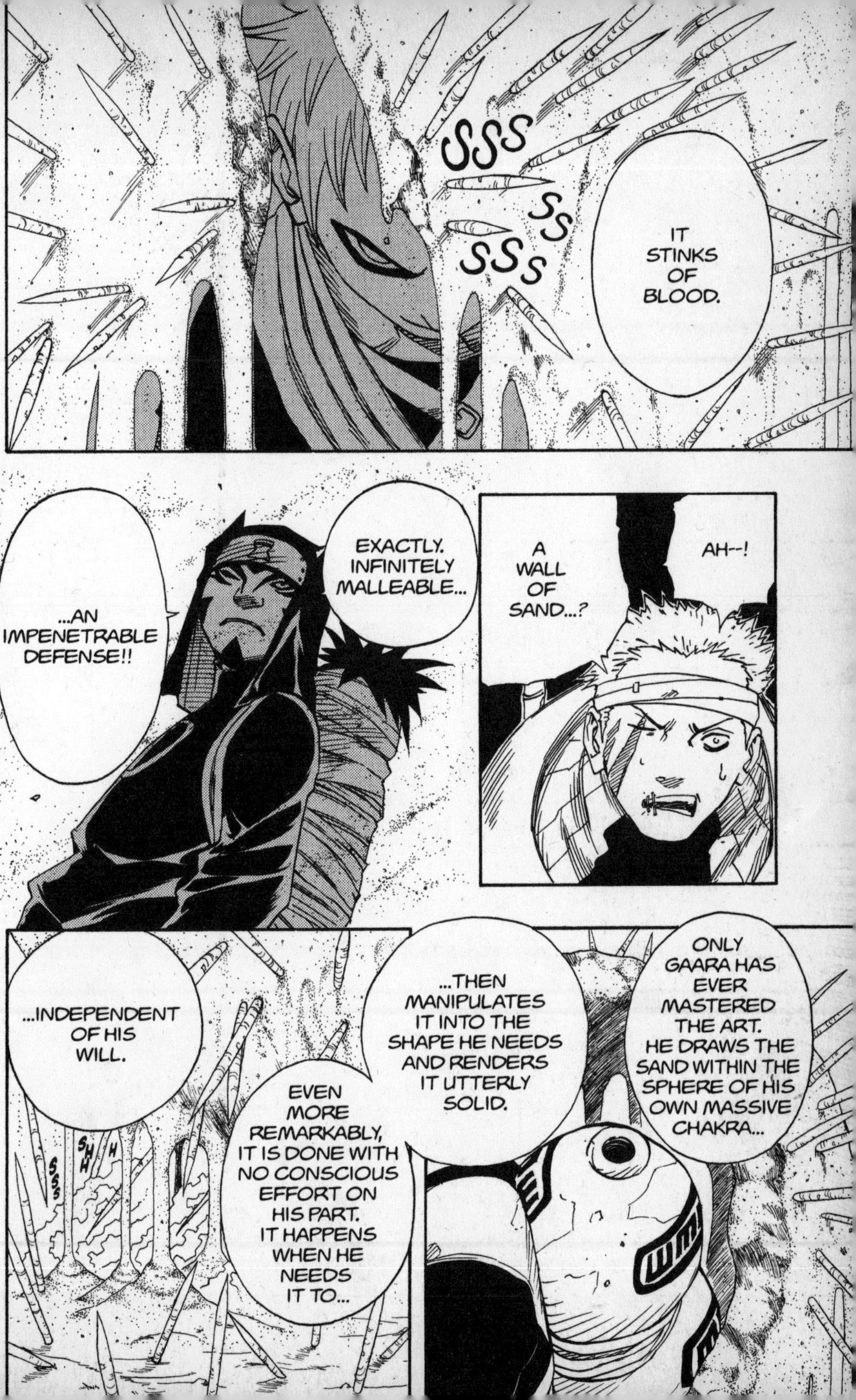
SSS
SS
SSS
IT STINKS OF BLOOD.
AH--!
A WALL OF SAND...?
EXACTLY. INFINITELY MALLEABLE...
...AN IMPENETRABLE DEFENSE!!
ONLY GAARA HAS EVER MASTERED THE ART. HE DRAWS THE SAND WITHIN THE SPHERE OF HIS OWN MASSIVE CHAKRA...
...THEN MANIPULATES IT INTO THE SHAPE HE NEEDS AND RENDERS IT UTTERLY SOLID.
EVEN MORE REMARKABLY, IT IS DONE WITH NO CONSCIOUS EFFORT ON HIS PART. IT HAPPENS WHEN HE NEEDS IT TO...
...INDEPENDENT OF HIS WILL.
SHH
SSS

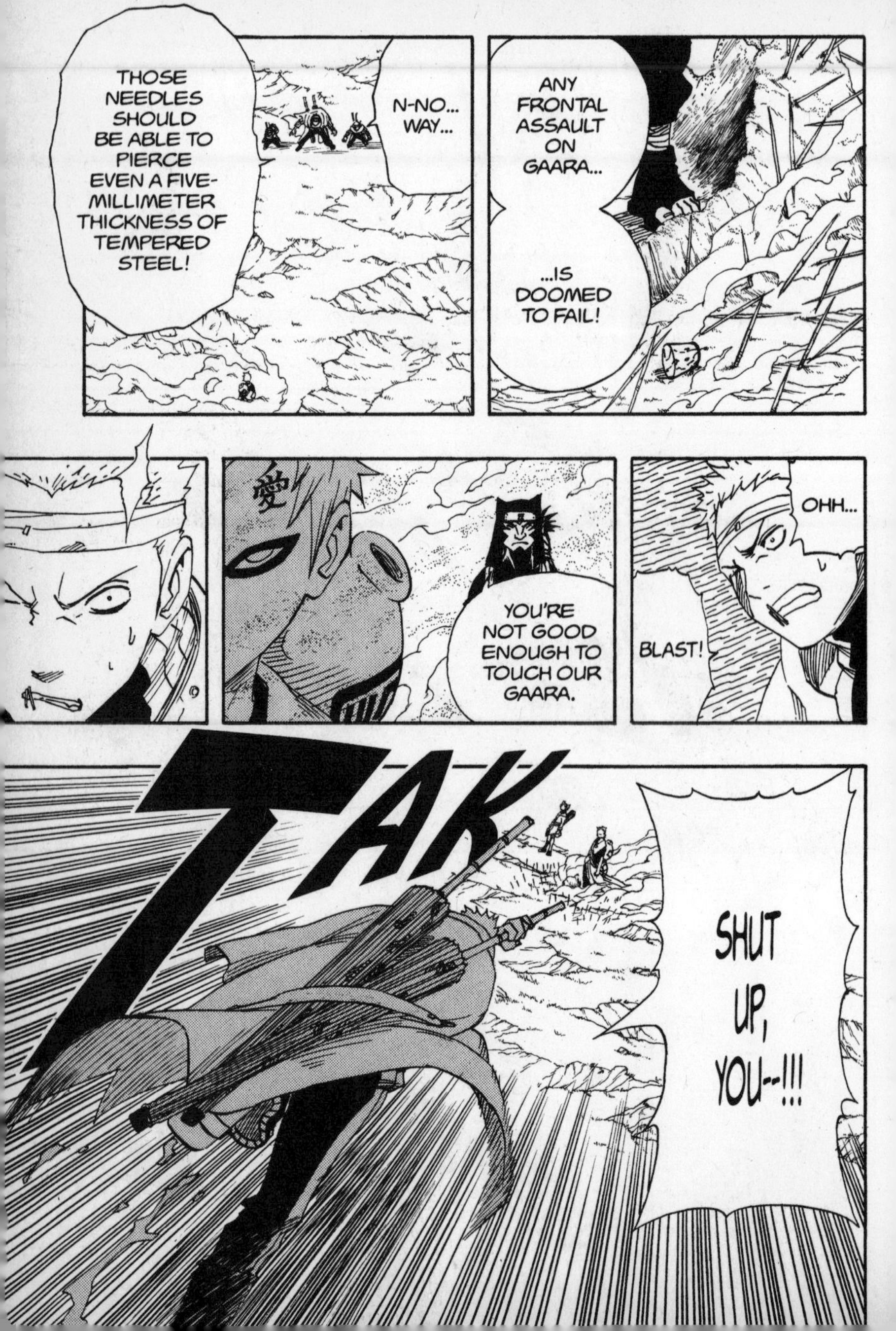
ANY FRONTAL ASSAULT ON GAARA...
...IS DOOMED TO FAIL!
N-NO... WAY...
THOSE NEEDLES SHOULD BE ABLE TO PIERCE EVEN A FIVE-MILLIMETER THICKNESS OF TEMPERED STEEL!
OHH...
BLAST!
YOU'RE NOT GOOD ENOUGH TO TOUCH OUR GAARA.
SHUT UP, YOU--!!!
TAK

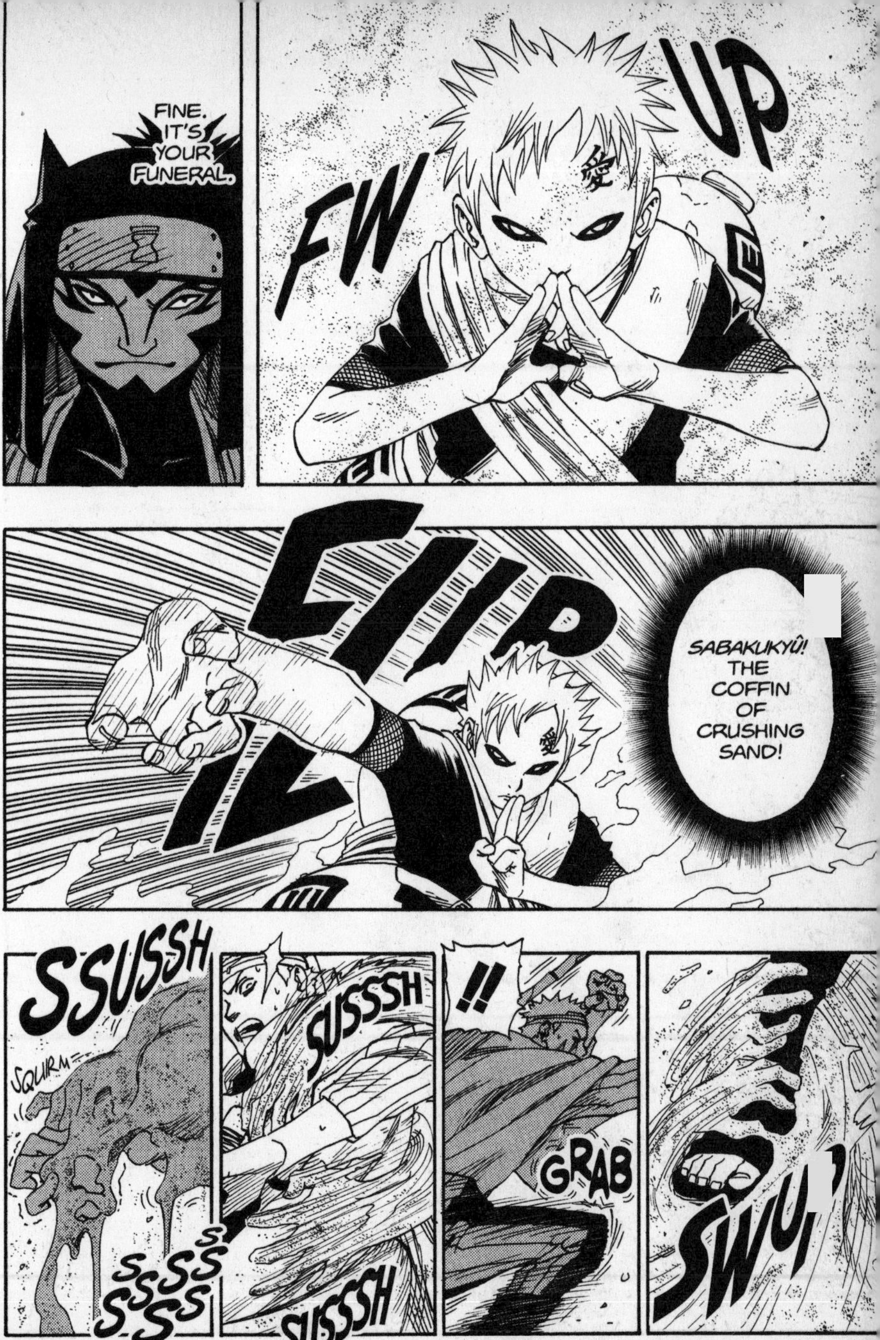
FW
UP
FINE. IT'S YOUR FUNERAL.
SABAKUKYÛ! THE COFFIN OF CRUSHING SAND!
!!
GRAB
SUSSSH
SUSSSH
SSUSSH
SQUIRM
SSSSSSSS

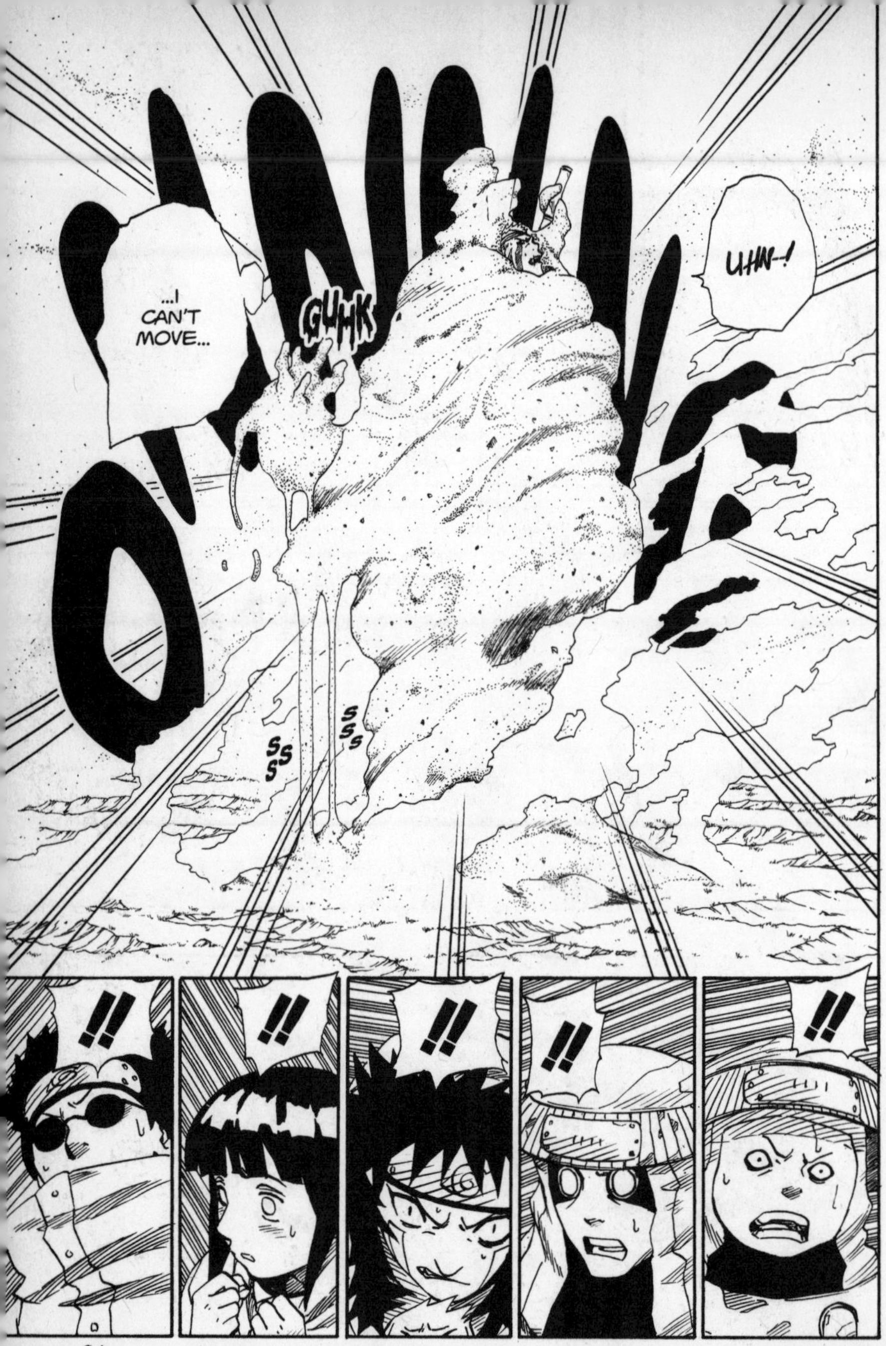
UHN-!
GUHK
...I CAN'T MOVE...
SSS
SSS
!!
!!
!!
!!
!!

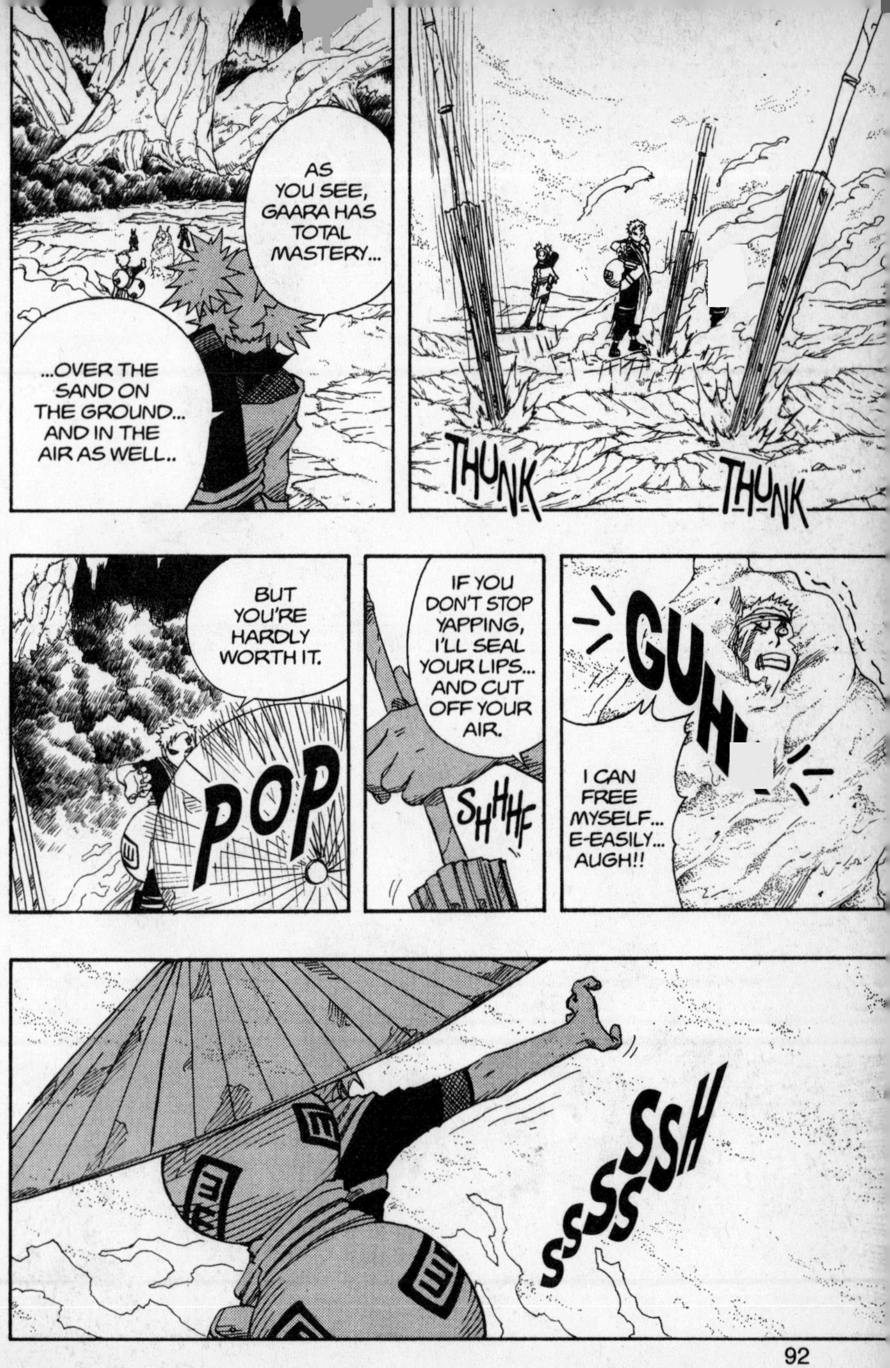
THUNK
THUNK
AS YOU SEE, GAARA HAS TOTAL MASTERY...
...OVER THE SAND ON THE GROUND... AND IN THE AIR AS WELL..
GUH
I CAN FREE MYSELF... E-EASILY... AUGH!!
IF YOU DON'T STOP YAPPING, I'LL SEAL YOUR LIPS... AND CUT OFF YOUR AIR.
SHHHF
BUT YOU'RE HARDLY WORTH IT.
POP
SSSSSSH

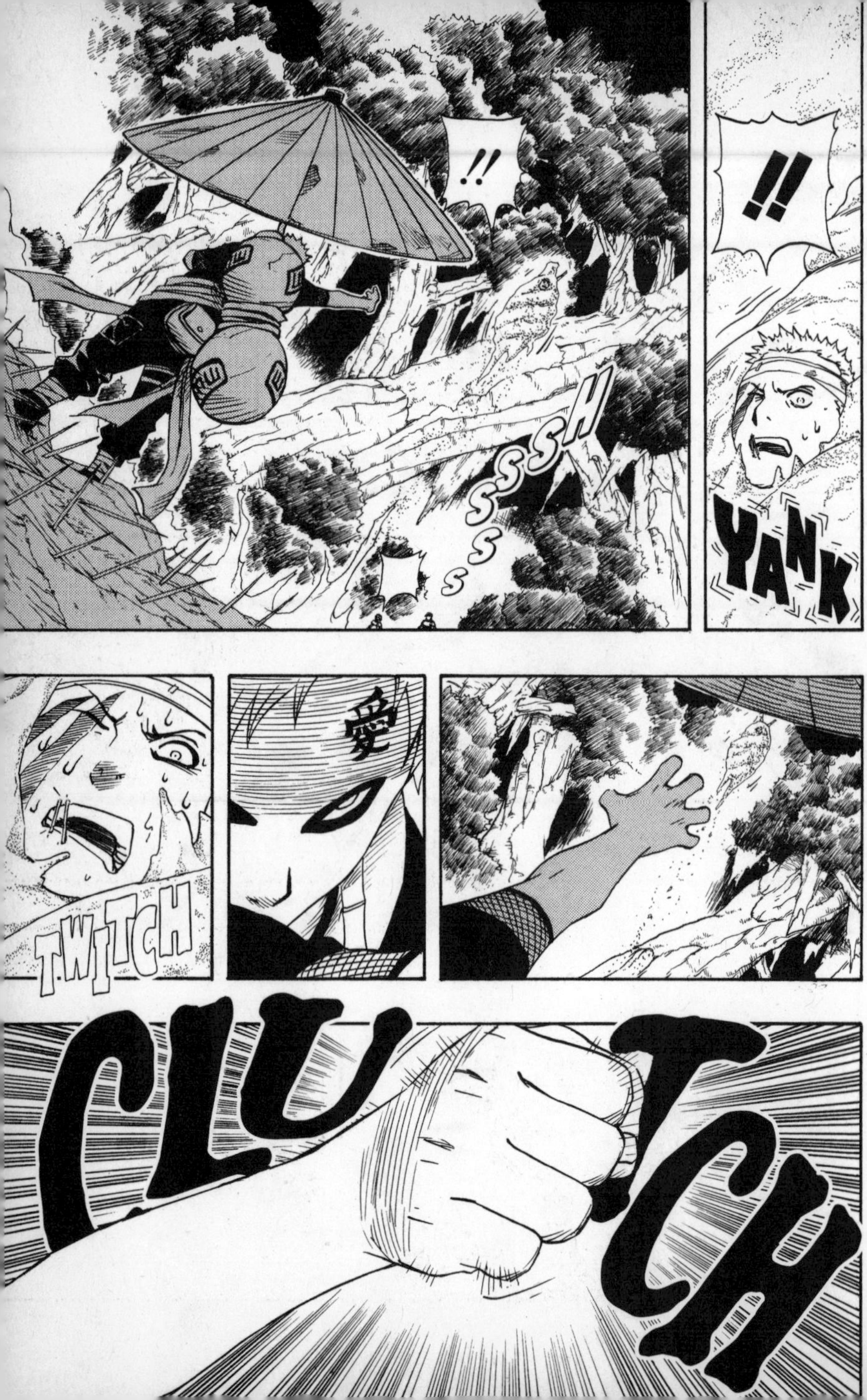
!!
YANK
!!
SSSSSH
愛
TWITCH
CLUTCH

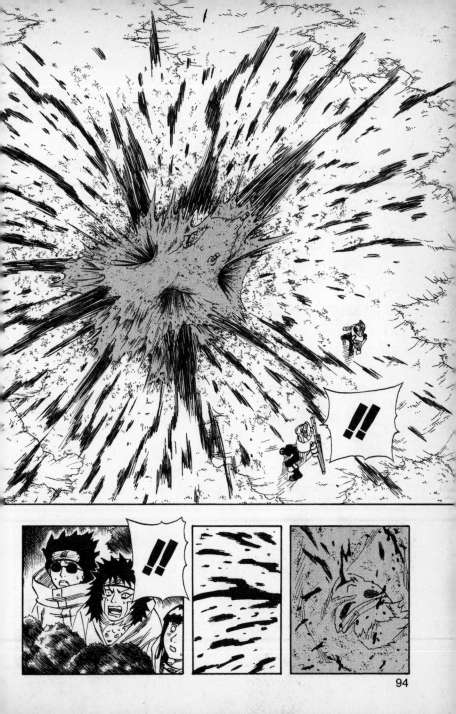

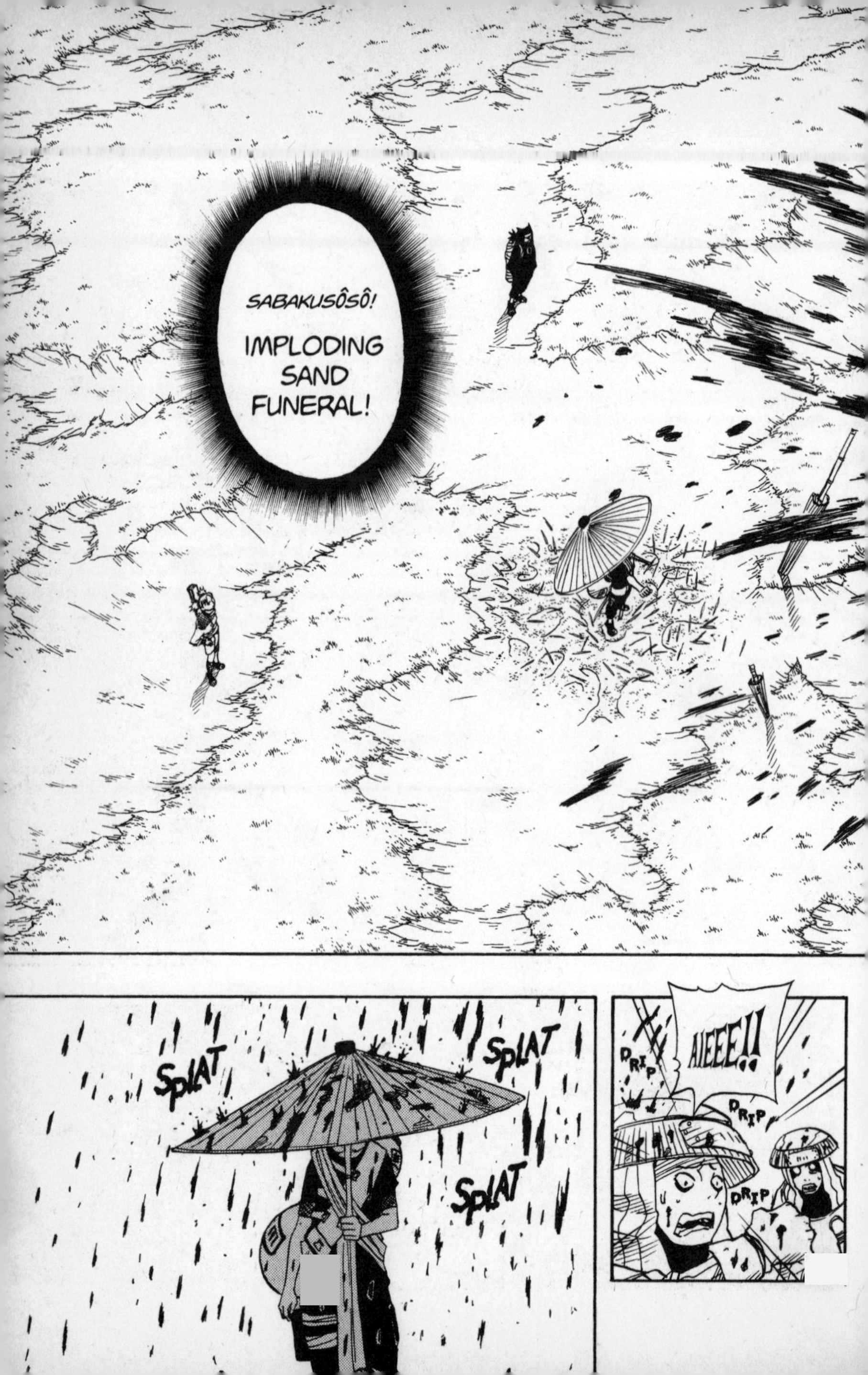
SABAKUSÔSÔ!
IMPLODING SAND FUNERAL!
DRIP
AIEEE!!
DRIP
DRIP
SPLAT
SPLAT
SPLAT

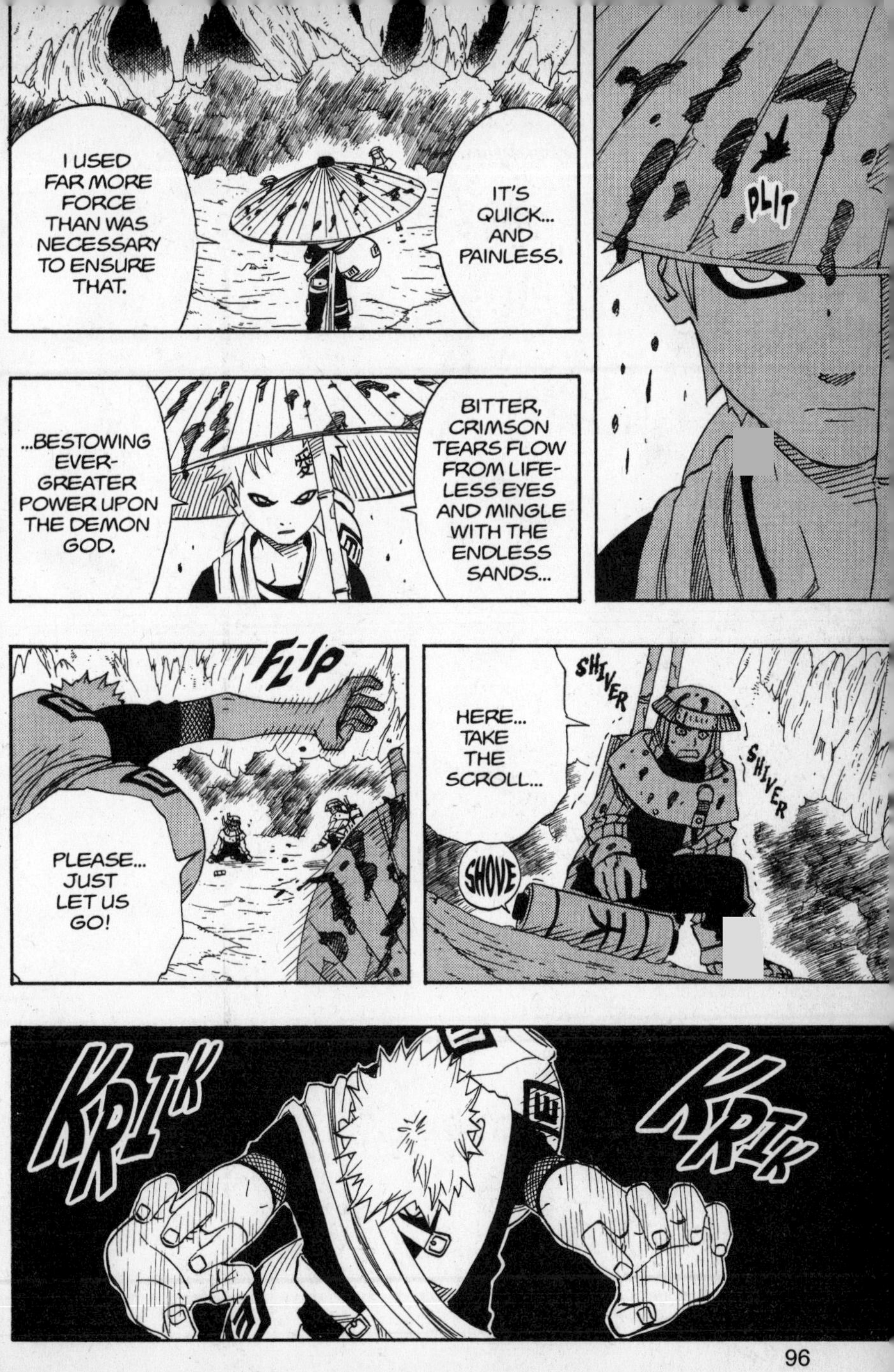
PLIT
IT'S QUICK... AND PAINLESS.
I USED FAR MORE FORCE THAN WAS NECESSARY TO ENSURE THAT.
BITTER, CRIMSON TEARS FLOW FROM LIFE-LESS EYES AND MINGLE WITH THE ENDLESS SANDS...
...BESTOWING EVER-GREATER POWER UPON THE DEMON GOD.
SHIVER
HERE... TAKE THE SCROLL...
SHIVER
SHOVE
FLIP
PLEASE... JUST LET US GO!
KRIK
KRIK

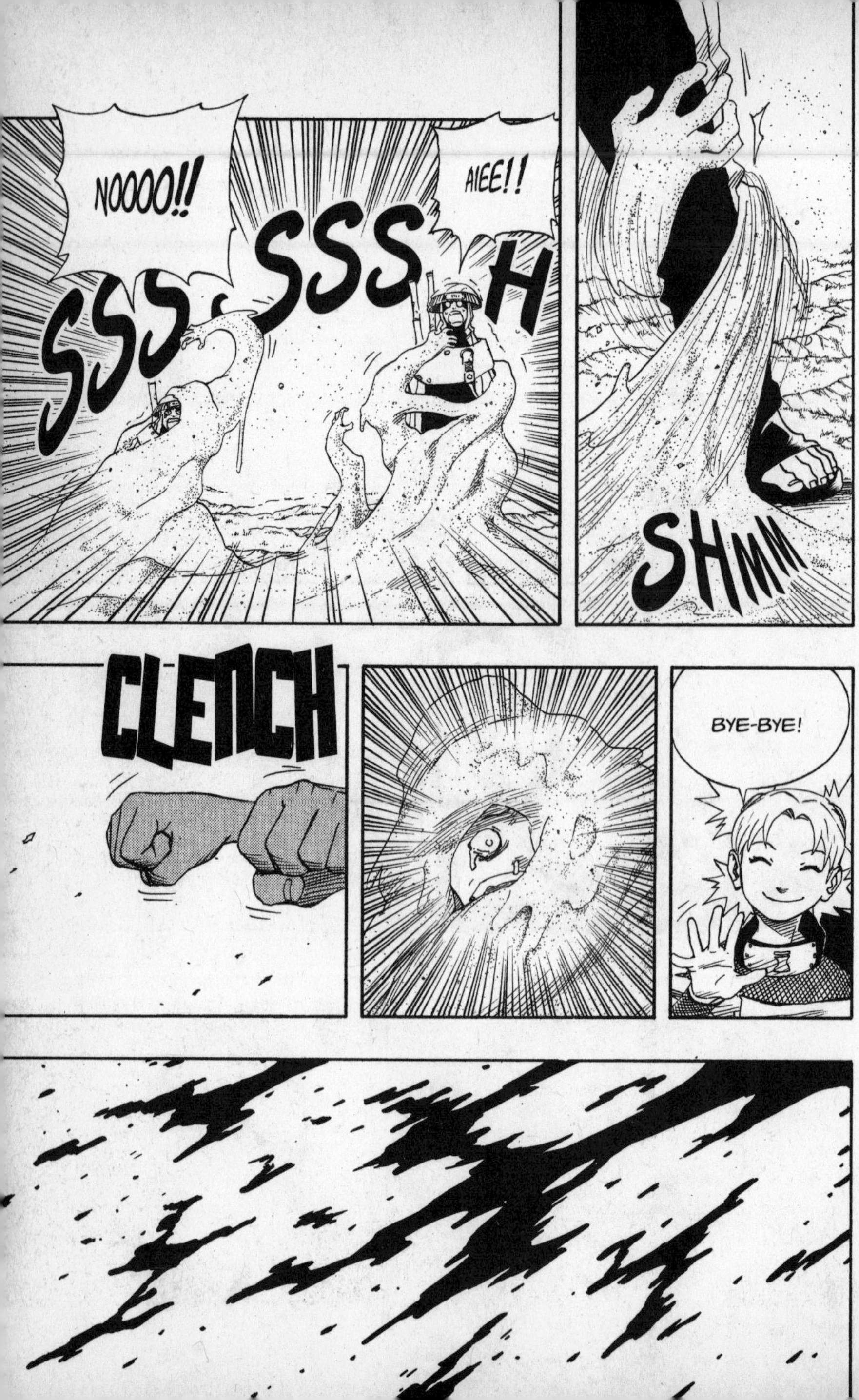
SHMM
AIEE!!
NOOOO!!
SSSSSSH
BYE-BYE!
CLENCH

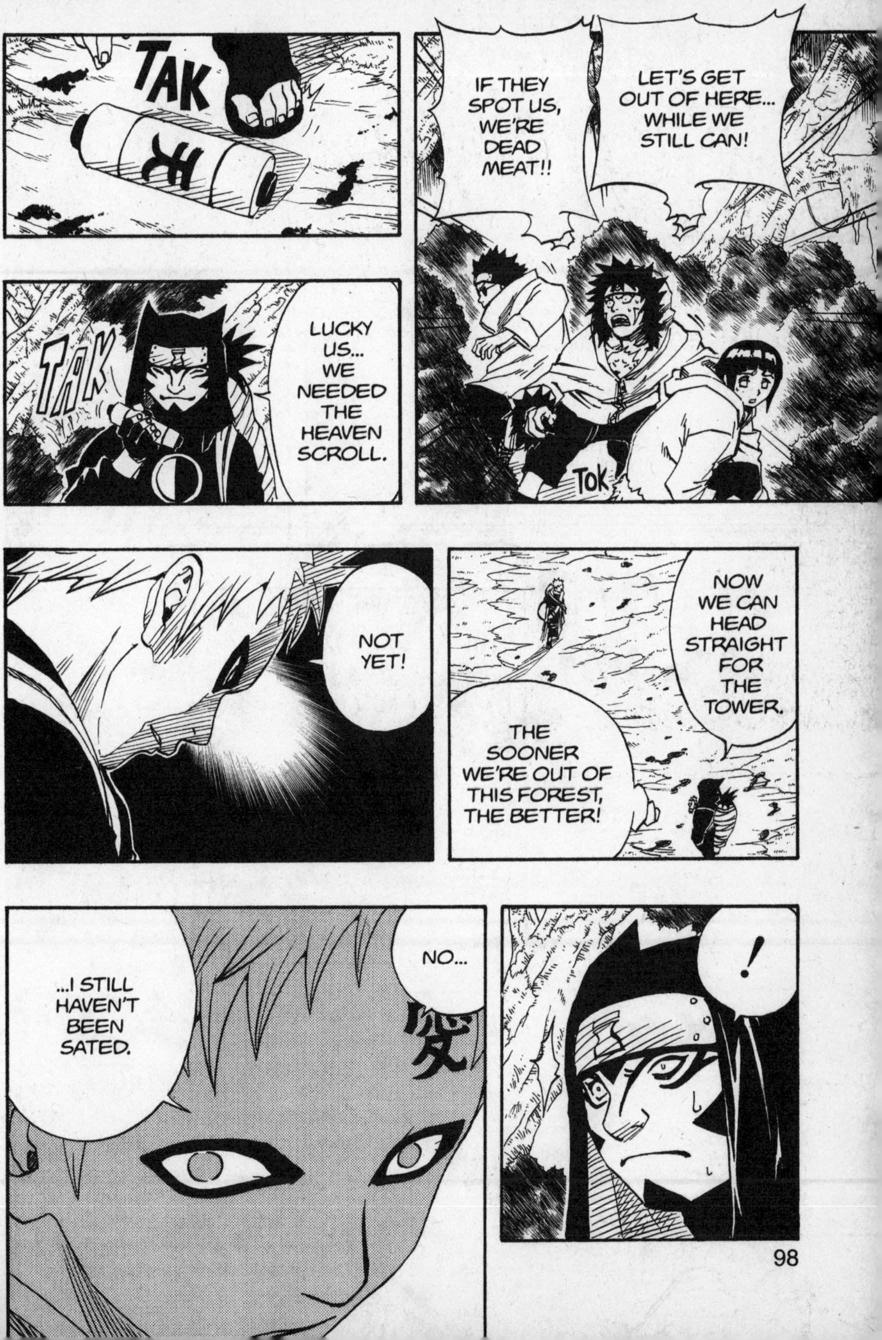
LET'S GET OUT OF HERE... WHILE WE STILL CAN!
IF THEY SPOT US, WE'RE DEAD MEAT!!
TOK
TAK
LUCKY US... WE NEEDED THE HEAVEN SCROLL.
TAK
NOW WE CAN HEAD STRAIGHT FOR THE TOWER.
THE SOONER WE'RE OUT OF THIS FOREST, THE BETTER!
NOT YET!
!
NO...
...I STILL HAVEN'T BEEN SATED.

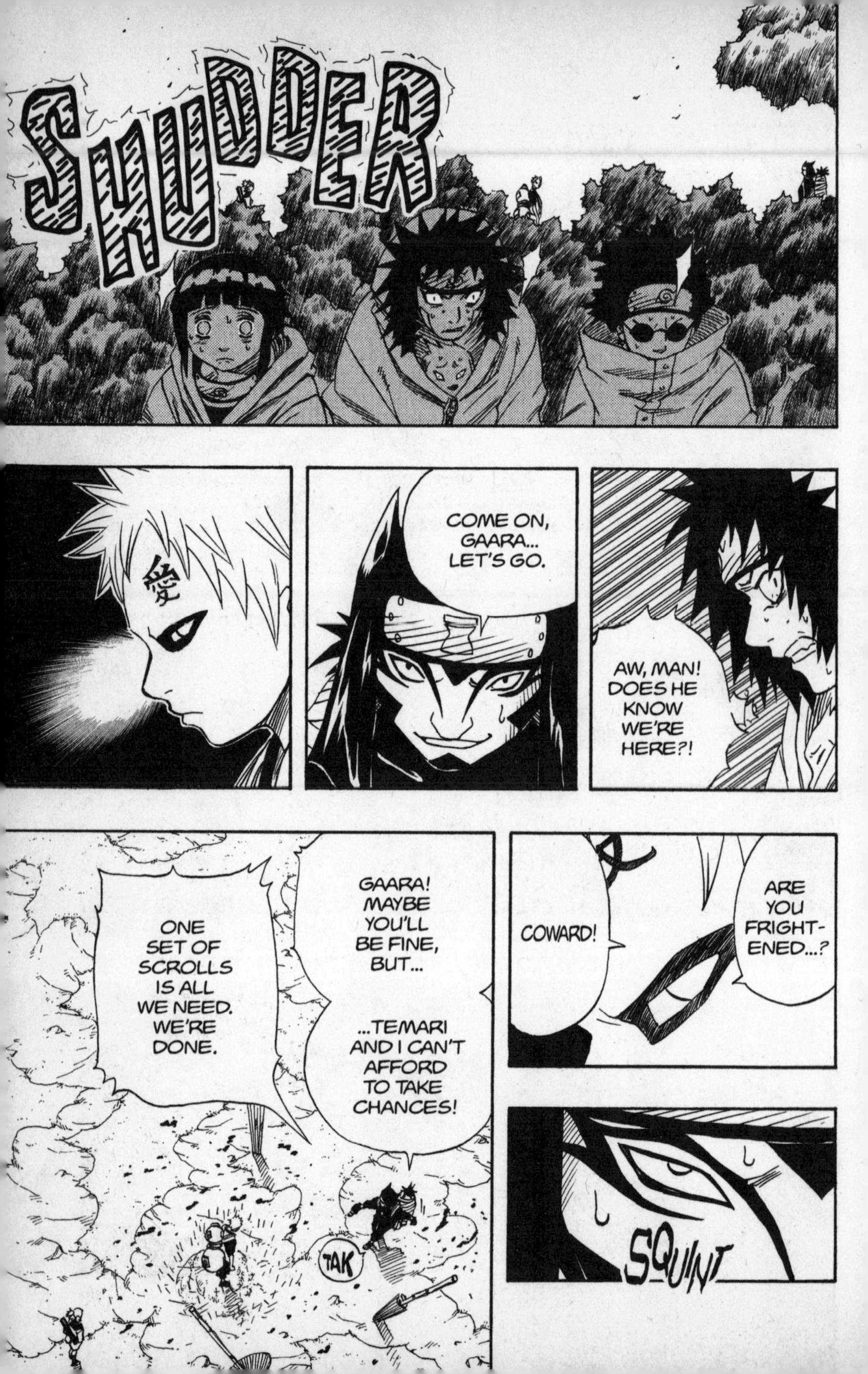
SHUDDER
AW, MAN! DOES HE KNOW WE'RE HERE?!
COME ON, GAARA... LET'S GO.
ARE YOU FRIGHTENED...?
COWARD!
SQUINT
GAARA! MAYBE YOU'LL BE FINE, BUT...
...TEMARI AND I CAN'T AFFORD TO TAKE CHANCES!
ONE SET OF SCROLLS IS ALL WE NEED. WE'RE DONE.
TAK

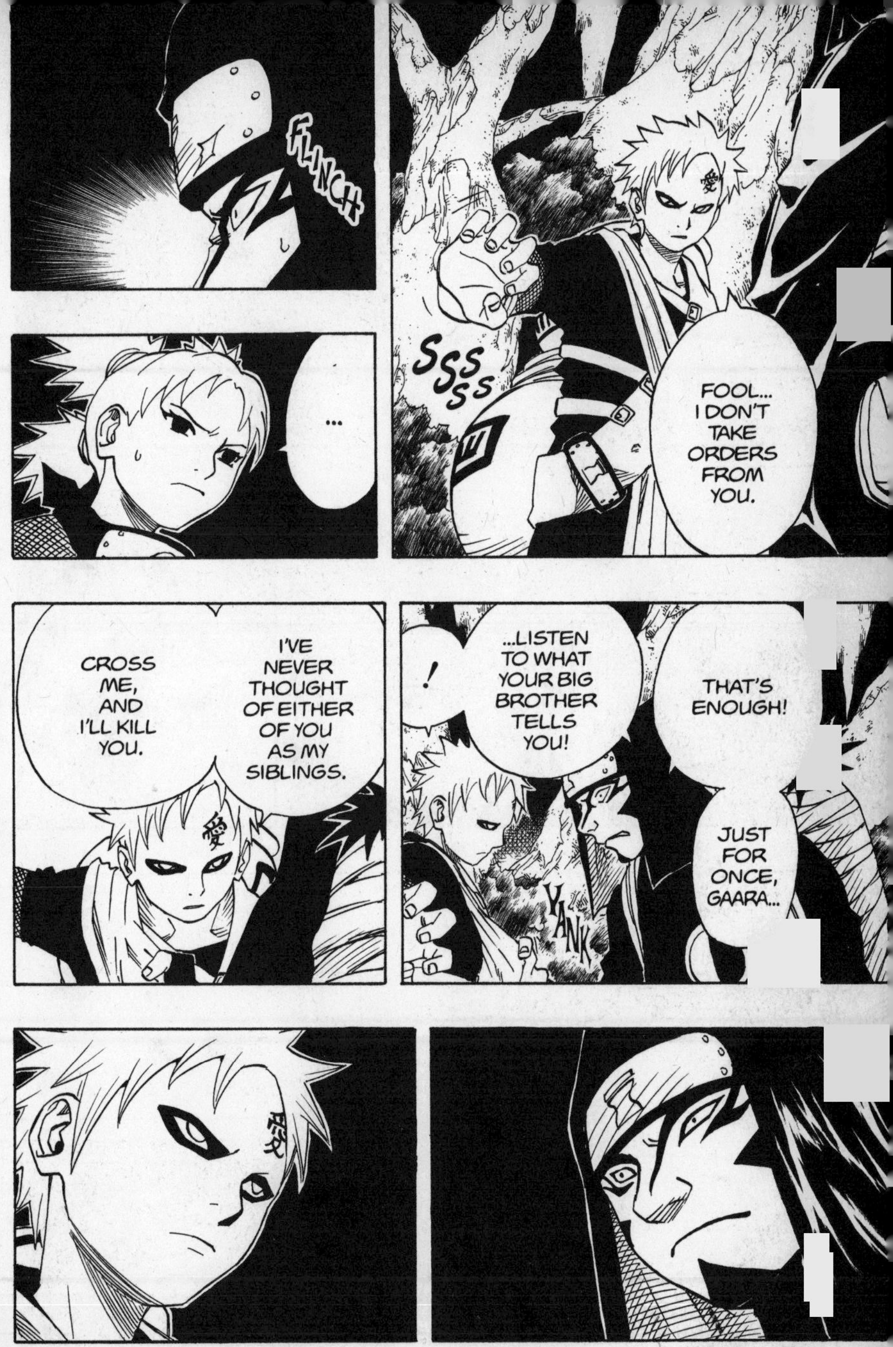
FOOL... I DON'T TAKE ORDERS FROM YOU.
SSSSS
FLINCH
...
THAT'S ENOUGH!
JUST FOR ONCE, GAARA...
...LISTEN TO WHAT YOUR BIG BROTHER TELLS YOU!
!
YANK
I'VE NEVER THOUGHT OF EITHER OF YOU AS MY SIBLINGS.
CROSS ME, AND I'LL KILL YOU.

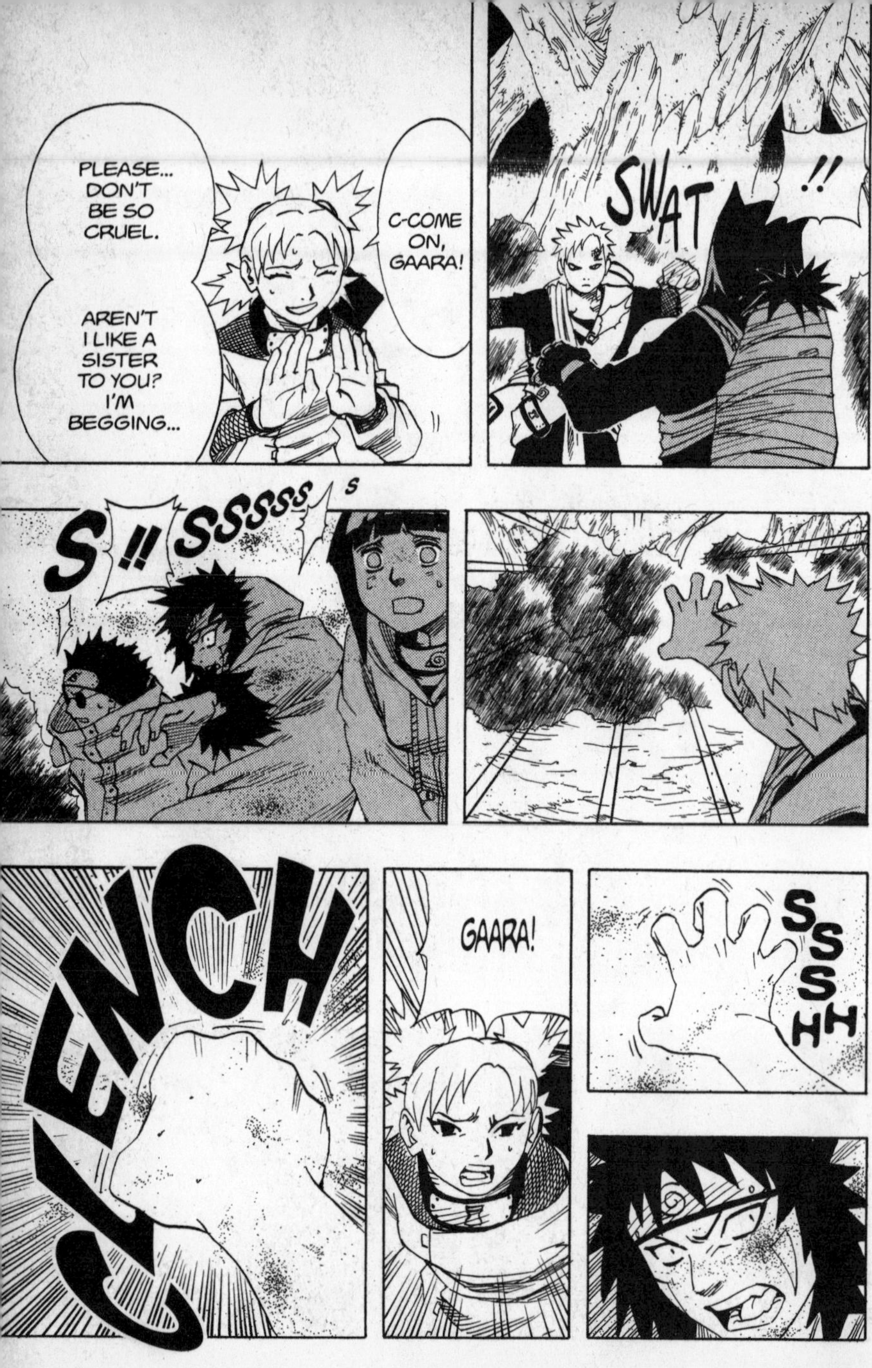
SWAT
!!
C-COME ON, GAARA!
PLEASE... DON'T BE SO CRUEL.
AREN'T I LIKE A SISTER TO YOU? I'M BEGGING...
S
!!
SSSSS
S
SSSH
GAARA!
ENCH

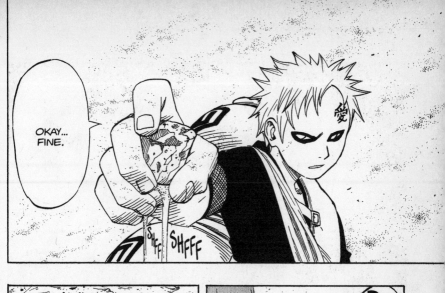

OKAY... FINE.

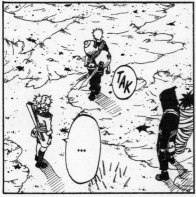

TAK

...

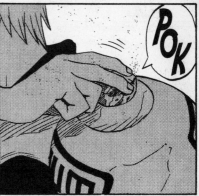

POK

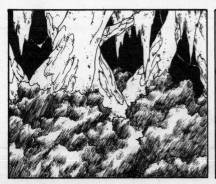

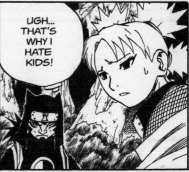

UGH... THAT'S WHY I HATE KIDS!

READ THIS WAY

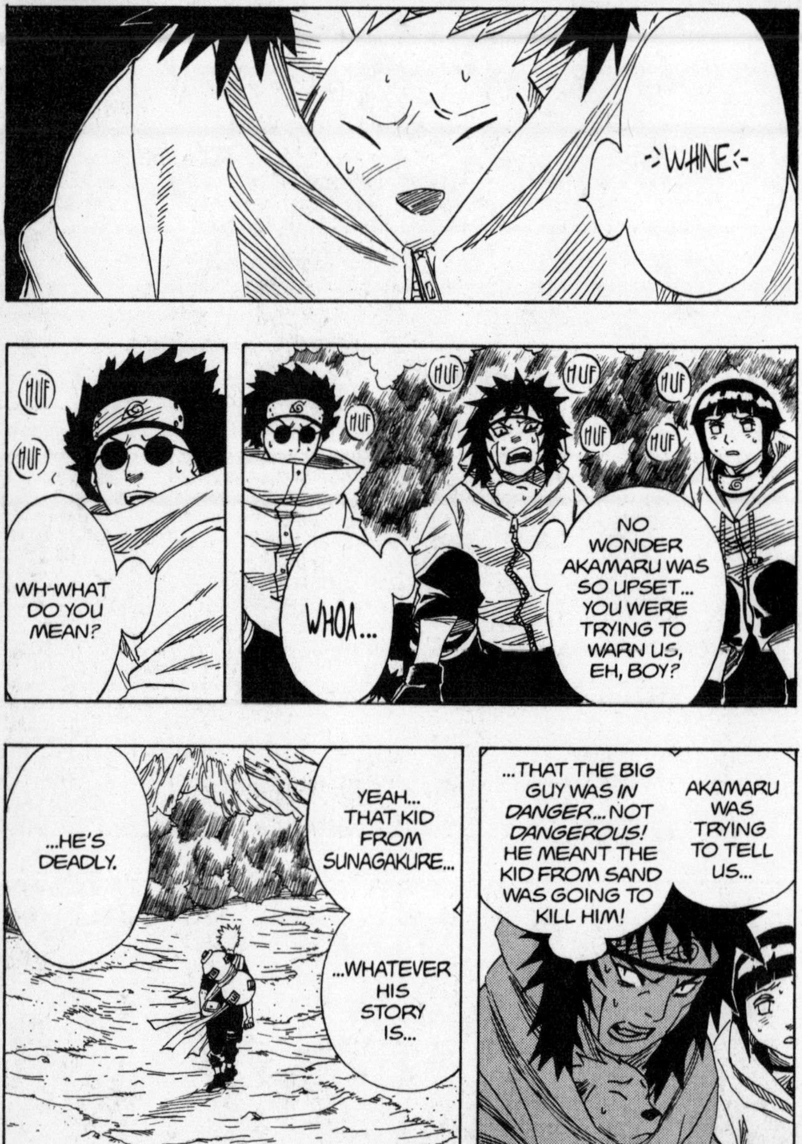

WHINE
HUF
HUF
HUF
HUF
HUF
NO WONDER AKAMARU WAS SO UPSET... YOU WERE TRYING TO WARN US, EH, BOY?
WHOA...
HUF
HUF
WH-WHAT DO YOU MEAN?
AKAMARU WAS TRYING TO TELL US...
...THAT THE BIG GUY WAS IN *DANGER*... NOT *DANGEROUS!* HE MEANT THE KID FROM SAND WAS GOING TO KILL HIM!
YEAH... THAT KID FROM SUNAGAKURE...
...WHATEVER HIS STORY IS...
...HE'S DEADLY.

THE WORLD OF KISHIMOTO MASASHI
MY PERSONAL HISTORY, PART THREE: PRIMARY SCHOOL

AS AN ELEMENTARY SCHOOLER, I SPENT A LOT OF
TIME EVERY DAY DOODLING IN MY "ANYTHING GOES"
SKETCHBOOK. EVEN WHEN I WAS OUT ON THE PLAY-
GROUND PLAYING TAG, I ALWAYS HID REALLY WELL IN
HOPES THAT WHOEVER WAS "IT" WOULDN'T FIND ME
AND SAT QUIETLY, DRAWING DORAEMON IN THE DIRT.

THEN ONE SUCH DAY, I SAW AN AMAZING TV SHOW.
"WHAT IN THE WORLD IS IT?" I WONDERED. "IT'S SO
COOL, AND THE ARTWORK IS AWESOME." THE SHOW
WAS... "MOBILE SUIT GUNDAM." AFTER THAT, MY
SKETCHBOOK WAS ALWAYS CRAMMED WITH DRAWINGS
OF ROBOTS CALLED MOBILE SUITS. ZAKU, GOUF, DOM,
GM, DOZLE ZABI... I FEVERISHLY DREW ALL KINDS OF
GUNDAM CHARACTERS.

THEN ON ANOTHER DAY, I SAW ANOTHER INCREDIBLE
TV SHOW AND THOUGHT, "W-WOW! THE ART IS AMAZING!
AND IT HAS SUCH STYLE!!" THE PROGRAM WAS "DR SLUMP:
ARALE-CHAN." FROM THAT POINT ON, ALL I WANTED TO
DRAW WAS ARALE-CHAN. I EVEN ENTERED A CRAYON
SKETCH OF ARALE-CHAN INTO AN ELEMENTARY SCHOOL
ART EXHIBITION. I CAN STILL REMEMBER MY MOTHER
SAYING, "IF THIS ARALE-CHAN IS A GIRL, THEN YOU HAVE
TO PUT LIPSTICK ON HER," AND JUST LIKE THAT, SHE
ADDED RED LIPSTICK TO MY DRAWING OF ARALE-CHAN.
I ALSO REMEMBER CLEARLY THAT THAT WAS THE FIRST
TIME IN MY LIFE THAT I COMPLETELY LOST MY TEMPER.

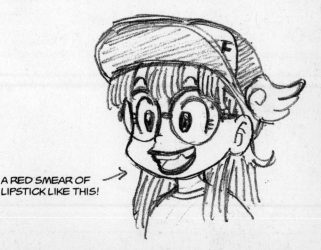

A RED SMEAR OF
LIPSTICK LIKE THIS!

Number 60: The Last Chance...!!

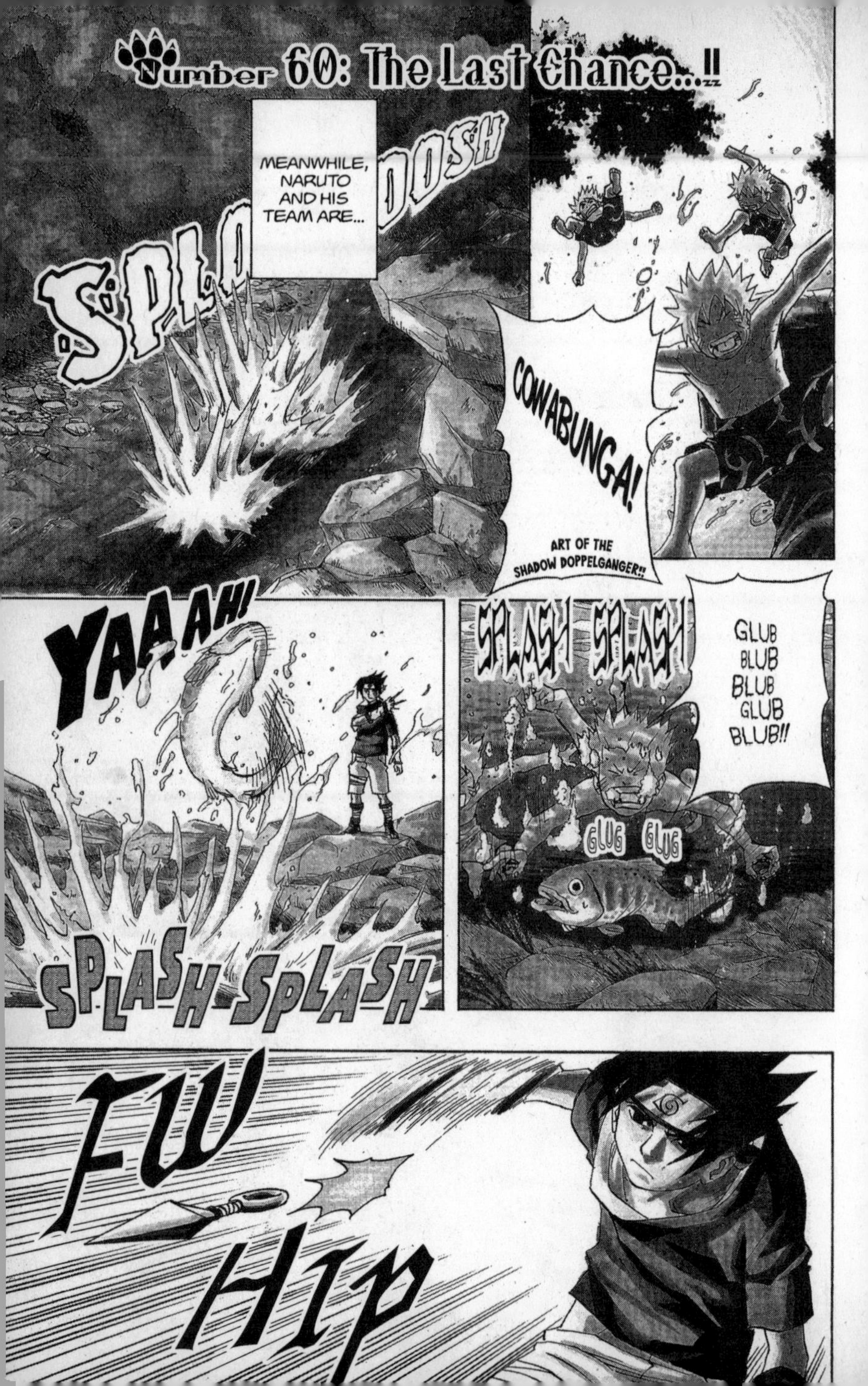
COWABUNGA!
ART OF THE SHADOW DOPPELGANGER!!
MEANWHILE, NARUTO AND HIS TEAM ARE...
SPL
DOOSH
SPLASH SPLASH
GLUB BLUB BLUB GLUB BLUB!!
GLUG GLUG
YAAAH!
SPLASH SPLASH
FW HIP

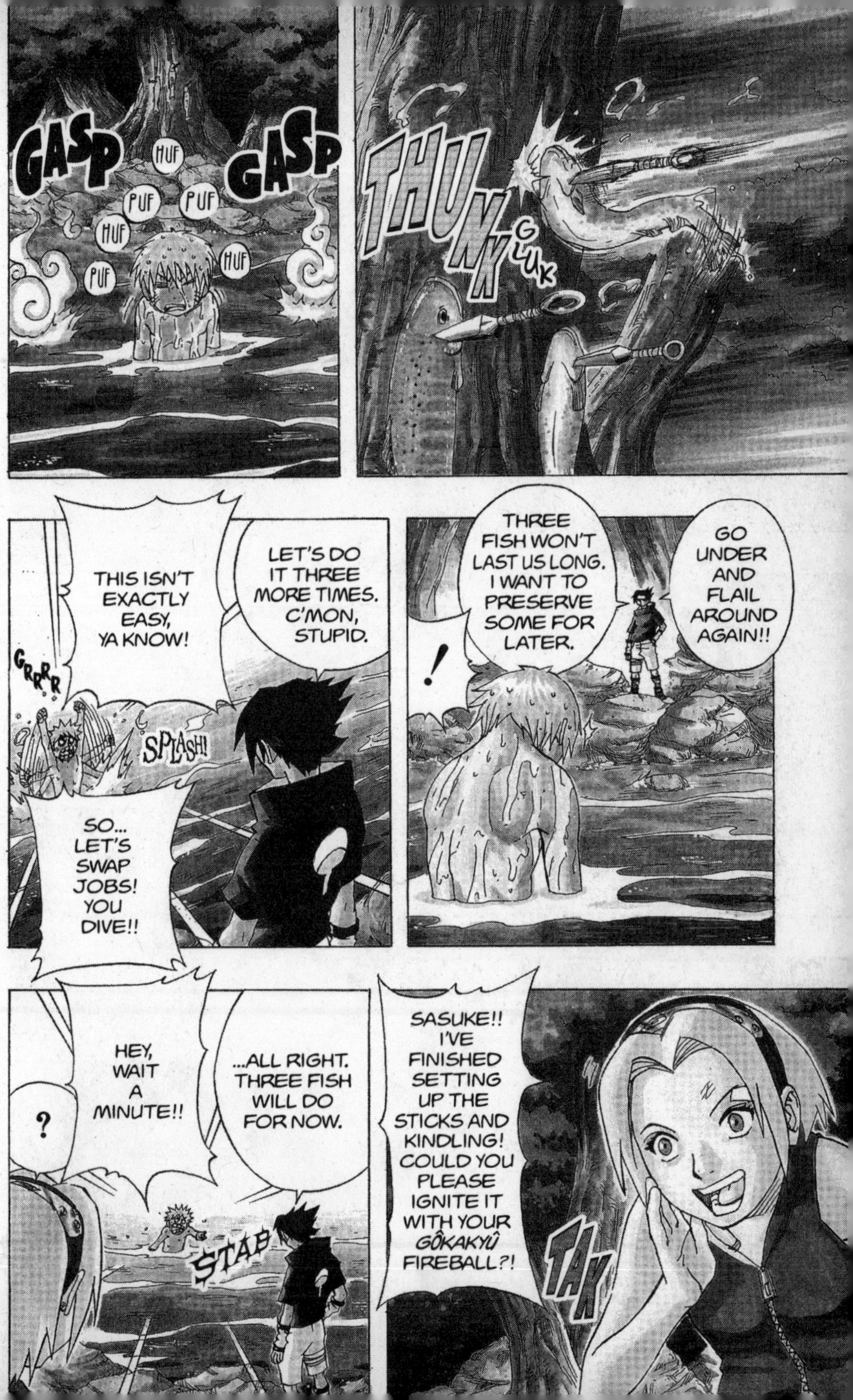
THUNK
GLUK
GASP
HUF
PUF
PUF
HUF
HUF
PUF
GASP
GO UNDER AND FLAIL AROUND AGAIN!!
THREE FISH WON'T LAST US LONG. I WANT TO PRESERVE SOME FOR LATER.
!
LET'S DO IT THREE MORE TIMES. C'MON, STUPID.
...
THIS ISN'T EXACTLY EASY, YA KNOW!
GRRRR
SPLASH!
SO... LET'S SWAP JOBS! YOU DIVE!!
SASUKE!! I'VE FINISHED SETTING UP THE STICKS AND KINDLING! COULD YOU PLEASE IGNITE IT WITH YOUR *GÔKAKYÛ* FIREBALL?!
TAK
...ALL RIGHT. THREE FISH WILL DO FOR NOW.
HEY, WAIT A MINUTE!!
?
STAB

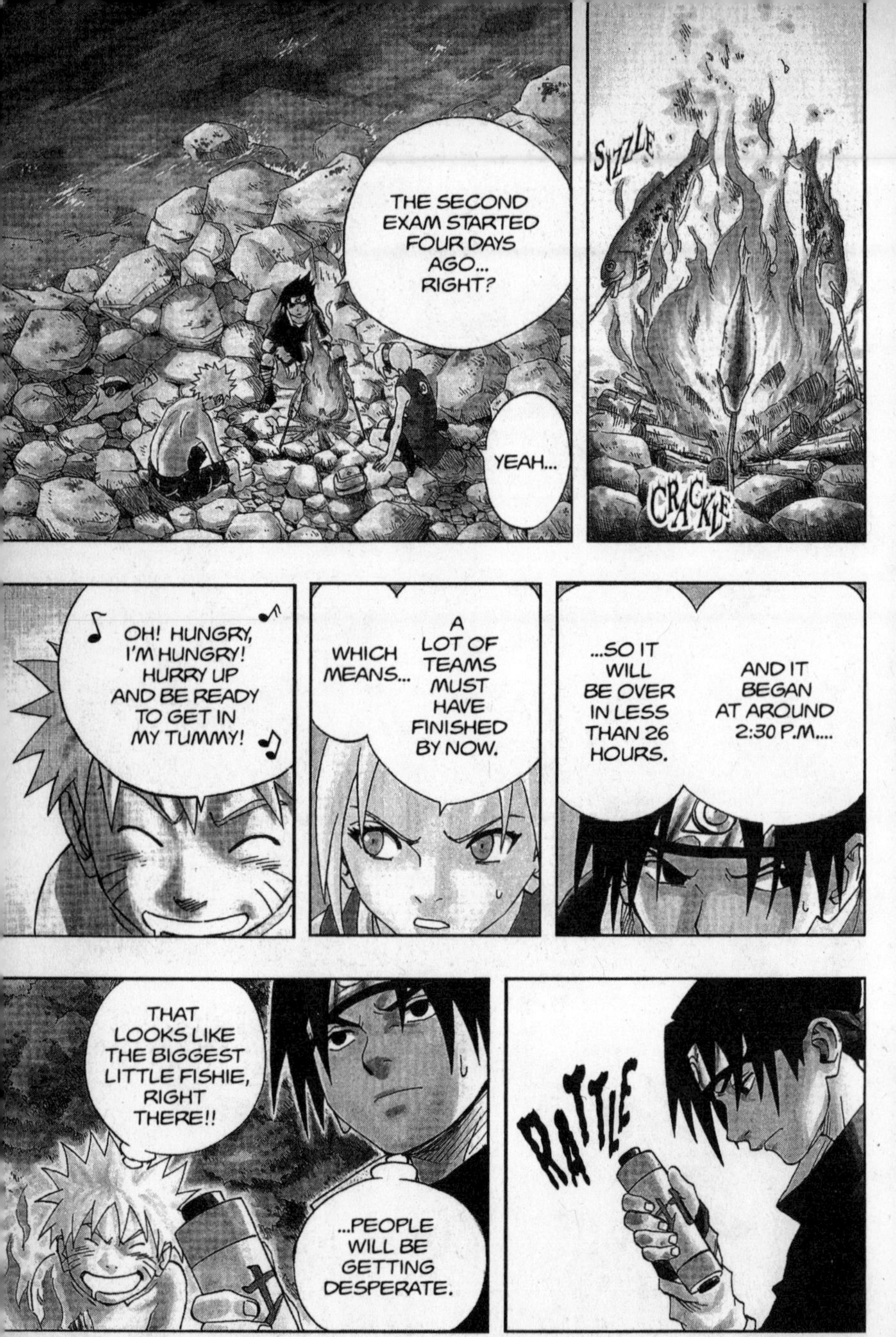
SIZZLE
CRACKLE
THE SECOND EXAM STARTED FOUR DAYS AGO... RIGHT?
YEAH...
AND IT BEGAN AT AROUND 2:30 P.M....
...SO IT WILL BE OVER IN LESS THAN 26 HOURS.
A LOT OF TEAMS MUST HAVE FINISHED BY NOW.
WHICH MEANS...
OH! HUNGRY, I'M HUNGRY! HURRY UP AND BE READY TO GET IN MY TUMMY!
RATTLE
THAT LOOKS LIKE THE BIGGEST LITTLE FISHIE, RIGHT THERE!!
...PEOPLE WILL BE GETTING DESPERATE.

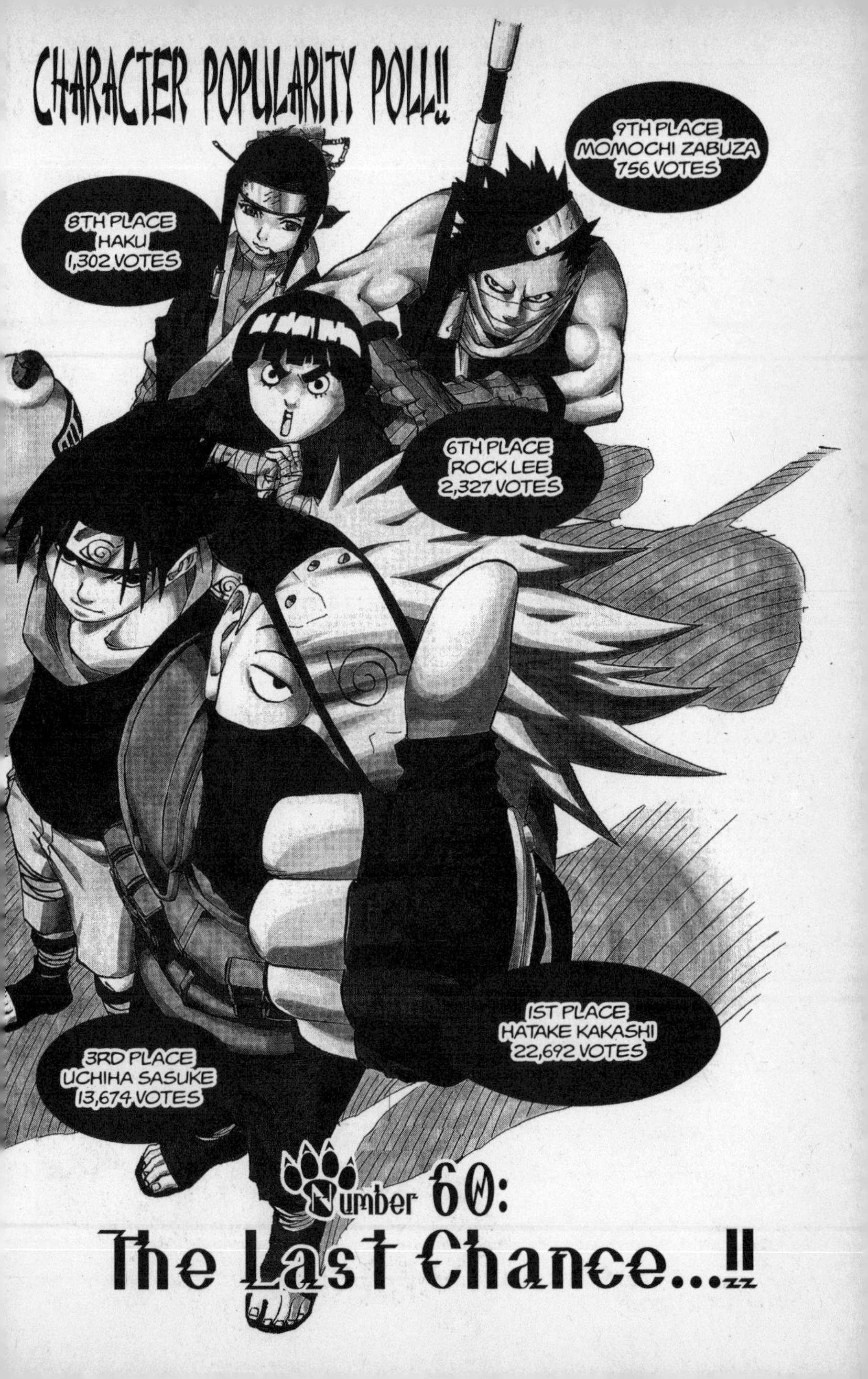
CHARACTER POPULARITY POLL!!
9TH PLACE MOMOCHI ZABUZA 756 VOTES
8TH PLACE HAKU 1,302 VOTES
6TH PLACE ROCK LEE 2,327 VOTES
1ST PLACE HATAKE KAKASHI 22,692 VOTES
3RD PLACE UCHIHA SASUKE 13,674 VOTES
Number 60:
The Last Chance...!!

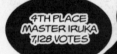

ANNOUNCING THE RESULTS OF OU

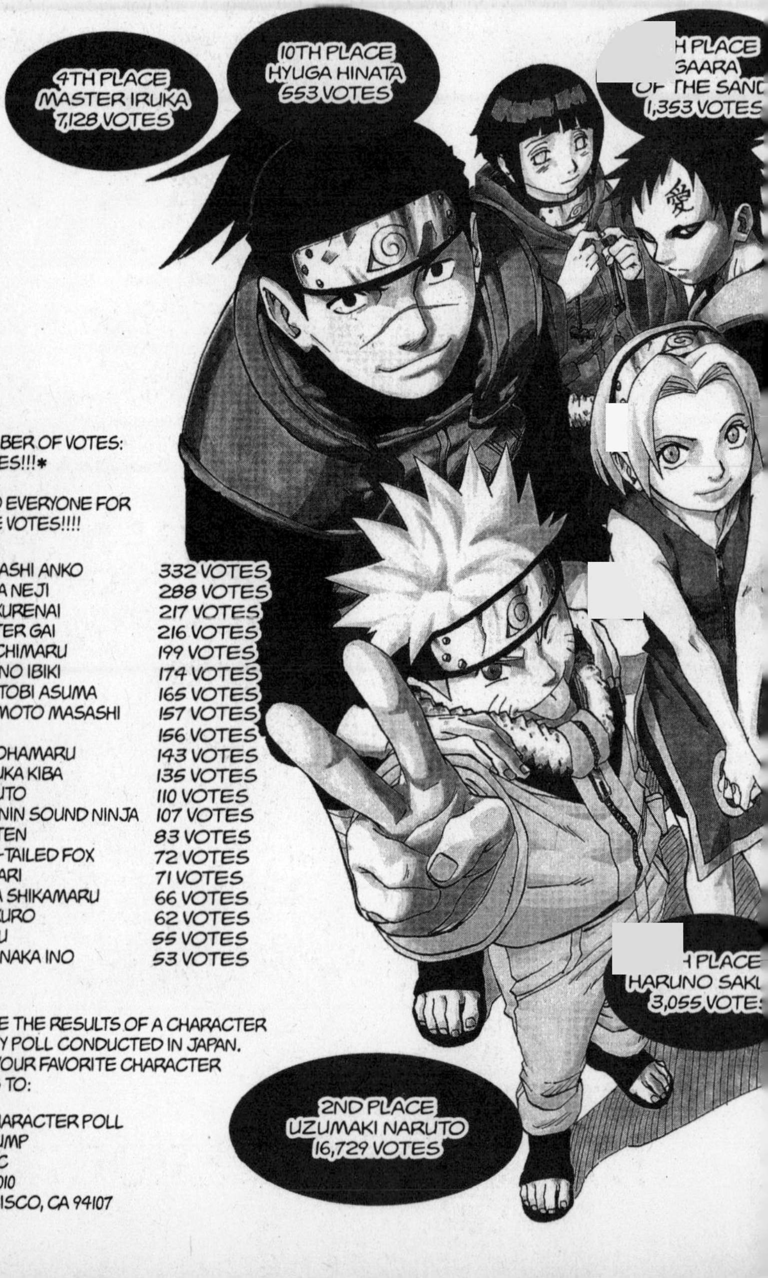

**4TH PLACE
MASTER IRUKA
7,128 VOTES**

**10TH PLACE
HYUGA HINATA
553 VOTES**

**H PLACE
GAARA
OF THE SAND
1,353 VOTES**

TOTAL NUMBER OF VOTES:
72,733 VOTES!!!*

THANKS TO EVERYONE FOR
ALL THOSE VOTES!!!!

11TH: MITARASHI ANKO	332 VOTES
12TH: HYUGA NEJI	288 VOTES
13TH: YUHI KURENAI	217 VOTES
14TH: MASTER GAI	216 VOTES
15TH: OROCHIMARU	199 VOTES
16TH: MORINO IBIKI	174 VOTES
17TH: SARUTOBI ASUMA	165 VOTES
18TH: KISHIMOTO MASASHI	157 VOTES
19TH: INARI	156 VOTES
20TH: KONOHAMARU	143 VOTES
21ST: INUZUKA KIBA	135 VOTES
22ND: KABUTO	110 VOTES
23RD: OTONIN SOUND NINJA	107 VOTES
24TH: TENTEN	83 VOTES
25TH: NINE-TAILED FOX	72 VOTES
26TH: TEMARI	71 VOTES
27TH: NARA SHIKAMARU	66 VOTES
28TH: KANKURO	62 VOTES
29TH: EBISU	55 VOTES
30TH: YAMANAKA INO	53 VOTES

*THESE ARE THE RESULTS OF A CHARACTER
POPULARITY POLL CONDUCTED IN JAPAN.
VOTE FOR YOUR FAVORITE CHARACTER
BY WRITING TO:

NARUTO CHARACTER POLL
SHONEN JUMP
C/O VIZ, LLC
P.O. BOX 77010
SAN FRANCISCO, CA 94107

**H PLACE
HARUNO SAKU
3,055 VOTES**

**2ND PLACE
UZUMAKI NARUTO
16,729 VOTES**

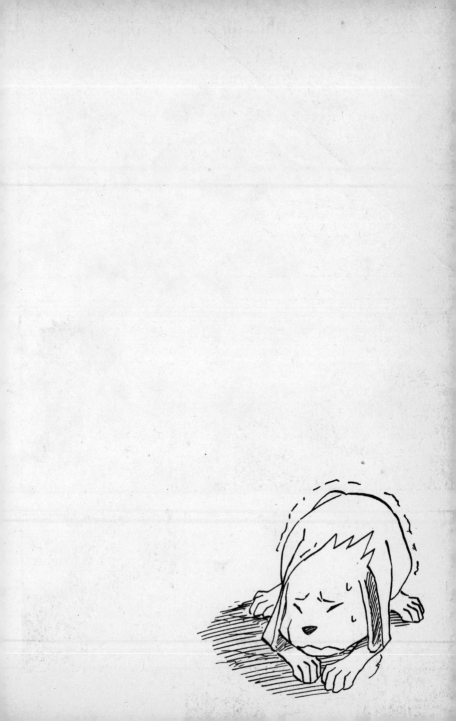

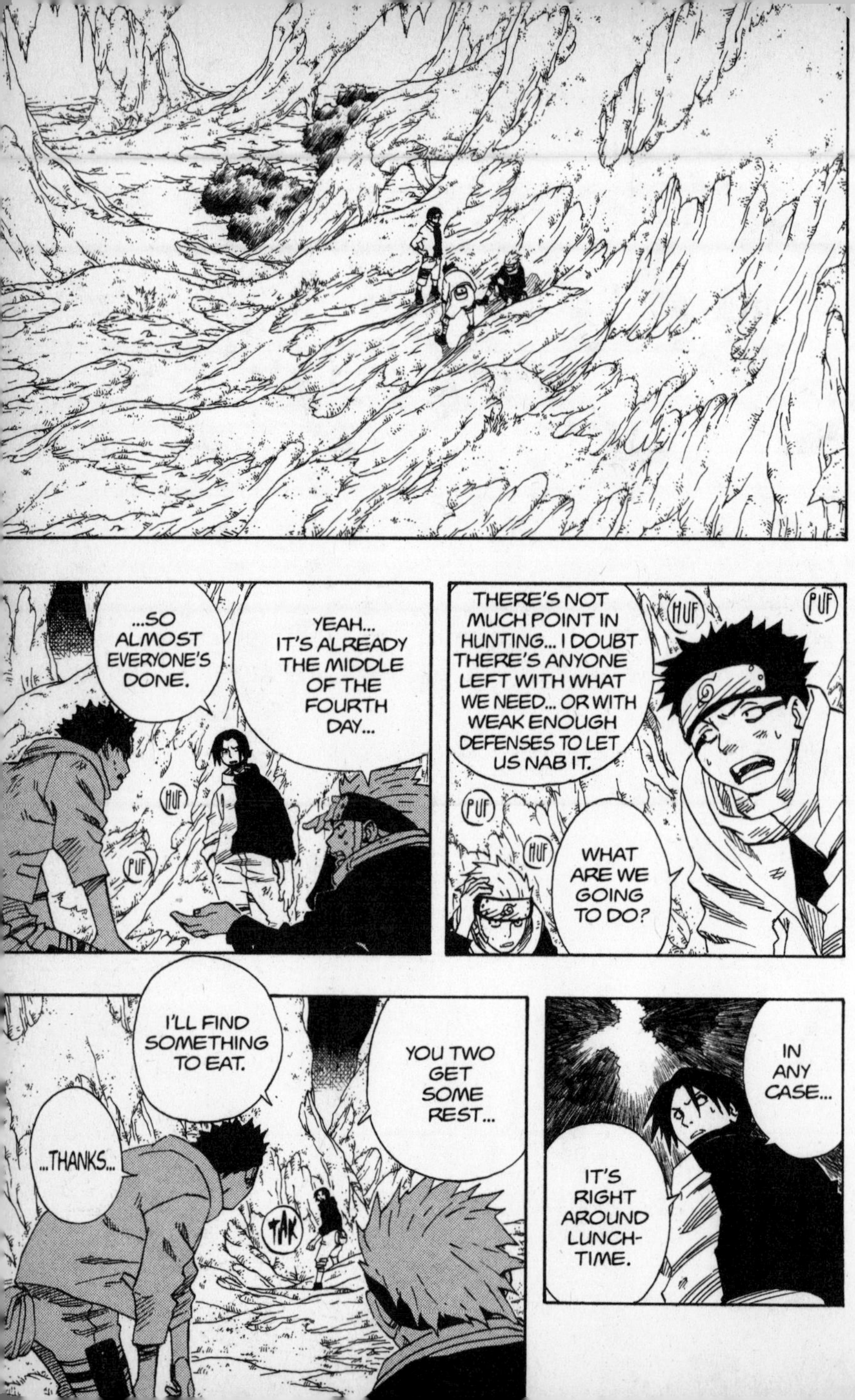
HUF
PUF
THERE'S NOT MUCH POINT IN HUNTING... I DOUBT THERE'S ANYONE LEFT WITH WHAT WE NEED... OR WITH WEAK ENOUGH DEFENSES TO LET US NAB IT.
PUF
HUF
WHAT ARE WE GOING TO DO?
YEAH... IT'S ALREADY THE MIDDLE OF THE FOURTH DAY...
...SO ALMOST EVERYONE'S DONE.
HUF
PUF
IN ANY CASE...
IT'S RIGHT AROUND LUNCH-TIME.
YOU TWO GET SOME REST...
I'LL FIND SOMETHING TO EAT.
TAK
...THANKS...

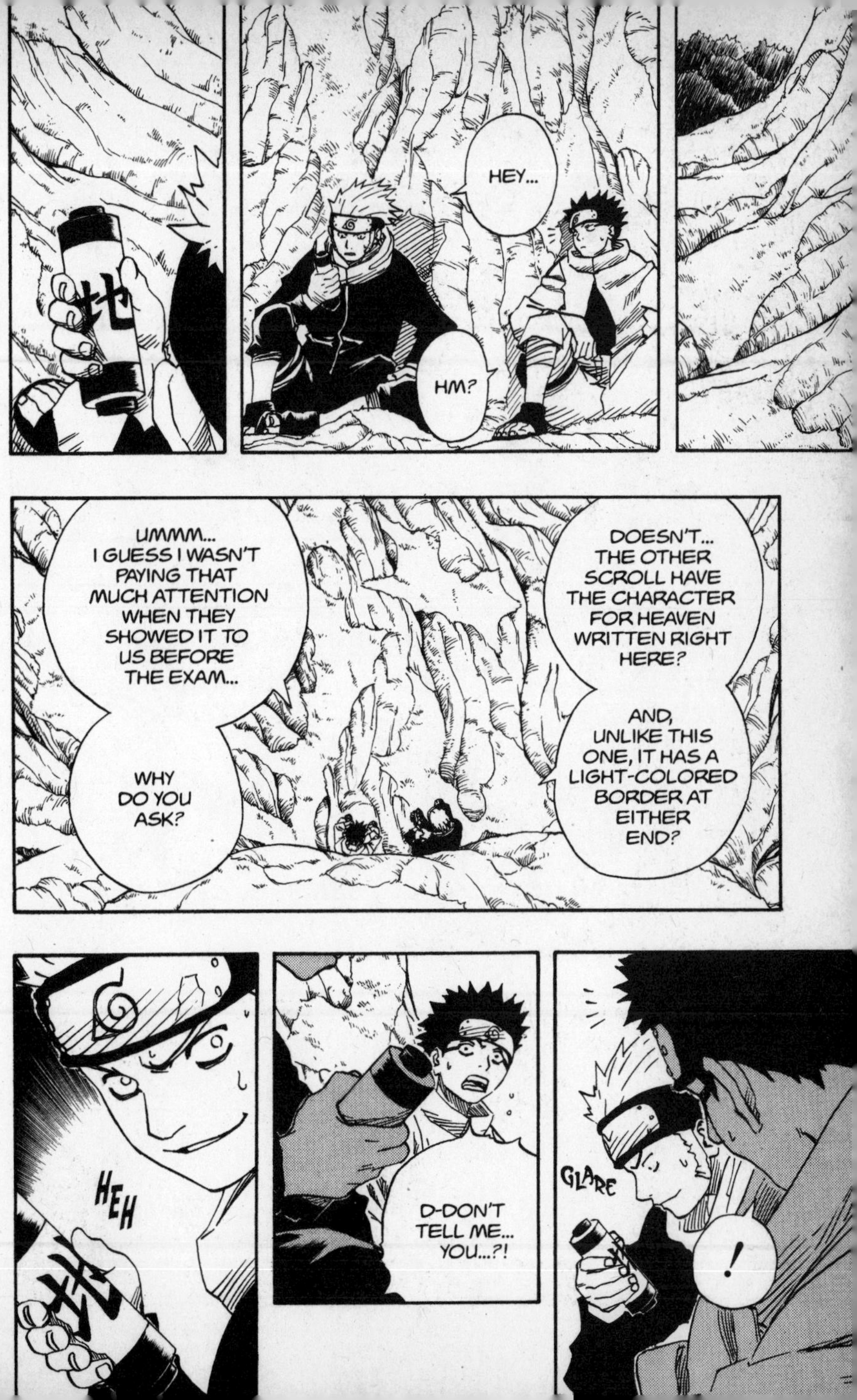
HEY...
HM?
地
DOESN'T... THE OTHER SCROLL HAVE THE CHARACTER FOR HEAVEN WRITTEN RIGHT HERE?
AND, UNLIKE THIS ONE, IT HAS A LIGHT-COLORED BORDER AT EITHER END?
UMMM... I GUESS I WASN'T PAYING THAT MUCH ATTENTION WHEN THEY SHOWED IT TO US BEFORE THE EXAM...
WHY DO YOU ASK?
GLARE
!
D-DON'T TELL ME... YOU...?!
HEH

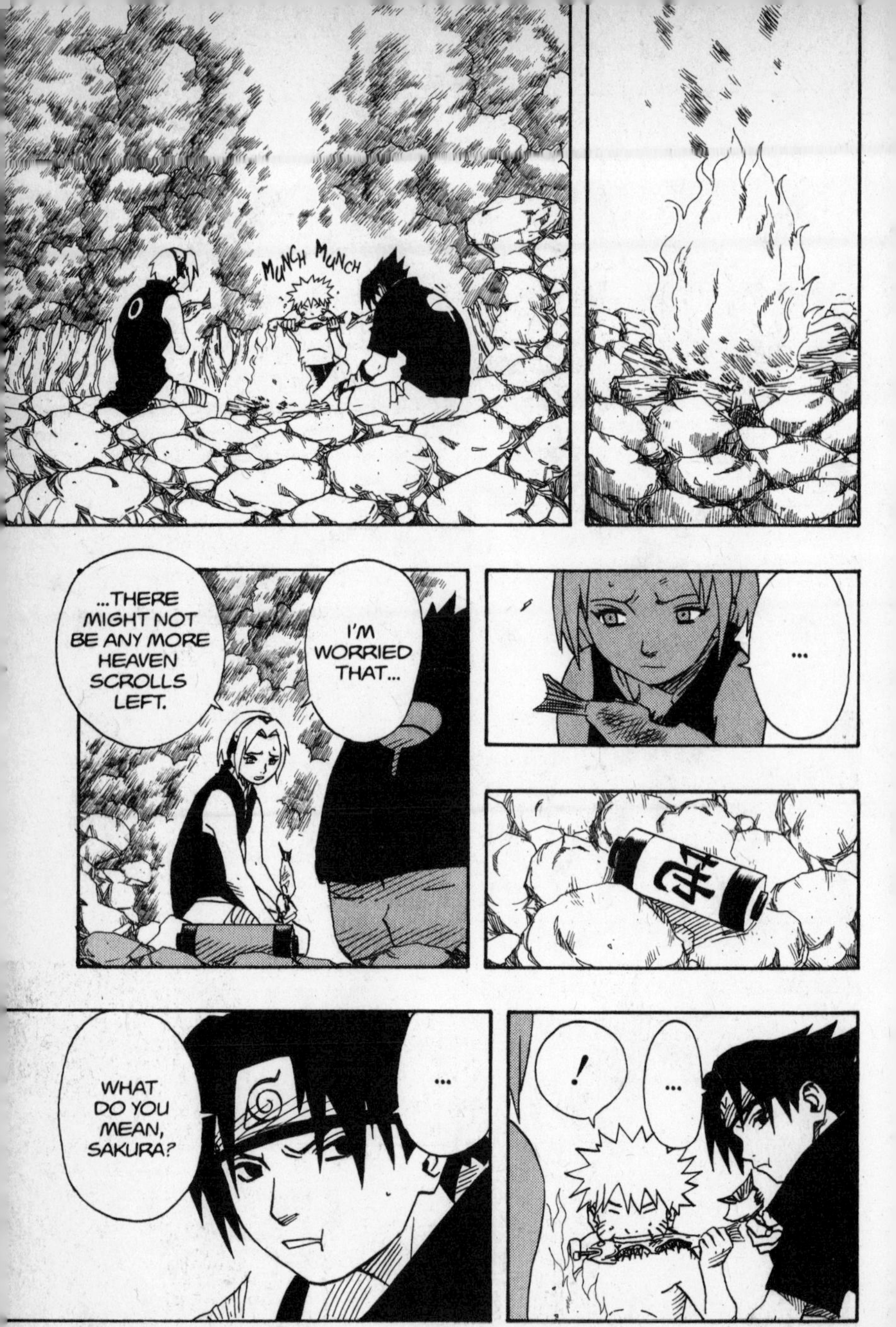
MUNCH MUNCH
...
I'M WORRIED THAT...
...THERE MIGHT NOT BE ANY MORE HEAVEN SCROLLS LEFT.
...
!
...
WHAT DO YOU MEAN, SAKURA?

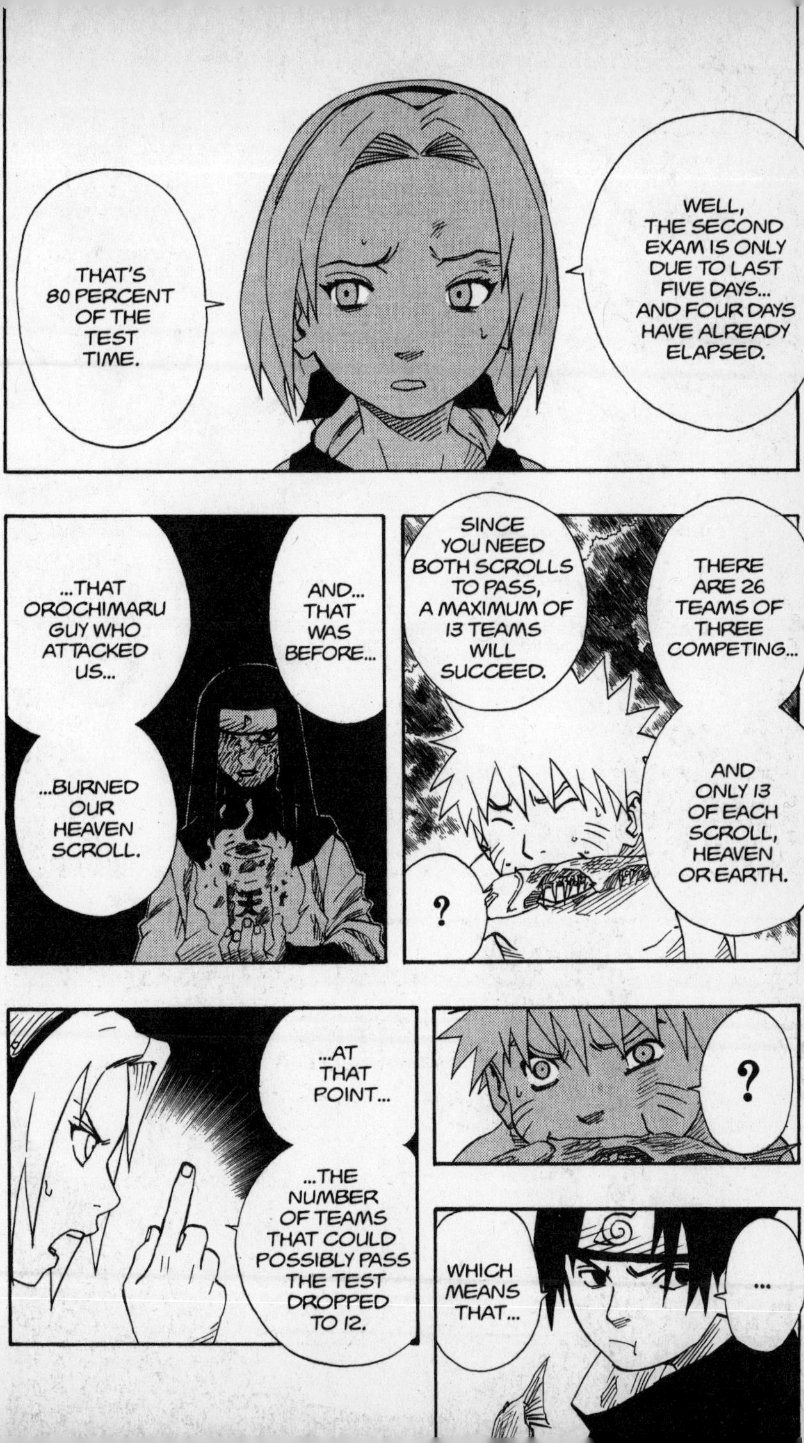
WELL, THE SECOND EXAM IS ONLY DUE TO LAST FIVE DAYS... AND FOUR DAYS HAVE ALREADY ELAPSED.
THAT'S 80 PERCENT OF THE TEST TIME.
THERE ARE 26 TEAMS OF THREE COMPETING...
SINCE YOU NEED BOTH SCROLLS TO PASS, A MAXIMUM OF 13 TEAMS WILL SUCCEED.
AND ONLY 13 OF EACH SCROLL, HEAVEN OR EARTH.
?
AND... THAT WAS BEFORE...
...THAT OROCHIMARU GUY WHO ATTACKED US...
...BURNED OUR HEAVEN SCROLL.
?
...
WHICH MEANS THAT...
...AT THAT POINT...
...THE NUMBER OF TEAMS THAT COULD POSSIBLY PASS THE TEST DROPPED TO 12.

READ THIS WAY

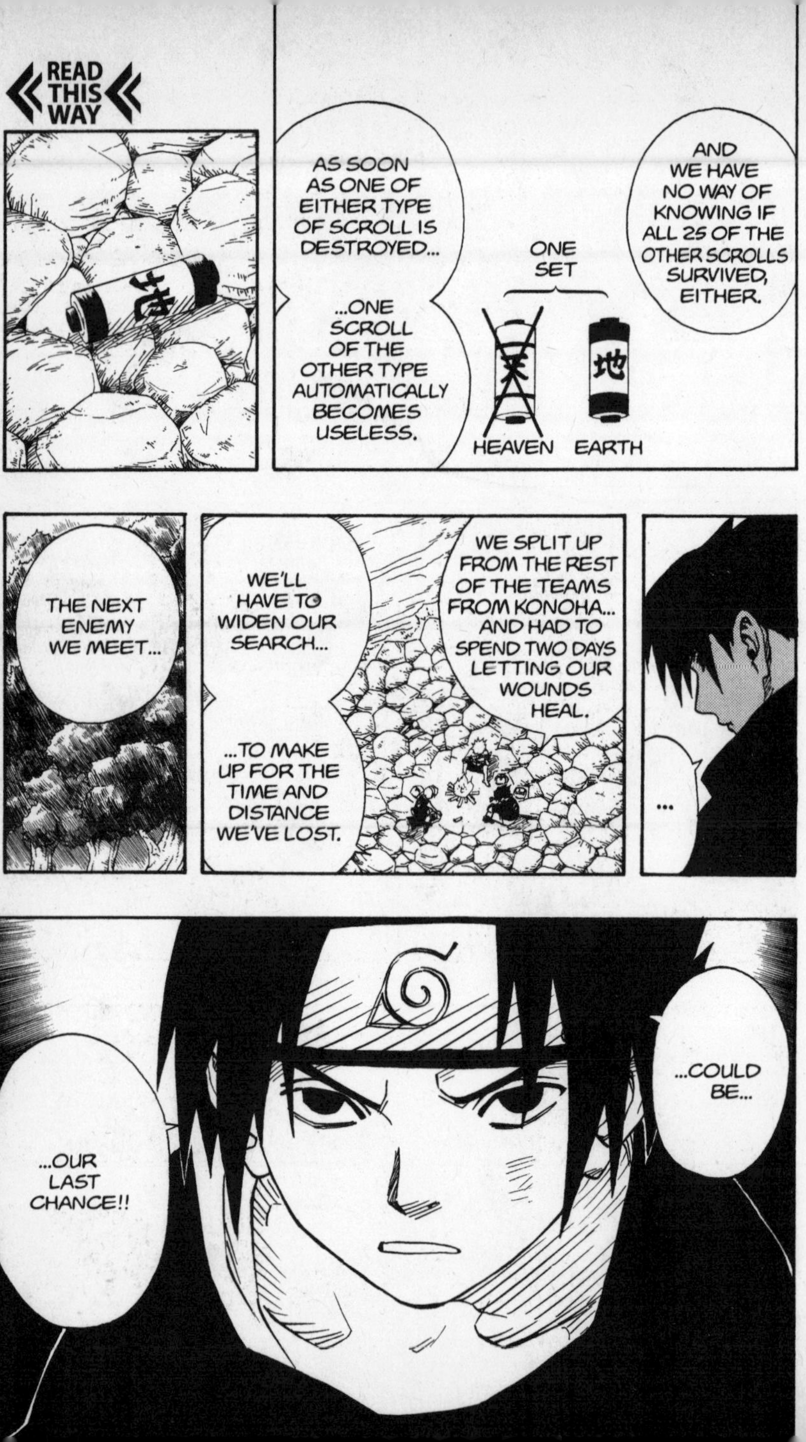
AS SOON AS ONE OF EITHER TYPE OF SCROLL IS DESTROYED...
...ONE SCROLL OF THE OTHER TYPE AUTOMATICALLY BECOMES USELESS.
ONE SET
HEAVEN
EARTH
AND WE HAVE NO WAY OF KNOWING IF ALL 25 OF THE OTHER SCROLLS SURVIVED, EITHER.
...
WE SPLIT UP FROM THE REST OF THE TEAMS FROM KONOHA... AND HAD TO SPEND TWO DAYS LETTING OUR WOUNDS HEAL.
WE'LL HAVE TO WIDEN OUR SEARCH...
...TO MAKE UP FOR THE TIME AND DISTANCE WE'VE LOST.
THE NEXT ENEMY WE MEET...
...COULD BE...
...OUR LAST CHANCE!!

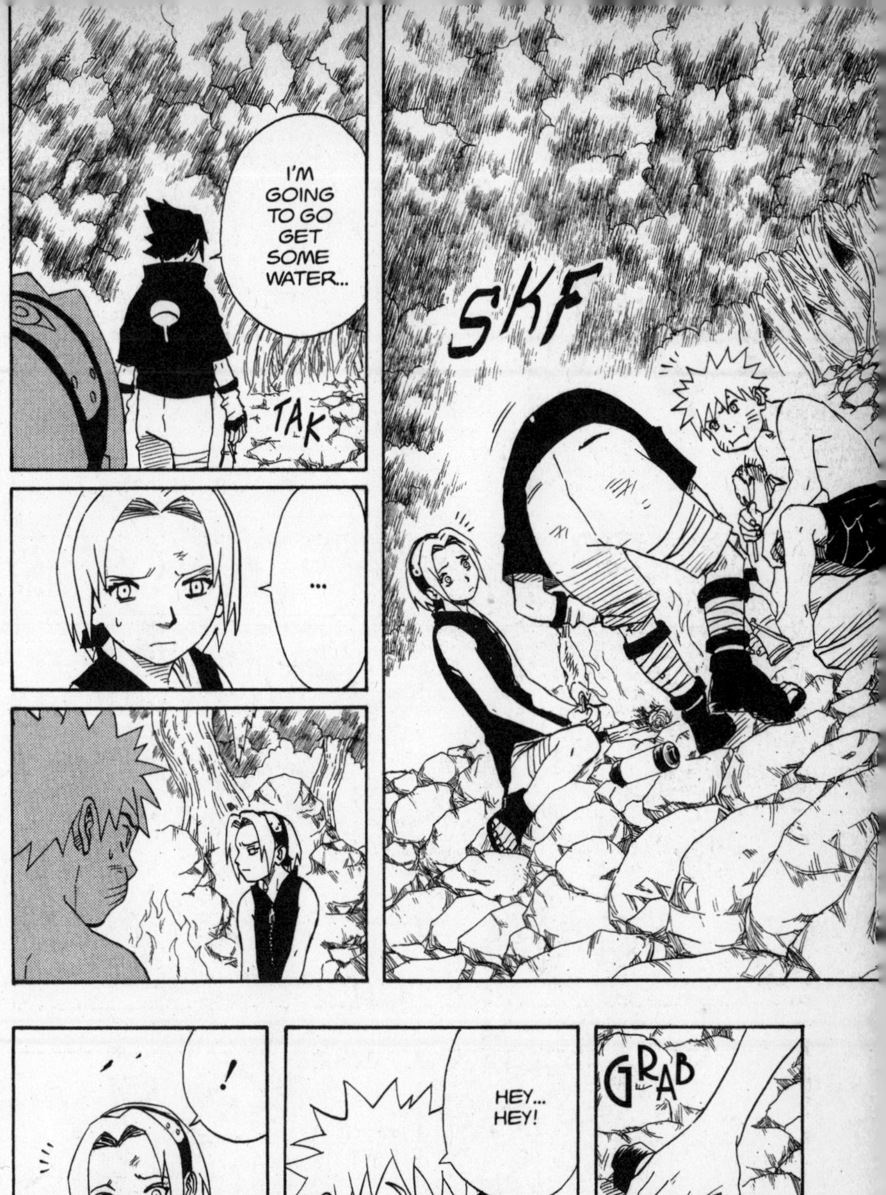
SKF
I'M GOING TO GO GET SOME WATER...
TAK
...
GRAB
HEY... HEY!
!

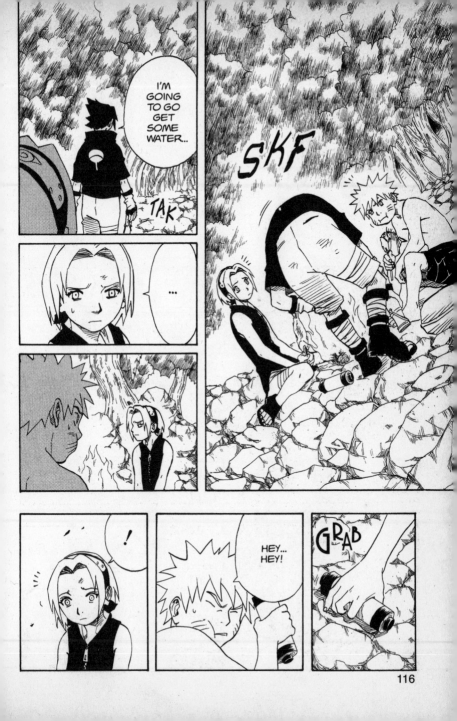

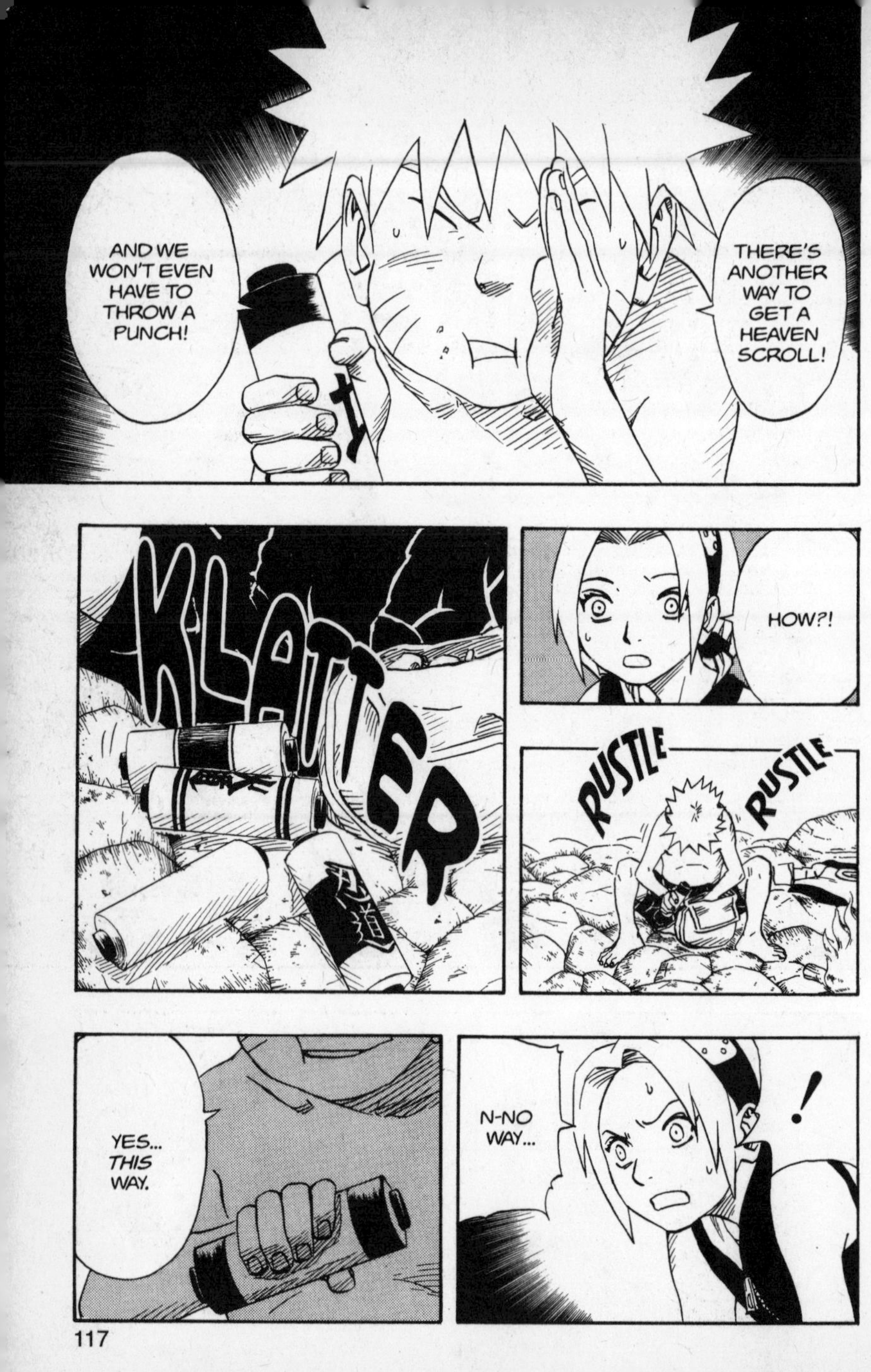
THERE'S ANOTHER WAY TO GET A HEAVEN SCROLL!
AND WE WON'T EVEN HAVE TO THROW A PUNCH!
HOW?!
RUSTLE
RUSTLE
KLATTER
!
N-NO WAY...
YES... THIS WAY.

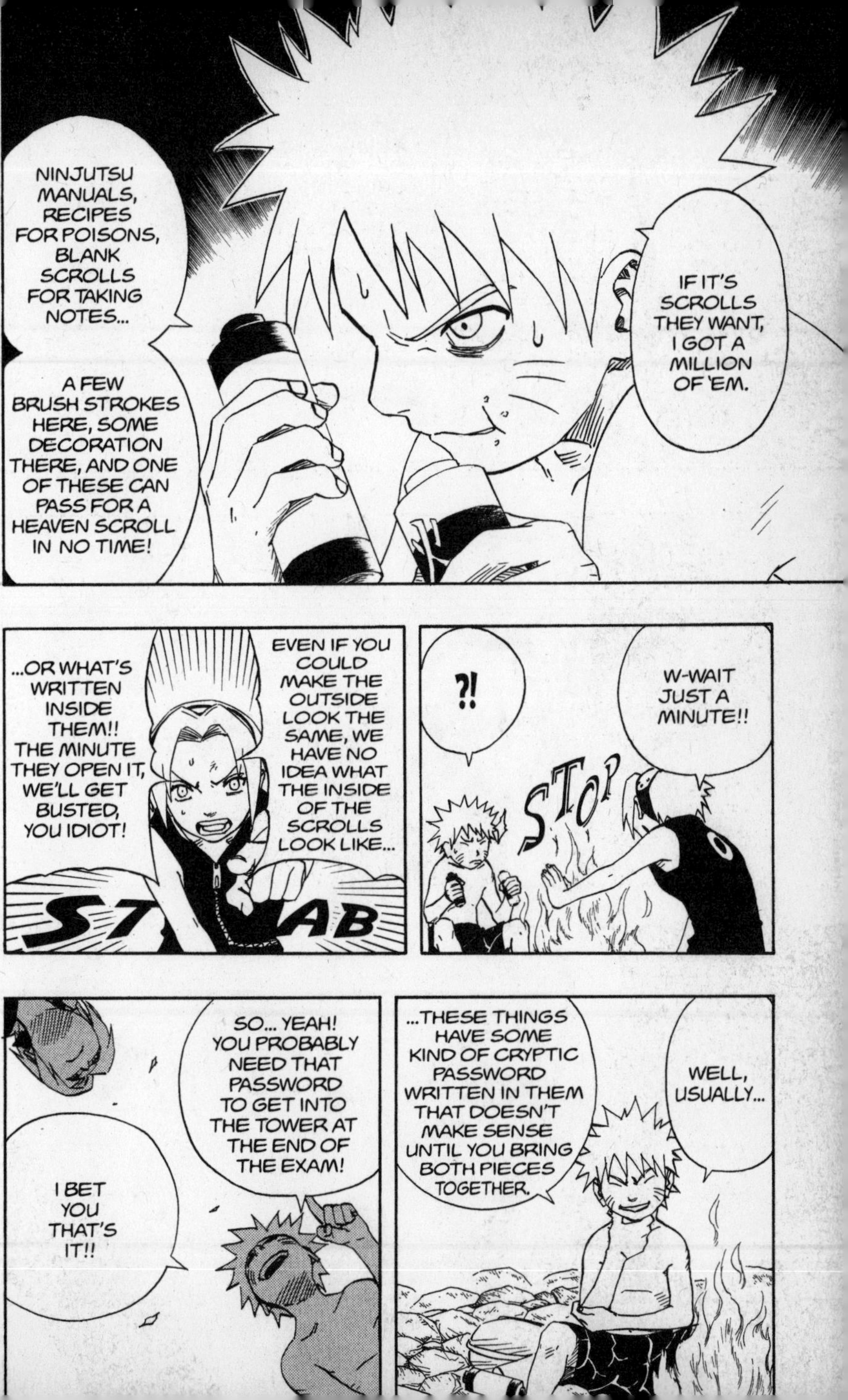
IF IT'S SCROLLS THEY WANT, I GOT A MILLION OF 'EM.
NINJUTSU MANUALS, RECIPES FOR POISONS, BLANK SCROLLS FOR TAKING NOTES...
A FEW BRUSH STROKES HERE, SOME DECORATION THERE, AND ONE OF THESE CAN PASS FOR A HEAVEN SCROLL IN NO TIME!
W-WAIT JUST A MINUTE!!
?!
STOP
EVEN IF YOU COULD MAKE THE OUTSIDE LOOK THE SAME, WE HAVE NO IDEA WHAT THE INSIDE OF THE SCROLLS LOOK LIKE...
...OR WHAT'S WRITTEN INSIDE THEM!! THE MINUTE THEY OPEN IT, WE'LL GET BUSTED, YOU IDIOT!
STAB
WELL, USUALLY...
...THESE THINGS HAVE SOME KIND OF CRYPTIC PASSWORD WRITTEN IN THEM THAT DOESN'T MAKE SENSE UNTIL YOU BRING BOTH PIECES TOGETHER.
SO... YEAH! YOU PROBABLY NEED THAT PASSWORD TO GET INTO THE TOWER AT THE END OF THE EXAM!
I BET YOU THAT'S IT!!

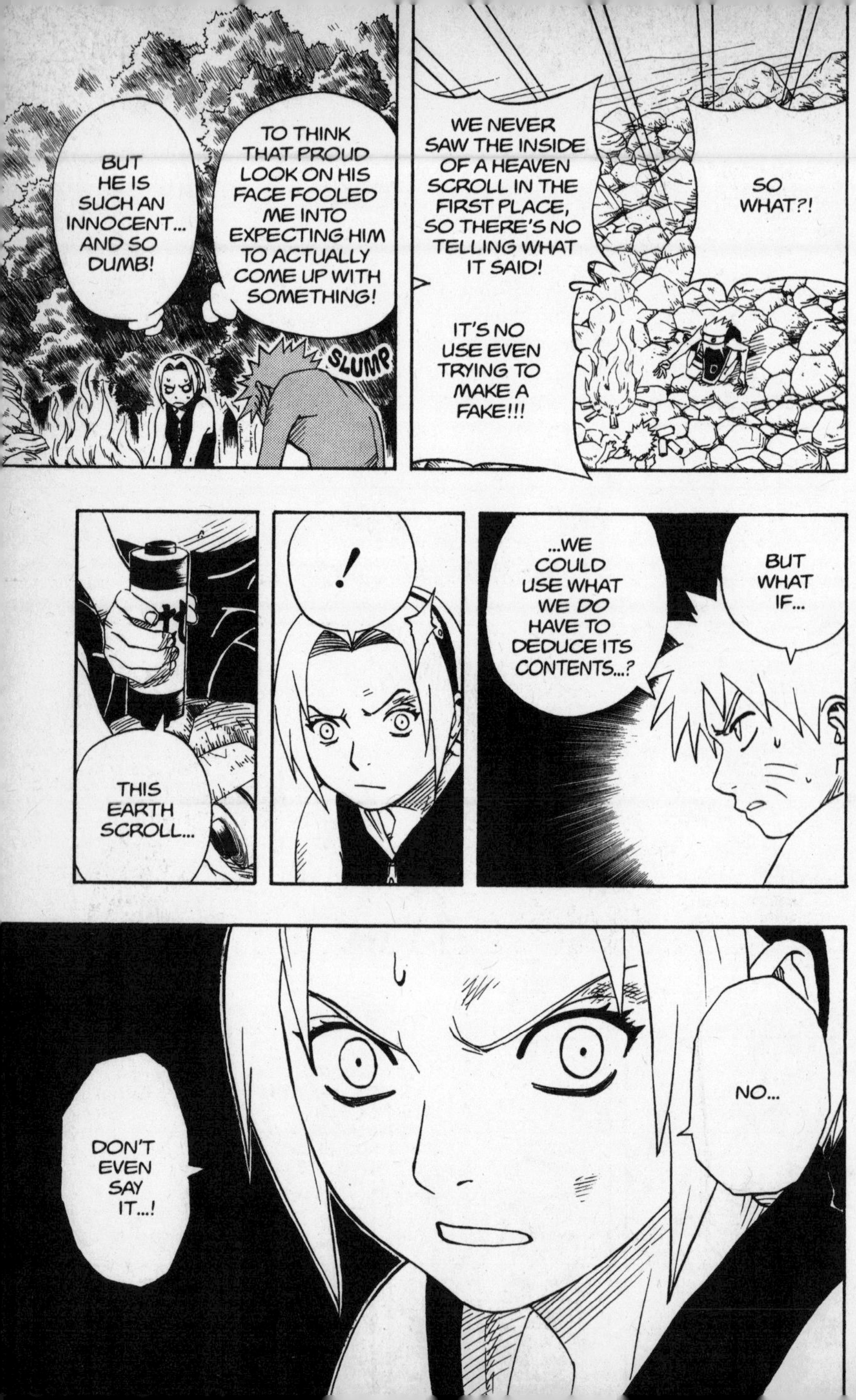
SO WHAT?!
WE NEVER SAW THE INSIDE OF A HEAVEN SCROLL IN THE FIRST PLACE, SO THERE'S NO TELLING WHAT IT SAID!
IT'S NO USE EVEN TRYING TO MAKE A FAKE!!!
TO THINK THAT PROUD LOOK ON HIS FACE FOOLED ME INTO EXPECTING HIM TO ACTUALLY COME UP WITH SOMETHING!
BUT HE IS SUCH AN INNOCENT... AND SO DUMB!
SLUMP
BUT WHAT IF...
...WE COULD USE WHAT WE *DO* HAVE TO DEDUCE ITS CONTENTS...?
!
THIS EARTH SCROLL...
NO...
DON'T EVEN SAY IT...!

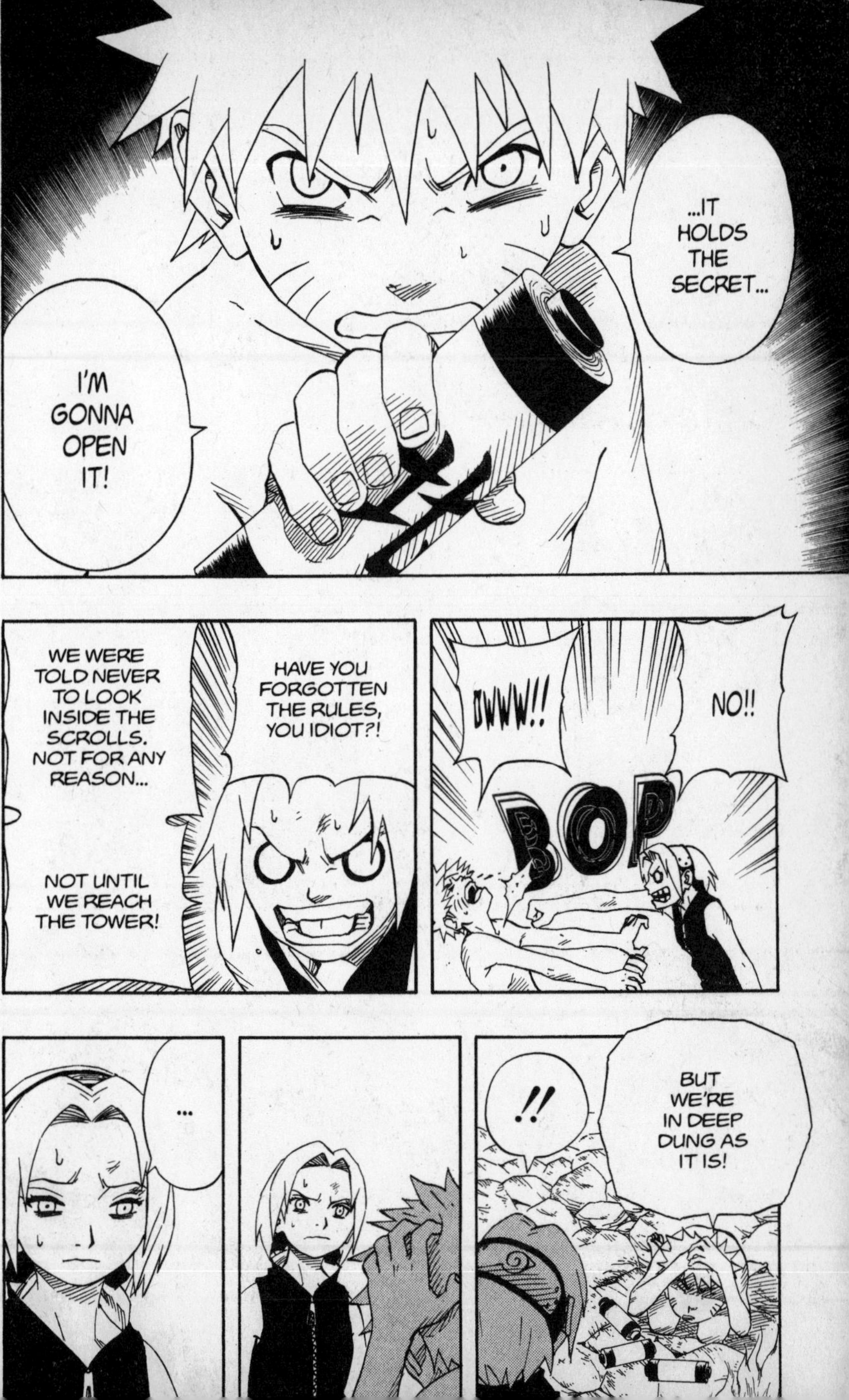
...IT HOLDS THE SECRET...
I'M GONNA OPEN IT!
NO!!
OWWW!!
BOP
HAVE YOU FORGOTTEN THE RULES, YOU IDIOT?!
WE WERE TOLD NEVER TO LOOK INSIDE THE SCROLLS. NOT FOR ANY REASON...
NOT UNTIL WE REACH THE TOWER!
BUT WE'RE IN DEEP DUNG AS IT IS!
!!
...

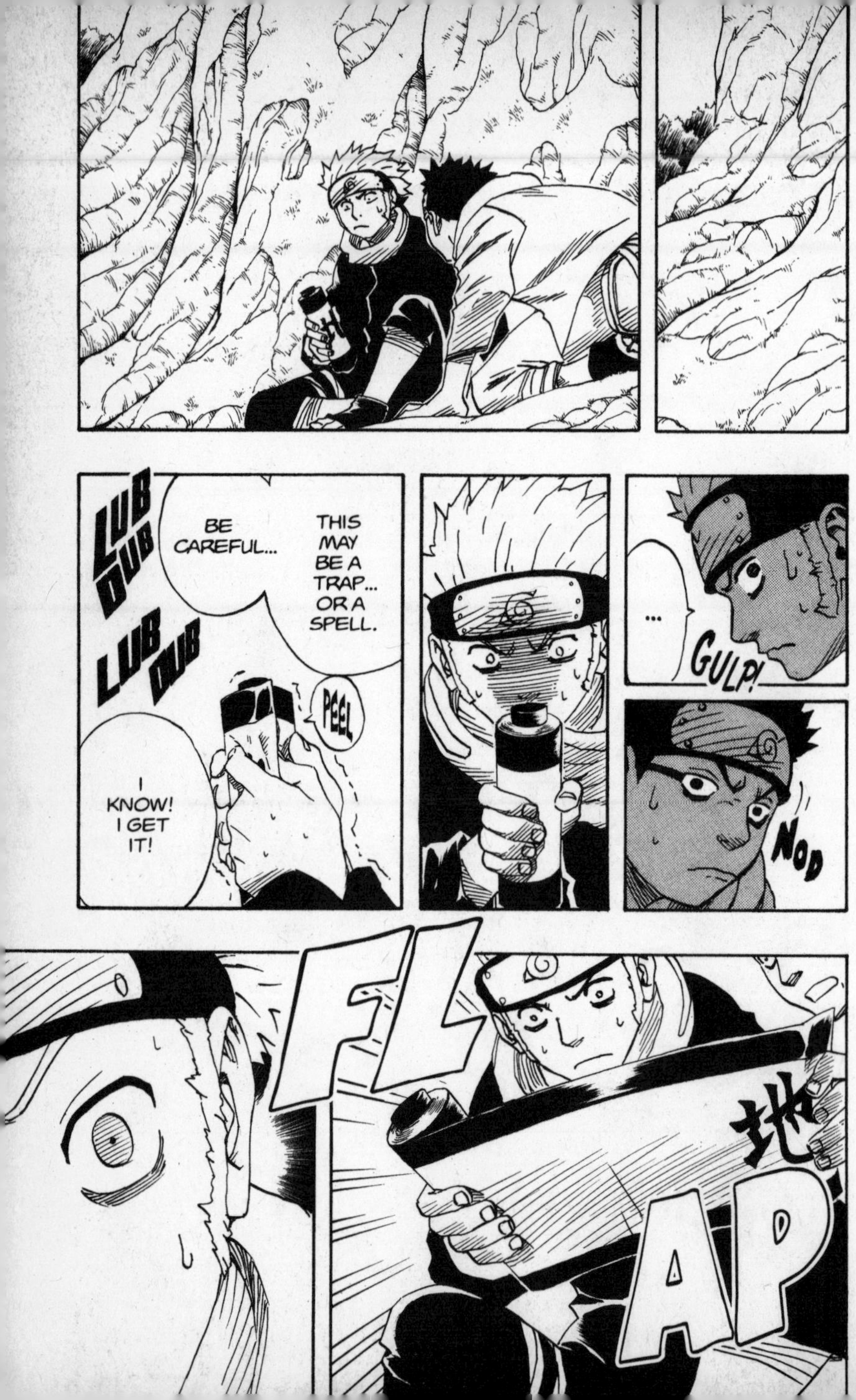
...
GULP!
NOD
LUB DUB LUB DUB
BE CAREFUL... THIS MAY BE A TRAP... OR A SPELL.
PEEL
I KNOW! I GET IT!
FLAP
地

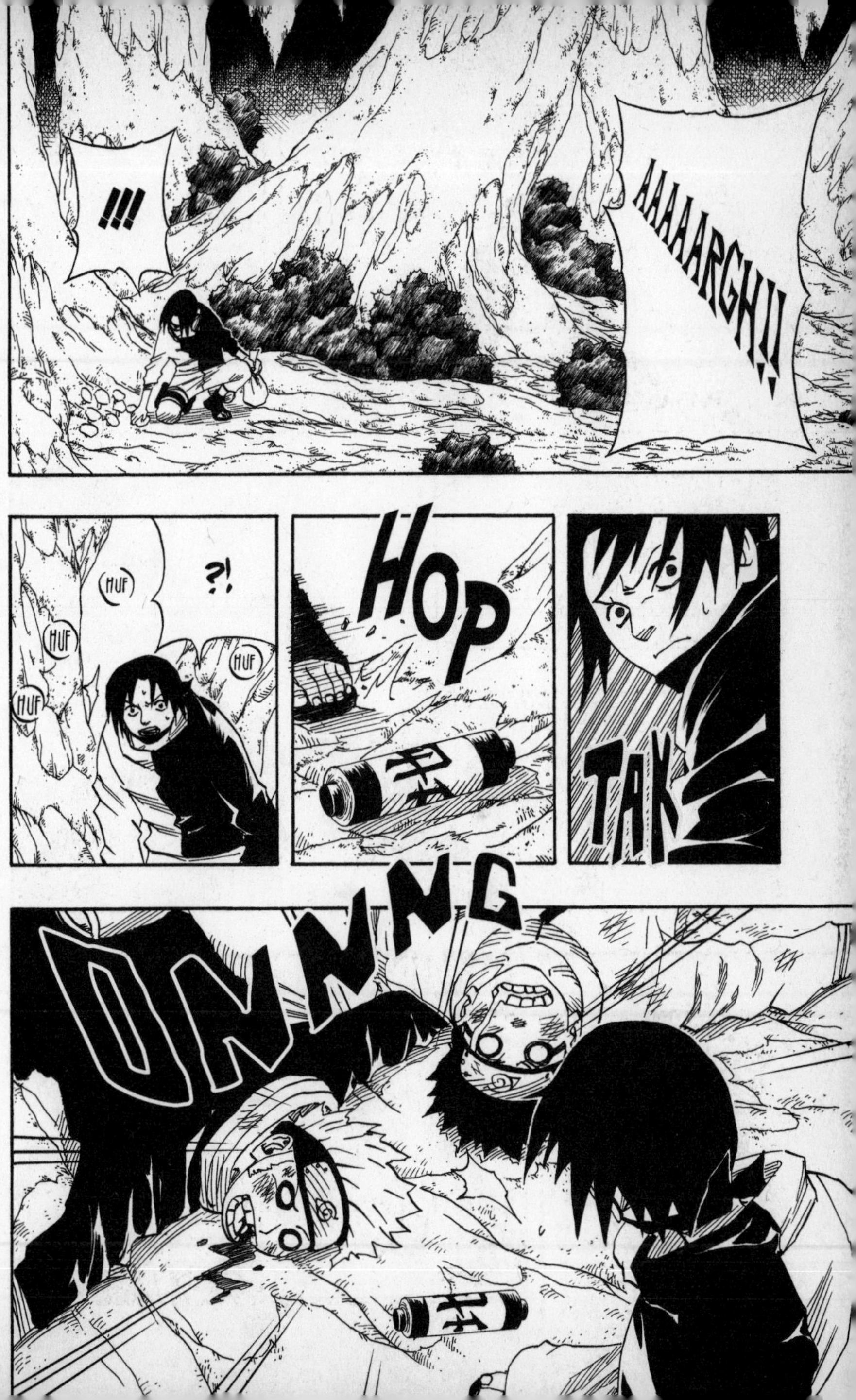
AAAAARGH!!
!!!
TAK
HOP
HUF
HUF
HUF
HUF
?!
DONNNG

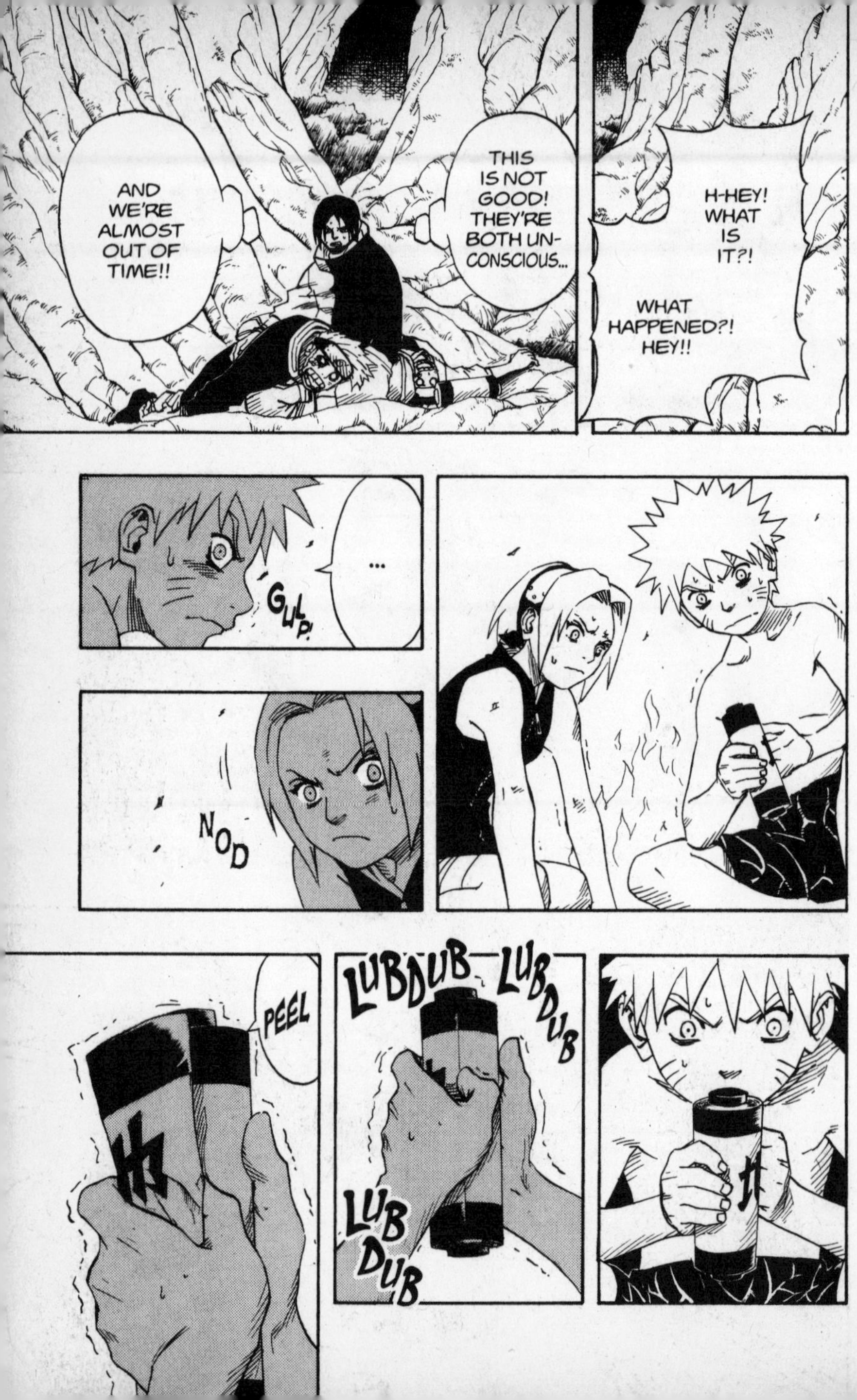
H-HEY! WHAT IS IT?!
WHAT HAPPENED?! HEY!!
THIS IS NOT GOOD! THEY'RE BOTH UN-CONSCIOUS...
AND WE'RE ALMOST OUT OF TIME!!
...
GULP!
NOD
LUBDUB LUBDUB
LUBDUB
PEEL

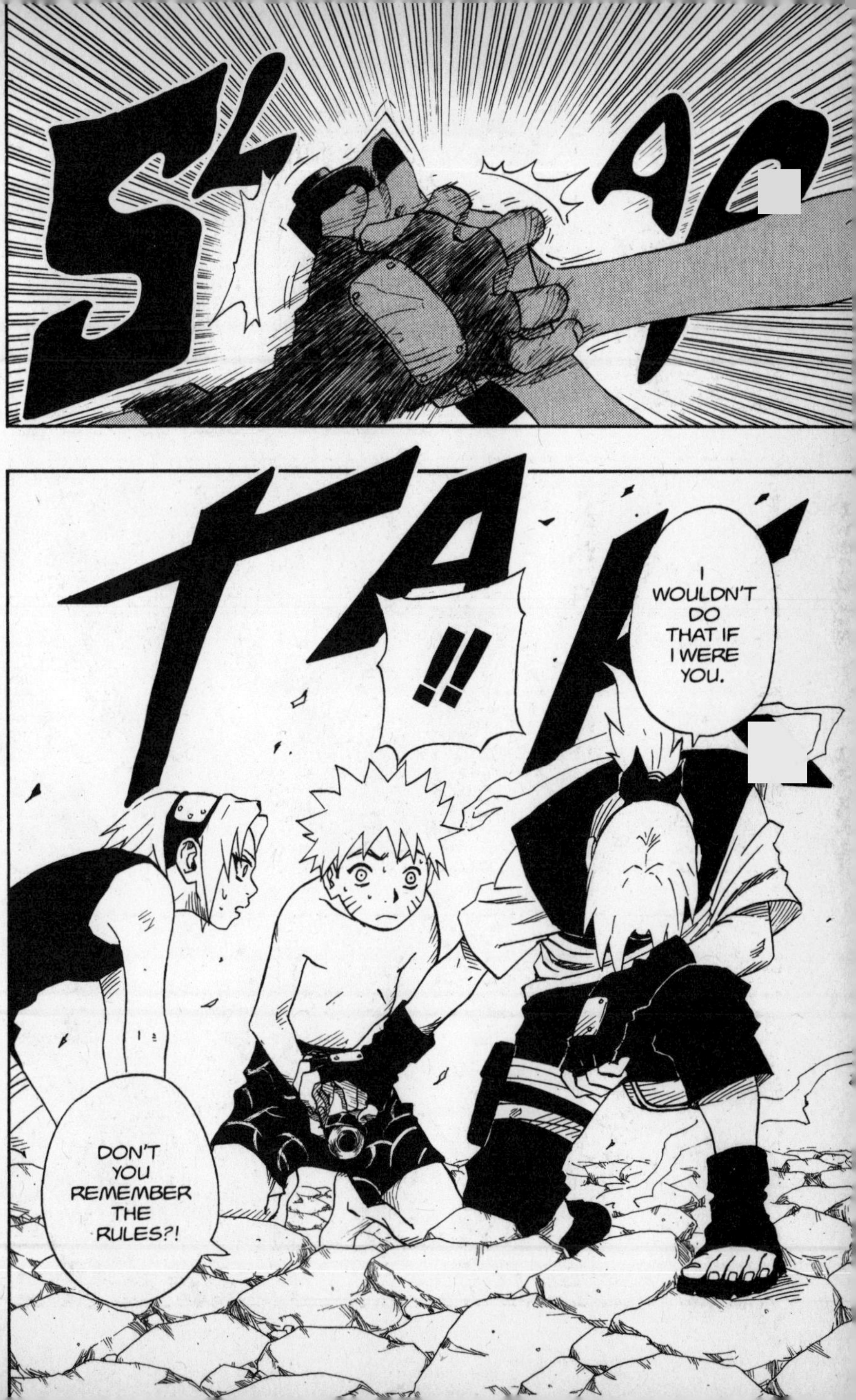
I WOULDN'T DO THAT IF I WERE YOU.
!!
DON'T YOU REMEMBER THE RULES?!

READ THIS WAY

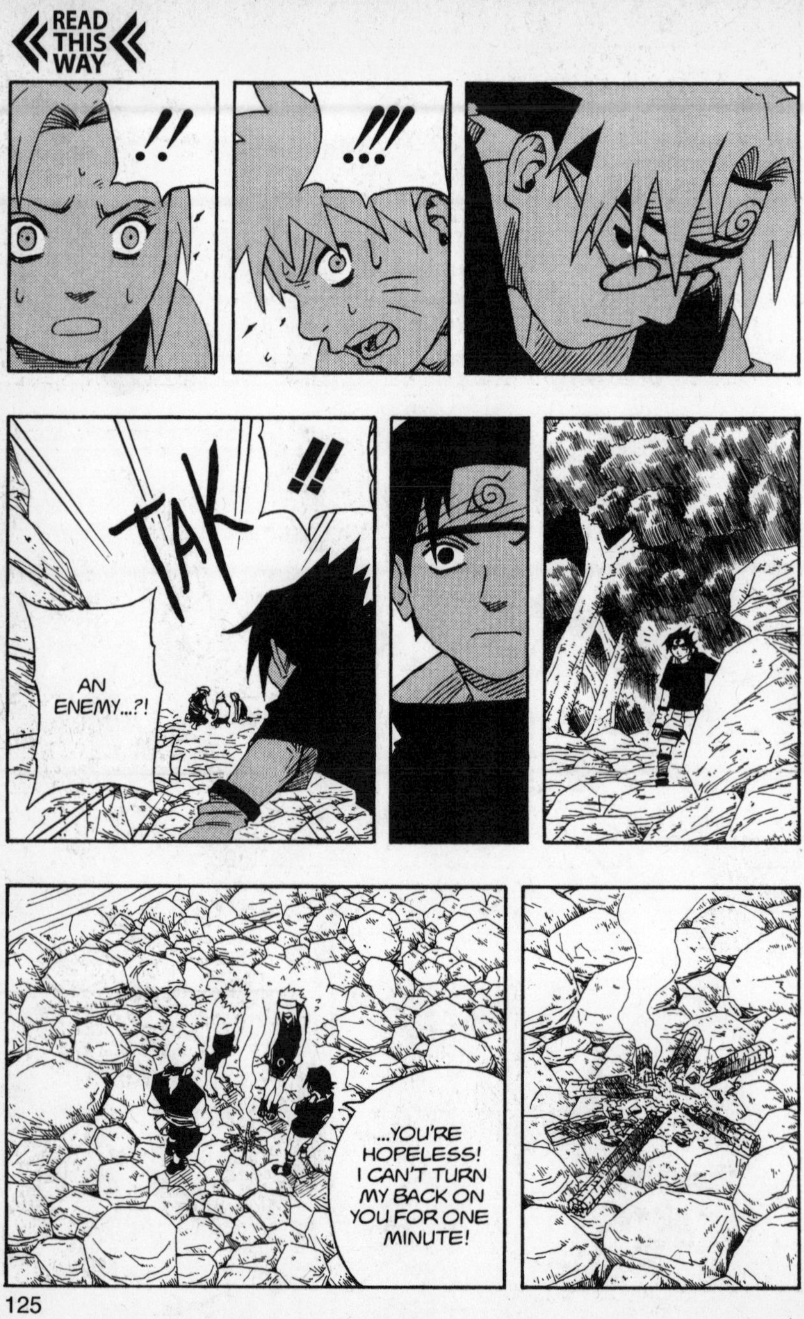
!!!
!!
TAK
!!
AN ENEMY...?!
...YOU'RE HOPELESS! I CAN'T TURN MY BACK ON YOU FOR ONE MINUTE!

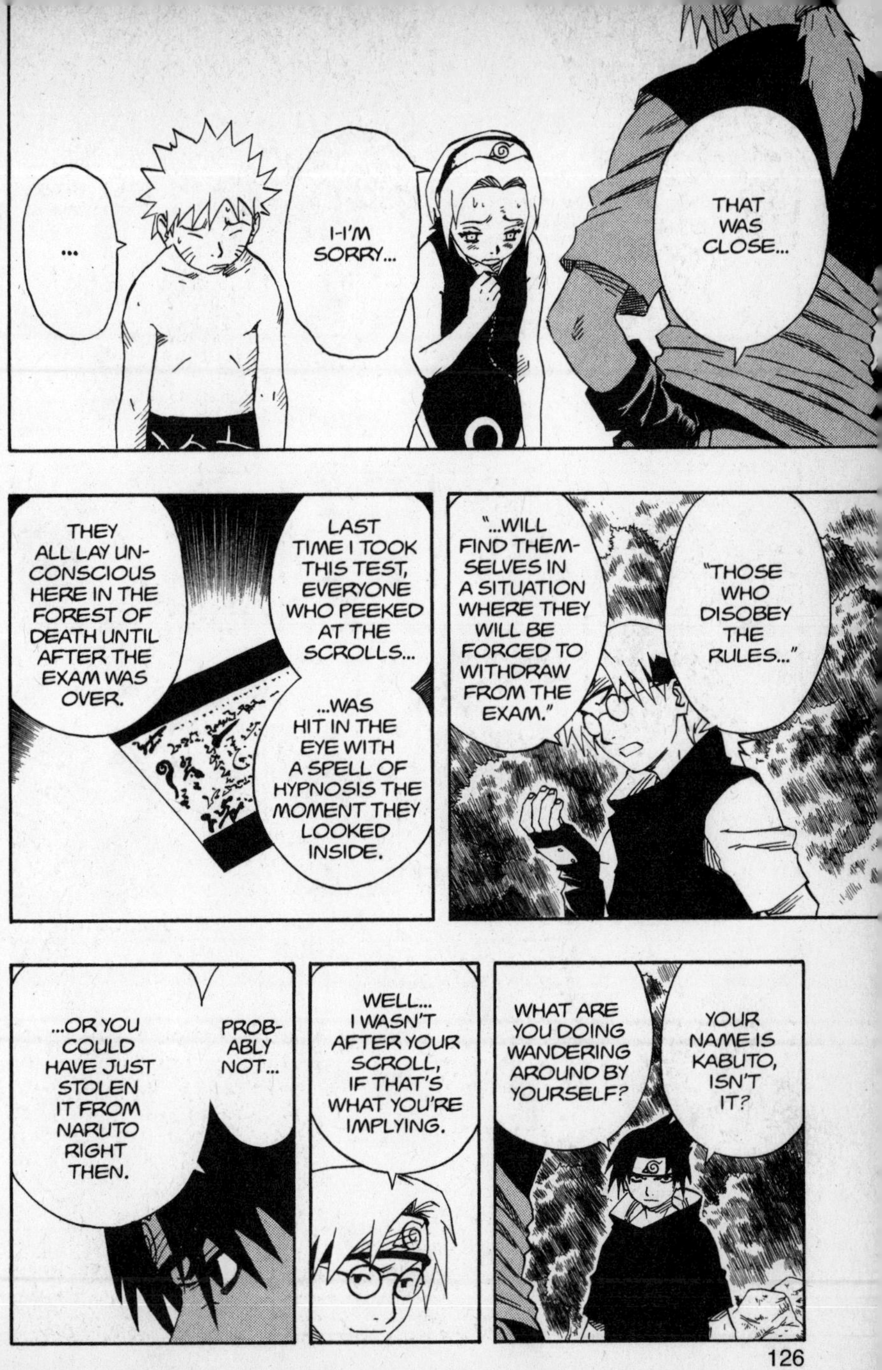
THAT WAS CLOSE...
I-I'M SORRY...
...
"THOSE WHO DISOBEY THE RULES..."
"...WILL FIND THEMSELVES IN A SITUATION WHERE THEY WILL BE FORCED TO WITHDRAW FROM THE EXAM."
LAST TIME I TOOK THIS TEST, EVERYONE WHO PEEKED AT THE SCROLLS...
...WAS HIT IN THE EYE WITH A SPELL OF HYPNOSIS THE MOMENT THEY LOOKED INSIDE.
THEY ALL LAY UNCONSCIOUS HERE IN THE FOREST OF DEATH UNTIL AFTER THE EXAM WAS OVER.
YOUR NAME IS KABUTO, ISN'T IT?
WHAT ARE YOU DOING WANDERING AROUND BY YOURSELF?
WELL... I WASN'T AFTER YOUR SCROLL, IF THAT'S WHAT YOU'RE IMPLYING.
PROBABLY NOT...
...OR YOU COULD HAVE JUST STOLEN IT FROM NARUTO RIGHT THEN.

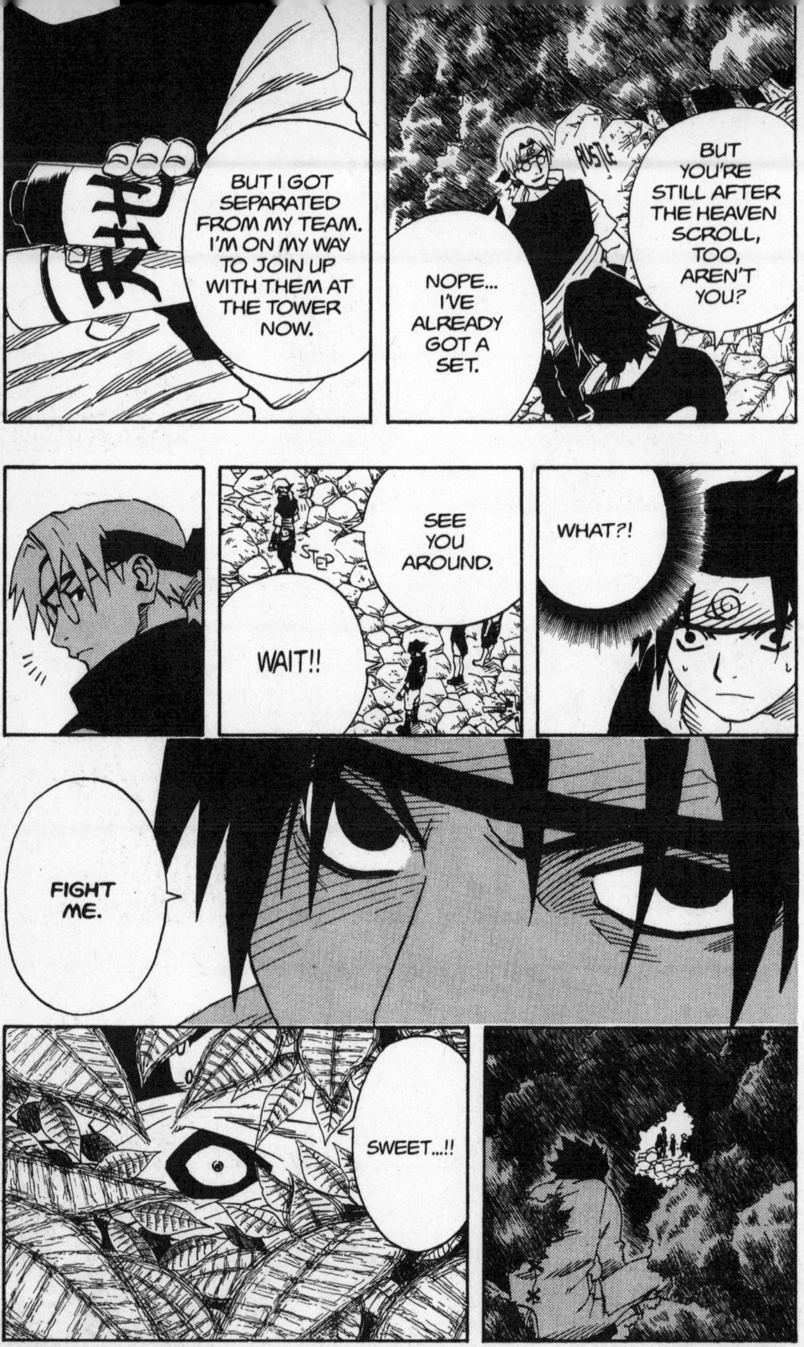
BUT YOU'RE STILL AFTER THE HEAVEN SCROLL, TOO, AREN'T YOU?
RUSTLE
NOPE... I'VE ALREADY GOT A SET.
BUT I GOT SEPARATED FROM MY TEAM. I'M ON MY WAY TO JOIN UP WITH THEM AT THE TOWER NOW.
WHAT?!
SEE YOU AROUND.
STEP
WAIT!!
FIGHT ME.
SWEET...!!

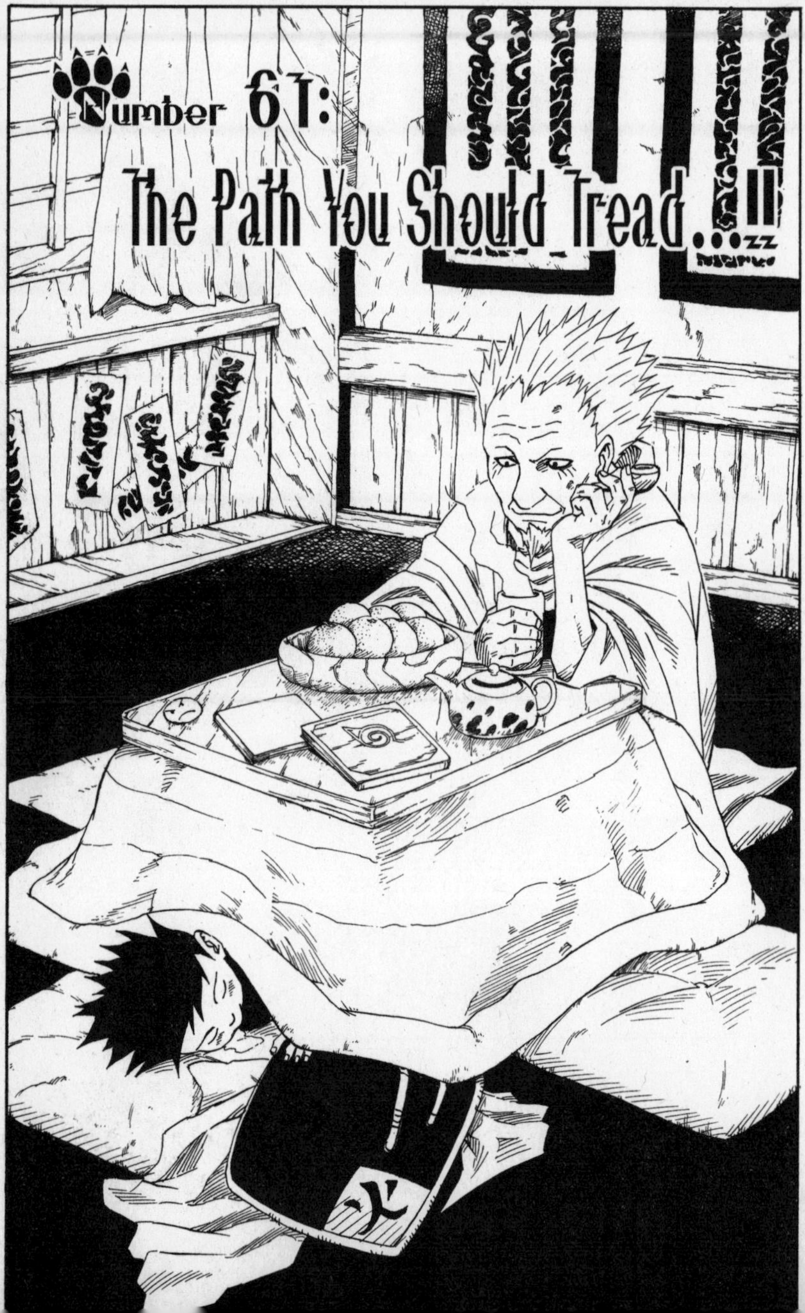
Number 61:
The Path You Should Tread...!!
zz

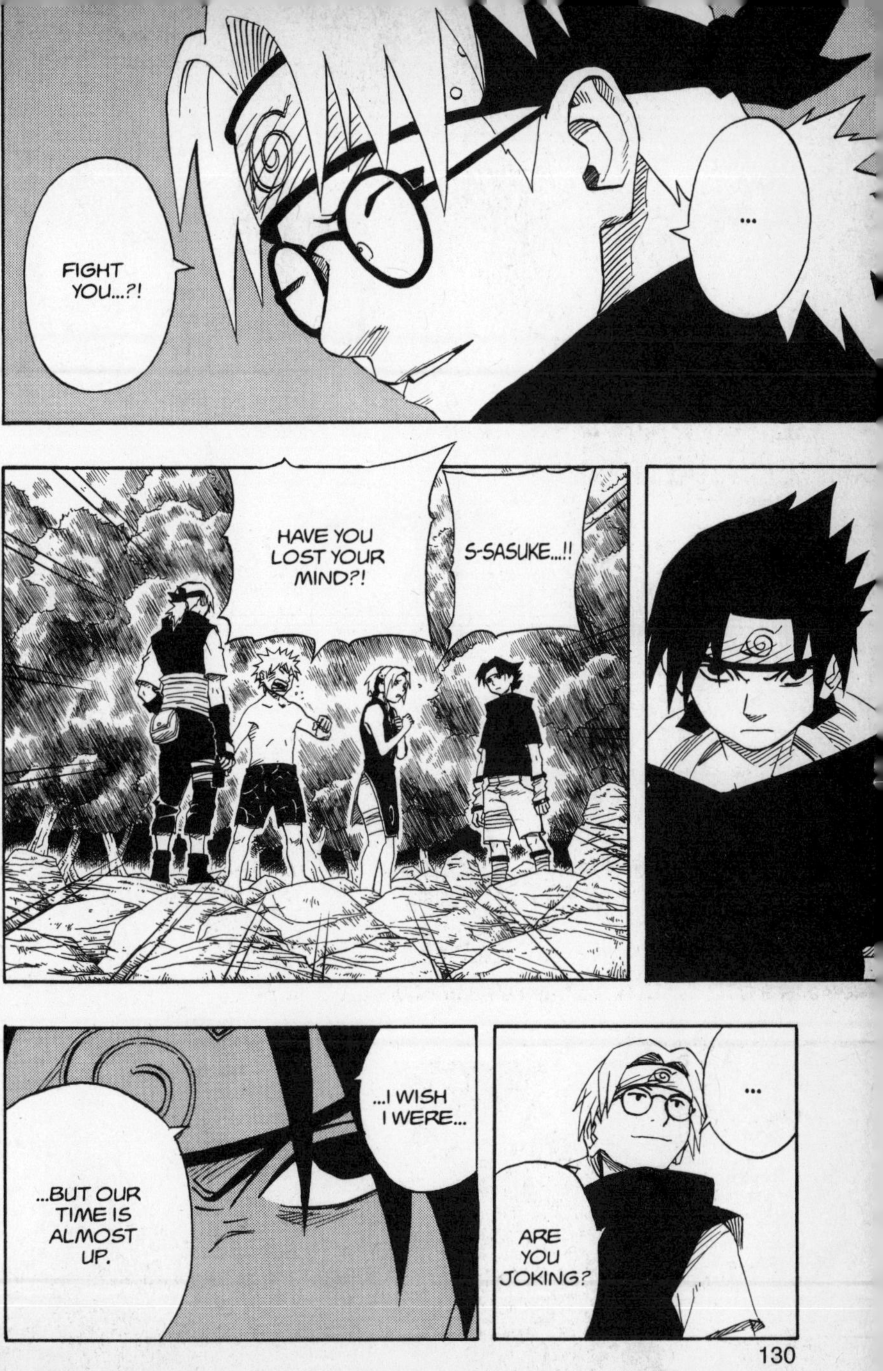
...
FIGHT YOU...?!
S-SASUKE...!!
HAVE YOU LOST YOUR MIND?!
...
ARE YOU JOKING?
...I WISH I WERE...
...BUT OUR TIME IS ALMOST UP.

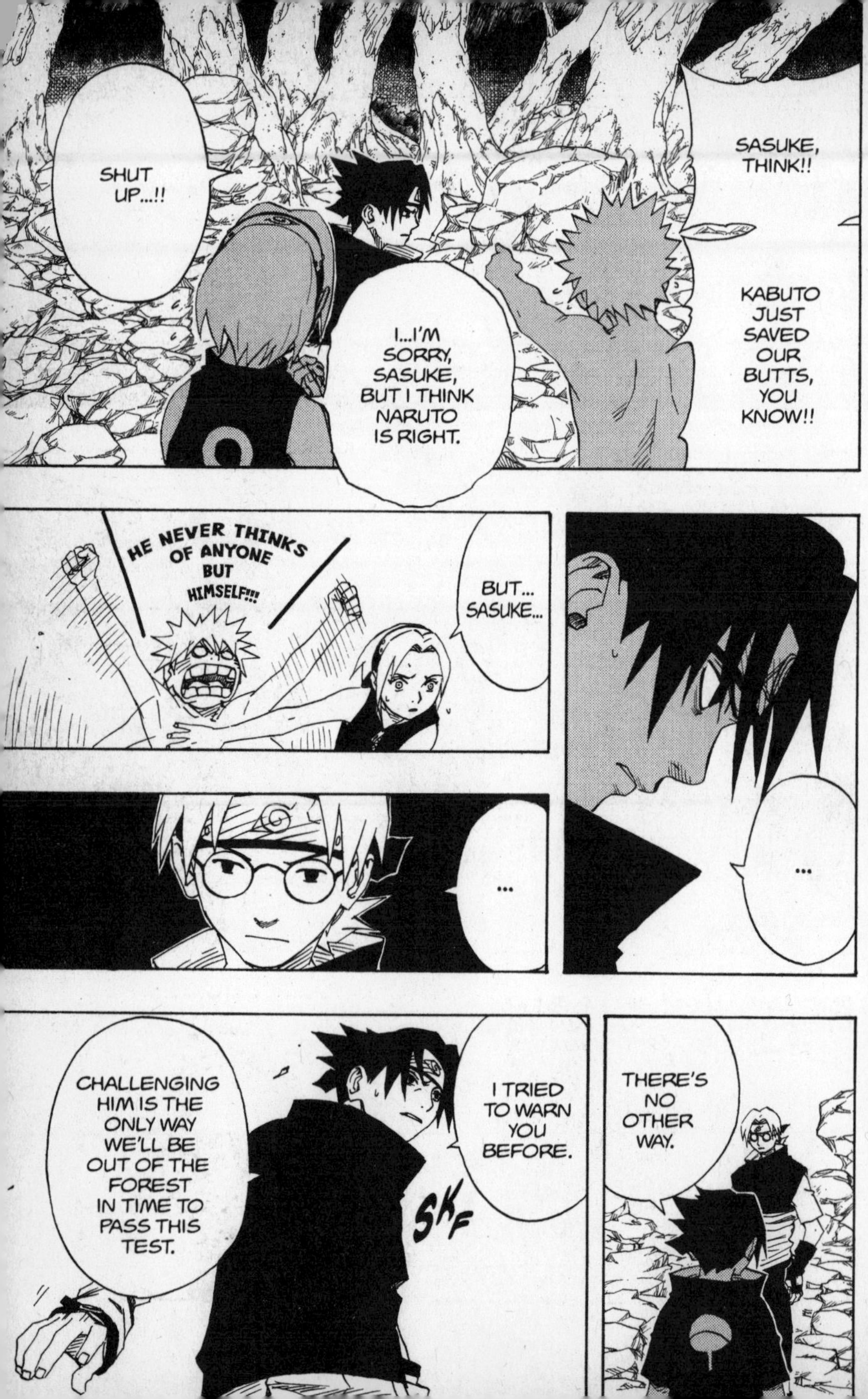
SASUKE, THINK!!
KABUTO JUST SAVED OUR BUTTS, YOU KNOW!!
I...I'M SORRY, SASUKE, BUT I THINK NARUTO IS RIGHT.
SHUT UP...!!
...
BUT... SASUKE...
HE NEVER THINKS OF ANYONE BUT HIMSELF!!!
...
THERE'S NO OTHER WAY.
I TRIED TO WARN YOU BEFORE.
SKF
CHALLENGING HIM IS THE ONLY WAY WE'LL BE OUT OF THE FOREST IN TIME TO PASS THIS TEST.

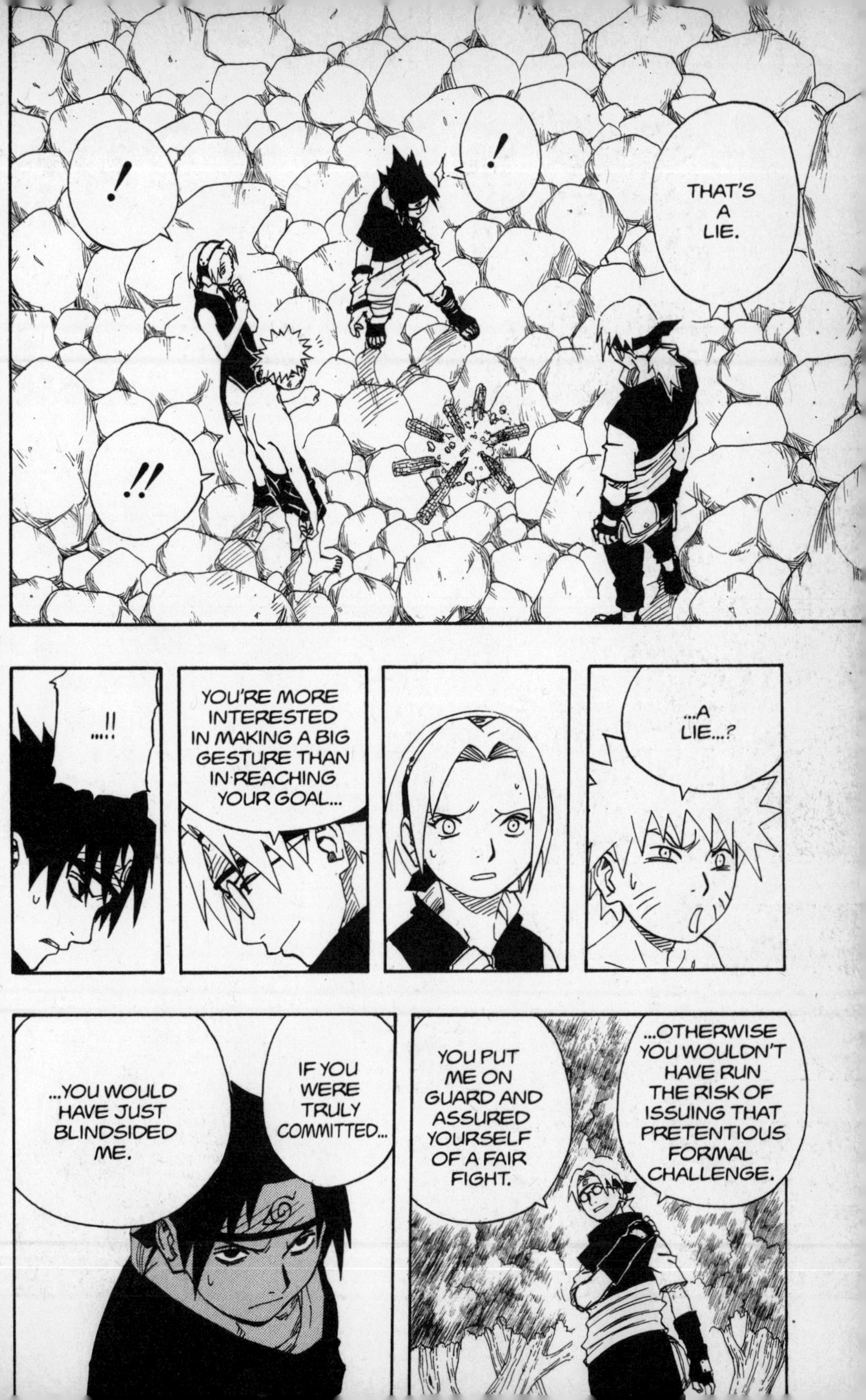
THAT'S A LIE.
!
!
!!
...A LIE...?
YOU'RE MORE INTERESTED IN MAKING A BIG GESTURE THAN IN REACHING YOUR GOAL...
...!!
...OTHERWISE YOU WOULDN'T HAVE RUN THE RISK OF ISSUING THAT PRETENTIOUS FORMAL CHALLENGE.
YOU PUT ME ON GUARD AND ASSURED YOURSELF OF A FAIR FIGHT.
IF YOU WERE TRULY COMMITTED...
...YOU WOULD HAVE JUST BLINDSIDED ME.

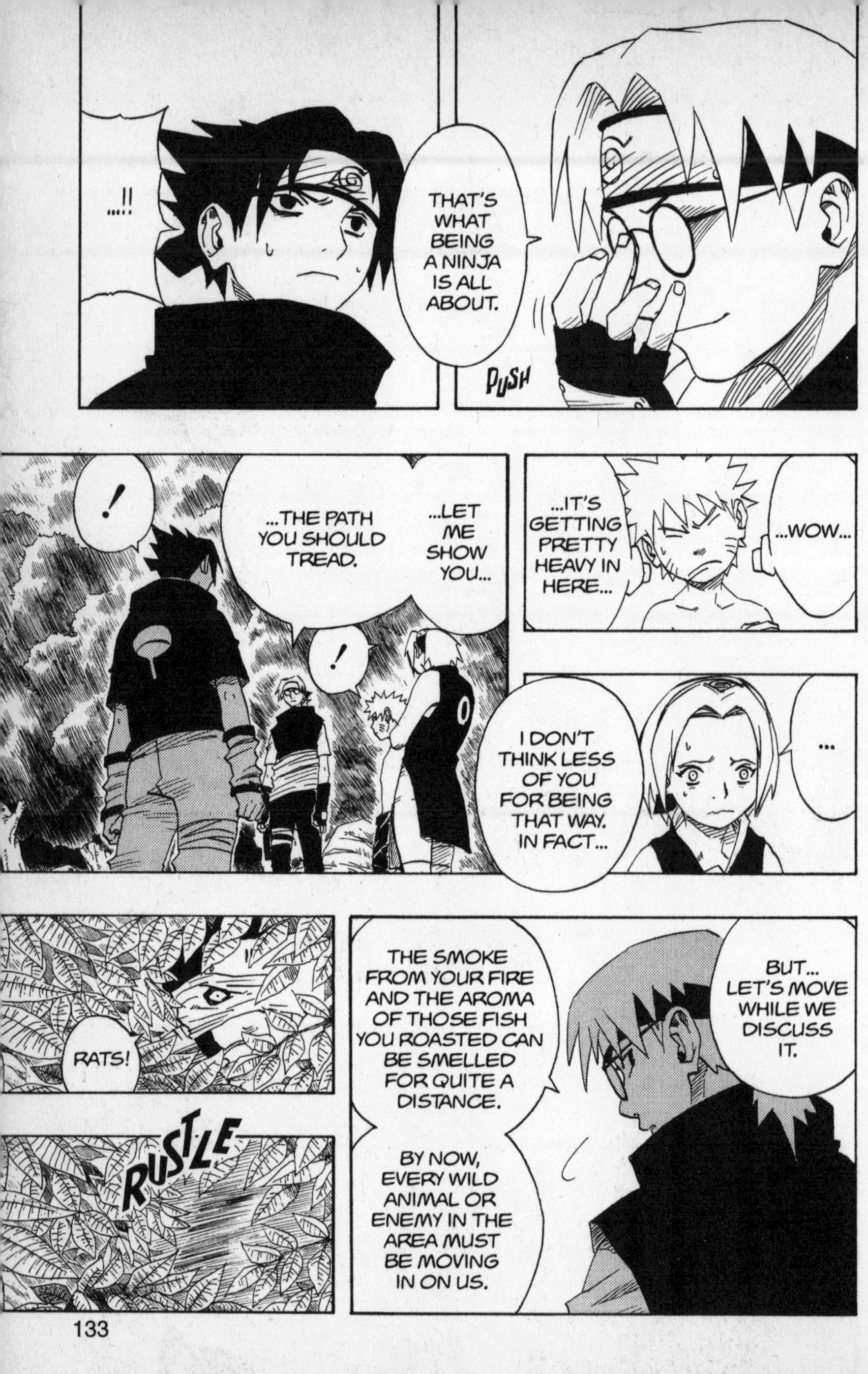
THAT'S WHAT BEING A NINJA IS ALL ABOUT.
PUSH
...!!
...WOW...
...IT'S GETTING PRETTY HEAVY IN HERE...
...
I DON'T THINK LESS OF YOU FOR BEING THAT WAY. IN FACT...
...LET ME SHOW YOU...
...THE PATH YOU SHOULD TREAD.
!
!
BUT... LET'S MOVE WHILE WE DISCUSS IT.
THE SMOKE FROM YOUR FIRE AND THE AROMA OF THOSE FISH YOU ROASTED CAN BE SMELLED FOR QUITE A DISTANCE.
BY NOW, EVERY WILD ANIMAL OR ENEMY IN THE AREA MUST BE MOVING IN ON US.
RATS!
RUSTLE

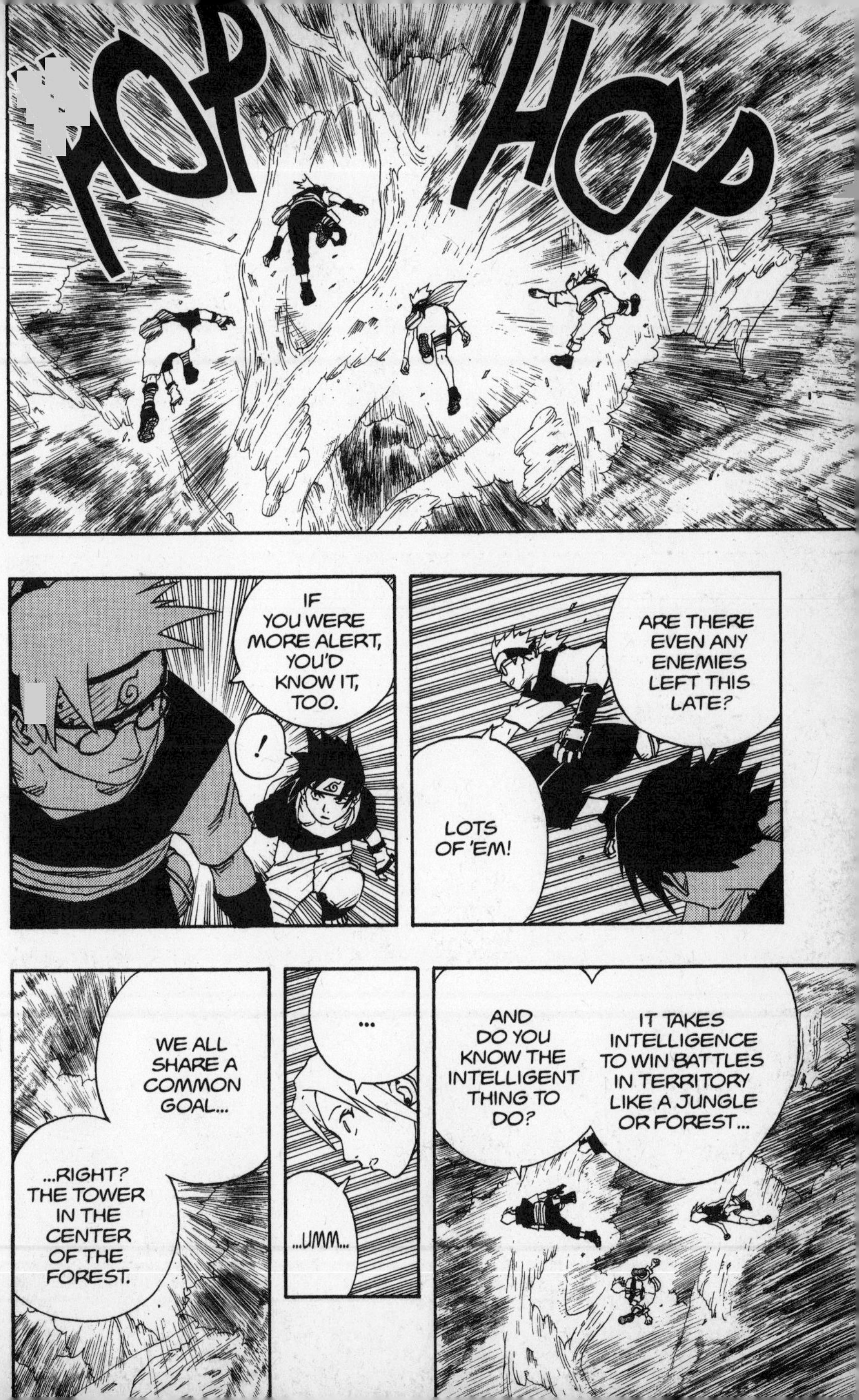
HOP
HOP
ARE THERE EVEN ANY ENEMIES LEFT THIS LATE?
LOTS OF 'EM!
IF YOU WERE MORE ALERT, YOU'D KNOW IT, TOO.
!
IT TAKES INTELLIGENCE TO WIN BATTLES IN TERRITORY LIKE A JUNGLE OR FOREST...
AND DO YOU KNOW THE INTELLIGENT THING TO DO?
...
...UMM...
WE ALL SHARE A COMMON GOAL...
...RIGHT? THE TOWER IN THE CENTER OF THE FOREST.

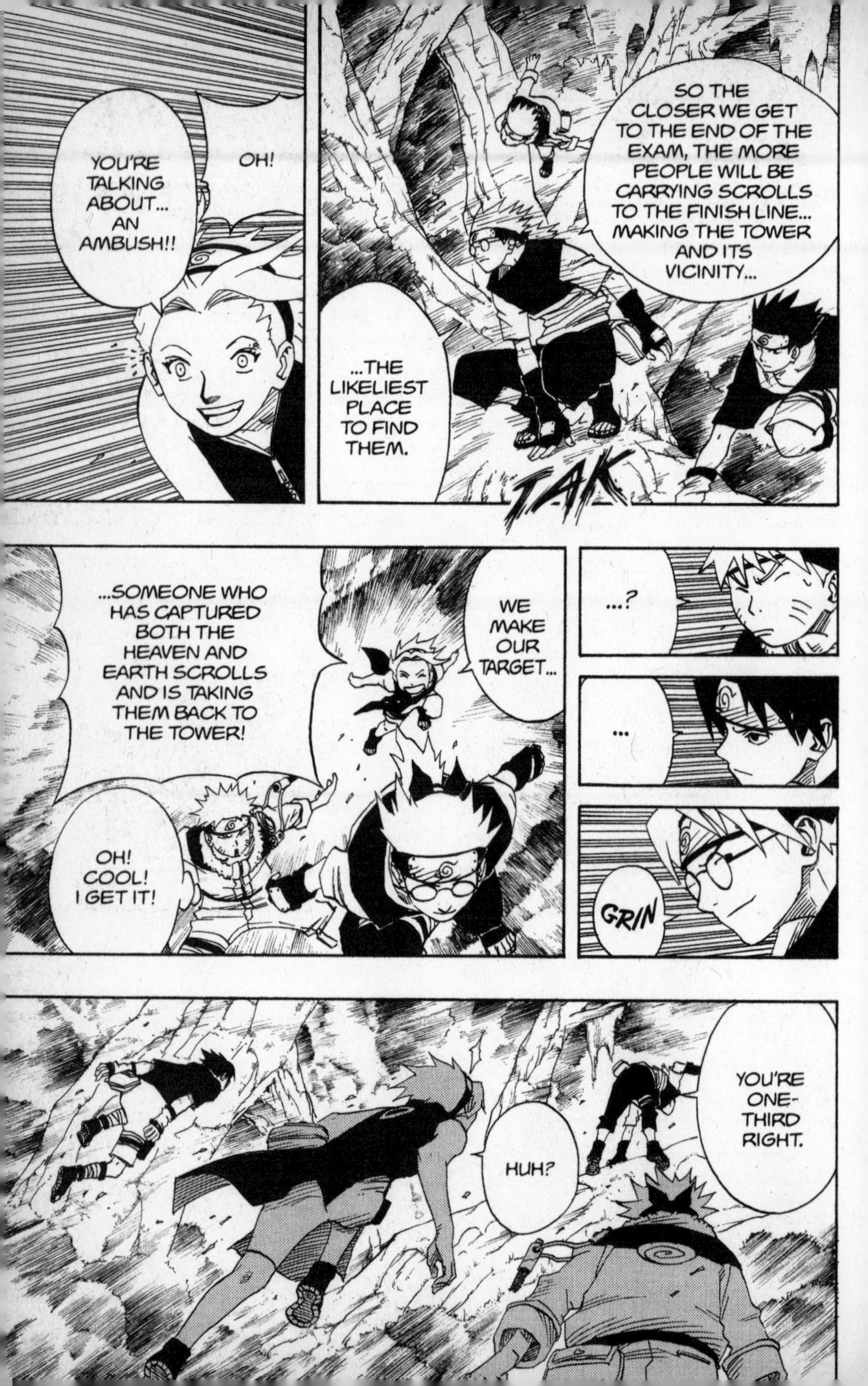
SO THE CLOSER WE GET TO THE END OF THE EXAM, THE MORE PEOPLE WILL BE CARRYING SCROLLS TO THE FINISH LINE... MAKING THE TOWER AND ITS VICINITY...
...THE LIKELIEST PLACE TO FIND THEM.
TAK
OH!
YOU'RE TALKING ABOUT... AN AMBUSH!!
...?
...
GRIN
WE MAKE OUR TARGET...
...SOMEONE WHO HAS CAPTURED BOTH THE HEAVEN AND EARTH SCROLLS AND IS TAKING THEM BACK TO THE TOWER!
OH! COOL! I GET IT!
YOU'RE ONE-THIRD RIGHT.
HUH?

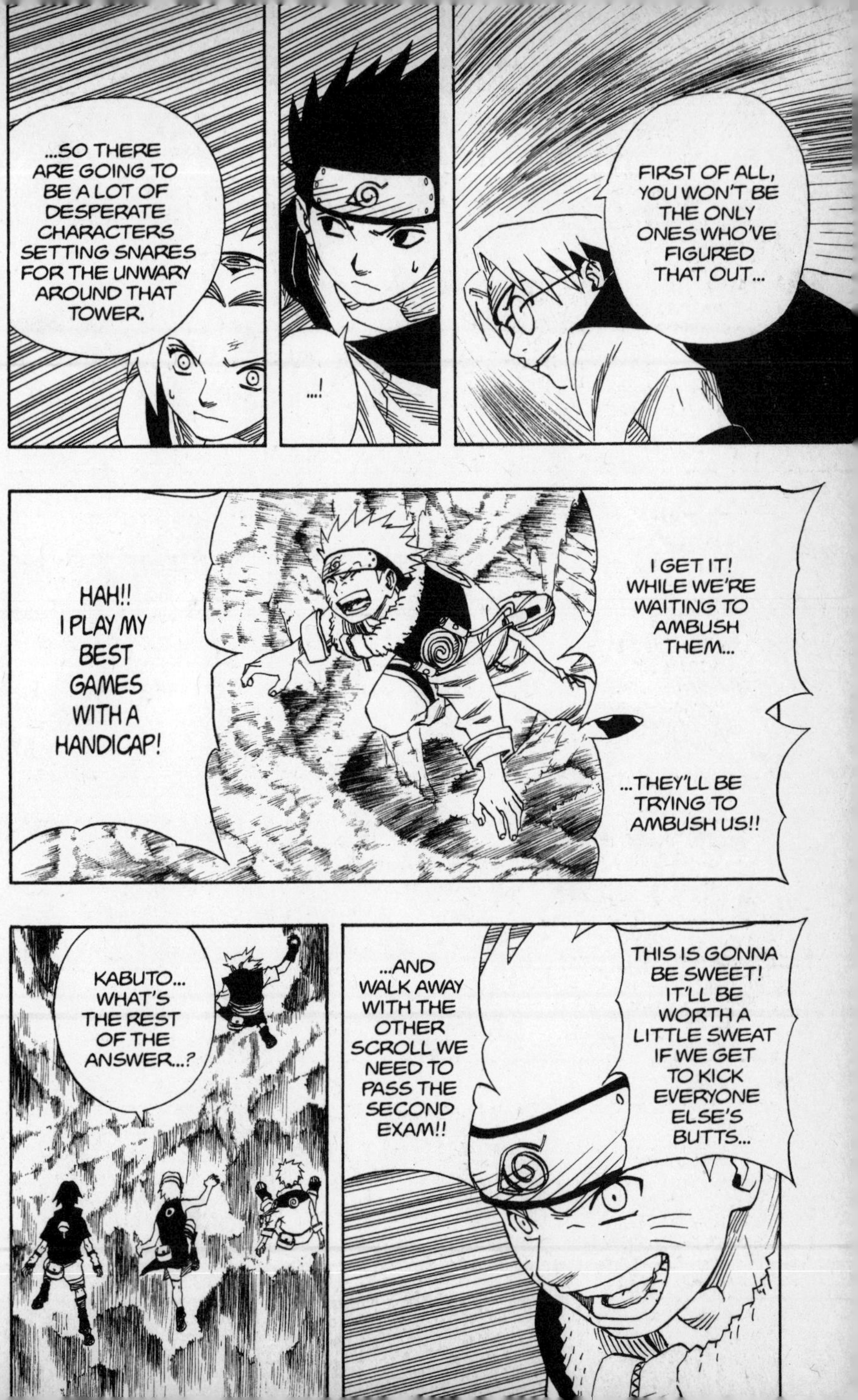
FIRST OF ALL, YOU WON'T BE THE ONLY ONES WHO'VE FIGURED THAT OUT...
...!
...SO THERE ARE GOING TO BE A LOT OF DESPERATE CHARACTERS SETTING SNARES FOR THE UNWARY AROUND THAT TOWER.
I GET IT! WHILE WE'RE WAITING TO AMBUSH THEM...
...THEY'LL BE TRYING TO AMBUSH US!!
HAH!! I PLAY MY BEST GAMES WITH A HANDICAP!
THIS IS GONNA BE SWEET! IT'LL BE WORTH A LITTLE SWEAT IF WE GET TO KICK EVERYONE ELSE'S BUTTS...
...AND WALK AWAY WITH THE OTHER SCROLL WE NEED TO PASS THE SECOND EXAM!!
KABUTO... WHAT'S THE REST OF THE ANSWER...?

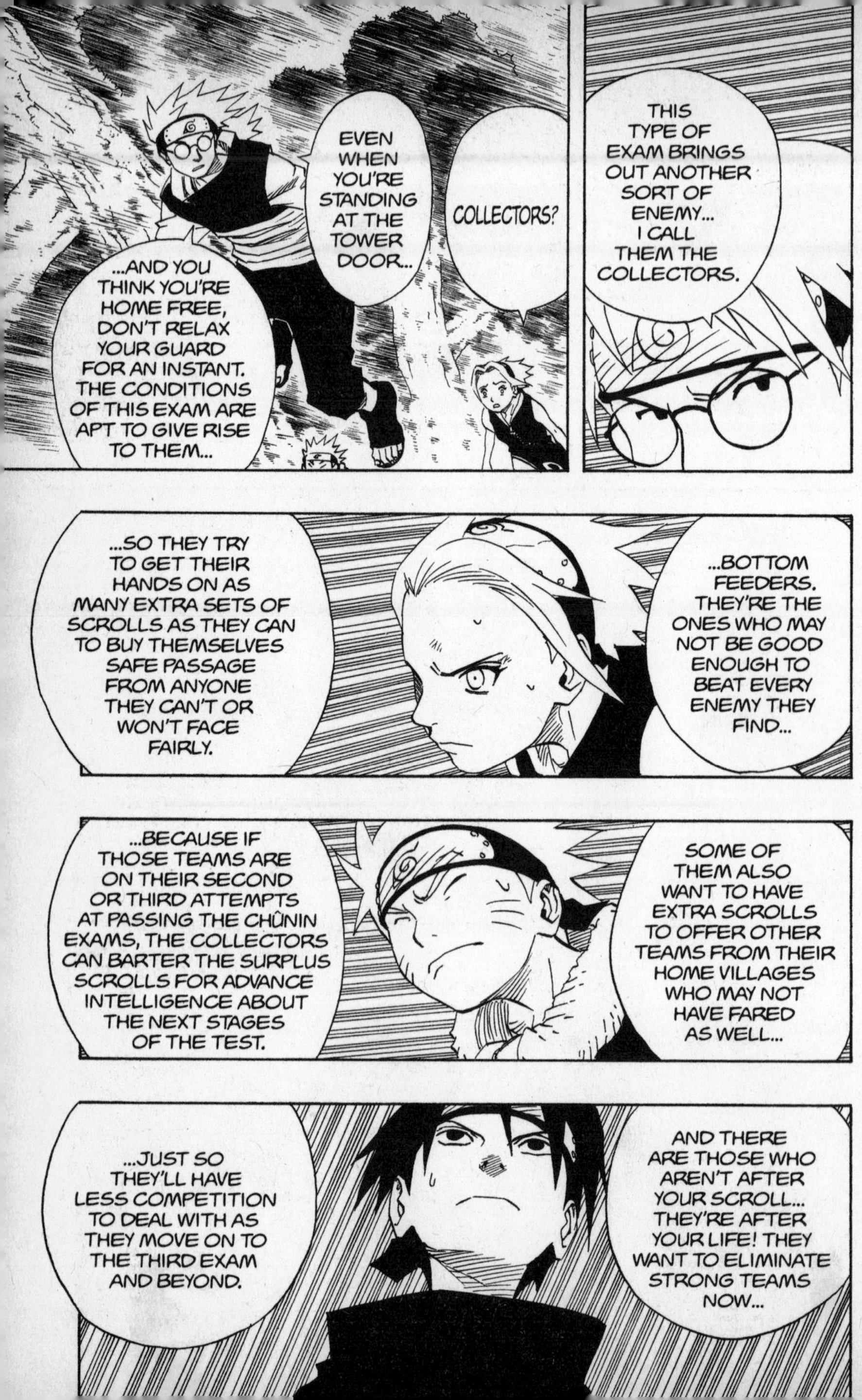
THIS TYPE OF EXAM BRINGS OUT ANOTHER SORT OF ENEMY... I CALL THEM THE COLLECTORS.
COLLECTORS?
EVEN WHEN YOU'RE STANDING AT THE TOWER DOOR...
...AND YOU THINK YOU'RE HOME FREE, DON'T RELAX YOUR GUARD FOR AN INSTANT. THE CONDITIONS OF THIS EXAM ARE APT TO GIVE RISE TO THEM...
...BOTTOM FEEDERS. THEY'RE THE ONES WHO MAY NOT BE GOOD ENOUGH TO BEAT EVERY ENEMY THEY FIND...
...SO THEY TRY TO GET THEIR HANDS ON AS MANY EXTRA SETS OF SCROLLS AS THEY CAN TO BUY THEMSELVES SAFE PASSAGE FROM ANYONE THEY CAN'T OR WON'T FACE FAIRLY.
SOME OF THEM ALSO WANT TO HAVE EXTRA SCROLLS TO OFFER OTHER TEAMS FROM THEIR HOME VILLAGES WHO MAY NOT HAVE FARED AS WELL...
...BECAUSE IF THOSE TEAMS ARE ON THEIR SECOND OR THIRD ATTEMPTS AT PASSING THE CHÛNIN EXAMS, THE COLLECTORS CAN BARTER THE SURPLUS SCROLLS FOR ADVANCE INTELLIGENCE ABOUT THE NEXT STAGES OF THE TEST.
AND THERE ARE THOSE WHO AREN'T AFTER YOUR SCROLL... THEY'RE AFTER YOUR LIFE! THEY WANT TO ELIMINATE STRONG TEAMS NOW...
...JUST SO THEY'LL HAVE LESS COMPETITION TO DEAL WITH AS THEY MOVE ON TO THE THIRD EXAM AND BEYOND.

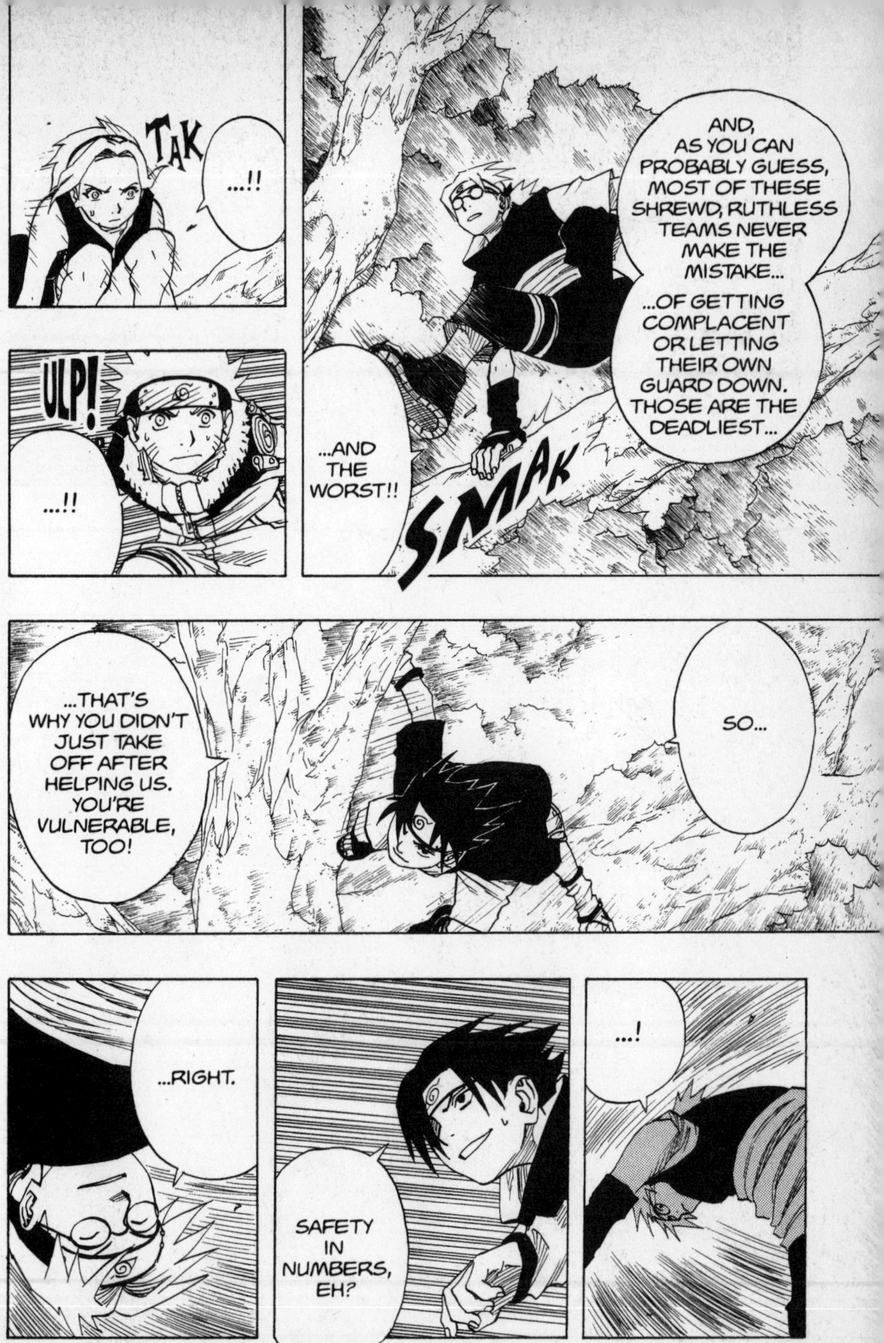
AND, AS YOU CAN PROBABLY GUESS, MOST OF THESE SHREWD, RUTHLESS TEAMS NEVER MAKE THE MISTAKE...
...OF GETTING COMPLACENT OR LETTING THEIR OWN GUARD DOWN. THOSE ARE THE DEADLIEST...
...AND THE WORST!!
SMAK
TAK
...!!
ULP!
...!!
SO...
...THAT'S WHY YOU DIDN'T JUST TAKE OFF AFTER HELPING US. YOU'RE VULNERABLE, TOO!
...!
SAFETY IN NUMBERS, EH?
...RIGHT.

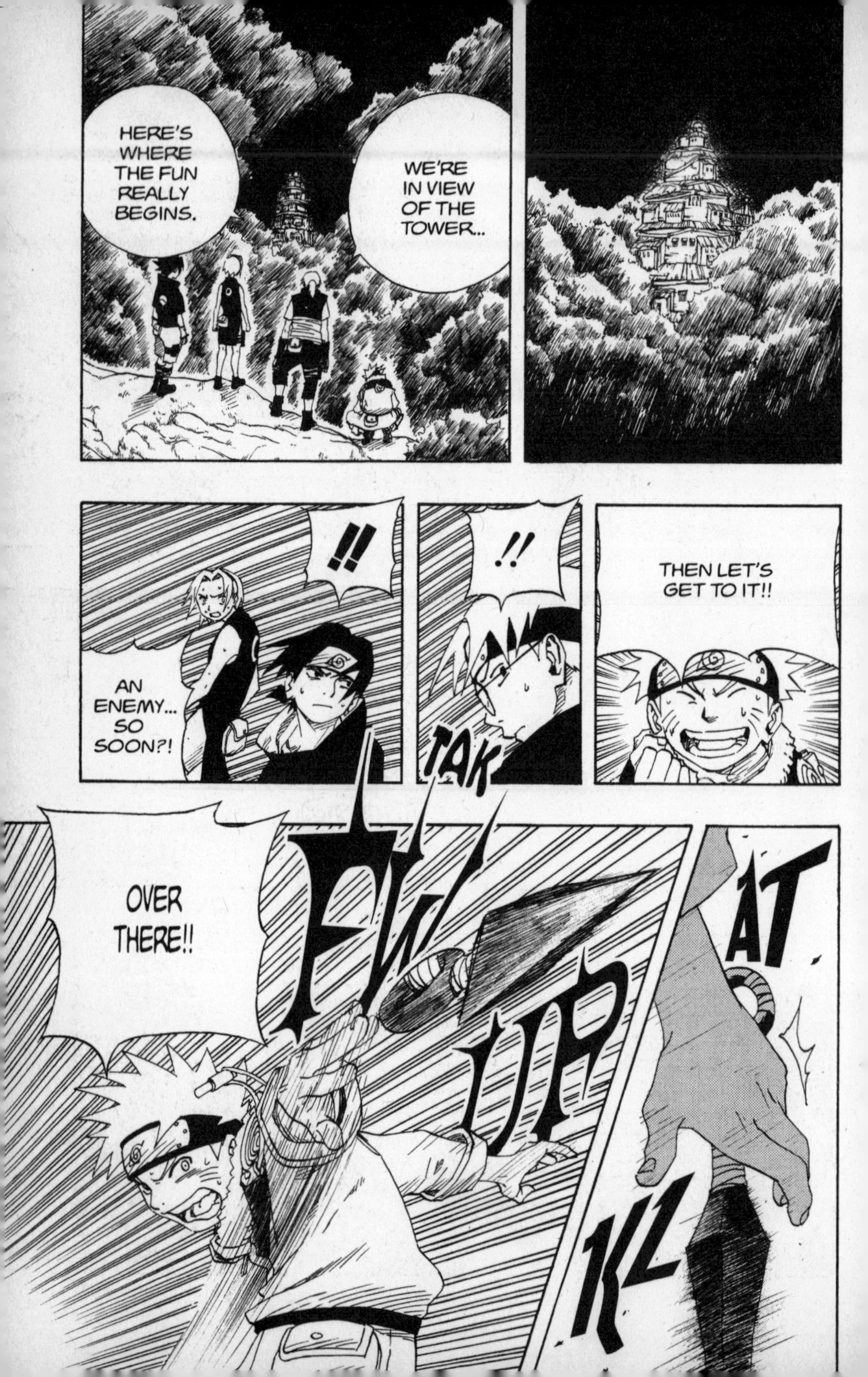
WE'RE IN VIEW OF THE TOWER...
HERE'S WHERE THE FUN REALLY BEGINS.
THEN LET'S GET TO IT!!
!!
TAK
!!
AN ENEMY... SO SOON?!
OVER THERE!!

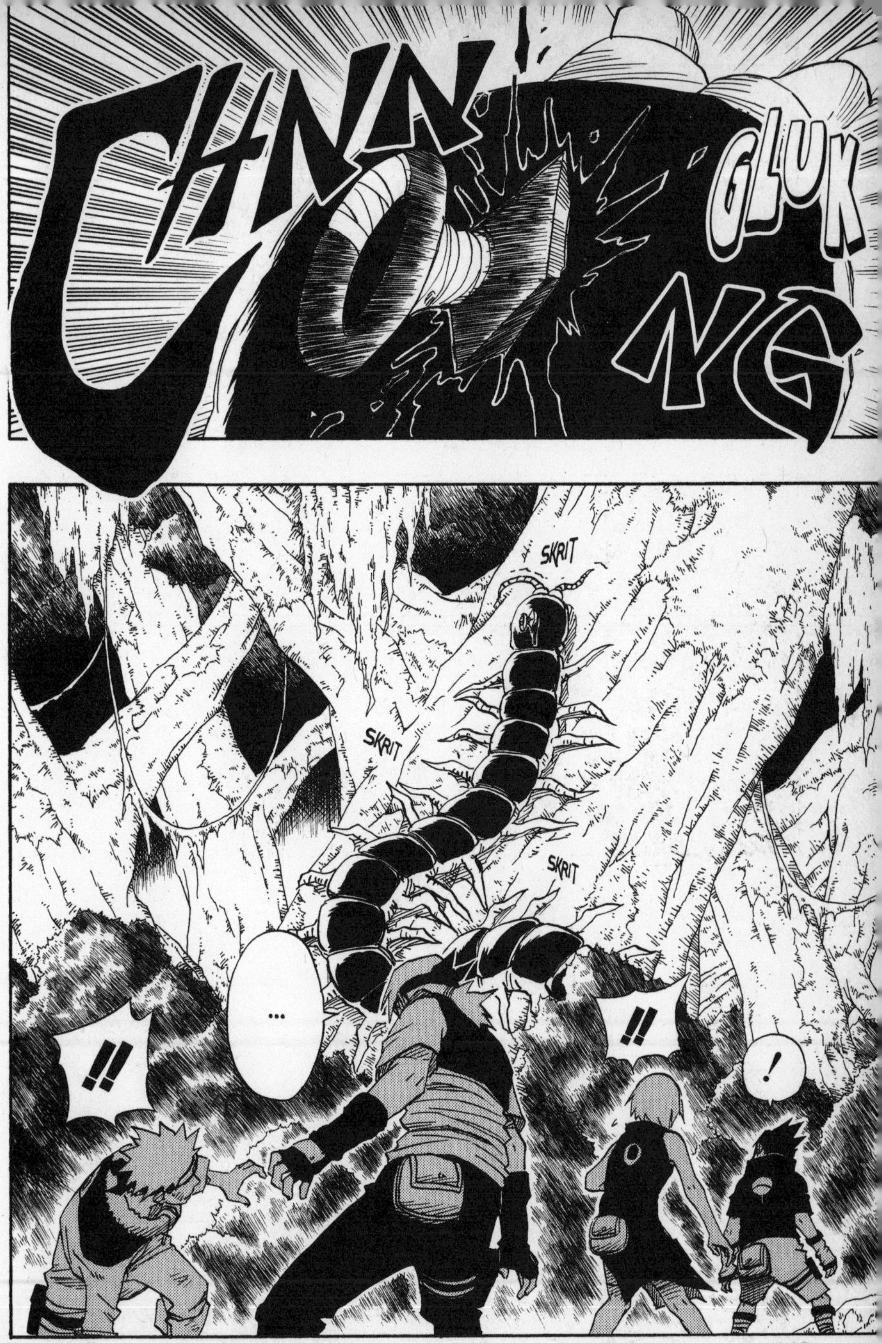
GLUK
NG
SKRIT
SKRIT
SKRIT
!
!!
...
!!

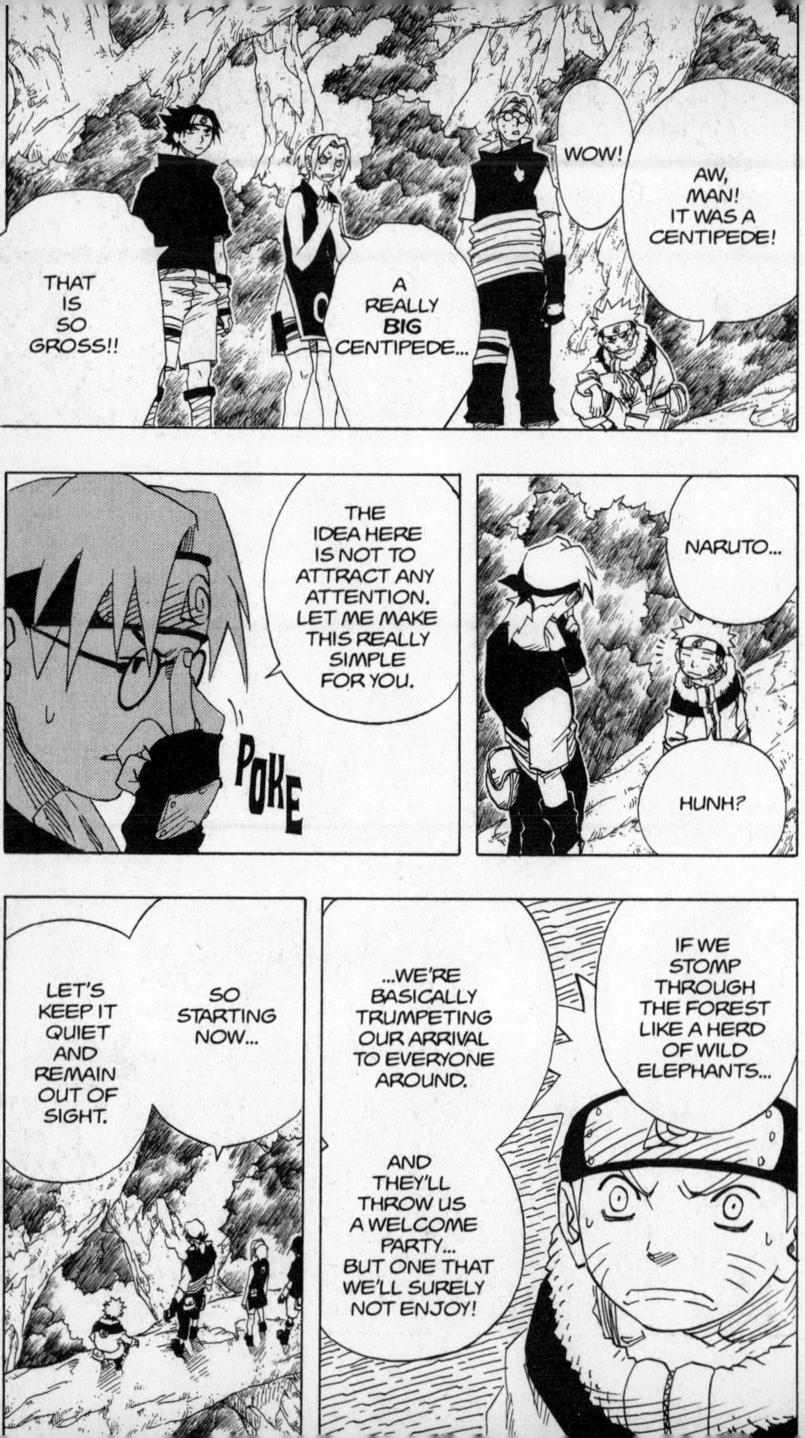
AW, MAN! IT WAS A CENTIPEDE!
WOW!
A REALLY **BIG** CENTIPEDE...
THAT IS SO GROSS!!
NARUTO...
HUNH?
THE IDEA HERE IS NOT TO ATTRACT ANY ATTENTION. LET ME MAKE THIS REALLY SIMPLE FOR YOU.
POKE
IF WE STOMP THROUGH THE FOREST LIKE A HERD OF WILD ELEPHANTS...
...WE'RE BASICALLY TRUMPETING OUR ARRIVAL TO EVERYONE AROUND.
AND THEY'LL THROW US A WELCOME PARTY... BUT ONE THAT WE'LL SURELY NOT ENJOY!
SO STARTING NOW...
LET'S KEEP IT QUIET AND REMAIN OUT OF SIGHT.

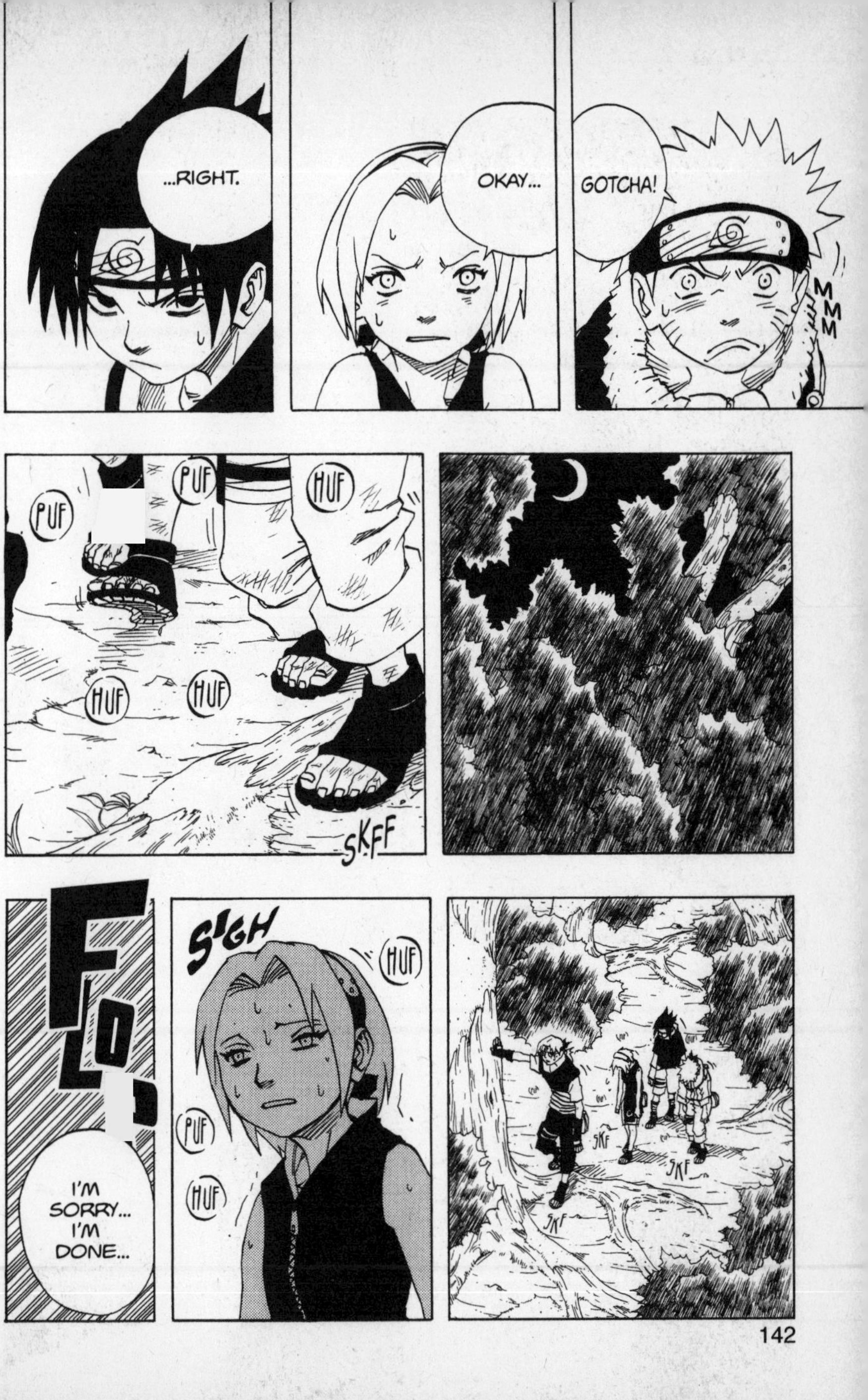
GOTCHA!
MMM
OKAY...
...RIGHT.
HUF
PUF
PUF
HUF
HUF
SKFF
SKF
SKF
SKF
SIGH
HUF
PUF
HUF
I'M SORRY... I'M DONE...

READ THIS WAY

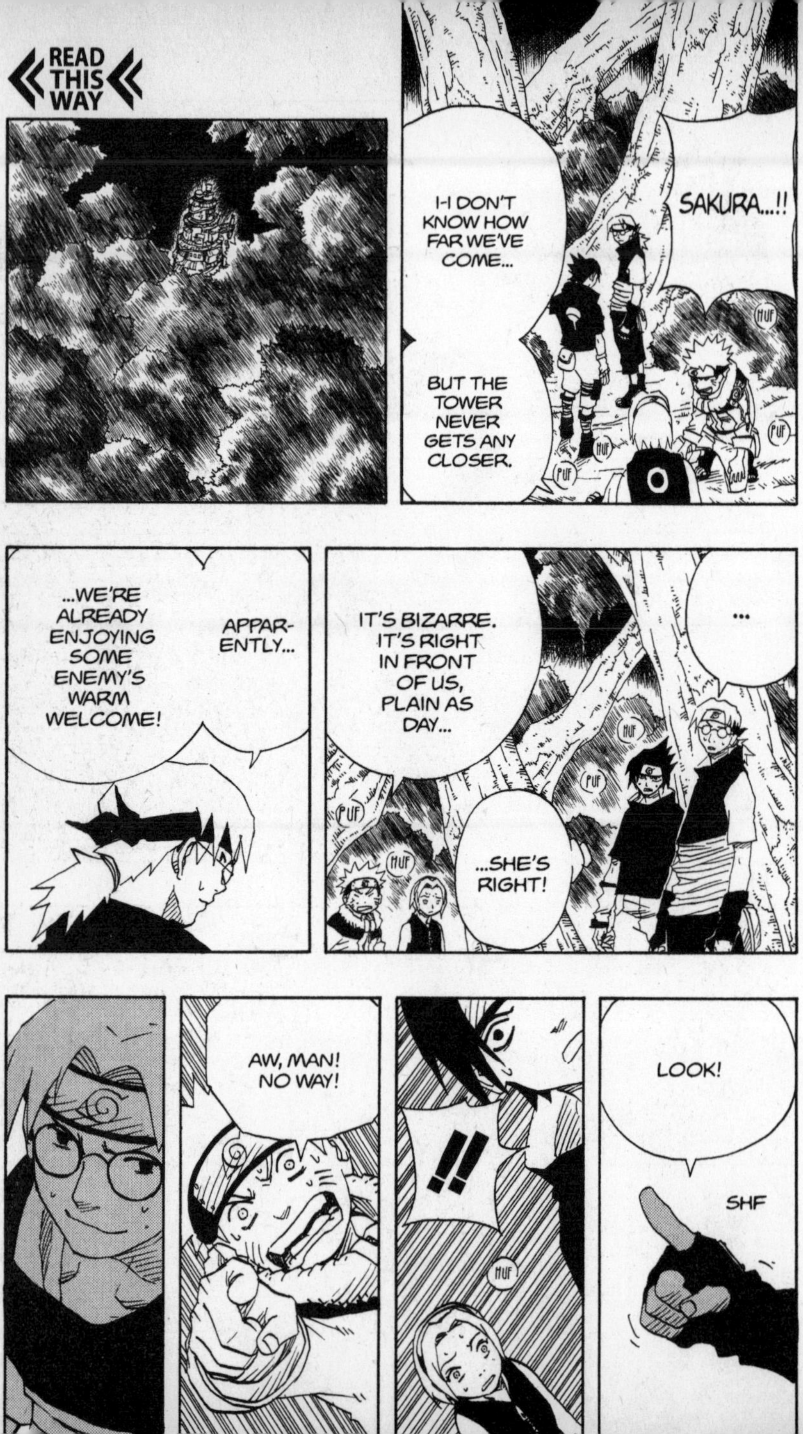
SAKURA...!!
I-I DON'T KNOW HOW FAR WE'VE COME...
BUT THE TOWER NEVER GETS ANY CLOSER.
HUF
PUF
...
IT'S BIZARRE. IT'S RIGHT IN FRONT OF US, PLAIN AS DAY...
...SHE'S RIGHT!
APPAR-ENTLY...
...WE'RE ALREADY ENJOYING SOME ENEMY'S WARM WELCOME!
LOOK!
SHF
!!
HUF
AW, MAN! NO WAY!

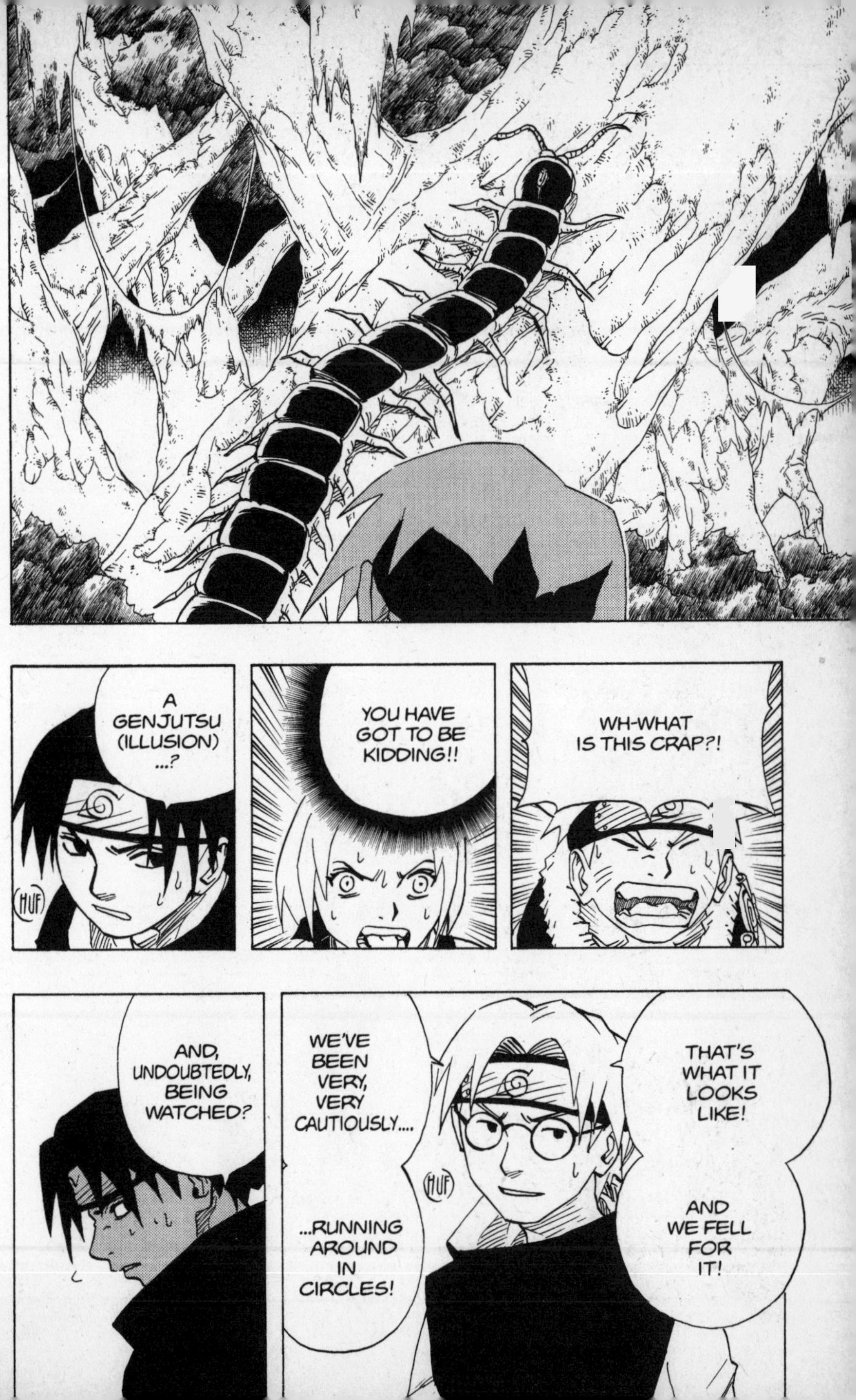
WH-WHAT IS THIS CRAP?!
YOU HAVE GOT TO BE KIDDING!!
A GENJUTSU (ILLUSION) ...?
HUF
THAT'S WHAT IT LOOKS LIKE!
AND WE FELL FOR IT!
HUF
WE'VE BEEN VERY, VERY CAUTIOUSLY....
...RUNNING AROUND IN CIRCLES!
AND, UNDOUBTEDLY, BEING WATCHED?

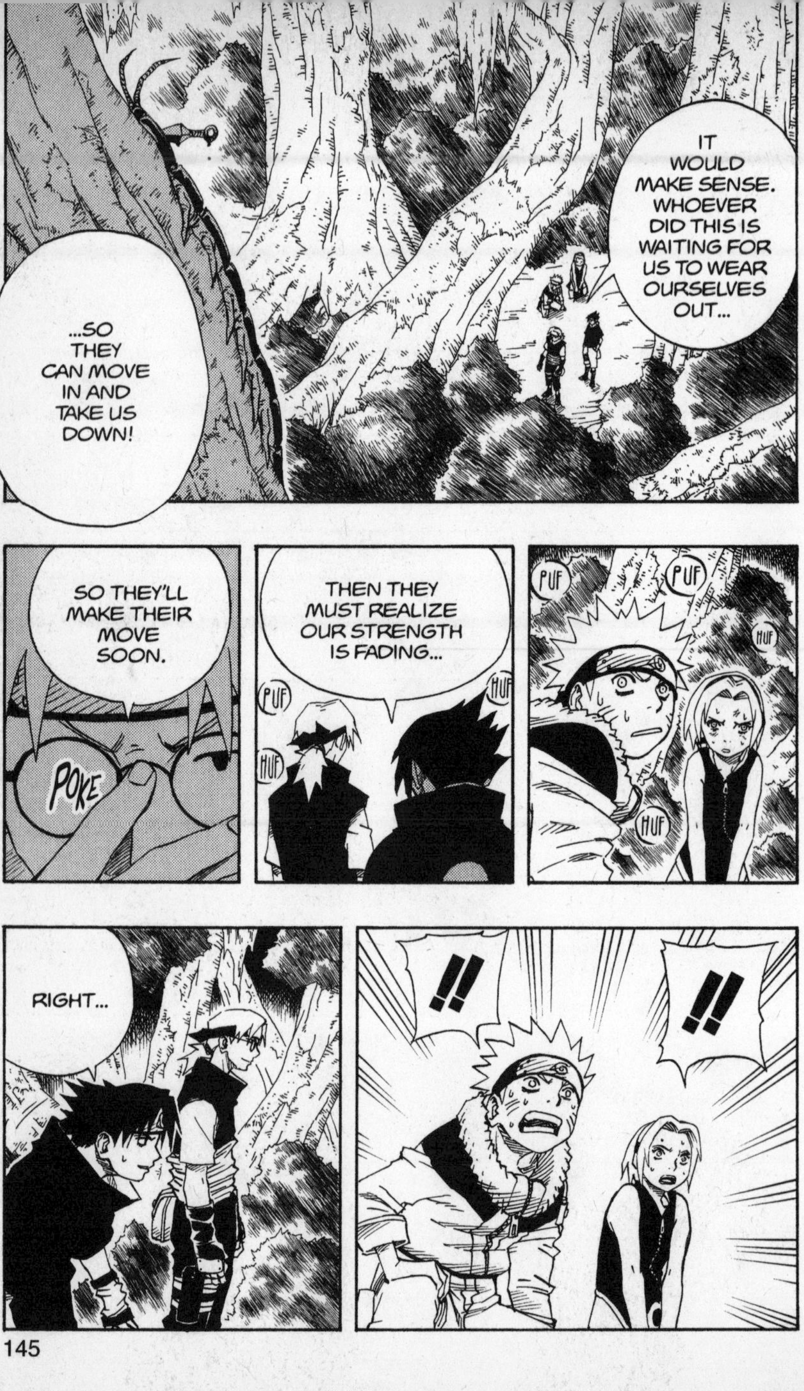

IT WOULD MAKE SENSE. WHOEVER DID THIS IS WAITING FOR US TO WEAR OURSELVES OUT...
...SO THEY CAN MOVE IN AND TAKE US DOWN!
PUF
PUF
HUF
HUF
THEN THEY MUST REALIZE OUR STRENGTH IS FADING...
HUF
PUF
HUF
SO THEY'LL MAKE THEIR MOVE SOON.
POKE
!!
!!
RIGHT...

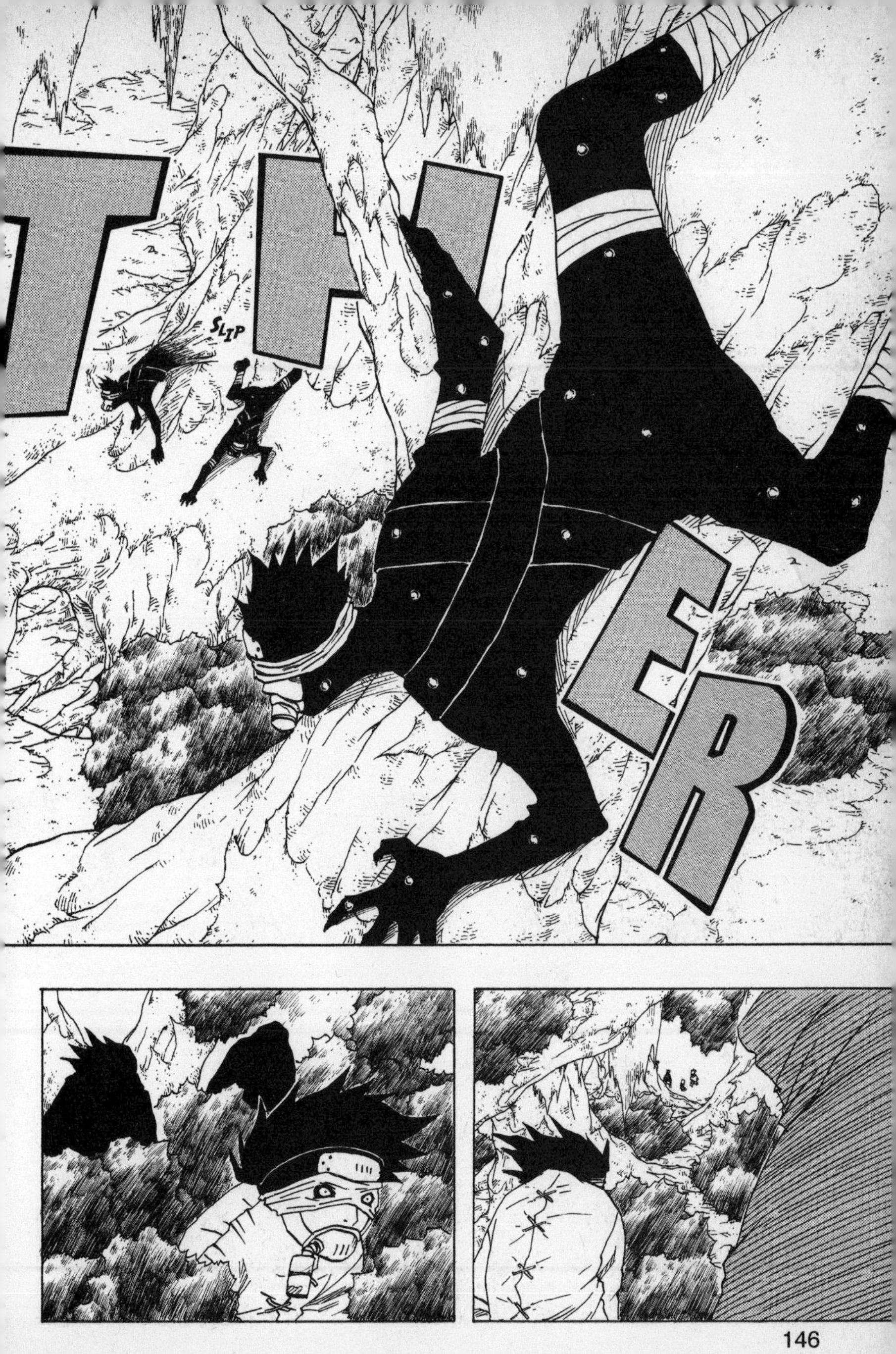
SLIP

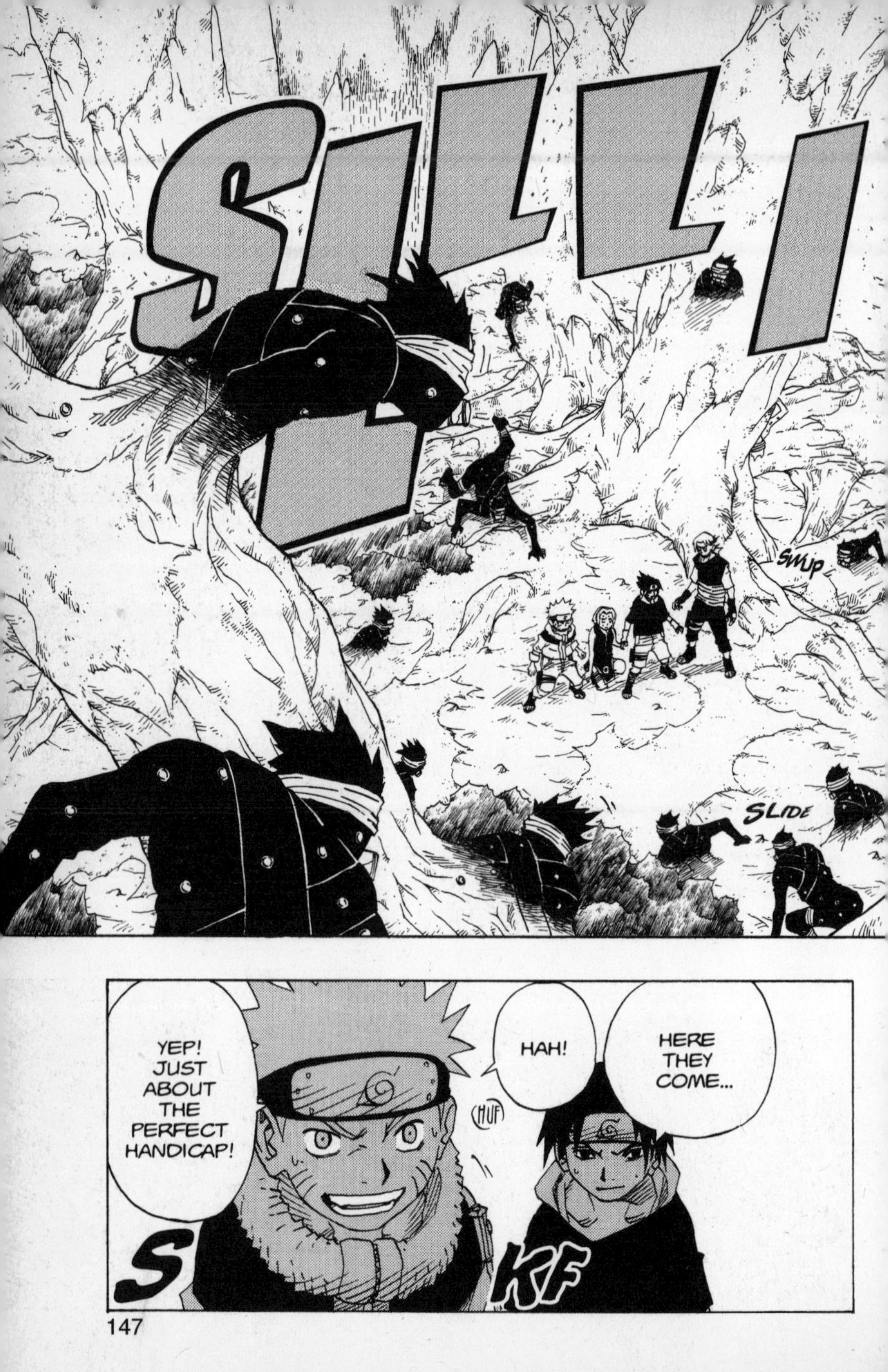
SWUP
SLIDE
HERE THEY COME...
HAH!
HUF
YEP! JUST ABOUT THE PERFECT HANDICAP!

THE WORLD OF KISHIMOTO MASASHI
MY PERSONAL HISTORY, PART 4: GRADE-SCHOOL OBSESSIONS

BY THE MIDDLE OF ELEMENTARY SCHOOL, MY INTEREST HAD GROWN TO INCLUDE SCULPTING AND MODEL-MAKING. INITIALLY, ANY TIME MY PARENTS WOULDN'T BUY ME A TOY I REALLY WANTED, I'D MAKE IT FOR MYSELF OUT OF CLAY. BUT THAT DIDN'T SATISFY ME FOR LONG, SO I TURNED TO THE PLASTIC MODELS BASED ON THE GUNDAM SERIES -- GUNPLA (GUNDAM PLASTIC) FOR SHORT. I GOT SOME FOR A NEW YEAR'S GIFT AND ASSEMBLED THEM IN AN ABSOLUTE FRENZY. THE NEXT FAD WAS PLAMORAJICON (OR PLARAJI) -- RADIO-CONTROLLED PLASTIC MODEL VEHICLES -- AND I JUMPED ON THAT PONY AS WELL (IN AMERICA, THESE WERE CALLED R/C CARS).

I NAMED MY PLARAJI "THE ELEPHANT," MADE AN ELEPHANT-SHAPED DECAL OUT OF SHEET PLASTIC, STUCK IT ON, AND RACED IT... DUE, NO DOUBT, TO THE INFLUENCE OF A POPULAR MANGA OF THE TIME CALLED "RAJICON BOY." THE PLARAJI I OWNED WAS BASED ON THE MITSUBISHI PAJERO, BUT IT WASN'T VERY FAST, AND WAS CONSTANTLY BEING OVERTAKEN BY THE PLARAJIS OF MY LITTLE BROTHER AND ALL OF MY FRIENDS. THIS ANNOYED ME VERY MUCH, SO I REMODELED MY PAJERO WITH THE "GRASSHOPPER UPGRADE KIT," WHICH WAS ACTUALLY DESIGNED FOR A DIFFERENT MODEL ENTIRELY. I MELTED THE PAJERO'S PLASTIC CHASSIS WITH A SOLDERING IRON -- NEVER GIVING A THOUGHT TO THE TOXIC FUMES BEING RELEASED INTO THE UNVENTILATED LITTLE ROOM -- AND WAS ECSTATIC WHEN I SUCCEEDED IN MAKING THE UPGRADE. BUT MY IDIOTIC ELATION WAS SHORT-LIVED, AS NEW PROBLEMS QUICKLY UNFOLDED!

BECAUSE I HAD FORCIBLY WELDED INCOMPATIBLE PARTS ONTO MY CAR, THE PAJERO'S BODY NO LONGER FIT WELL ONTO THE CHASSIS. I WAS TERRIBLY DEPRESSED OVER THE IRREVERSIBLE DAMAGE I'D DONE TO MY CAR, WITH THE BODY LEANING OFF THE CHASSIS AT ABOUT A TEN-DEGREE ANGLE, BUT I INSISTED THAT APPEARANCE MEANT NOTHING. A PLARAJI SHOULD BE JUDGED BY HOW IT PERFORMS, NOT HOW IT LOOKS! BUT WHEN WE RACED AGAIN, THE OTHERS OUTMATCHED MY POOR LITTLE CAR IN BOTH SPEED **AND** APPEARANCE.

UNDAUNTED EVEN AFTER GETTING HIT WITH THIS ONE-TWO COMBINATION OF DISAPPOINTMENTS, I MANAGED TO GET MY HANDS ON AN INCREDIBLE MOTOR CALLED THE "BLACK MOTOR ANGELS" AND INSTALLED IT IN THE PAJERO. "I'LL NEVER LOSE AGAIN!" I SAID, AND FINALLY WON THE RACING VICTORY THAT HAD BEEN MY HEART'S DESIRE. BUT THE MOTOR WAS SO POWERFUL THAT SUDDENLY SMOKE BEGAN POURING OUT OF THE CONTROLS. THE PAJERO WOULD NEVER ENTER ANOTHER RACE. I KEPT IT ON DISPLAY IN MY ROOM, BUT IN MY HEART I WAS DESPONDENT AND FULL OF REGRET ABOUT EVER HAVING TRIED THE GRASSHOPPER UPGRADE KIT.

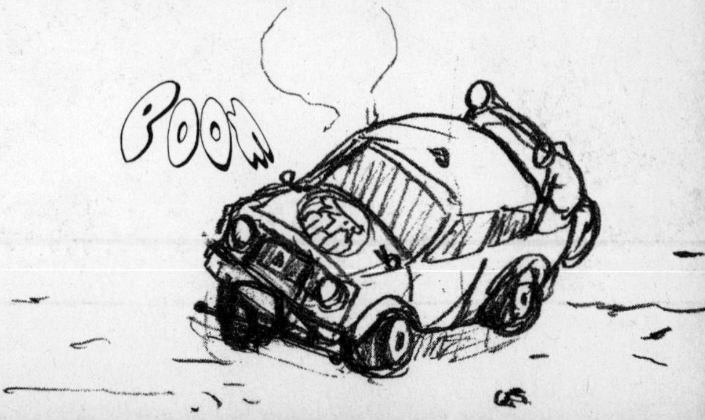
POOM

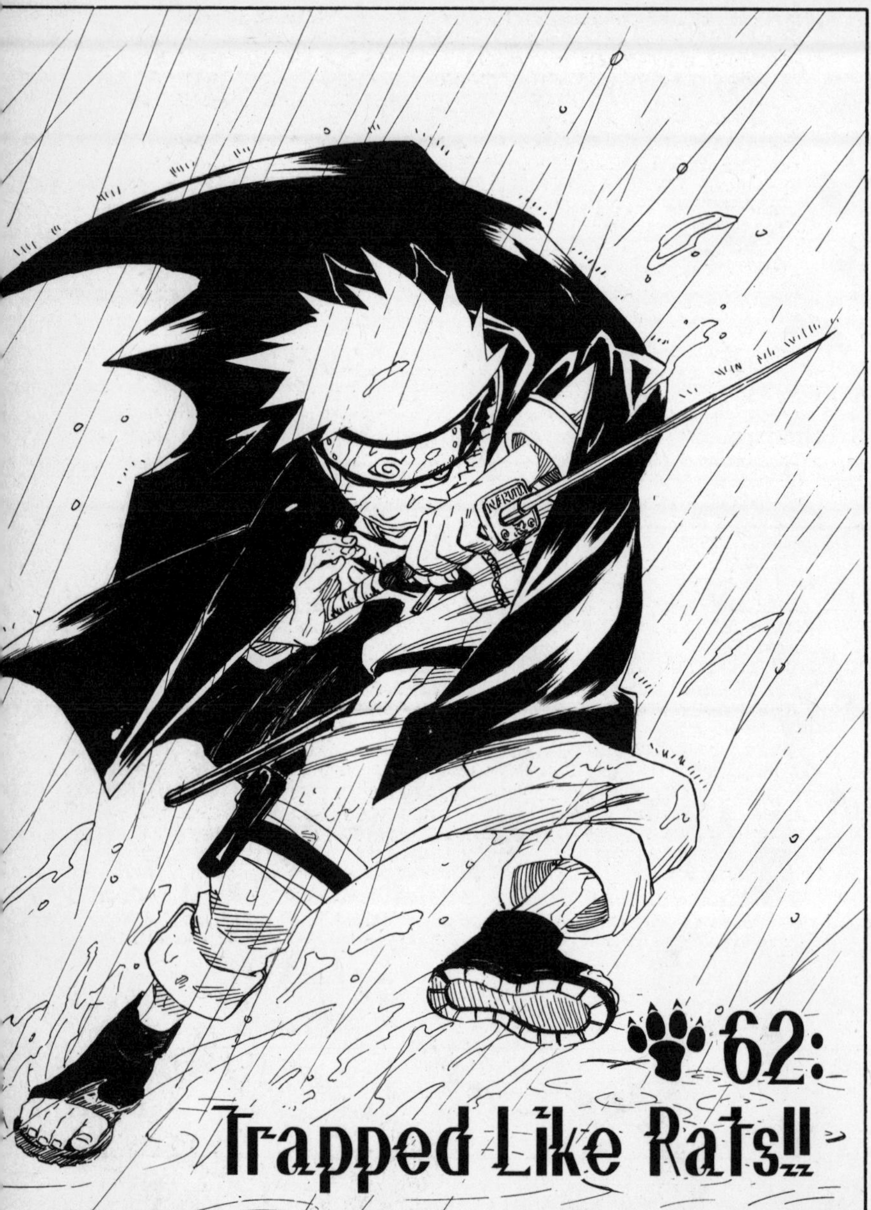
62:
Trapped Like Rats!!

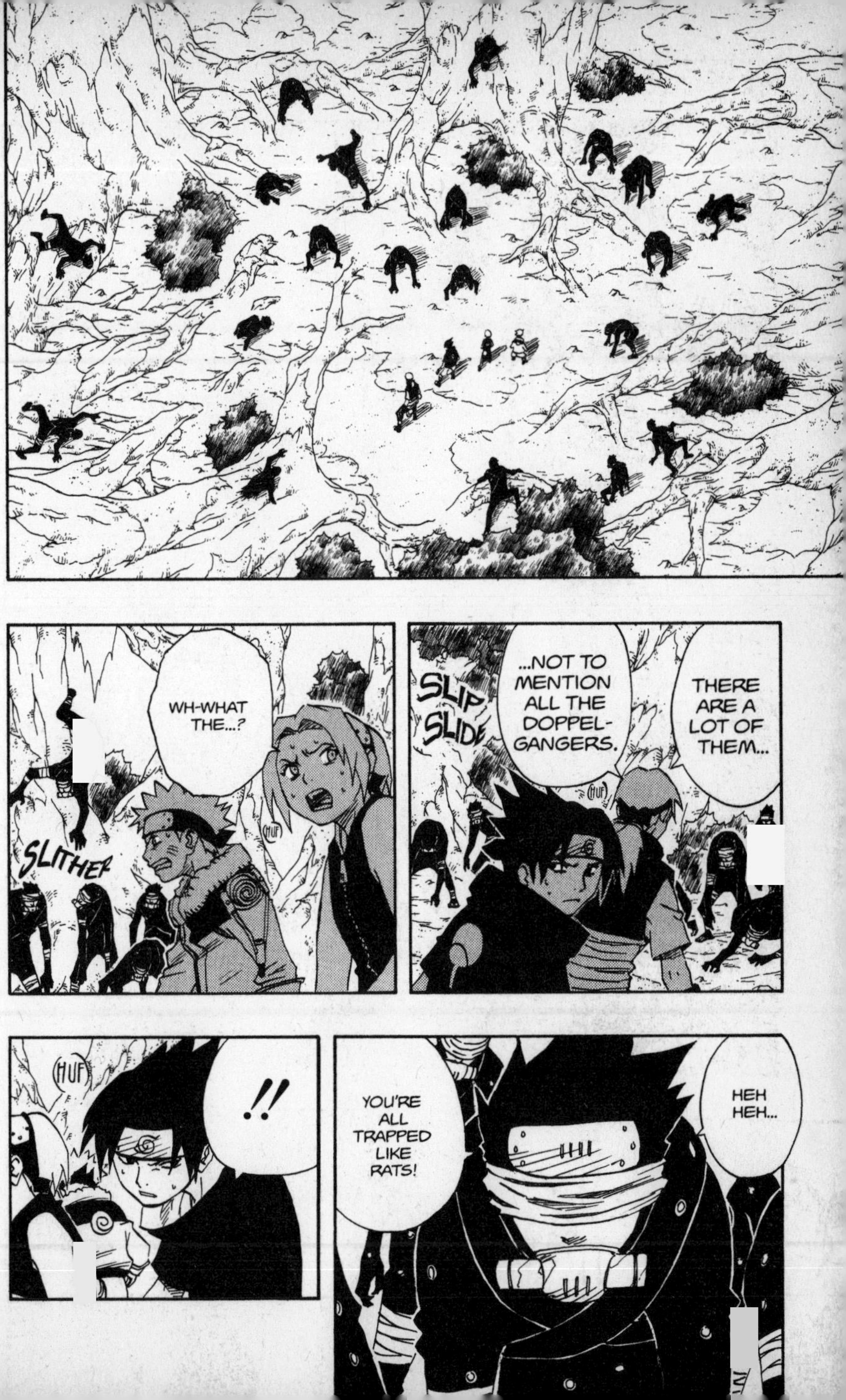
THERE ARE A LOT OF THEM...
...NOT TO MENTION ALL THE DOPPEL-GANGERS.
HUF
SLIP SLIDE
WH-WHAT THE...?
HUF
SLITHER
HEH HEH...
YOU'RE ALL TRAPPED LIKE RATS!
!!
HUF

READ THIS WAY

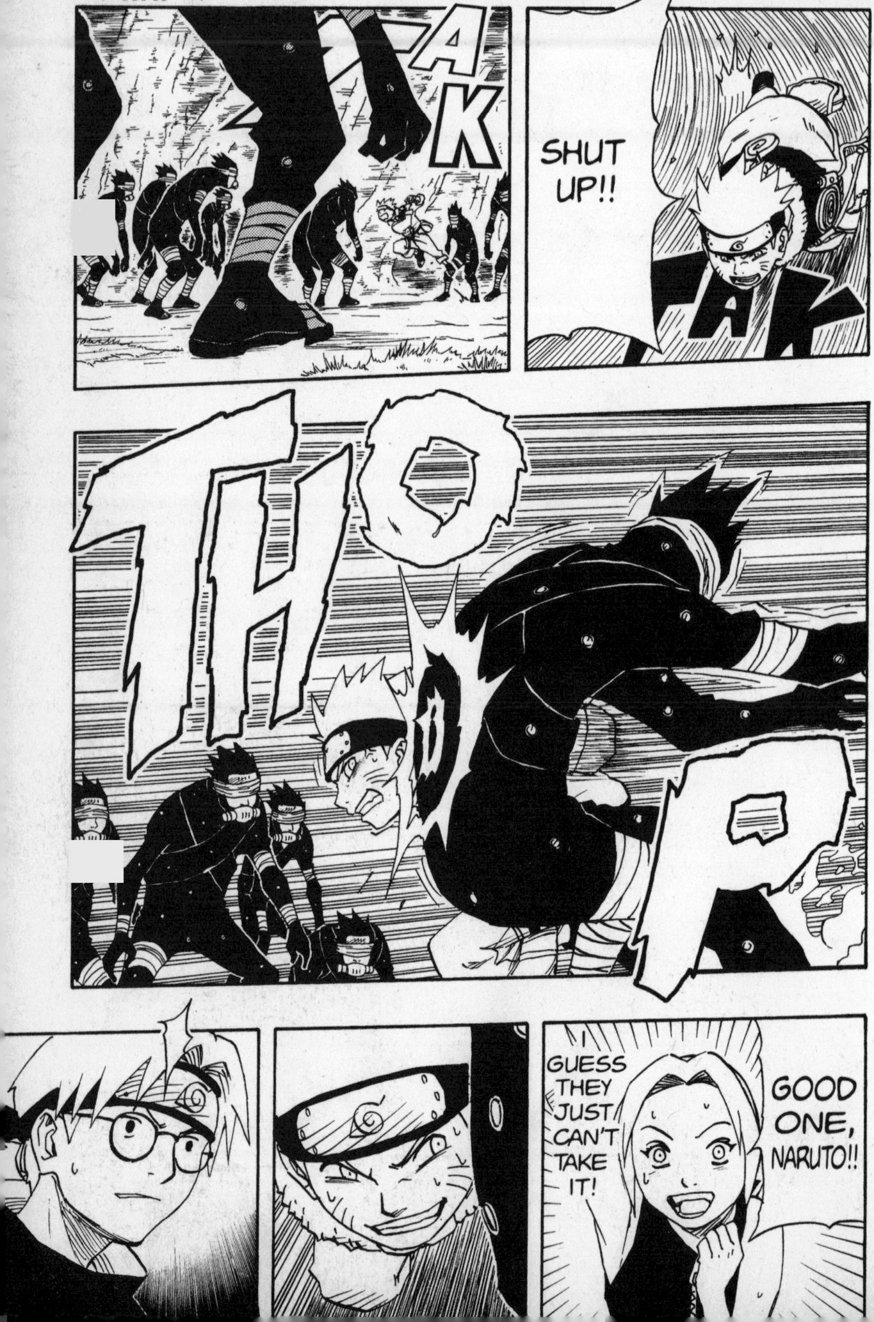
SHUT UP!!
AK
THOP
GOOD ONE, NARUTO!!
I GUESS THEY JUST CAN'T TAKE IT!

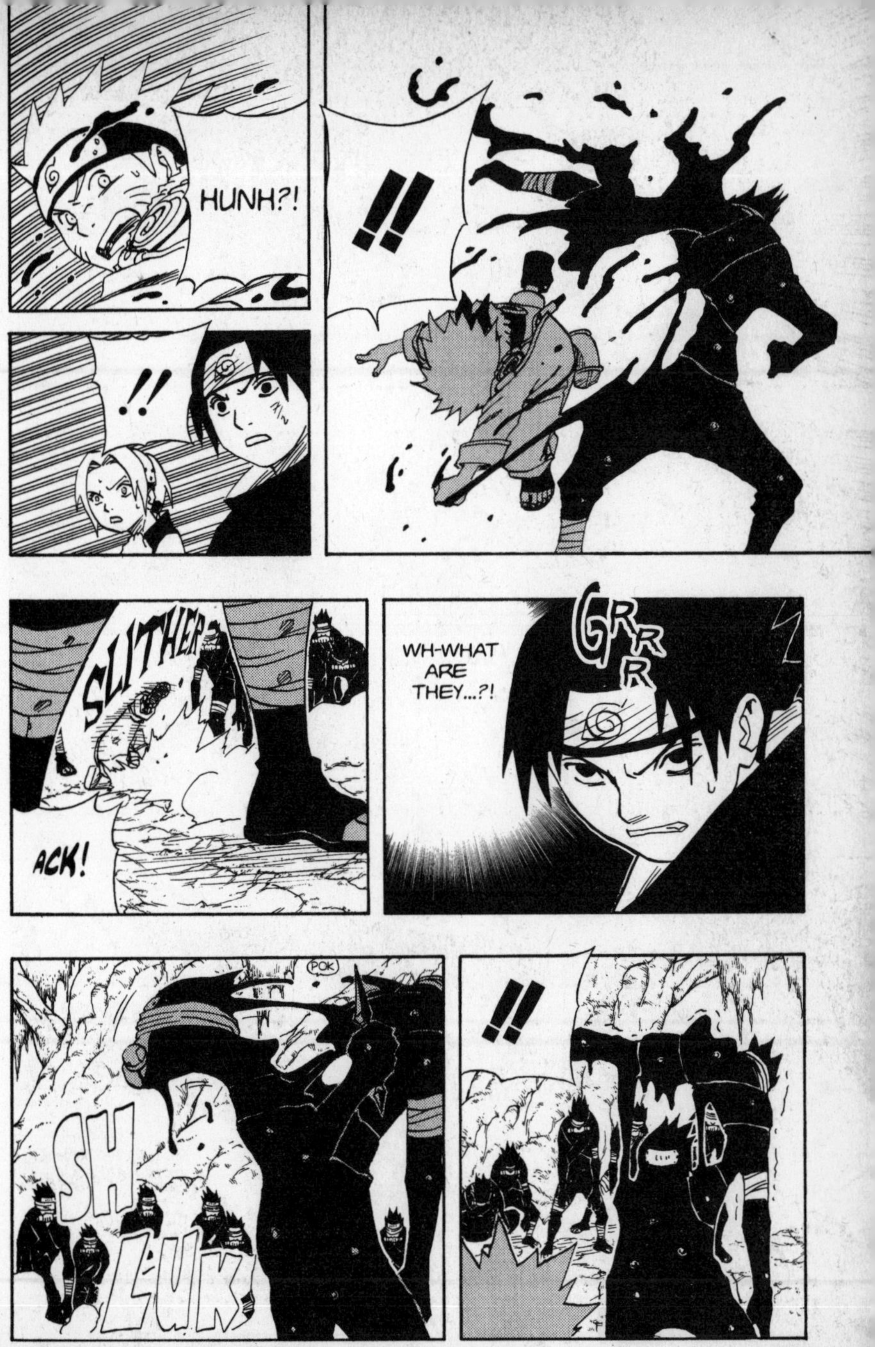
!!
HUNH?!
!!
GRRR
WH-WHAT ARE THEY...?!
SLITHER
ACK!
!!
POK
SHLUK

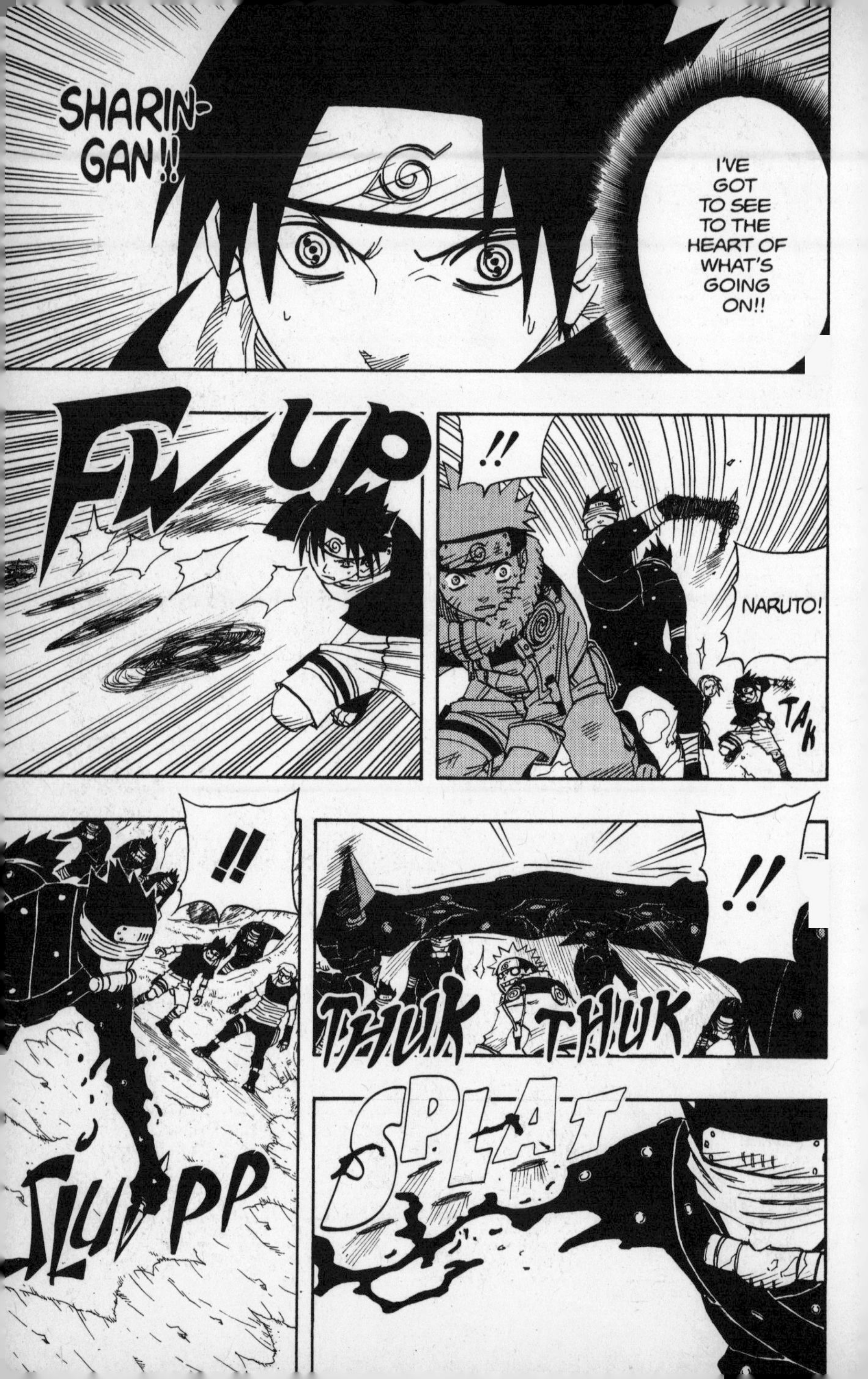

I'VE GOT TO SEE TO THE HEART OF WHAT'S GOING ON!!
SHARIN-GAN!!
!!
NARUTO!
TAK
FWUP
!!
THUK THUK
SPLAT
!!
SLUPP

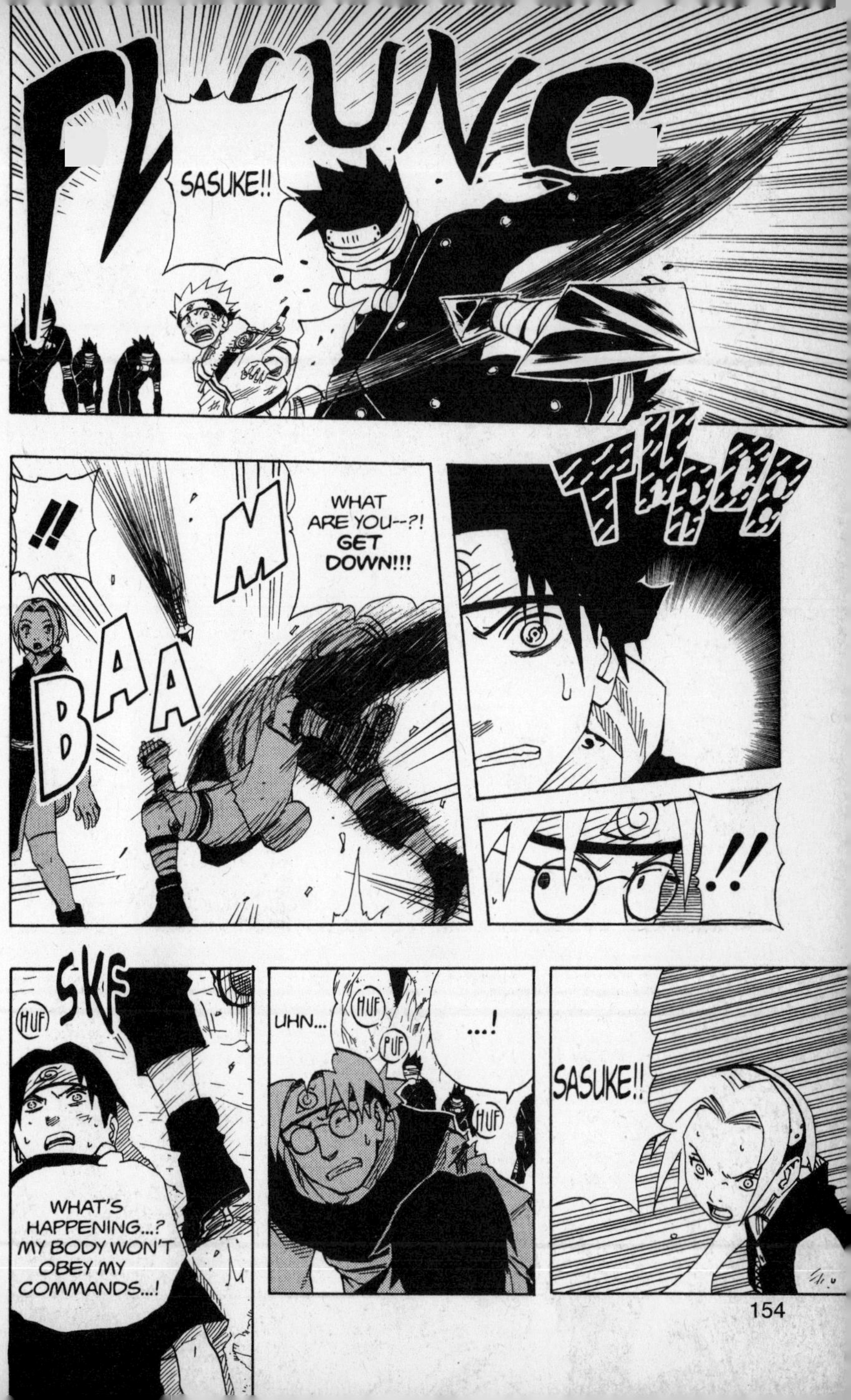
SASUKE!!
!!
WHAT ARE YOU--?! GET DOWN!!!
BAAM
!!
SASUKE!!
...!
HUF
PUF
UHN...
HUF
SKF
HUF
WHAT'S HAPPENING...? MY BODY WON'T OBEY MY COMMANDS...!

READ THIS WAY

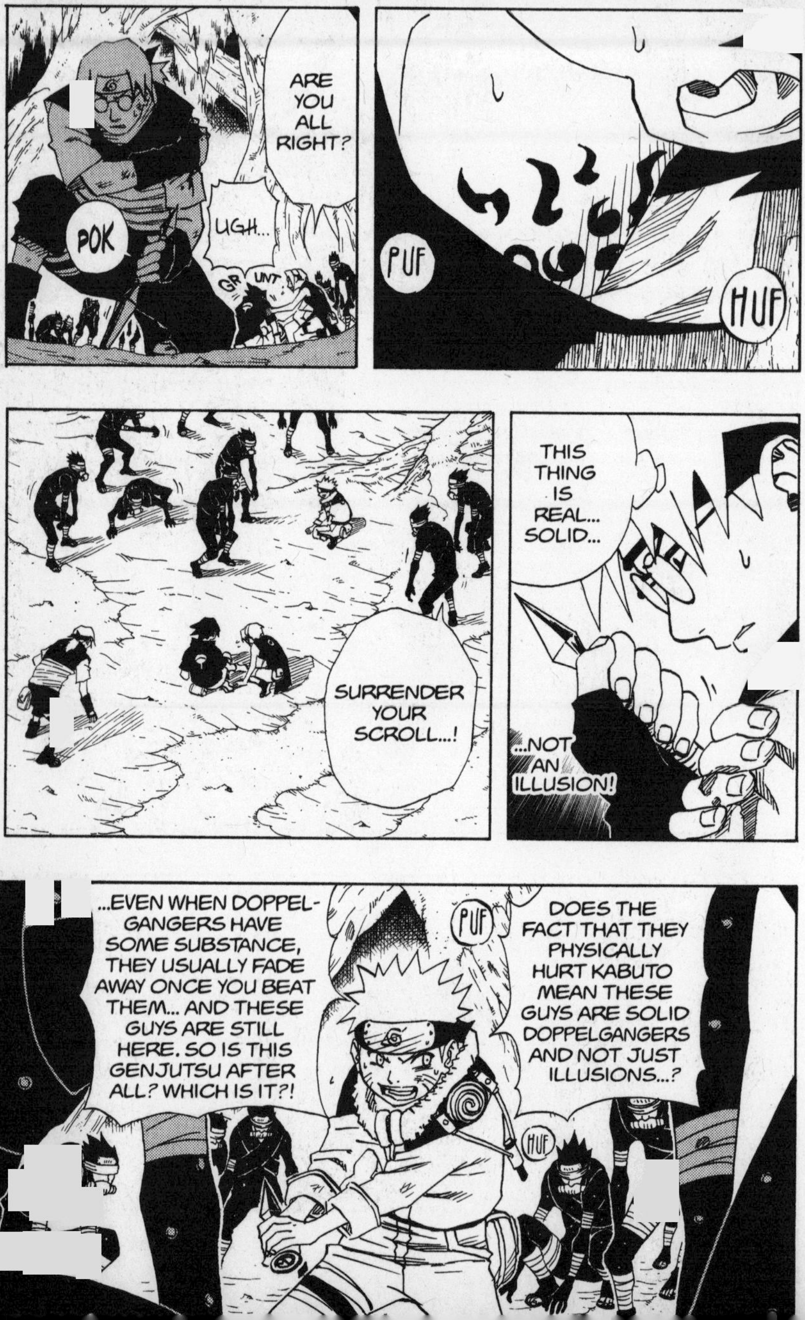
PUF
HUF
ARE YOU ALL RIGHT?
UGH...
GRUNT
POK
THIS THING IS REAL... SOLID...
...NOT AN ILLUSION!
SURRENDER YOUR SCROLL...!
DOES THE FACT THAT THEY PHYSICALLY HURT KABUTO MEAN THESE GUYS ARE SOLID DOPPELGANGERS AND NOT JUST ILLUSIONS...?
PUF
...EVEN WHEN DOPPEL-GANGERS HAVE SOME SUBSTANCE, THEY USUALLY FADE AWAY ONCE YOU BEAT THEM... AND THESE GUYS ARE STILL HERE. SO IS THIS GENJUTSU AFTER ALL? WHICH IS IT?!
HUF

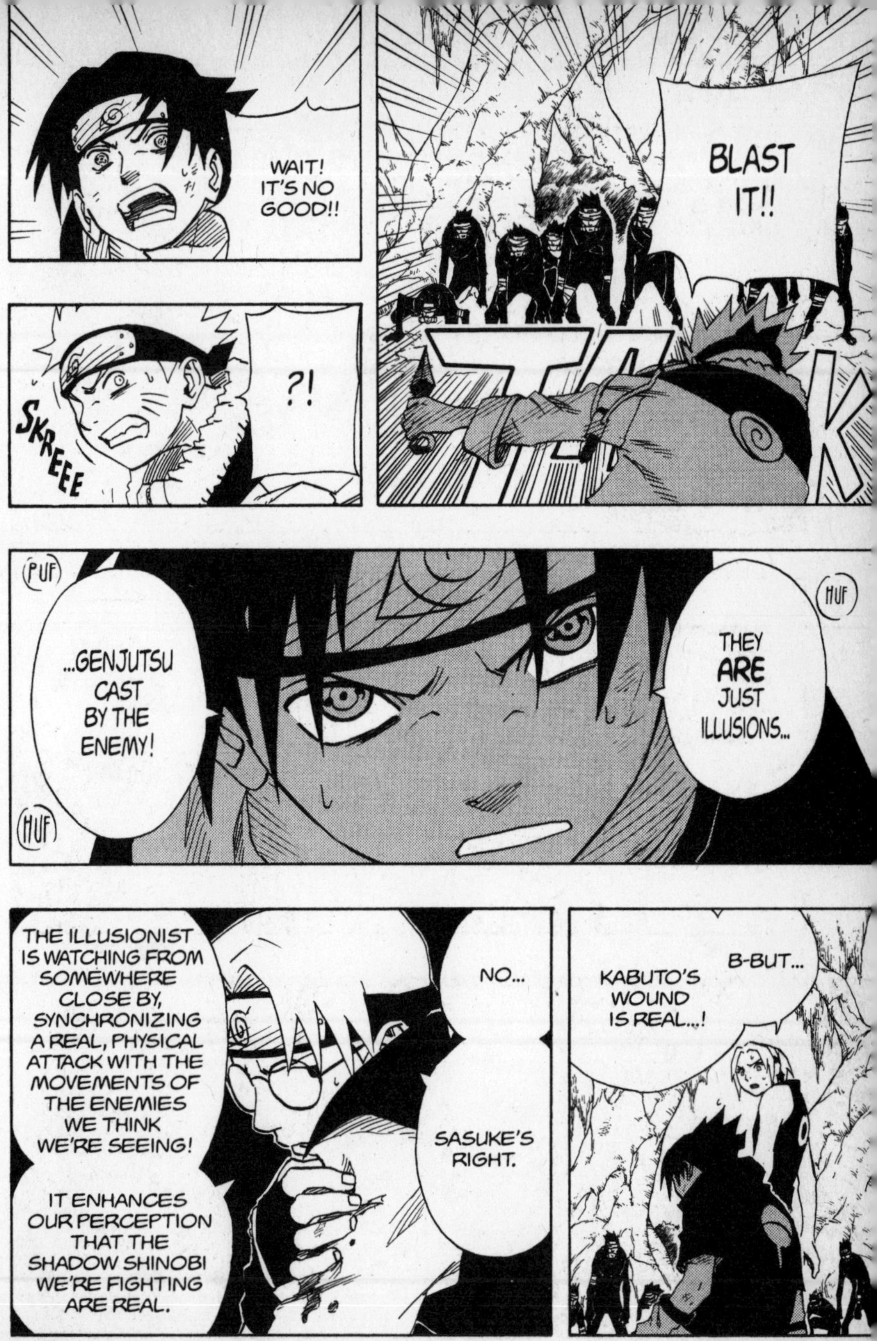
BLAST IT!!
TAK
WAIT! IT'S NO GOOD!!
?!
SKREEE
HUF
THEY ARE JUST ILLUSIONS...
PUF
...GENJUTSU CAST BY THE ENEMY!
HUF
B-BUT...
KABUTO'S WOUND IS REAL...!
NO...
SASUKE'S RIGHT.
THE ILLUSIONIST IS WATCHING FROM SOMEWHERE CLOSE BY, SYNCHRONIZING A REAL, PHYSICAL ATTACK WITH THE MOVEMENTS OF THE ENEMIES WE THINK WE'RE SEEING!
IT ENHANCES OUR PERCEPTION THAT THE SHADOW SHINOBI WE'RE FIGHTING ARE REAL.

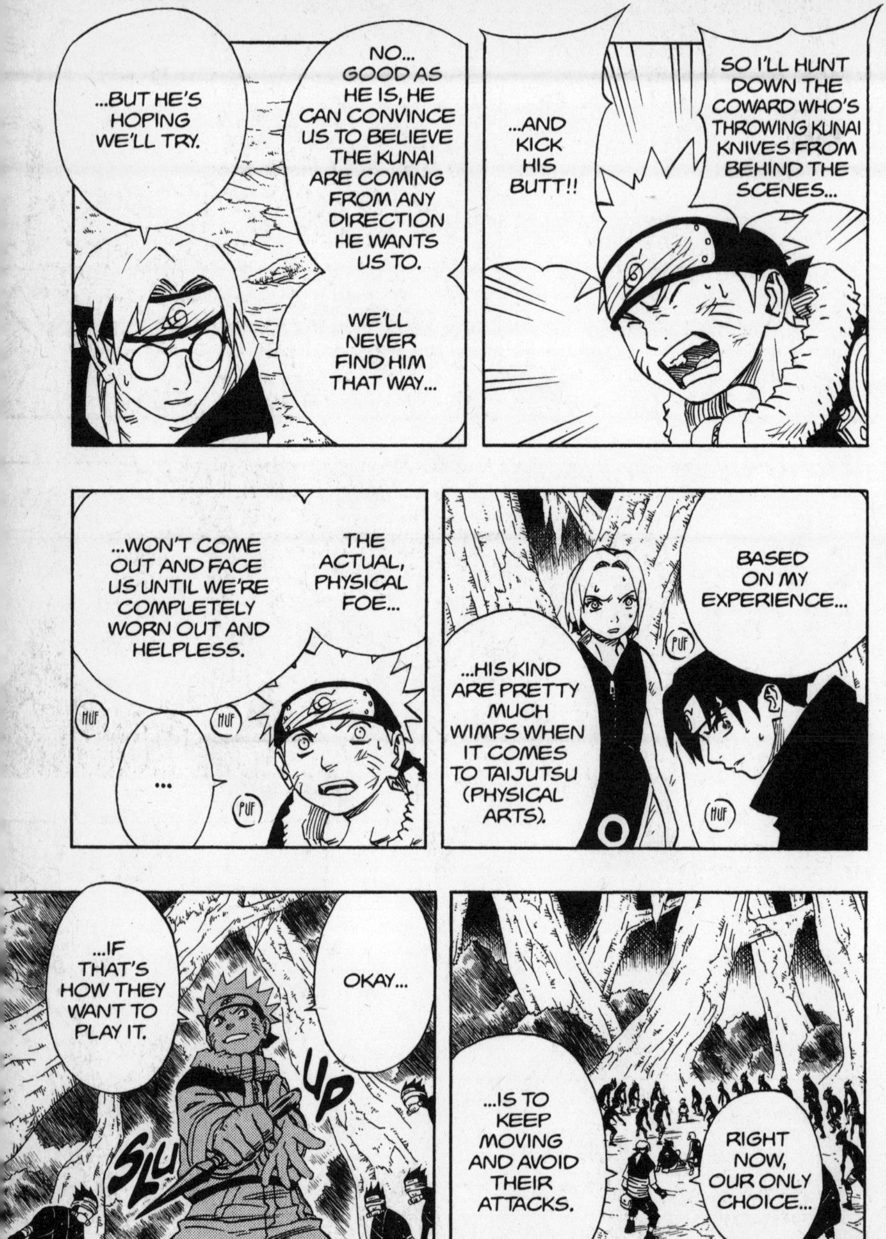
SO I'LL HUNT DOWN THE COWARD WHO'S THROWING KUNAI KNIVES FROM BEHIND THE SCENES...
...AND KICK HIS BUTT!!
NO... GOOD AS HE IS, HE CAN CONVINCE US TO BELIEVE THE KUNAI ARE COMING FROM ANY DIRECTION HE WANTS US TO.
WE'LL NEVER FIND HIM THAT WAY...
...BUT HE'S HOPING WE'LL TRY.
BASED ON MY EXPERIENCE...
PUF
...HIS KIND ARE PRETTY MUCH WIMPS WHEN IT COMES TO TAIJUTSU (PHYSICAL ARTS).
HUF
THE ACTUAL, PHYSICAL FOE...
...WON'T COME OUT AND FACE US UNTIL WE'RE COMPLETELY WORN OUT AND HELPLESS.
HUF
PUF
...
HUF
RIGHT NOW, OUR ONLY CHOICE...
...IS TO KEEP MOVING AND AVOID THEIR ATTACKS.
OKAY...
...IF THAT'S HOW THEY WANT TO PLAY IT.
UP
SLU

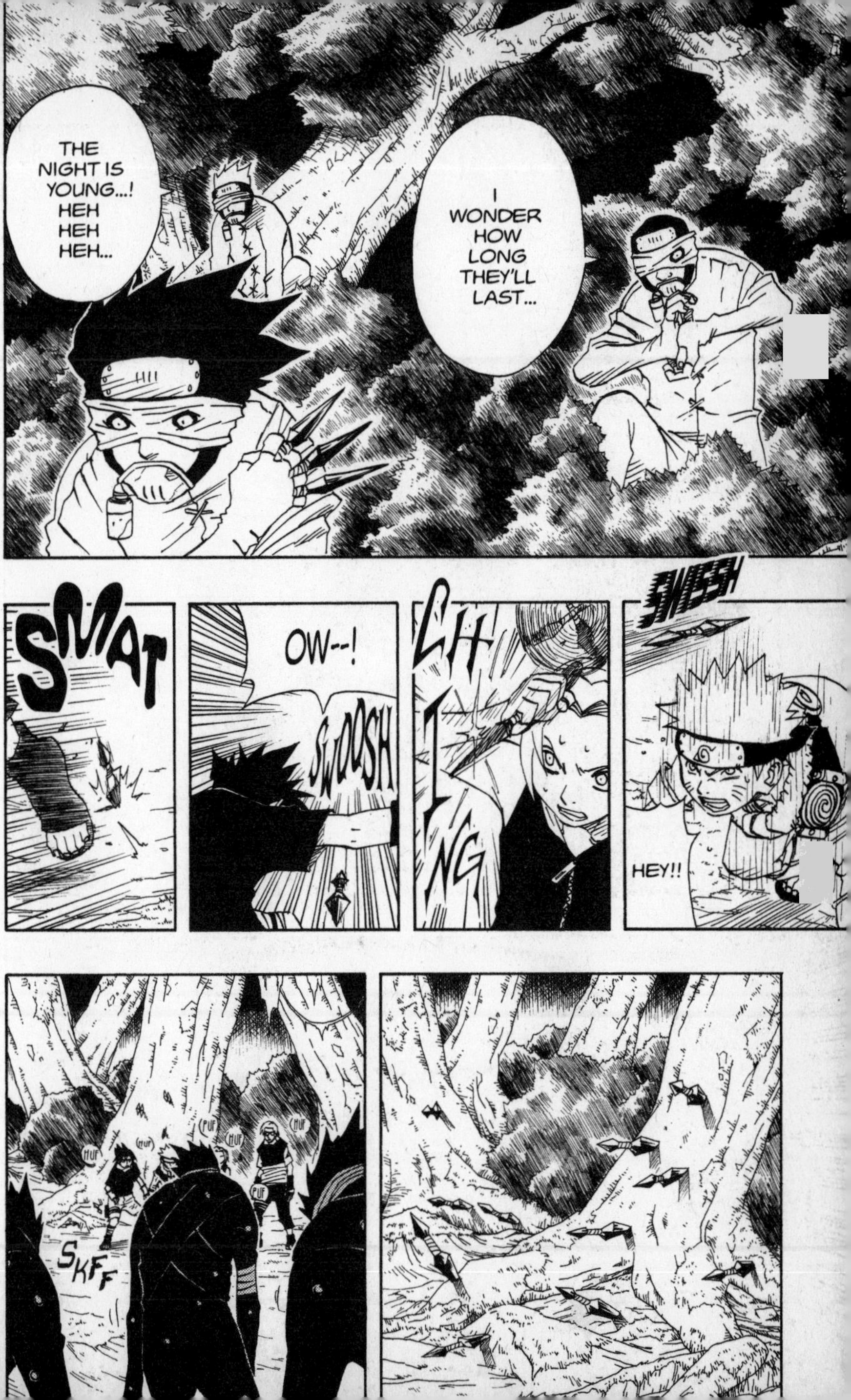
I WONDER HOW LONG THEY'LL LAST...
THE NIGHT IS YOUNG...! HEH HEH HEH...
SWISSH
HEY!!
CLING
OW--!
SWOOSH
SMAT
HUF
HUF
PUF
SKFF

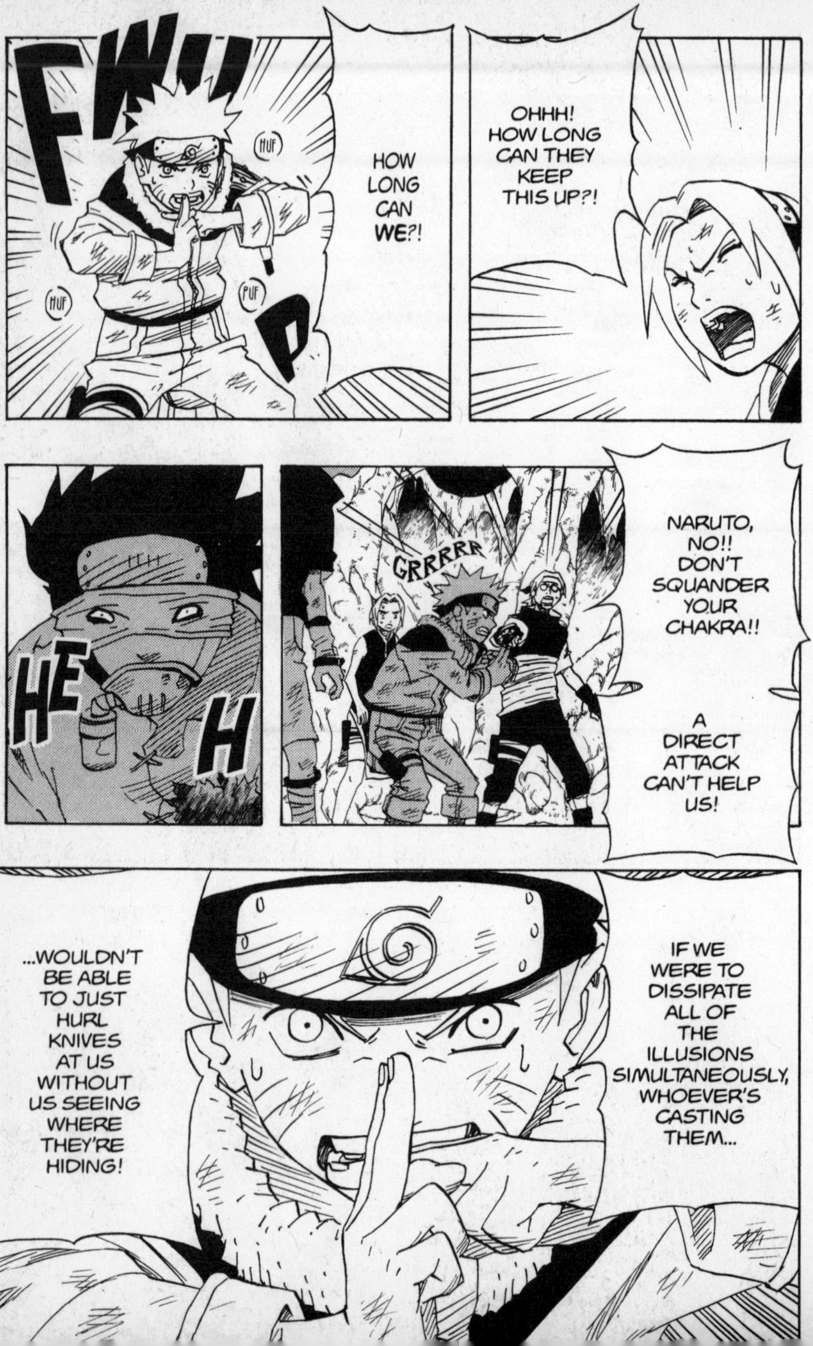
OHHH! HOW LONG CAN THEY KEEP THIS UP?!
HOW LONG CAN WE?!
FWIP
HUF
PUF
HUF
NARUTO, NO!! DON'T SQUANDER YOUR CHAKRA!!
A DIRECT ATTACK CAN'T HELP US!
GRRRRR
HEH
IF WE WERE TO DISSIPATE ALL OF THE ILLUSIONS SIMULTANEOUSLY, WHOEVER'S CASTING THEM...
...WOULDN'T BE ABLE TO JUST HURL KNIVES AT US WITHOUT US SEEING WHERE THEY'RE HIDING!

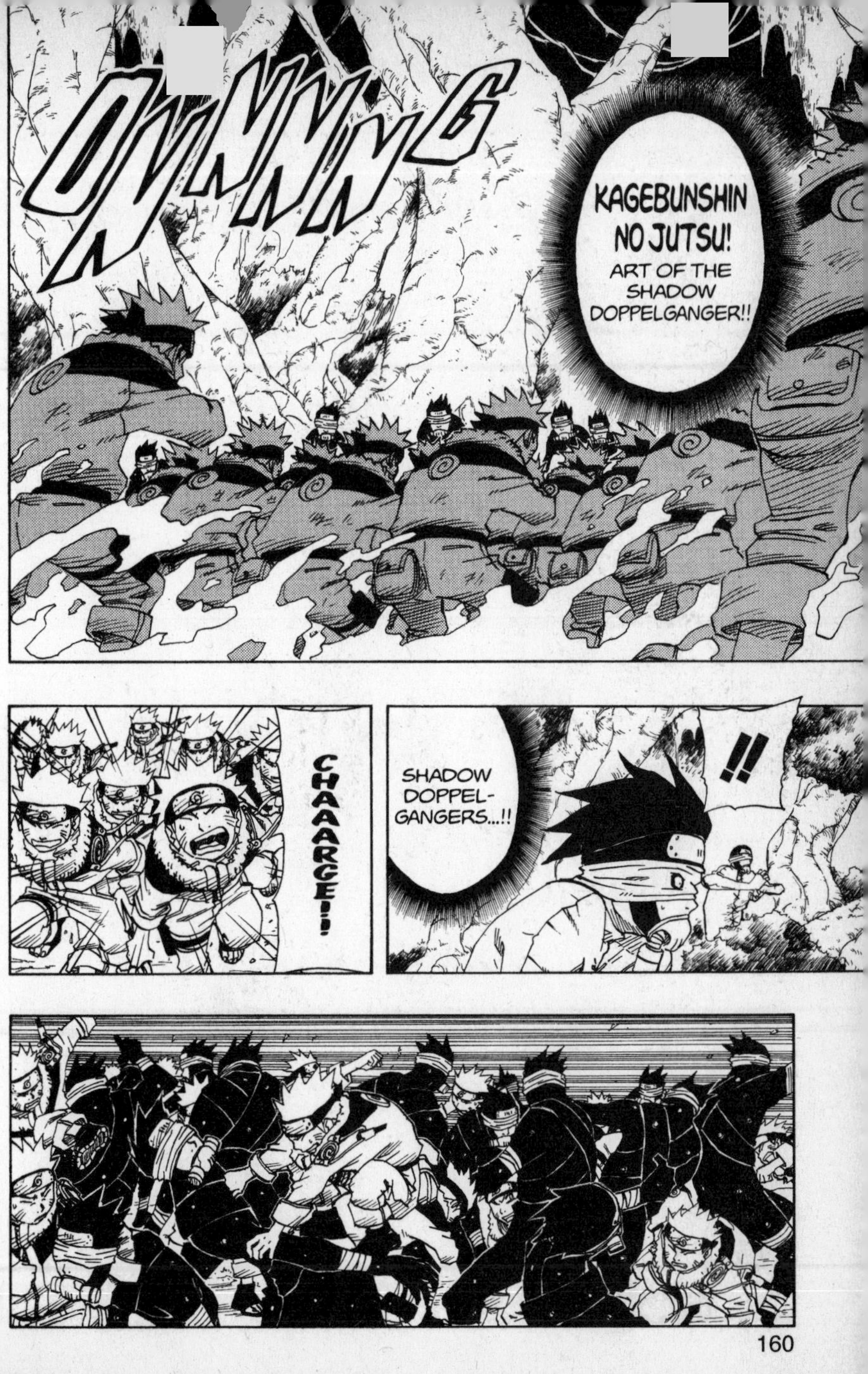
KAGEBUNSHIN NO JUTSU!
ART OF THE SHADOW DOPPELGANGER!!
!!
SHADOW DOPPEL-GANGERS...!!
CHAAARGE!!!

READ THIS WAY

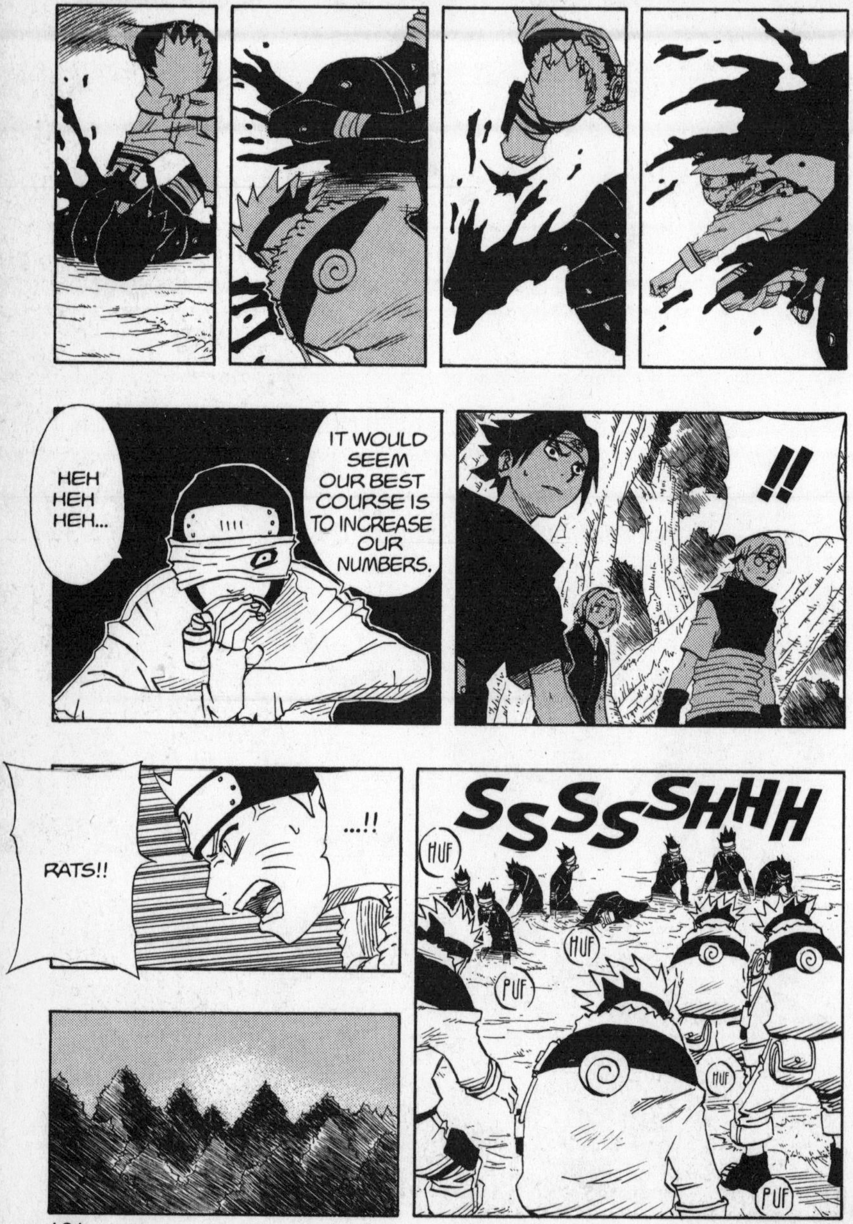
!!
IT WOULD SEEM OUR BEST COURSE IS TO INCREASE OUR NUMBERS.
HEH HEH HEH...
SSSSSHHHH
HUF
HUF
PUF
HUF
PUF
...!!
RATS!!

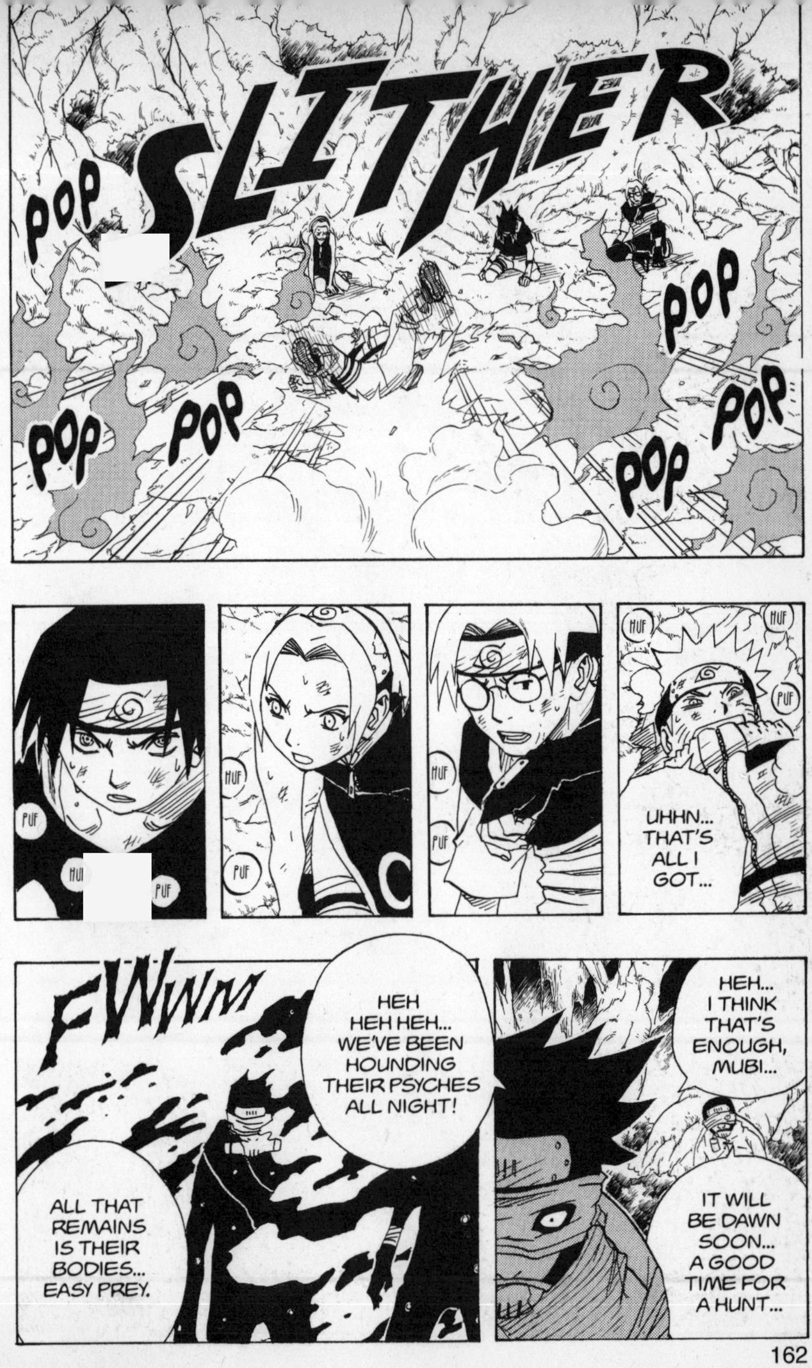
SLITHER
POP
POP
POP
POP
POP
POP
HUF
HUF
PUF
UHHN... THAT'S ALL I GOT...
HUF
PUF
HUF
PUF
PUF
PUF
HEH... I THINK THAT'S ENOUGH, MUBI...
IT WILL BE DAWN SOON... A GOOD TIME FOR A HUNT...
FWMM
HEH HEH HEH... WE'VE BEEN HOUNDING THEIR PSYCHES ALL NIGHT!
ALL THAT REMAINS IS THEIR BODIES... EASY PREY.

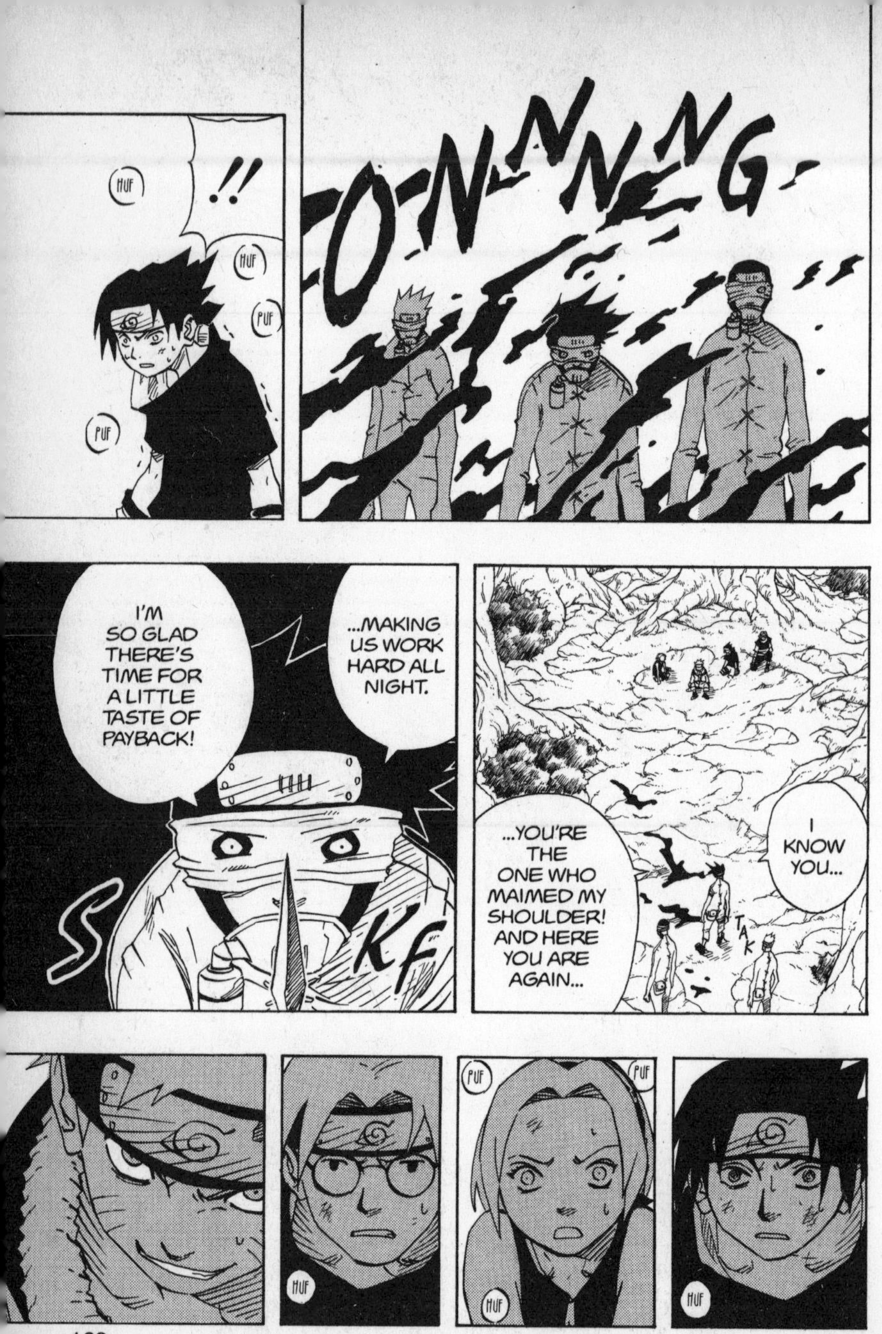

O-N-N-N-N-G
!!
HUF
HUF
PUF
PUF
I KNOW YOU...
...YOU'RE THE ONE WHO MAIMED MY SHOULDER! AND HERE YOU ARE AGAIN...
TAK
...MAKING US WORK HARD ALL NIGHT.
I'M SO GLAD THERE'S TIME FOR A LITTLE TASTE OF PAYBACK!
S
KF
HUF
PUF
PUF
HUF
HUF

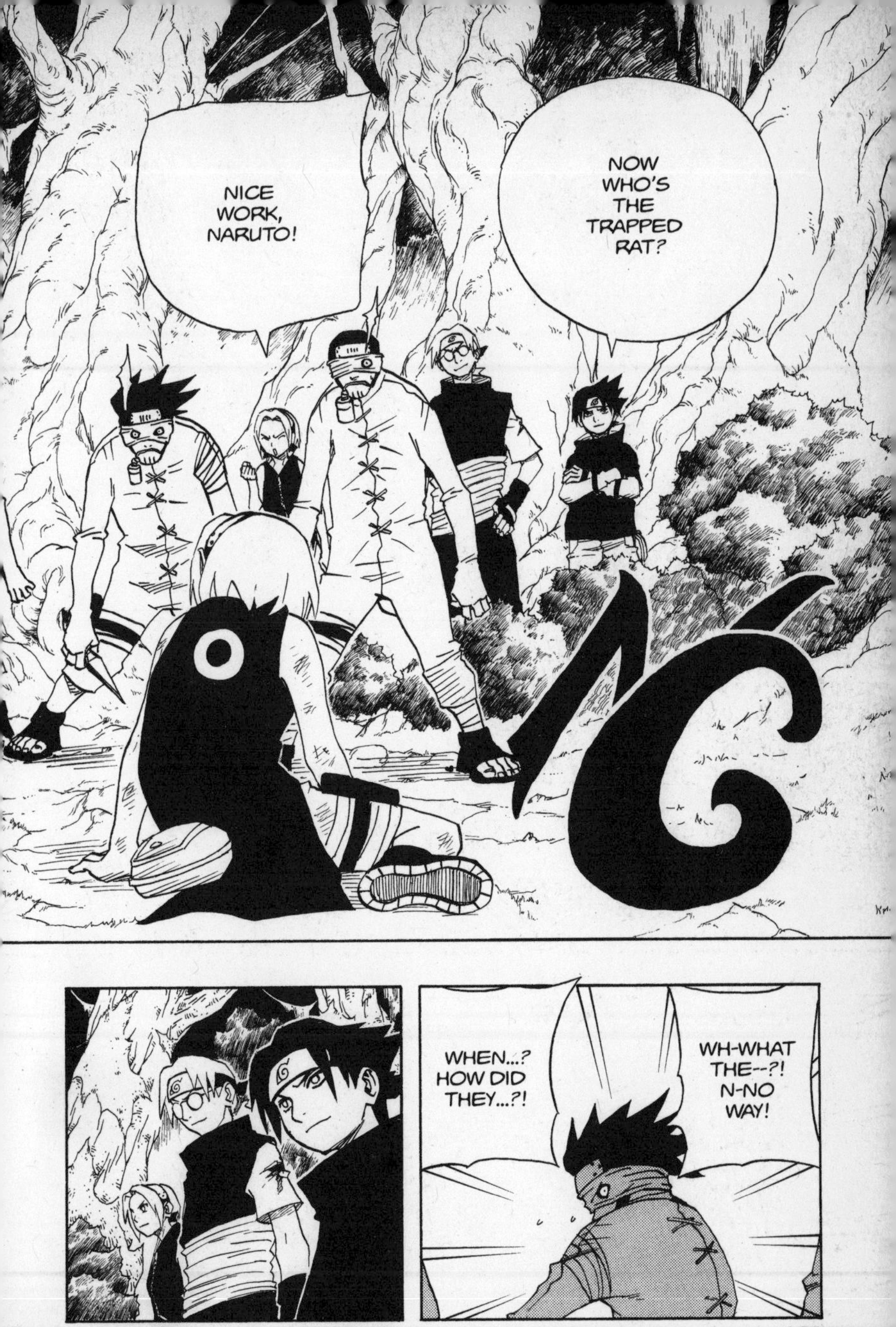
NOW WHO'S THE TRAPPED RAT?
NICE WORK, NARUTO!
WH-WHAT THE--?! N-NO WAY!
WHEN...? HOW DID THEY...?!

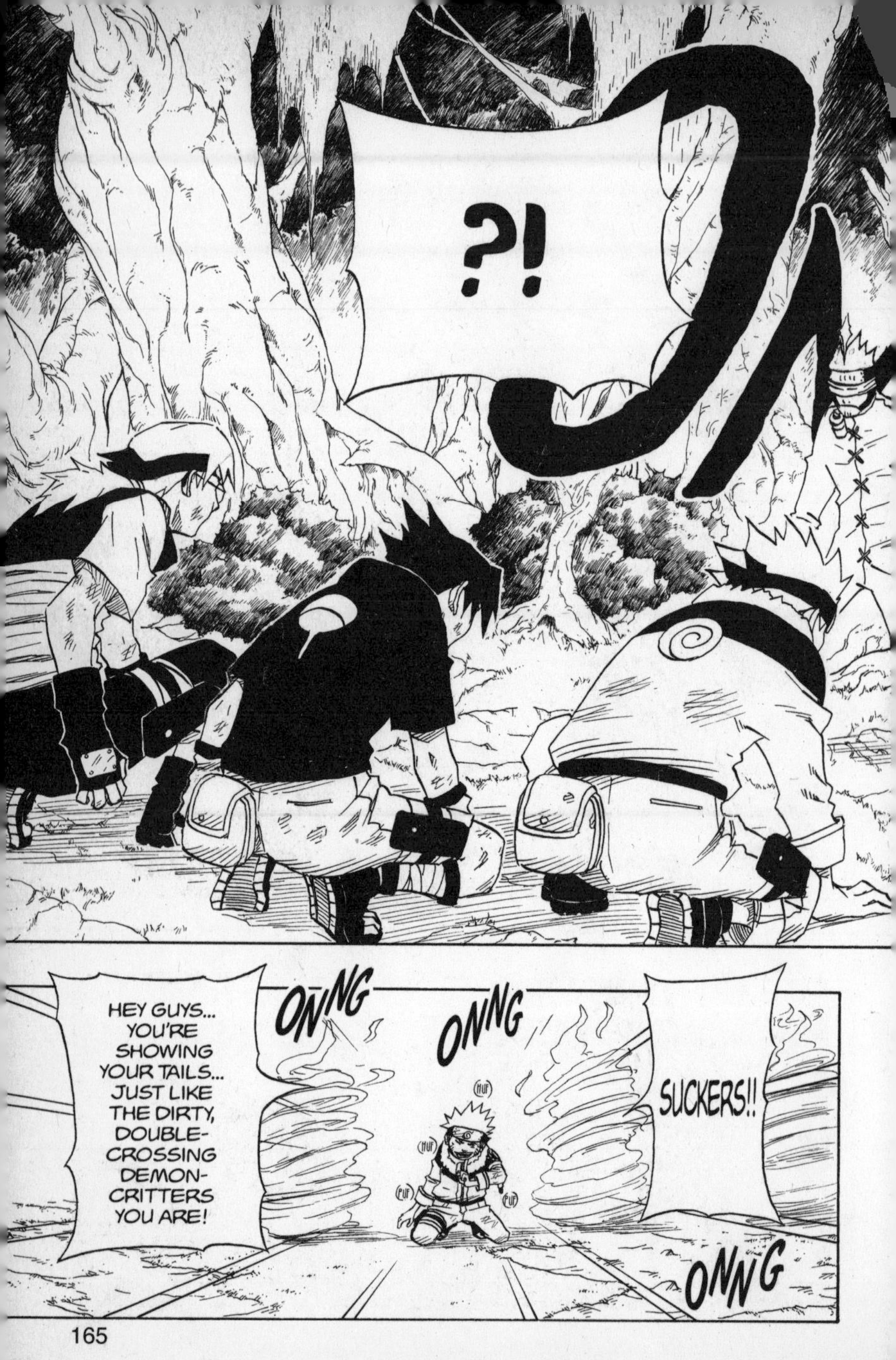
?!
SUCKERS!!
ONNG
ONNG
ONNG
HUF
HUF
PUF
PUF
HEY GUYS... YOU'RE SHOWING YOUR TAILS... JUST LIKE THE DIRTY, DOUBLE-CROSSING DEMON-CRITTERS YOU ARE!

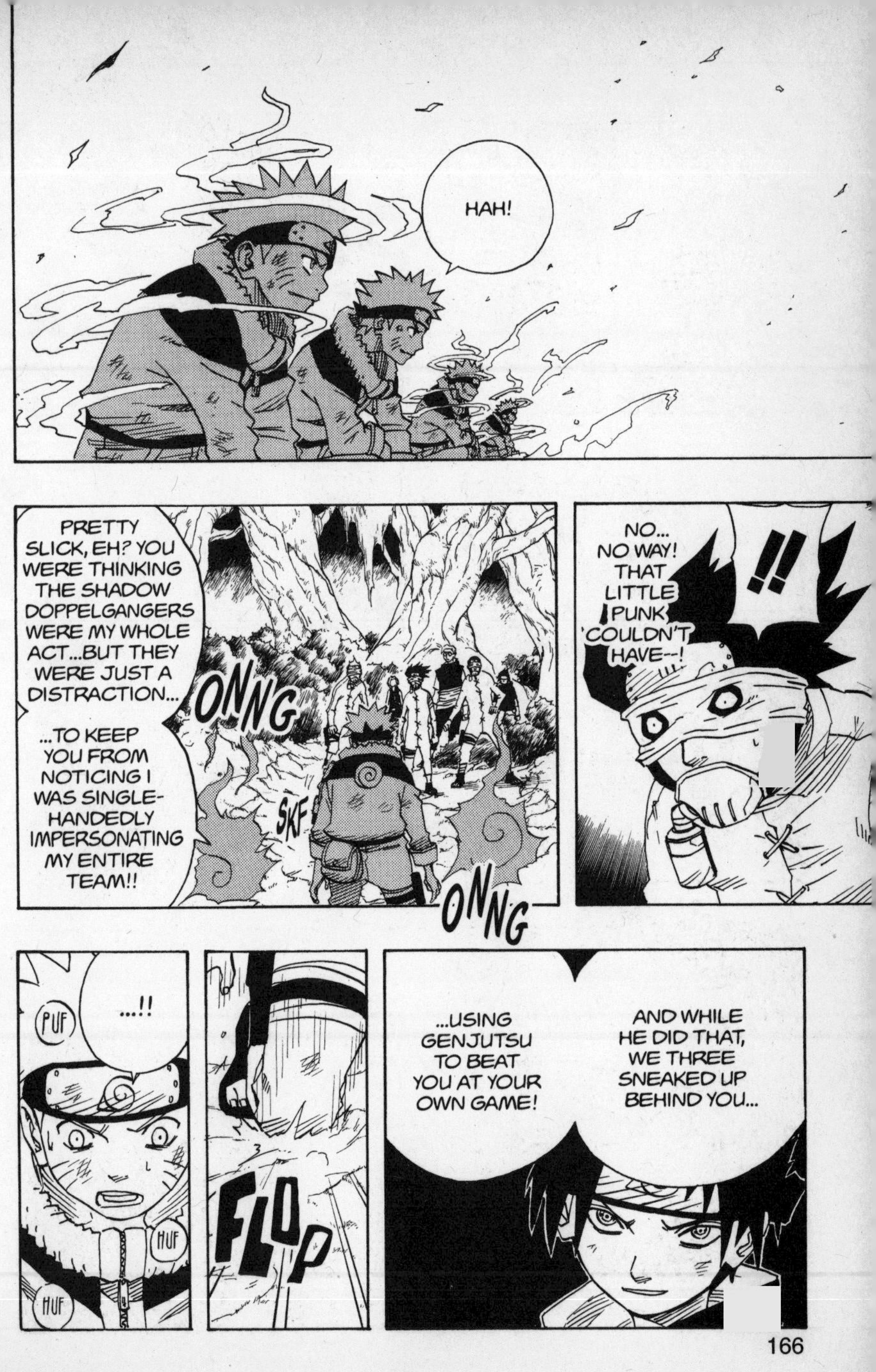
HAH!
!!
NO... NO WAY! THAT LITTLE PUNK COULDN'T HAVE--!
PRETTY SLICK, EH? YOU WERE THINKING THE SHADOW DOPPELGANGERS WERE MY WHOLE ACT...BUT THEY WERE JUST A DISTRACTION...
...TO KEEP YOU FROM NOTICING I WAS SINGLE-HANDEDLY IMPERSONATING MY ENTIRE TEAM!!
ONNG
SKF
ONNG
AND WHILE HE DID THAT, WE THREE SNEAKED UP BEHIND YOU...
...USING GENJUTSU TO BEAT YOU AT YOUR OWN GAME!
FLOP
PUF
...!!
HUF
HUF

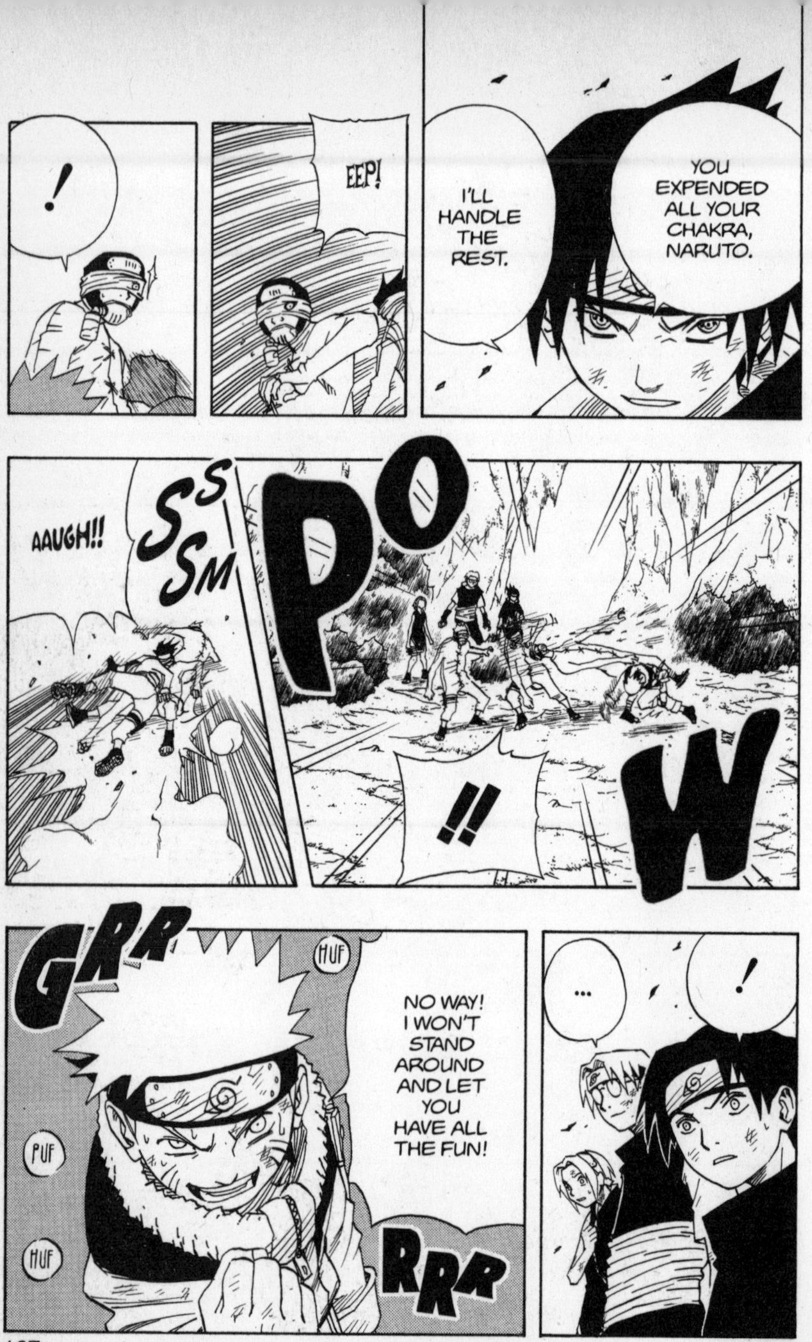
YOU EXPENDED ALL YOUR CHAKRA, NARUTO.
I'LL HANDLE THE REST.
EEP!
!
POW
!!
SSSM
AAUGH!!
!
...
HUF
GRR
NO WAY! I WON'T STAND AROUND AND LET YOU HAVE ALL THE FUN!
PUF
HUF
RRR

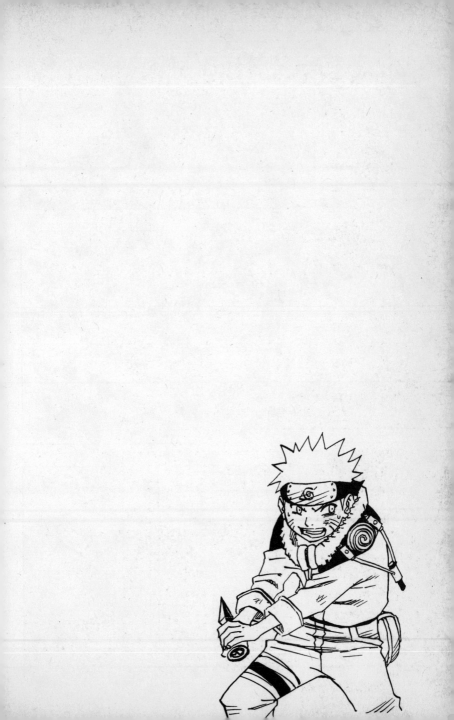

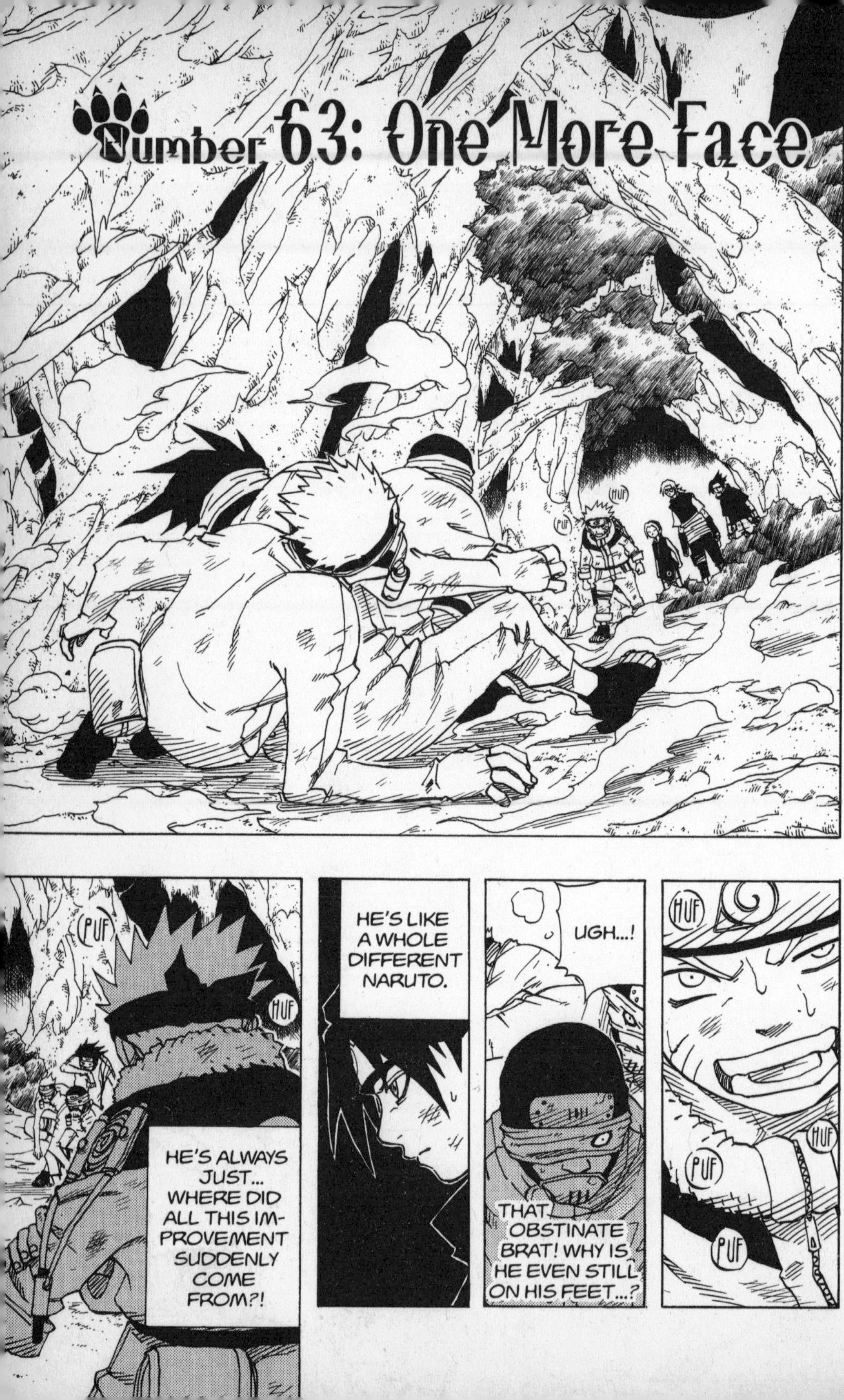
Number 63: One More Face
HUF
PUF
HUF
HUF
PUF
PUF
UGH...!
THAT OBSTINATE BRAT! WHY IS HE EVEN STILL ON HIS FEET...?
HE'S LIKE A WHOLE DIFFERENT NARUTO.
PUF
HUF
HE'S ALWAYS JUST... WHERE DID ALL THIS IM-PROVEMENT SUDDENLY COME FROM?!

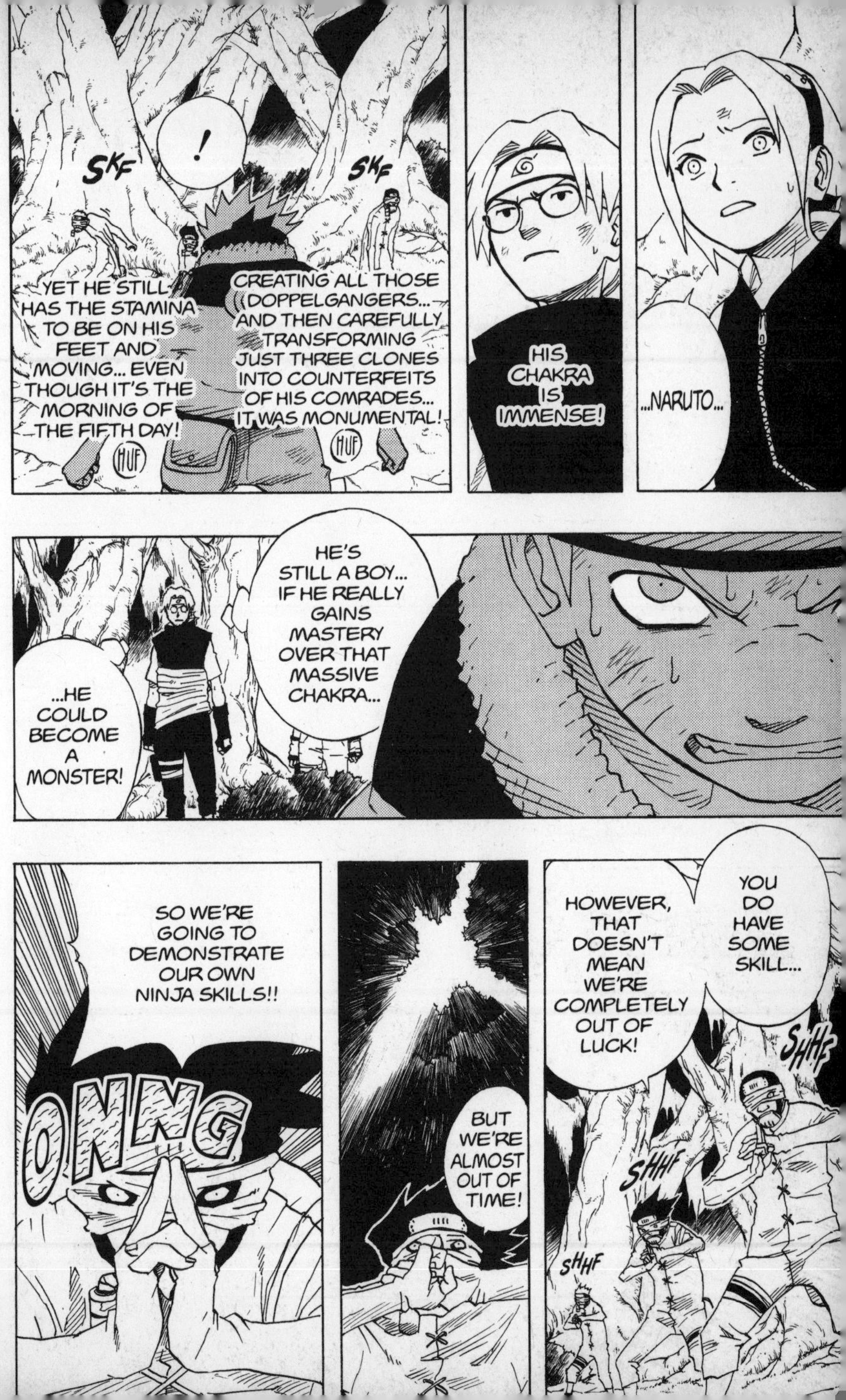
...NARUTO...
HIS CHAKRA IS IMMENSE!
!
SKF
SKF
CREATING ALL THOSE DOPPELGANGERS... AND THEN CAREFULLY TRANSFORMING JUST THREE CLONES INTO COUNTERFEITS OF HIS COMRADES... IT WAS MONUMENTAL!
YET HE STILL HAS THE STAMINA TO BE ON HIS FEET AND MOVING... EVEN THOUGH IT'S THE MORNING OF THE FIFTH DAY!
HUF
HUF
HE'S STILL A BOY... IF HE REALLY GAINS MASTERY OVER THAT MASSIVE CHAKRA...
...HE COULD BECOME A MONSTER!
YOU DO HAVE SOME SKILL...
HOWEVER, THAT DOESN'T MEAN WE'RE COMPLETELY OUT OF LUCK!
SHHF
SHHF
SHHF
BUT WE'RE ALMOST OUT OF TIME!
SO WE'RE GOING TO DEMONSTRATE OUR OWN NINJA SKILLS!!
ONNG

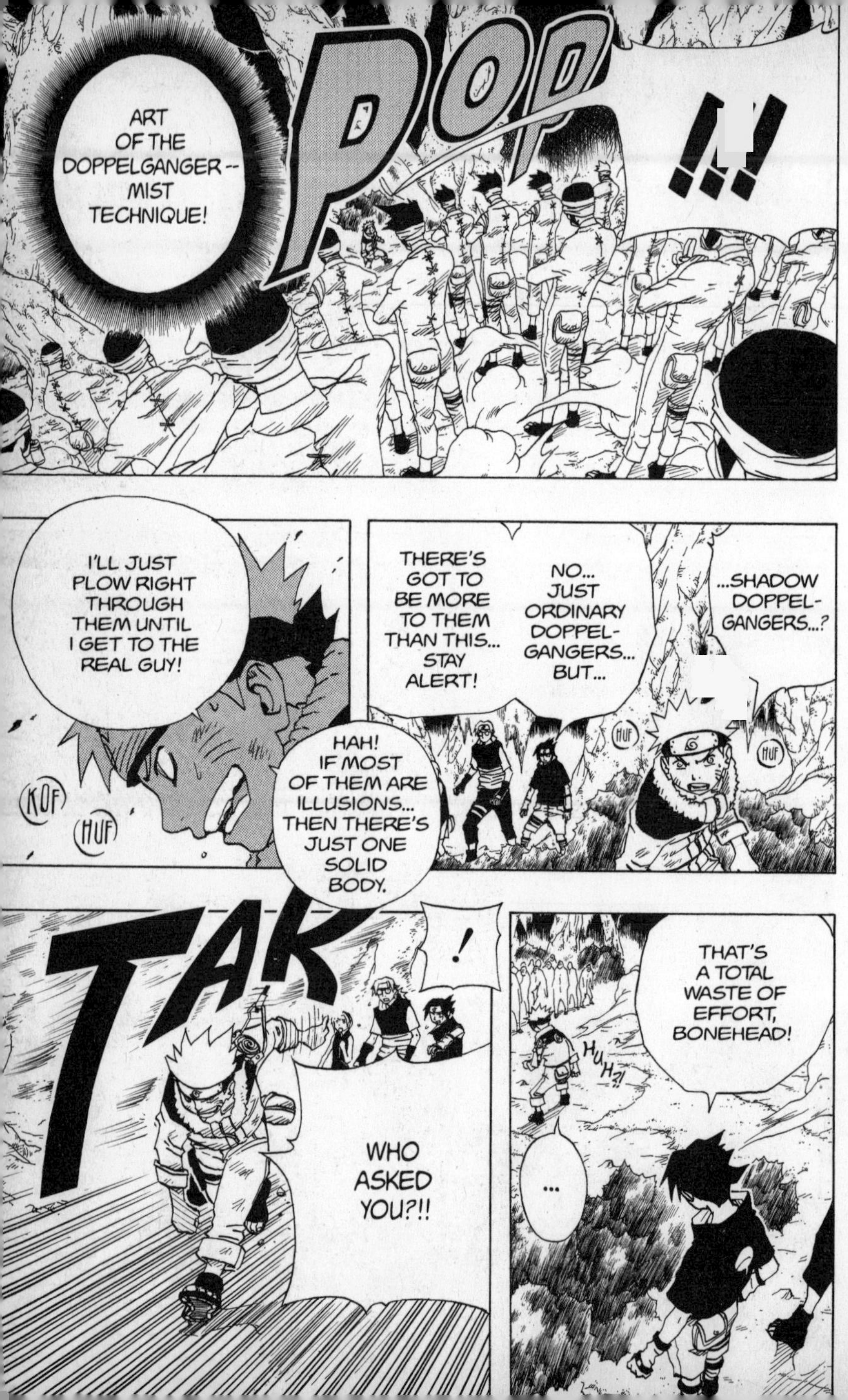
ART OF THE DOPPELGANGER -- MIST TECHNIQUE!
POP!!!
...SHADOW DOPPELGANGERS...?
HUF
HUF
NO... JUST ORDINARY DOPPELGANGERS... BUT...
THERE'S GOT TO BE MORE TO THEM THAN THIS... STAY ALERT!
HAH! IF MOST OF THEM ARE ILLUSIONS... THEN THERE'S JUST ONE SOLID BODY.
I'LL JUST PLOW RIGHT THROUGH THEM UNTIL I GET TO THE REAL GUY!
KOF
HUF
THAT'S A TOTAL WASTE OF EFFORT, BONEHEAD!
HUH?!
...
TAK
!
WHO ASKED YOU?!!

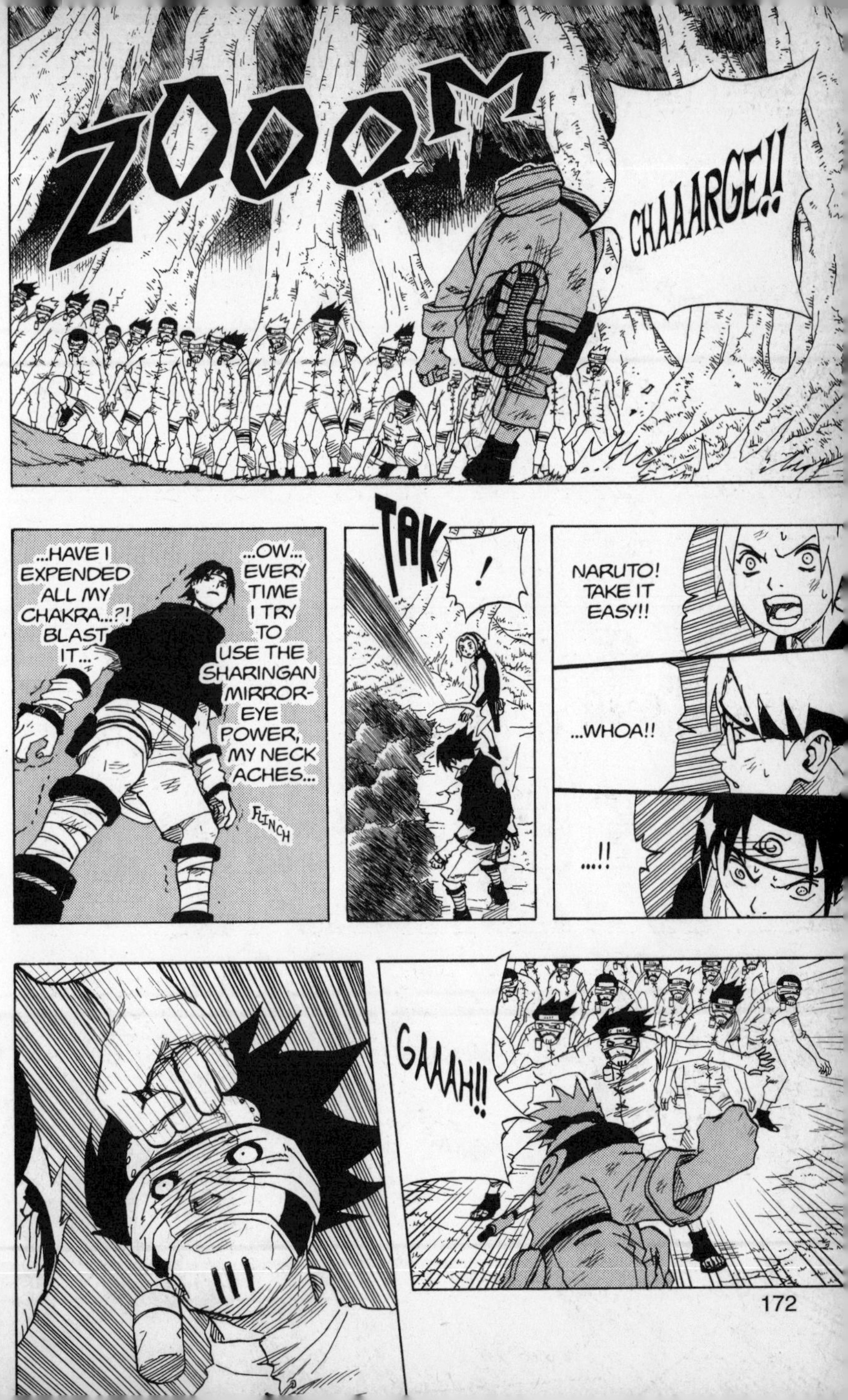
ZOOOM
CHAAARGE!!
NARUTO! TAKE IT EASY!!
...WHOA!!
...!!
TAK
!
...OW... EVERY TIME I TRY TO USE THE SHARINGAN MIRROR-EYE POWER, MY NECK ACHES...
FLINCH
...HAVE I EXPENDED ALL MY CHAKRA...?! BLAST IT...
GAAAH!!

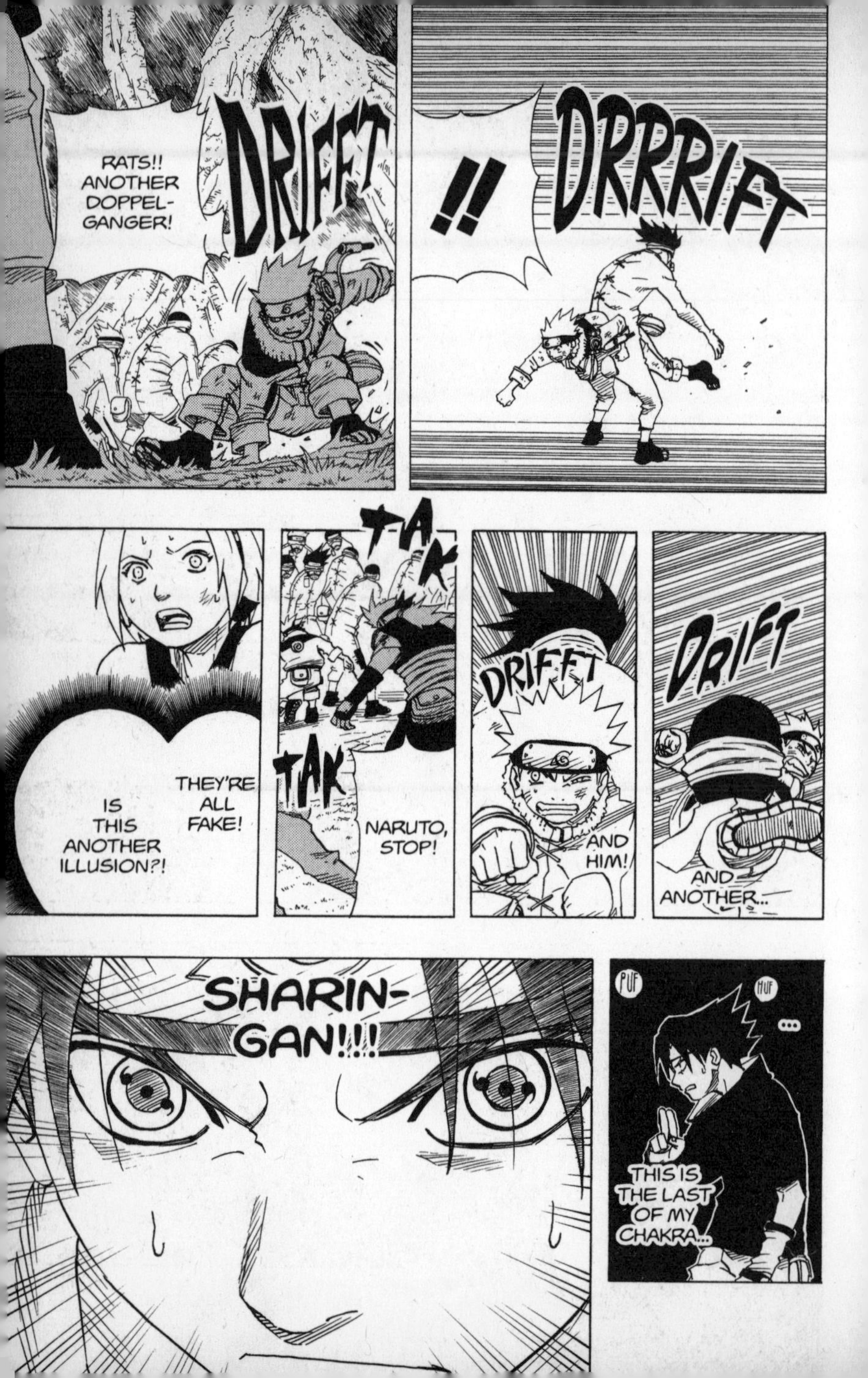
DRRRIFT
!!
DRIFFT
RATS!! ANOTHER DOPPEL-GANGER!
DRIFT
AND ANOTHER...
DRIFFT
AND HIM!
TAK
TAK
NARUTO, STOP!
THEY'RE ALL FAKE!
IS THIS ANOTHER ILLUSION?!
PUF
HUF
...
THIS IS THE LAST OF MY CHAKRA...
SHARIN-GAN!!!

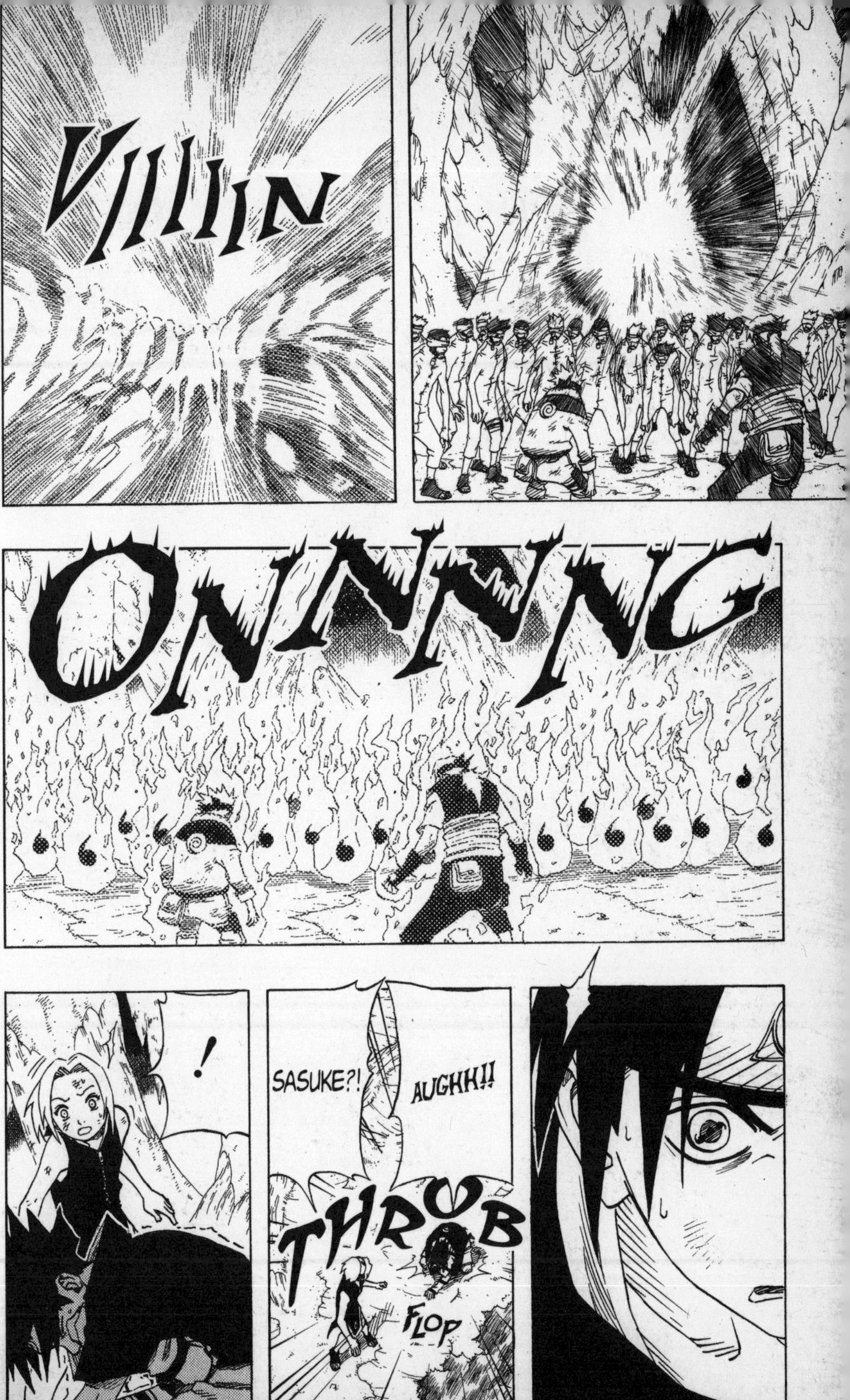
VIIIIN
ONNNG
AUGHH!!
SASUKE?!
THROB
FLOP
!

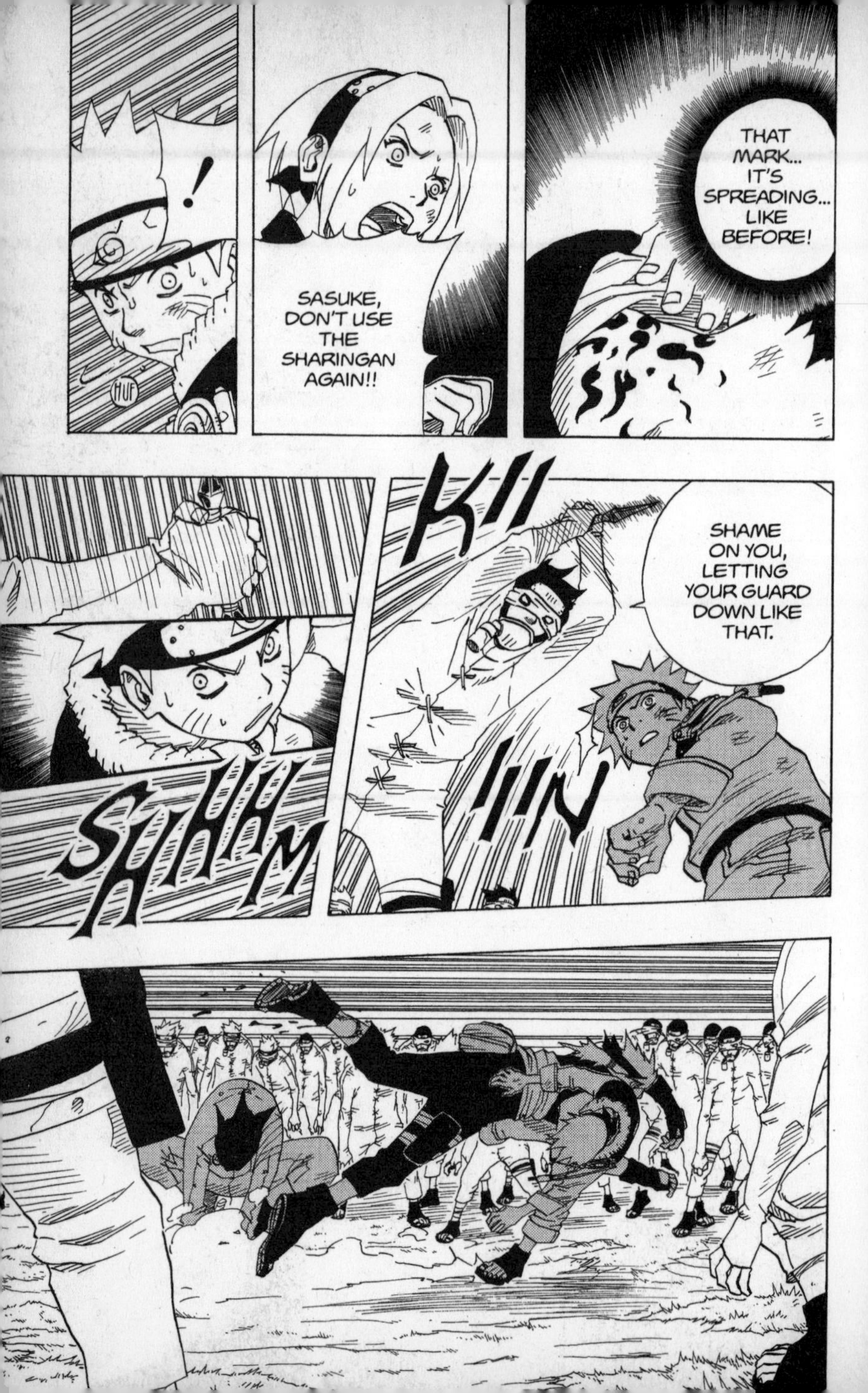
THAT MARK... IT'S SPREADING... LIKE BEFORE!
SASUKE, DON'T USE THE SHARINGAN AGAIN!!
!
HUF
SHAME ON YOU, LETTING YOUR GUARD DOWN LIKE THAT.
KII
IIN
SHHHM

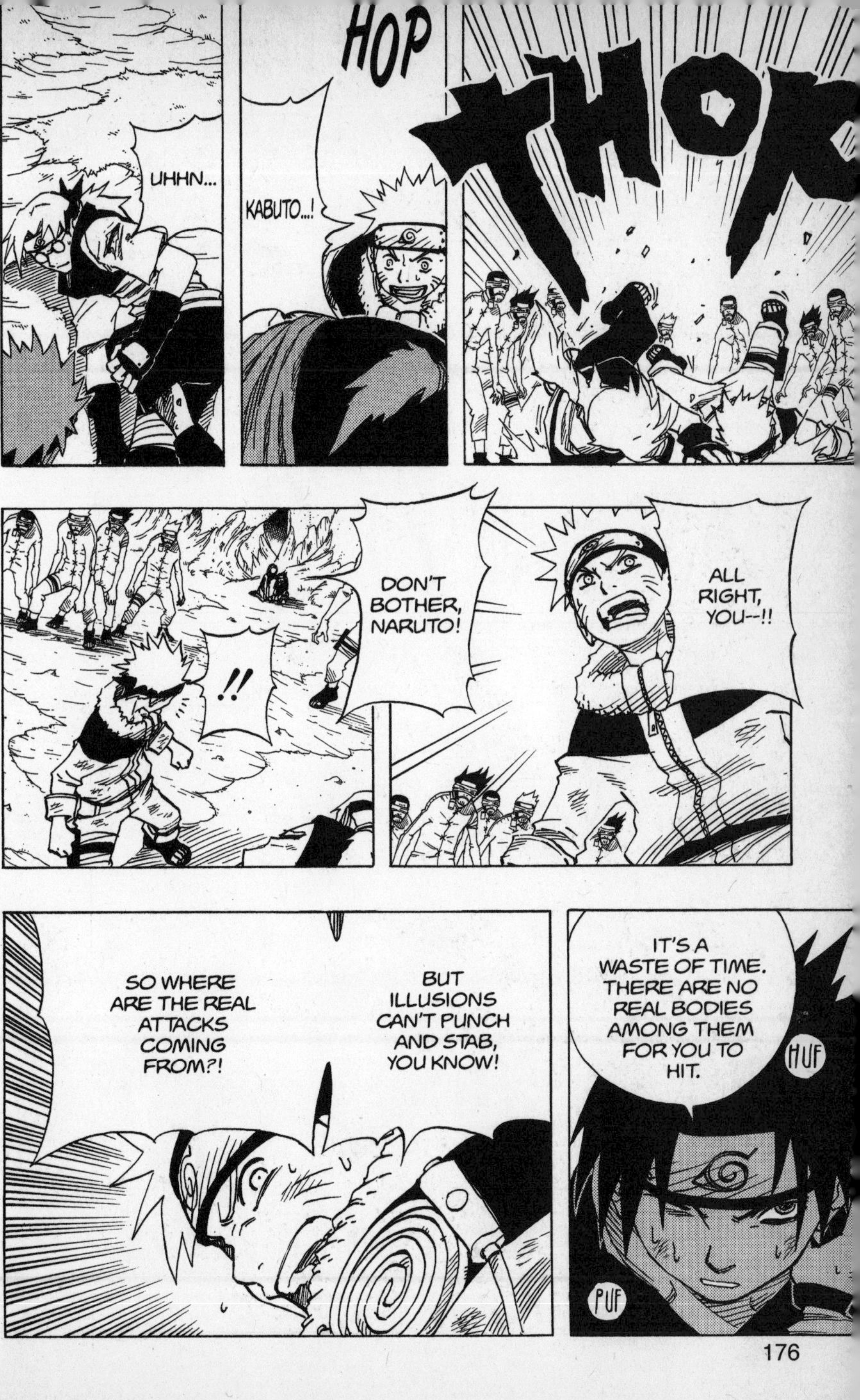
THO
HOP
KABUTO...!
UHHN...
ALL RIGHT, YOU--!!
DON'T BOTHER, NARUTO!
!!
IT'S A WASTE OF TIME. THERE ARE NO REAL BODIES AMONG THEM FOR YOU TO HIT.
HUF
PUF
BUT ILLUSIONS CAN'T PUNCH AND STAB, YOU KNOW!
SO WHERE ARE THE REAL ATTACKS COMING FROM?!

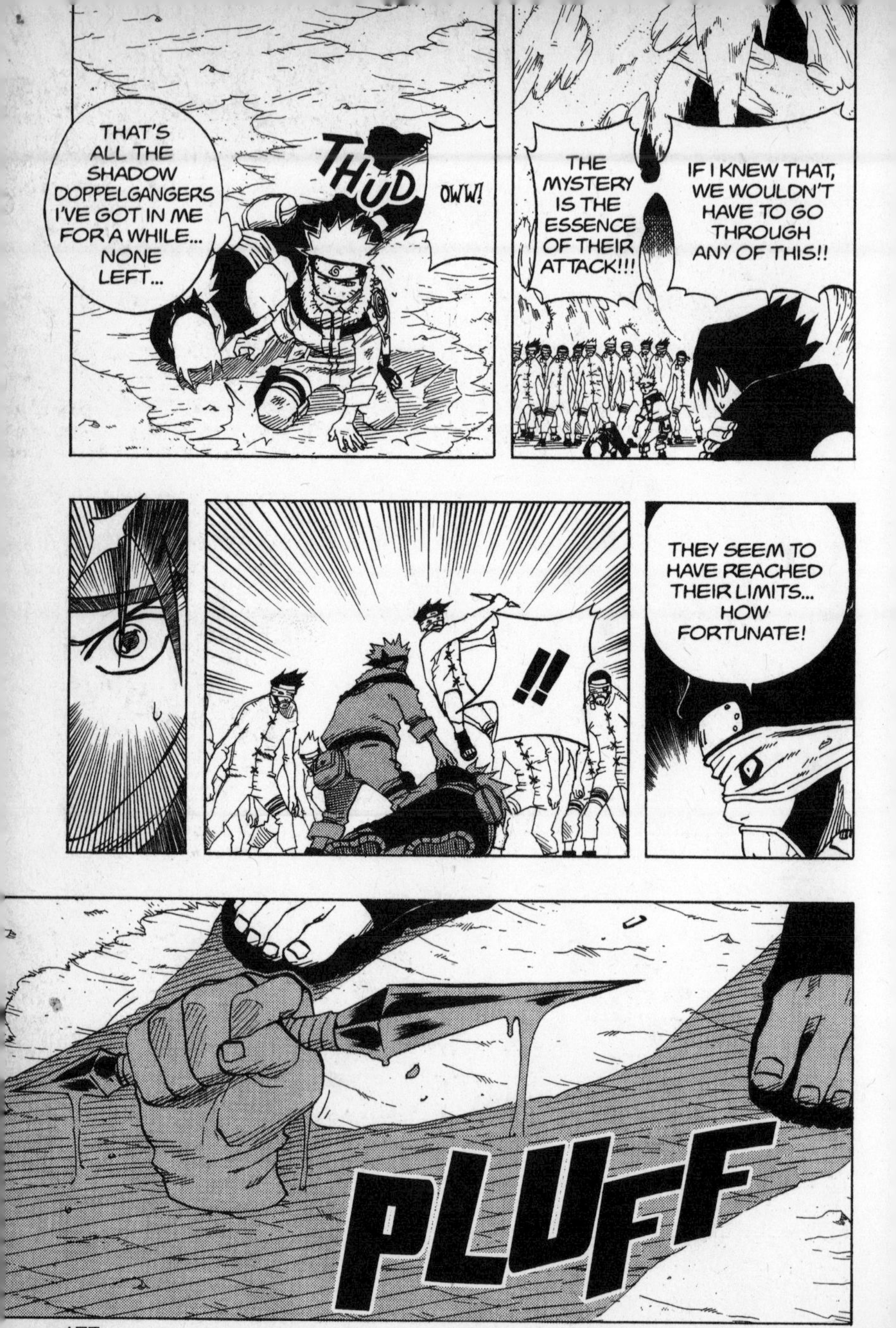
IF I KNEW THAT, WE WOULDN'T HAVE TO GO THROUGH ANY OF THIS!!
THE MYSTERY IS THE ESSENCE OF THEIR ATTACK!!!
THUD
OWW!
THAT'S ALL THE SHADOW DOPPELGANGERS I'VE GOT IN ME FOR A WHILE... NONE LEFT...
THEY SEEM TO HAVE REACHED THEIR LIMITS... HOW FORTUNATE!
!!
PLUFF

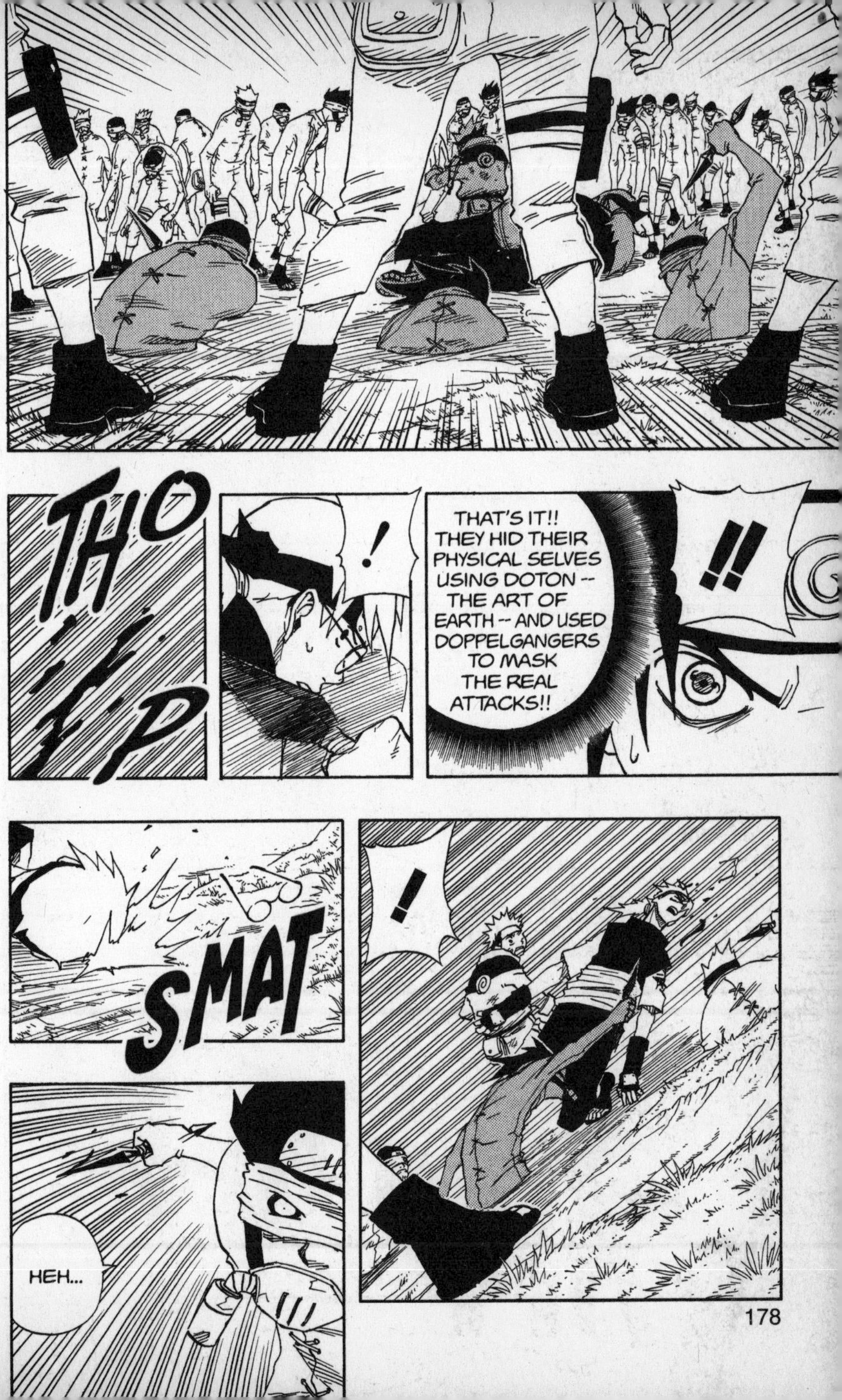
!!
THAT'S IT!! THEY HID THEIR PHYSICAL SELVES USING DOTON -- THE ART OF EARTH -- AND USED DOPPELGANGERS TO MASK THE REAL ATTACKS!!
!
THO
P
!
SMAT
HEH...

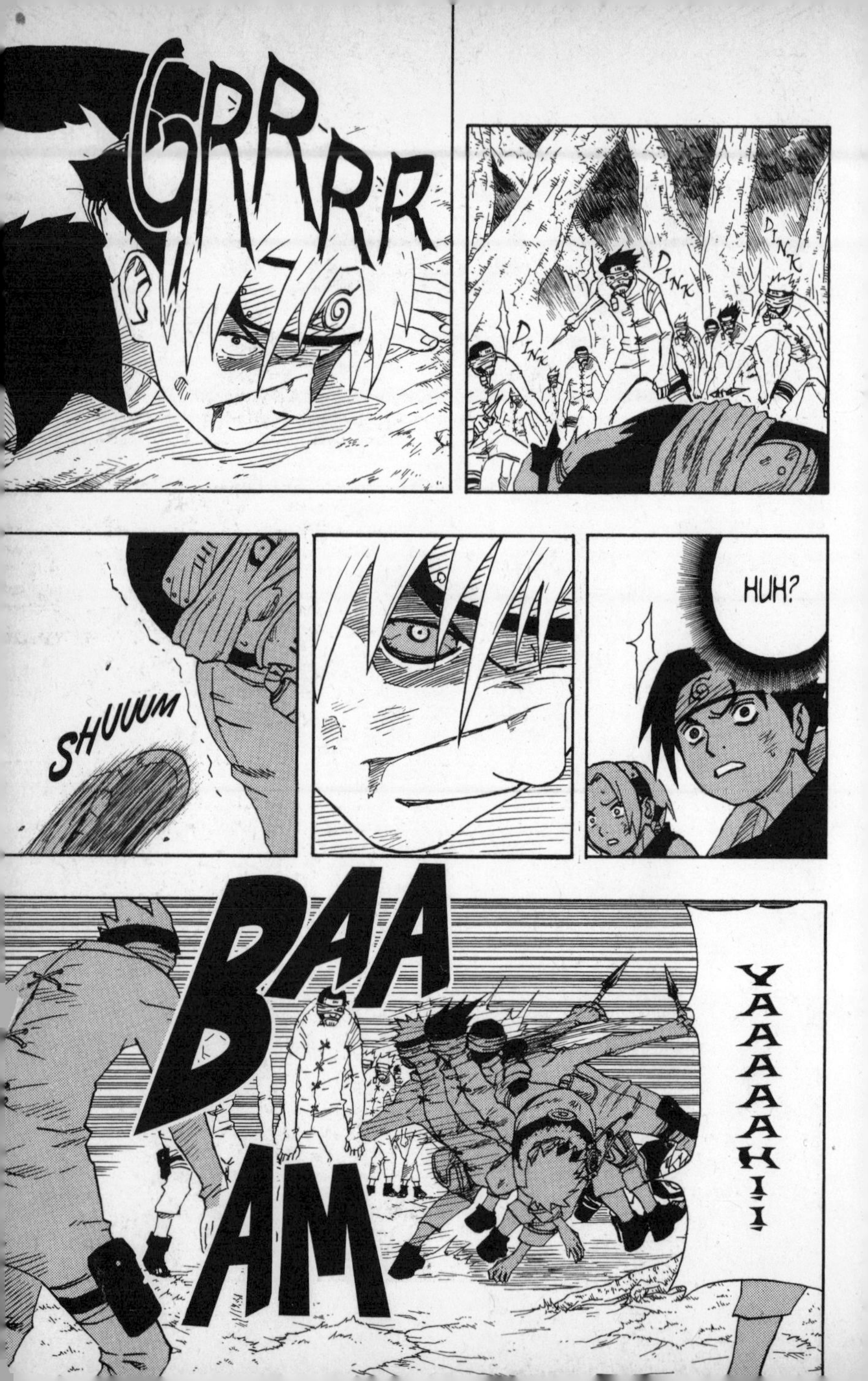
DINK
DINK
DINK
GRRRR
HUH?
SHUUUM
YAAAAAH!!
BAAAM

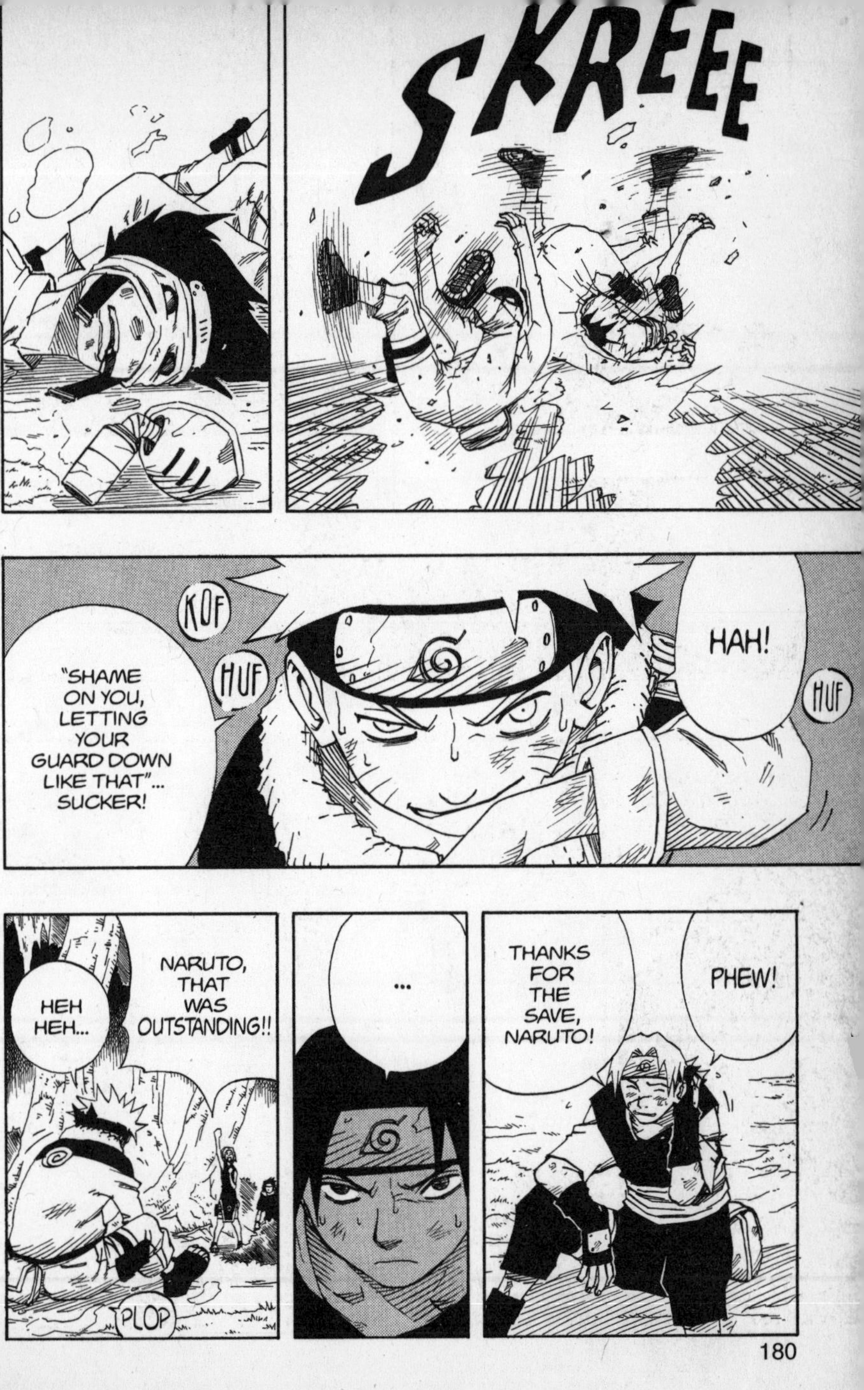
SKREEE
HAH!
HUF
KOF
HUF
"SHAME ON YOU, LETTING YOUR GUARD DOWN LIKE THAT"... SUCKER!
PHEW!
THANKS FOR THE SAVE, NARUTO!
...
NARUTO, THAT WAS OUTSTANDING!!
HEH HEH...
PLOP

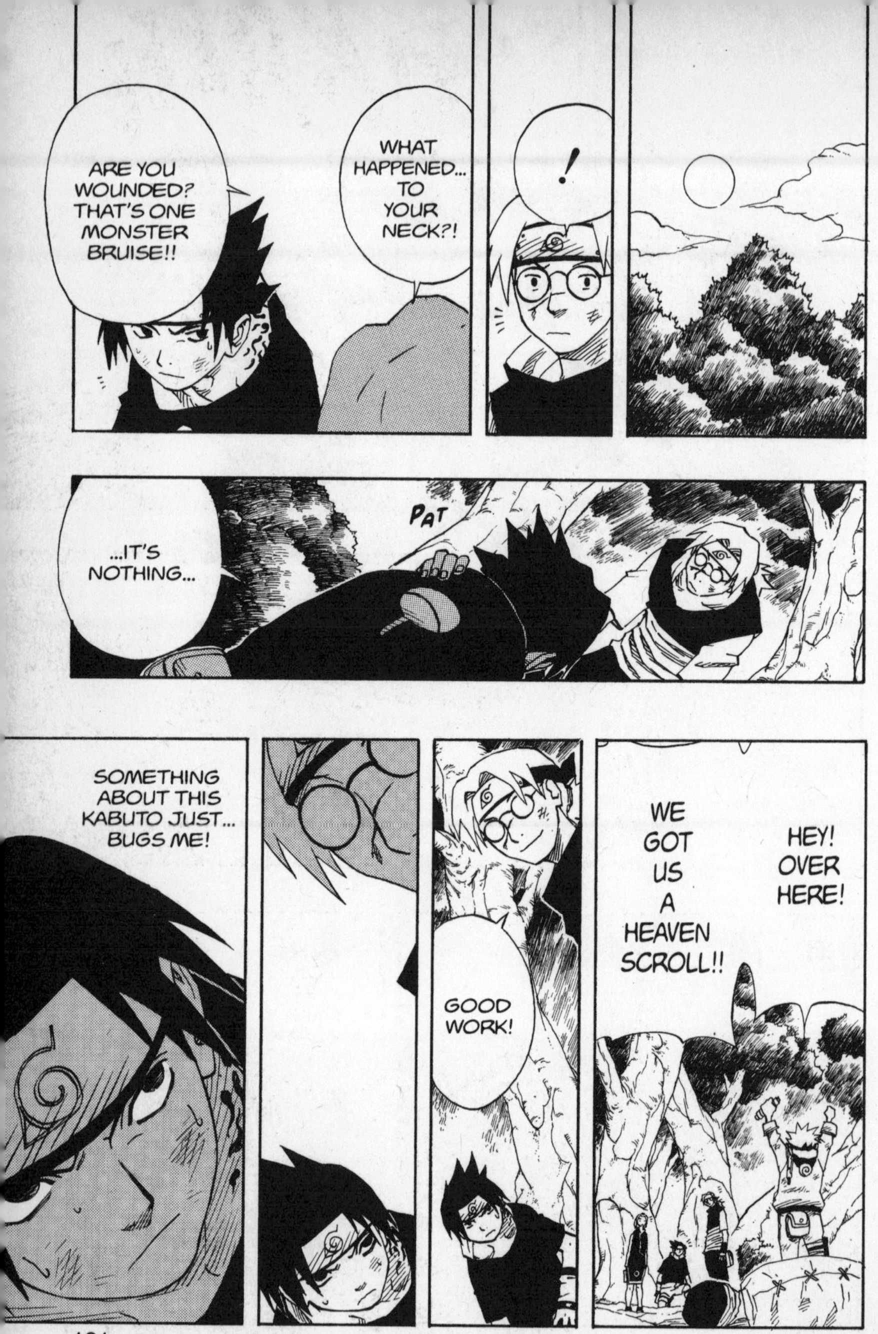
!
WHAT HAPPENED... TO YOUR NECK?!
ARE YOU WOUNDED? THAT'S ONE MONSTER BRUISE!!
PAT
...IT'S NOTHING...
HEY! OVER HERE!
WE GOT US A HEAVEN SCROLL!!
GOOD WORK!
SOMETHING ABOUT THIS KABUTO JUST... BUGS ME!

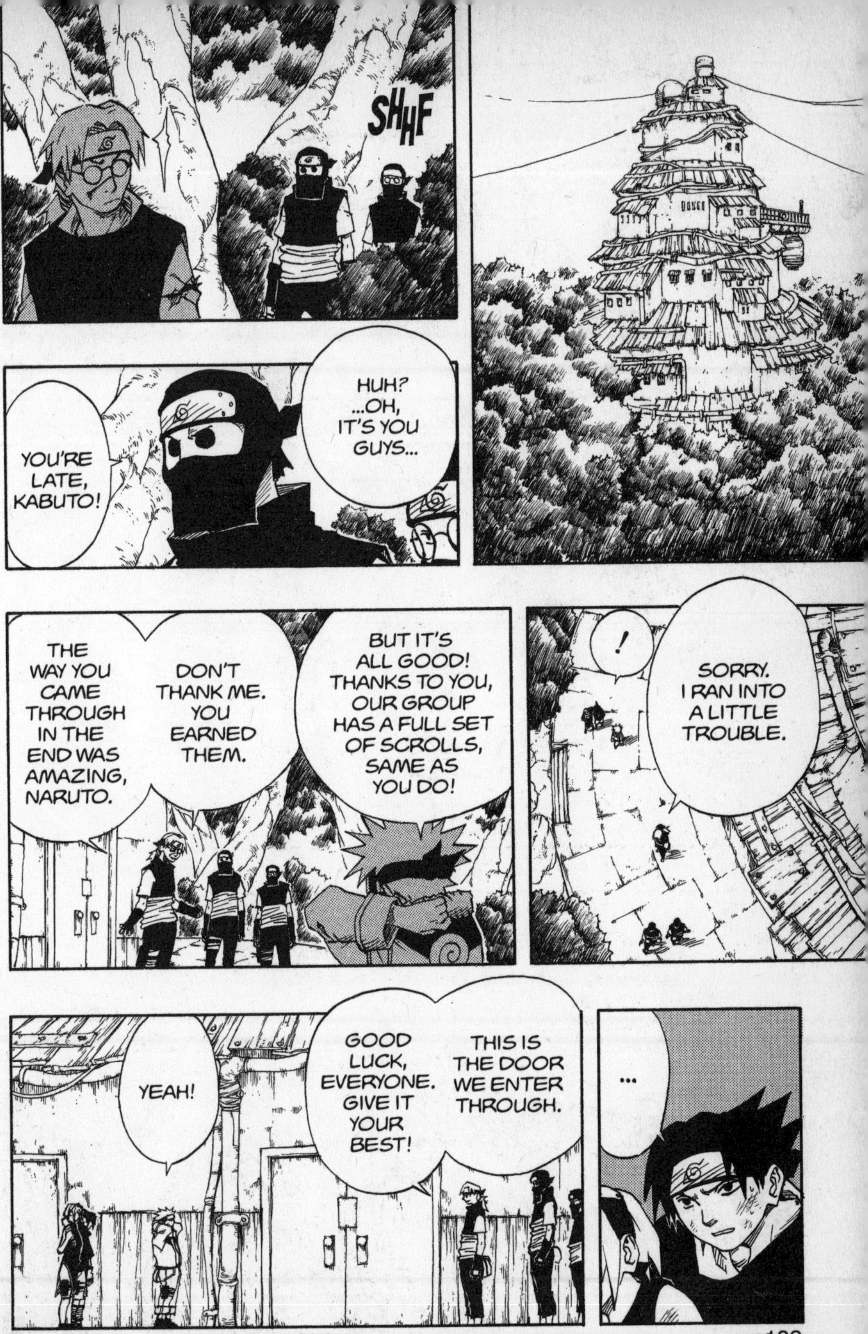
SHHF
HUH? ...OH, IT'S YOU GUYS...
YOU'RE LATE, KABUTO!
SORRY. I RAN INTO A LITTLE TROUBLE.
!
BUT IT'S ALL GOOD! THANKS TO YOU, OUR GROUP HAS A FULL SET OF SCROLLS, SAME AS YOU DO!
DON'T THANK ME. YOU EARNED THEM.
THE WAY YOU CAME THROUGH IN THE END WAS AMAZING, NARUTO.
...
THIS IS THE DOOR WE ENTER THROUGH.
GOOD LUCK, EVERYONE. GIVE IT YOUR BEST!
YEAH!

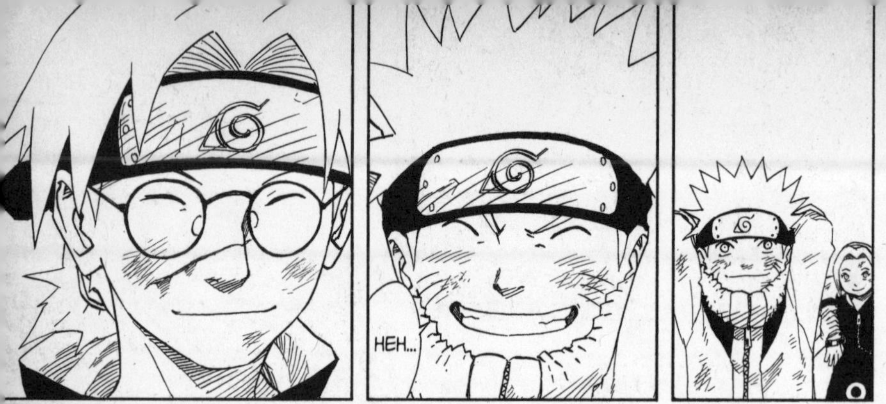
HEH...

THE SEAL ON THE DOOR SAYS "OPEN."

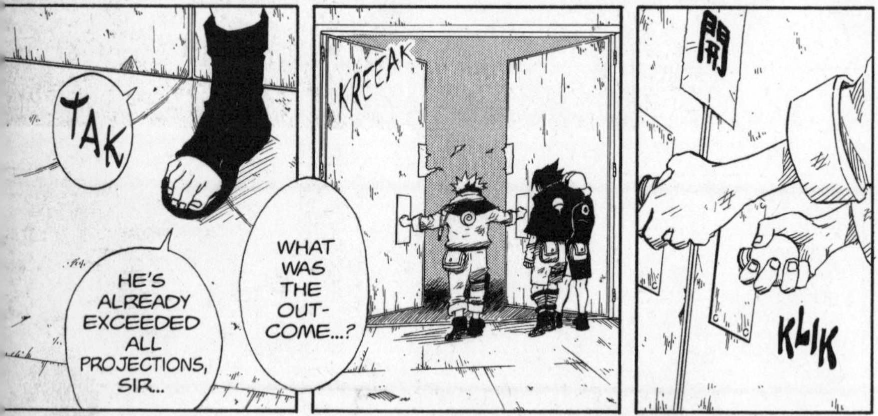
KLIK
KREEAK
WHAT WAS THE OUT-COME...?
TAK
HE'S ALREADY EXCEEDED ALL PROJECTIONS, SIR...

THE CHARACTER ON THE CARD SAYS "SHINOBI."

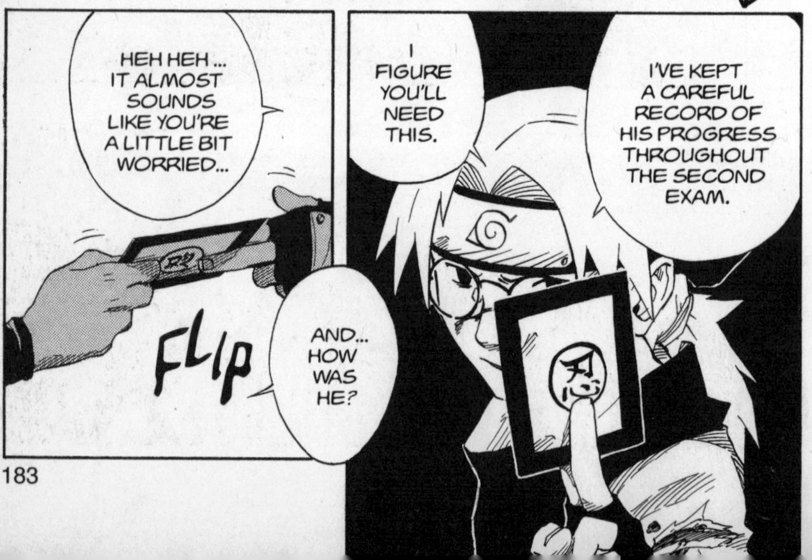
I'VE KEPT A CAREFUL RECORD OF HIS PROGRESS THROUGHOUT THE SECOND EXAM.
I FIGURE YOU'LL NEED THIS.
HEH HEH... IT ALMOST SOUNDS LIKE YOU'RE A LITTLE BIT WORRIED...
AND... HOW WAS HE?
FLIP

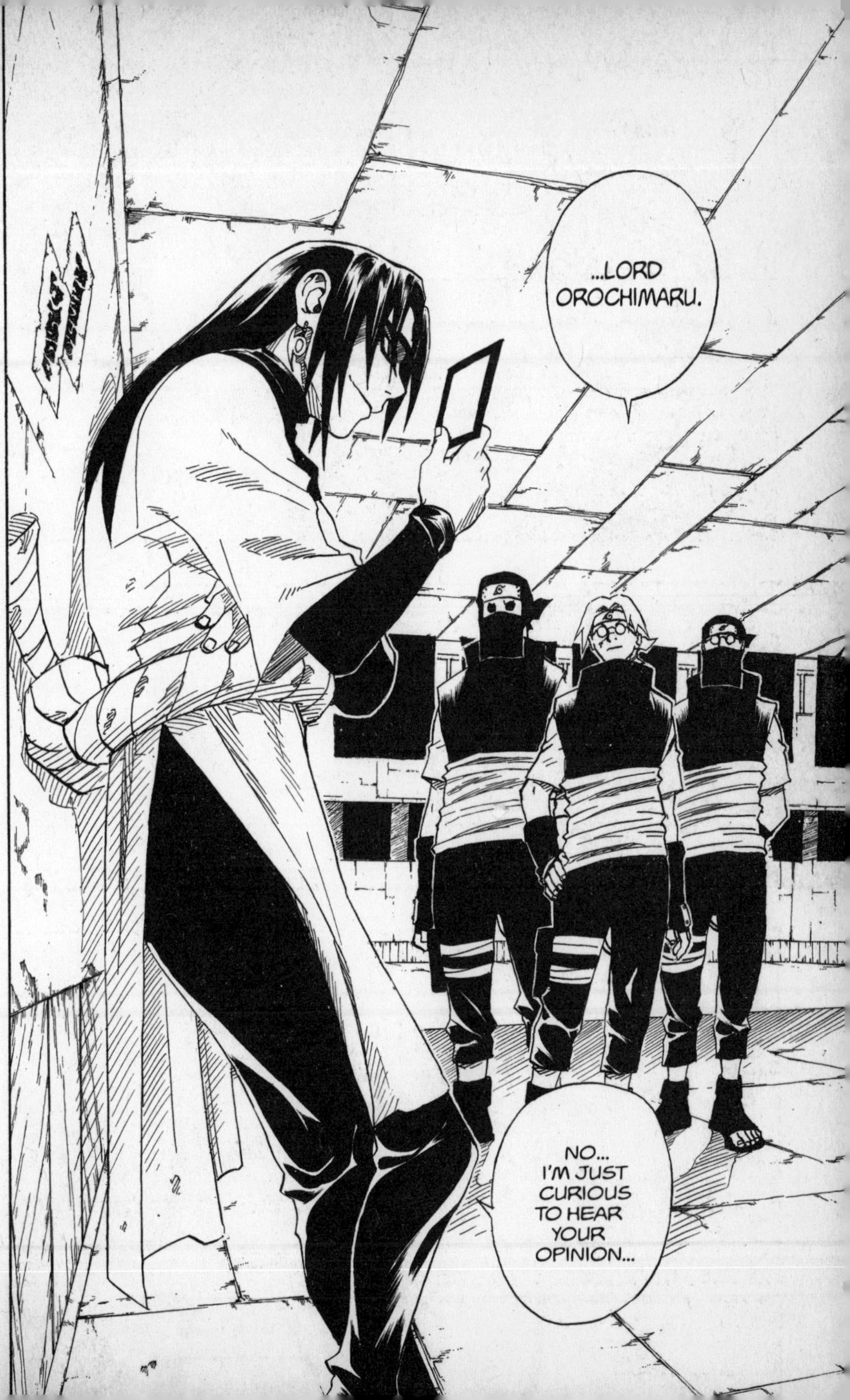
...LORD OROCHIMARU.
NO... I'M JUST CURIOUS TO HEAR YOUR OPINION...

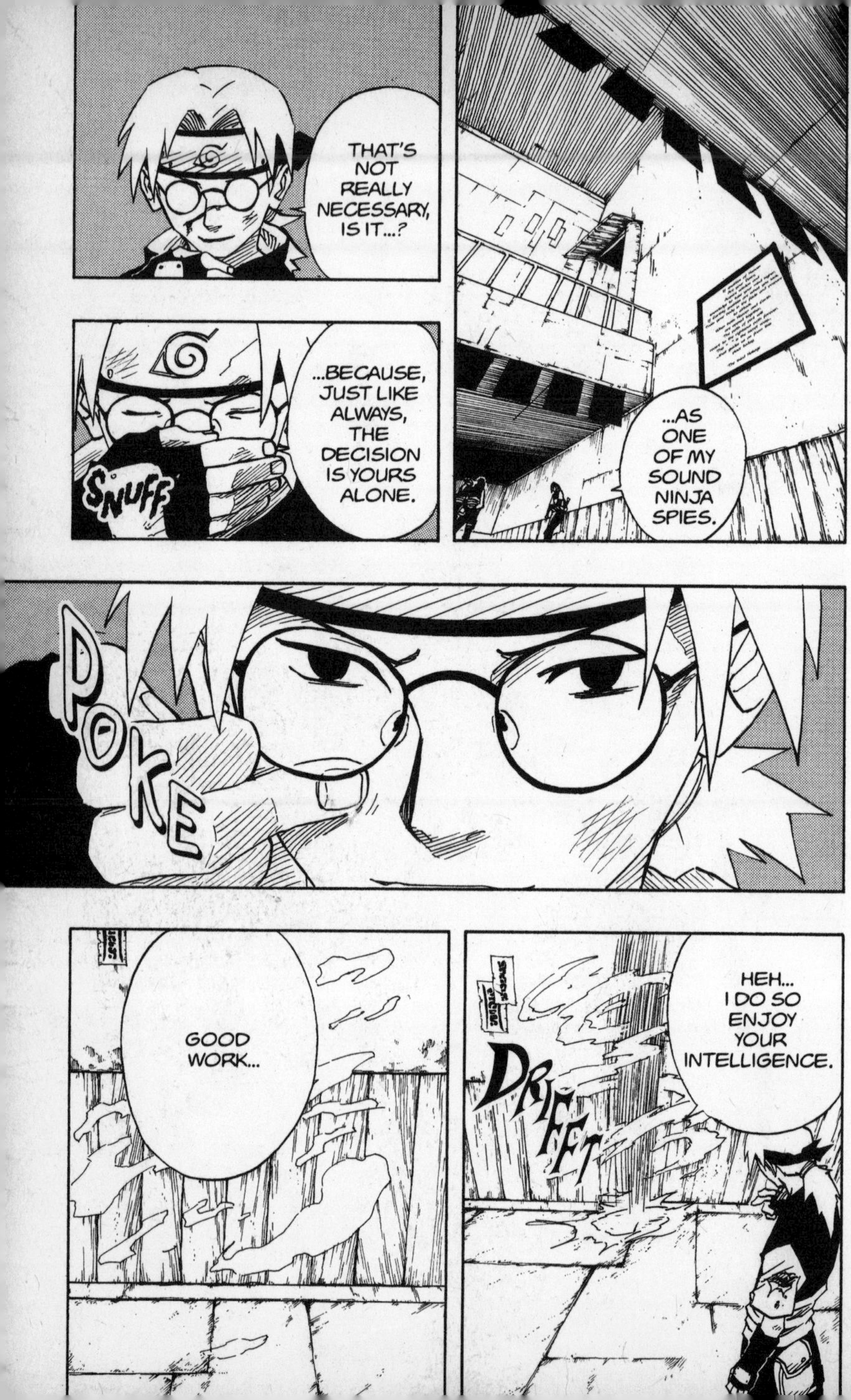
...AS ONE OF MY SOUND NINJA SPIES.
THAT'S NOT REALLY NECESSARY, IS IT...?
...BECAUSE, JUST LIKE ALWAYS, THE DECISION IS YOURS ALONE.
SNUFF
POKE
HEH... I DO SO ENJOY YOUR INTELLIGENCE.
DRIFFT
GOOD WORK...

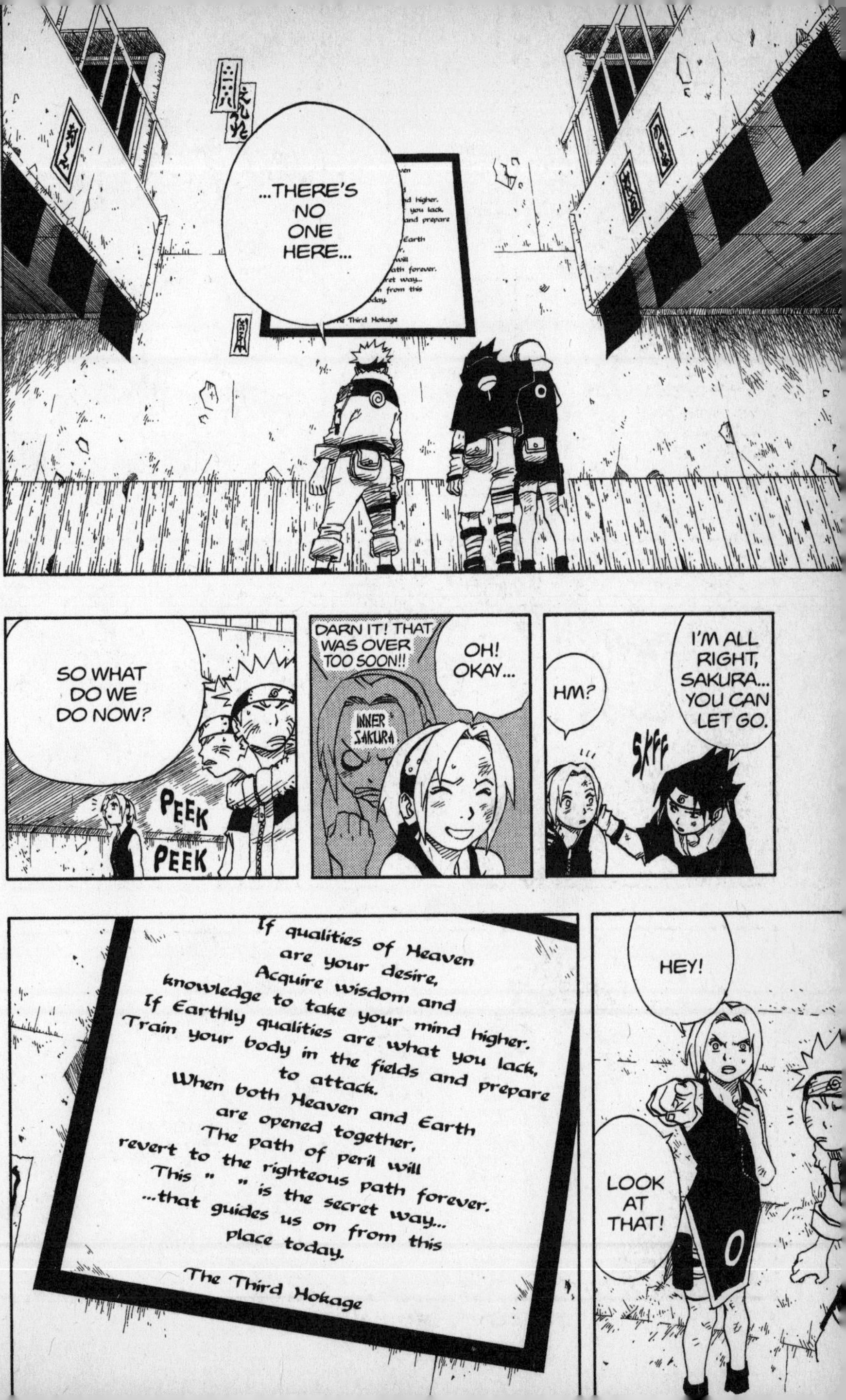
...THERE'S NO ONE HERE...
I'M ALL RIGHT, SAKURA... YOU CAN LET GO.
HM?
SKFF
OH! OKAY...
DARN IT! THAT WAS OVER TOO SOON!!
INNER SAKURA
SO WHAT DO WE DO NOW?
PEEK PEEK
HEY!
LOOK AT THAT!
If qualities of Heaven are your desire,
Acquire wisdom and knowledge to take your mind higher.
If Earthly qualities are what you lack,
Train your body in the fields and prepare to attack.
When both Heaven and Earth are opened together,
The path of peril will revert to the righteous path forever.
This " " is the secret way...
...that guides us on from this place today.
The Third Hokage

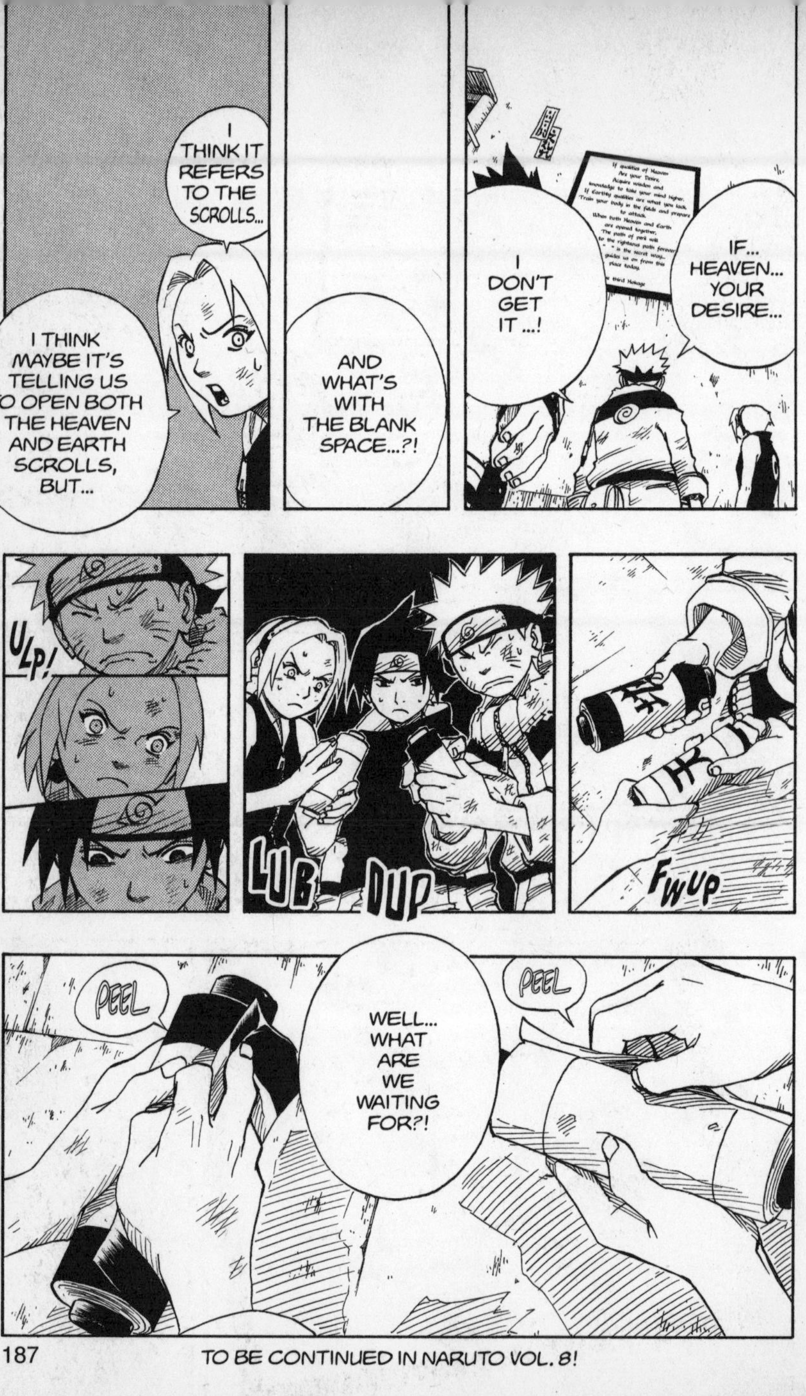
If qualities of Heaven
Are your Desire,
Acquire wisdom and
knowledge to take your mind higher.
If Earthly qualities are what you lack,
Train your body in the fields and prepare
to attack.
When both Heaven and Earth
are opened together,
The path of peril will
to the righteous path forever.
" " is the secret way...
guides us on from this
place today.
third Hokage
IF... HEAVEN... YOUR DESIRE...
I DON'T GET IT ...!
AND WHAT'S WITH THE BLANK SPACE...?!
I THINK IT REFERS TO THE SCROLLS...
I THINK MAYBE IT'S TELLING US TO OPEN BOTH THE HEAVEN AND EARTH SCROLLS, BUT...
FWUP
LUB
DUP
ULP!
PEEL
WELL... WHAT ARE WE WAITING FOR?!
PEEL

TO BE CONTINUED IN NARUTO VOL. 8!

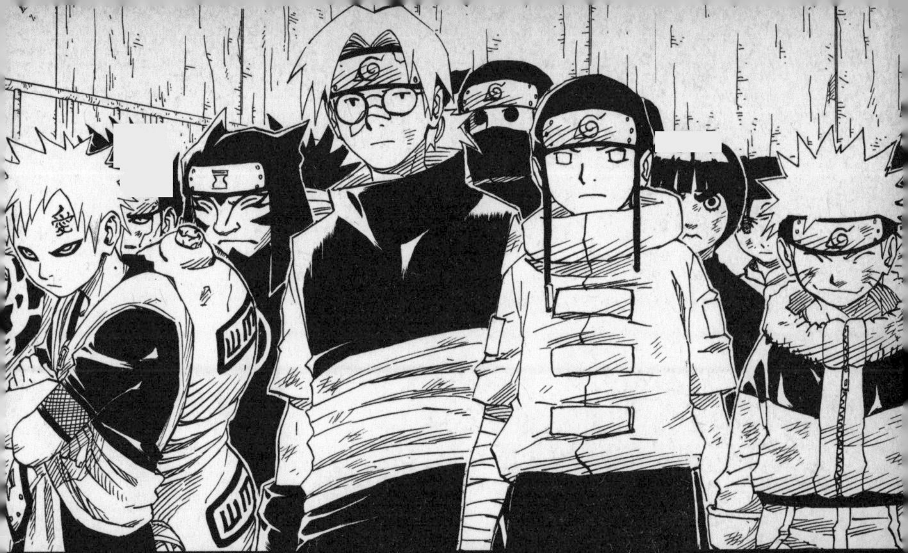

IN THE NEXT VOLUME...

What's inside those stinkin' scrolls, anyway?! As the test in the Forest of Death finally comes to a close, Naruto and the gang receive a cryptic message from the Lord Hokage! So...what comes next? The Third Exam, of course, which brings together the survivors from the previous stage to engage in harrowing one-on-one combat! Sasuke is still battling the effects of Orochimaru's curse...so can he hold his own in a no-holds-barred fight? And when Orochimaru himself reappears, will he reveal his true intentions?

AVAILABLE NOW!

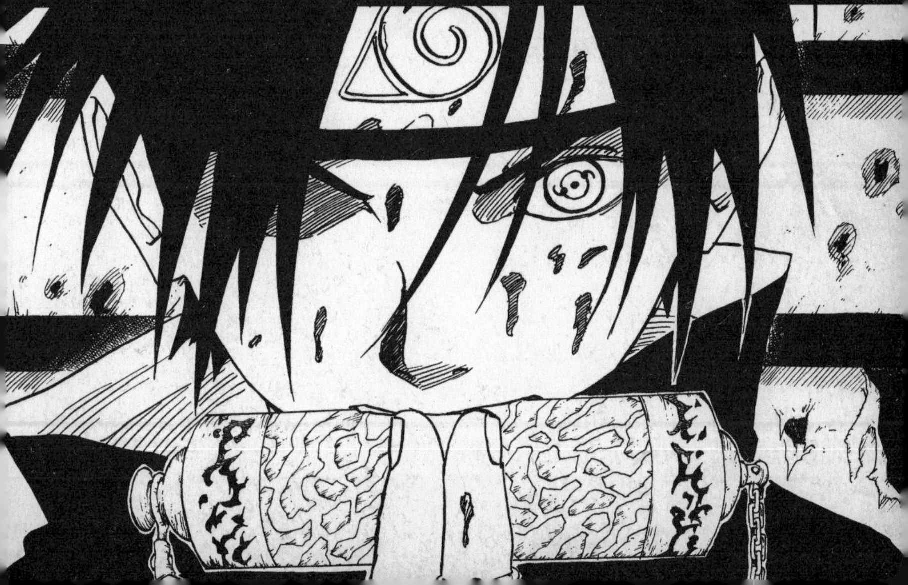

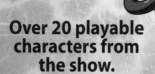

Tell us what you think about SHONEN JUMP manga!

Our survey is now available online.
Go to: www.SHONENJUMP.com/mangasurvey

Help us make our product offering better!

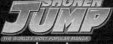

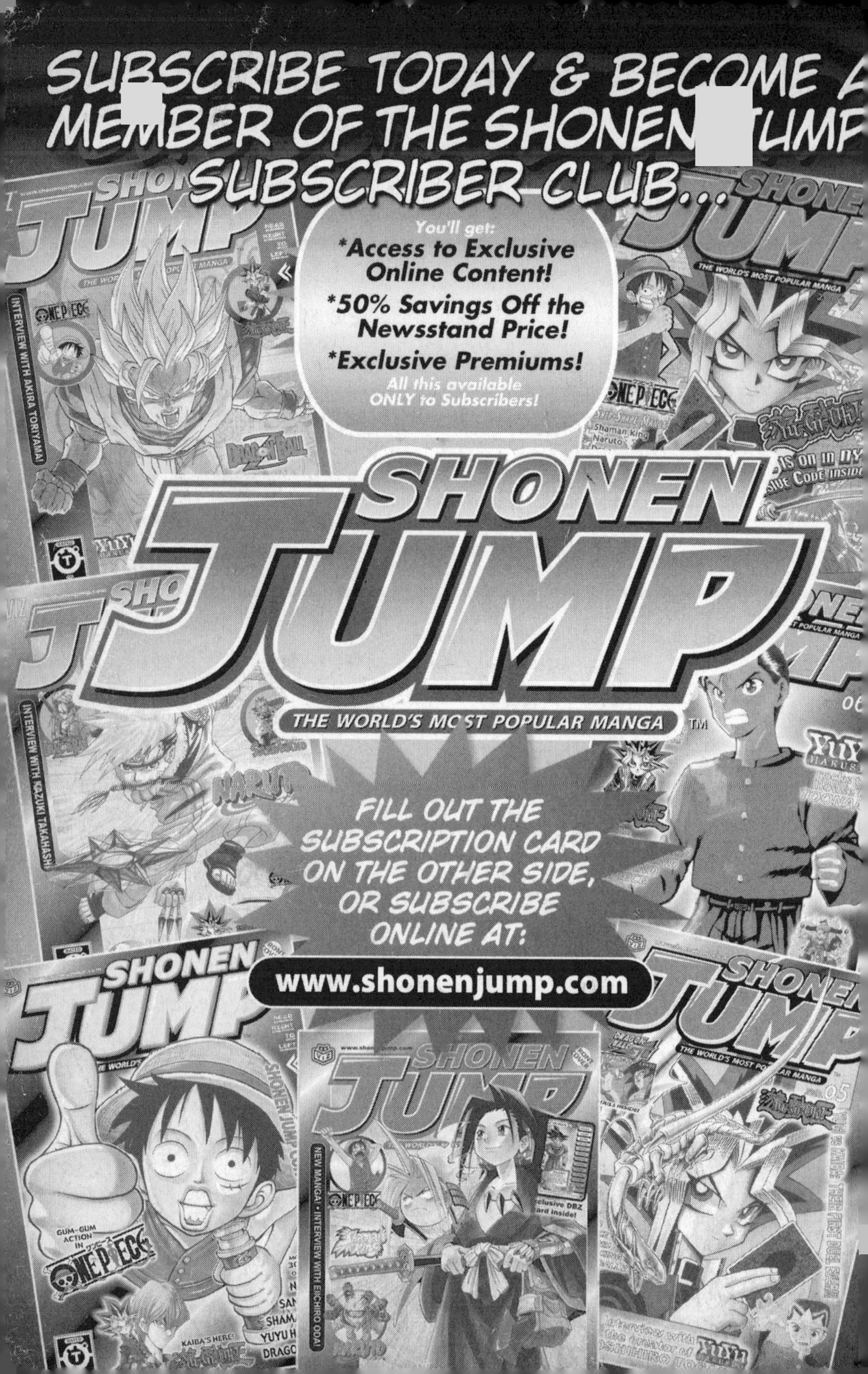
SUBSCRIBE TODAY & BECOME A MEMBER OF THE SHONEN JUMP SUBSCRIBER CLUB...
You'll get:
*Access to Exclusive Online Content!
*50% Savings Off the Newsstand Price!
*Exclusive Premiums!
All this available ONLY to Subscribers!
SHONEN JUMP
THE WORLD'S MOST POPULAR MANGA™
FILL OUT THE SUBSCRIPTION CARD ON THE OTHER SIDE, OR SUBSCRIBE ONLINE AT:
www.shonenjump.com